D0515064

Literacy
in the
Information
Age

Inquiries
Into
Meaning Making
With New
Technologies

BERTRAM C. BRUCE, EDITOR

University of Illinois at Urbana-Champaign
Champaign, Illinois, USA

STANFORD UNIVERSITY LIBRARIES

WITHDRAWN

INTERNATIONAL
Reading Association
800 Barksdale Road, PO Box 8139
Newark, Delaware 19714-8139, USA
www.reading.org

IRA BOARD OF DIRECTORS

Jerry L. Johns, Northern Illinois University, DeKalb, Illinois, *President* • Lesley Mandel Morrow, Rutgers University, New Brunswick, New Jersey, *President-Elect* • MaryEllen Vogt, California State University Long Beach, Long Beach, California, *Vice President* • Rita M. Bean, University of Pittsburgh, Pittsburgh, Pennsylvania • Rebecca L. Olness, Black Diamond, Washington • Doris Walker-Dalhouse, Minnesota State University Moorhead, Moorhead, Minnesota • Patricia L. Anders, University of Arizona, Tucson, Arizona • Timothy V. Rasinski, Kent State University, Kent, Ohio • Ann-Sofie Selin, Cygnaeus School, Åbo, Finland • Cathy Collins Block, Texas Christian University, Fort Worth, Texas • James Flood, San Diego State University, San Diego, California • Victoria J. Risko, Peabody College of Vanderbilt University, Nashville, Tennessee • Alan E. Farstrup, *Executive Director*

The International Reading Association attempts, through its publications, to provide a forum for a wide spectrum of opinions on reading. This policy permits divergent viewpoints without implying the endorsement of the Association.

Director of Publications   Joan M. Irwin
Editorial Director, Books and Special Projects   Matthew W. Baker
Production Editor   Shannon Benner
Permissions Editor   Janet S. Parrack
Acquisitions and Communications Coordinator   Corinne M. Mooney
Associate Editor, Books and Special Projects   Sara J. Murphy
Assistant Editor   Charlene M. Nichols
Administrative Assistant   Michele Jester
Senior Editorial Assistant   Tyanna L. Collins
Production Department Manager   Iona Sauscermen
Supervisor, Electronic Publishing   Anette Schütz
Senior Electronic Publishing Specialist   Cheryl J. Strum
Electronic Publishing Specialist   R. Lynn Harrison
Proofreader   Elizabeth C. Hunt

Project Editor   Charlene M. Nichols

Cover   Design, Linda Steere; Image, Creatas

Copyright 2003 by the International Reading Association, Inc.

All rights reserved. No part of this publication may be reproduced or transmitted in any form or by any means, electronic or mechanical, including photocopy, or any information storage and retrieval system, without permission from the publisher.

Library of Congress Cataloging-in-Publication Data

Literacy in the information age : inquiries into meaning making with new technologies / International Reading Association.

   p. cm.

ISBN 0-87207-003-4

1. Computers and literacy. 2. Media literacy. 3. Information technology. 4. Internet in education. I. International Reading Association.

LC149.5.L577 2003

302.2'244--dc21

2002155848

To Emily and Stephen, who have shown how important it is
to see literacy as a living, growing thing

CONTENTS

FOREWORD

This book isn't really about technology. It's as much about how schools and educational institutions can engage with the cultural and pedagogical, cognitive and social challenges that accompany new technologies.

We've been here before. In the mid to late 19th century, the U.S. economy began a slow but steady shift from an agricultural, rural economy to an industrial one. People moved from hinterlands in search of work in the industrial and service metropolises of the North and East. New formations, spaces, and identities emerged in the contexts of urbanization and industrialization: Family structures shifted from extended to nuclear, individuals lived "singly" in urban settings, "adolescents" and gangs appeared on the streets of Boston and New York, and diasporic ex-slaves and migrants claimed urban communities as their own. But this time the movement is on a global scale and it is much, much more rapid.

The emergence of new forms of human *techne*, not just steam engines, foundries and steel mills, cotton gins and factories, but also emergent modes of transportation, communication, and information have the power to compress and reorganize space and time. This, communications theorists such as Harold Innis (1951) taught us, has the effect of creating new "knowledge economies and monopolies" and destabilizing longstanding beliefs and ideologies, everyday lives and practices. With 19th and early 20th century industrialization and urbanization, people faced new economies, new cultures, and new life pathways. In response, they sought simple truths, literal readings, and new moral and epistemological anchors, often in the form of millenarian religions.

In schools and universities, we face challenges, wrought not by new technologies per se but by the complex effects of cultural and economic globalization: heterogeneous student bodies, with cultural and linguistic diversity as the norm rather than exception; new public pedagogies of mass media and mass culture; but also risky new life pathways to and from communities to school to work and back, linked closely to volatile employment markets. In the face of this, it is not surprising that youth engagement with digital technologies, ICTs (information and communication technologies) as they are called currently, has become both a scapegoat for educational risk and change, and a deficit for some who would return us "back to basics" of phonics, moral education, and so forth. At the same time, these same technologies are presented by their advocates, vendors, and corporate sponsors as the means for schools to generate new forms of "human capital" required by information economies.

For print-trained teachers and teacher educators, what is to be done? If Chip Bruce and his colleagues have done their work in this volume, you will find no new model of information and communications technology, no simple package or formula on how to digitalize your classroom. What you will find are hard-won approaches to pedagogy and curriculum, human community and communications, and new elaborations and articulations that range from John Dewey and Lev Vygotsky, circa 1920, to more current work on zines, cybraries, and cyberidentities, circa 2020.

These pieces were originally published in the *Journal of Adolescent & Adult Literacy* between 1998 and 2002. But they remain works in progress, morphing on the static, linear page. This is because they are genuinely interactive, working reflexively with a field of knowledge and social practice that has been and remains in very real flux, with practice reinvented daily in classrooms and online. Further, they model the very kind of multivoiced dialogue that educational reform and new technologies should generate—bringing together teachers and students, parents and academics, library scientists and weird scientists, prestructuralists and poststructuralists, practitioners, and public intellectuals, world citizens, and writers who have never left Kansas. The result is a kind of educational Creole—a unique blending of ideas and vernaculars, modes and modalities about, around, and through new technologies and media drawn from very different cultural places and theoretical spaces.

To mix metaphors even further, Chip Bruce is as close to a Renaissance scholar as we have working within the field. Trained as a computer scientist, working from cognitive theory, educational philosophy, interactional sociolinguistics and critical social and discourse theories, he began his work with information technologies more than two decades ago. But consider for a moment the very possibility of a Renaissance approach to the ubiquitous ICTs that now are at the heart of every professional development and teacher training program, every institution's "vision statement" and strategic plan. The power of the European work of the 12th to 14th centuries—culminating in the emergence of the then revolutionary information technology: the printing press—was that it brought together, reframed, and opened for critical scrutiny the textual archive of human knowledge. Thinkers and writers worked across fields, combining aesthetics and sciences, secular and nonsecular beliefs to explain the world in novel ways. As is often the case when the unsaid is said and the unthinkable becomes thinkable, existing power and knowledge relations began to unravel, as the likes of Galileo found out.

In this light, consider this question about historical changes in communications technologies. Centuries later, are we left with a "theory of the manuscript" or "theory of the printing press" or "theory of television"? Quite the contrary. Communications media enable multiple new theorizations and understandings, hosts of new social and textual and linguistic practices, an expanded archive of human knowledge, and pedagogical uses of these technologies that nobody could have predicted. I would argue that the push now to define and theorize educational technology as a field in and of itself is misled. Digital information technologies are communications technologies, new modalities and media of human communications, nothing more and nothing less. Their emergence—and the host of sophisticated social practices of inscription, memory, re/presentations, and mediation that they enable—encourages reframings of knowledge and power, new fields and rules of intellectual and social exchange. This is occurring in the wired classrooms and living rooms of advanced capitalist economies and globalized cultures as we speak. Children, parents, and teachers—often in that order—are experimenting with new designs, working through identities, desires, aspirations, and problems. Because we are for once genuinely "learning by doing" well in advance of accumulated curriculum wisdom, the current situation is disruptive and, for many in the field, slightly scary.

The new educational/information/communications technologies are, among other things, hosts of problem-solving and goal-seeking practices. In *Art as Experience* (1958), a work that deals explicitly neither with education nor literacy, John Dewey makes a defining pedagogical statement. He argues that art arises from organism/environment disequilibria. These generate responses, social behaviors, affect, and representations by means of which we render problems coherent. Dewey's position is that the aim of art, like the task of philosophy more generally, is to make our world coherent, to take what he referred to as "incohate" responses to disequilibria and willfully resolve them through shape, form, and design. In this regard, aesthetics is not the product of a will to the "beautiful" per se, but a way of dialectically reconciling our relationships with our social and environmental Others, in the same sense that we remediate or dialogically engage with our worlds, to draw from the more contemporary models of pedagogy discussed here.

Any pedagogy of multiliteracies is an attempt to capture via designs and redesigns what Anthony Wilden (1981) once called the intrinsically goal-seeking and problem-solving nature of human communications. Chip Bruce and colleagues here document an extraordinary educational moment, one in which learners are using communications technologies for such goal seeking and problem solving, for identifying and making "cohate" conflict, struggle, and disequilibria in their social worlds, institutional fields, and intellectual lives. This is a pedagogical universe where learners are actually inventing new genres and discourses, where some teachers are learning about the new technologies from kids, and where the archives and networks of knowledge are expanding exponentially beyond any government or corporation's immediate control or profit, try as much as they might. Put on your seatbelts, sign waivers bequeathing paradigms and packages, and get reading.

Allan Luke
University of Queensland
Brisbane, Australia

REFERENCES

Dewey, J. (1958). *Art as experience*. New York: Capricorn. (Original work published 1932)
Innis, H.A. (1951). *The bias of communication*. Toronto: University of Toronto Press.
Wilden, A. (1981). *System and structure: Essays in communication and exchange* (2nd ed.). London: Tavistock.

ACKNOWLEDGMENTS

The journey to create a book may feel solitary at times, but it is never the work of one person. Shared experiences and the thoughts, interests, and support of others infuse every stage of the process. For a book such as this one, the collective enterprise is all the more evident. Not only does it include specific contributions of others, but during the four years of column writing more people than I can name played a part in its creation.

This process undoubtedly began nearly three decades ago with colleagues at Bolt, Beranek, and Newman and Boston-area universities who were interested in new technologies for literacy learning. Andee Rubin, Allan Collins, Cindy Steinberg, Wally Feurzeig, Marilyn Adams, John Seely Brown, Ray Nickerson, Sarah Michaels, Courtney Cazden, Jim Gee, Don Graves, and Jim Squire, among many others, shaped the ideas and precursors to the technologies discussed in this book. Other colleagues at the Center for the Study of Reading at the University of Illinois—David Pearson, Rand Spiro, Taffy Raphael, Bill Brewer, and Dick Anderson, to name just a few—pushed those ideas further. More help came from other colleagues at Illinois, including those at the College of Education, the Center for Writing Studies, and the National Center for Supercomputing Applications—Jim Levin, Nick Burbules, Paul Prior, Renee Clift, Margery Osborne, Jack Easley, Liora Bresler, and Ken Travers, among many others. Some (Gail Hawisher and Umesh Thakkar) became column authors. These have been long-term collaborations that continue to this day. Equally important are the collaborations with students. A very incomplete list of those who shaped the views here includes Jianxia Du, Anna Li, Beena Choksi, Hui-Ju Huang, Shihkuan Hsu, Ina Gabler, Junghyun An, David Marcovitz, Dean Grosshandler, Christine Wang, and Shobha Sinha. Several of these students (Maureen Hogan, Jo Williamson, Kevin Leander, Michelle Hinn, and Karen Lunsford) also coauthored columns.

In 1996–1997, I was fortunate to have a sabbatical abroad, which provided the incubation, and toward the end, the direct impetus for the columns. In Beijing, I saw what was happening with computers and the Internet in a rapidly developing country. Colleagues at Peking University (Wei Xin and Min Weifang, among many) at Beijing Normal University (Chen Qi, Shu Hua, and Sang Xin Min), Beijing University of Aeronautics and Astronautics (Zhang Yan Tong), and

University of Montreal (Paul Gauthier) greatly expanded my perspective on learning and technology. In Brisbane, I was fortunate to work with Carmen Luke, Carolyn Baker, Colin Lankshear, Michele Knobel, and Peter Freebody, among others at the University of Queensland, Griffith University, and Queensland University of Technology. Students such as Daisy Webster were equally influential, as can be seen in the columns that follow.

It was in Brisbane that John Elkins and Allan Luke asked me to write the Technology department column for the *Journal of Adolescent & Adult Literacy*. Without their guidance and risk-taking, this book never would have happened. Once the columns began to appear, I heard from readers, who became collaborators through their comments and suggestions.

As the columns developed, I benefited from discussions with too many people to mention. I moved to the Graduate School of Library and Information Science (GSLIS) at the University of Illinois and connected with a wonderful group of colleagues with interests in this area. I would need to name essentially all the faculty, staff, and students to acknowledge their contributions properly, but I would like to note that Leigh Estabrook, Dan Schiller, and Ann Bishop made especially helpful comments on the text, and Ann authored two of the columns. The GSLIS Literacies Research Group (including Christine Jenkins and Betsy Hearne) has inspired and extended the ideas here, as have the Distributed Knowledge Research Collaborative (including Caroline Haythornthwaite, Geof Bowker, and others) and the Inquiry Project (Bryan Heidorn, Michael Twidale, Lisa Hinchliffe, Mihye Won, Alexia Benson, Jenny Robins, Trudy Morritz, Juna Snow, and others). Students such as Cece Merkel, Michele Kazmer, Rae Ann Montague, Keren Moses, Wei Li, and Norma Linton have added greatly to the intellectual climate for the book. Colleagues elsewhere including Deb Dillon, Donna Alvermann, Joy Peyton, Trent Batson, David Reinking, Cynthia Selfe, Suzanne Damarin, and others also shaped the work.

I could not fail to mention the role of the Literacy in the Information Age class. This is a university capstone course for an Information Technology Studies minor, which I teach each semester. The questions students asked, the ideas they brought, the experiences they shared, and the projects they undertook provided a continual source of inspiration. Three then-undergraduates (Bernhard Jungwirth, Michael Brunelle, and Marc Wielansky) became column authors.

The nonstandard format of the columns placed a heavy demand on the editors at the International Reading Association. I am grateful to June Hollins, James

Henderson, and Kate Tyler Wall for helping me (more or less) meet the deadlines and cope with the frustrations of rapidly changing URLs. I also thank Anne Fullerton and Cindy Held, who ably managed the nontrivial task of converting the columns to their *Reading Online* versions. I want to thank the *Reading Online* editors (Martha Dillner, Lynne Anderson-Inman, Bridget Dalton, and Dana Grisham) as well, for making a space for the columns. Matt Baker and Charlene Nichols took on the major task of pulling a set of texts written over five years into what we hope is now a cohesive book.

As I discuss in the Introduction, the Technology department would have been much less without the significant contribution from the guest authors. They expanded on ideas I barely touched and provided alternative perspectives. I appreciate their willingness and ability to write within hard deadlines and to catch the multimedia spirit of the columns. Most of all, I value their commitment to the project and the excellent columns they created.

Anyone who knows me knows how important my family is to me. Their general support has been absolutely vital, but in many specific ways they helped the project move from idea to reality. My daughter, Emily, who was 11 at the time of the sabbatical, began writing her own column on similar topics for the local newspaper about the time I started writing for the *Journal of Adolescent & Adult Literacy*. I worked hard to move beyond the feeling that her column ("Hit Return!") was livelier, more pertinent, and more widely read than my own, to instead learn from her and Stephen, Emily's one-year-younger brother. Both Emily and Stephen critique my writing and share what they and their contemporaries do in the online world. Their ideas are very much a part of this book. I especially have to thank my wife, Susan, who carried me through the dark times when the monthly column just wasn't coming together. She read each of the columns before it went out and helped me reshape clumsy sentences and sharpen ideas. Without her love and support, both emotional and intellectual, this book never could have happened.

INTRODUCTION

I teach a course for undergraduate students titled *Literacy in the Information Age* (see the conclusion for a discussion of what that title means). In the course, we explore how the nature of texts is changing as they are re-presented through online communities, websites, video, hypermedia, virtual reality, robotics, and other new technologies. These changes call on us to ask questions about readers, writers, and texts and what they mean for our intellectual, cultural, political, ethical, and personal lives.

One key question concerns the impact on young people themselves: How do they make meaning as they both respond to and create texts with the new media? A complementary question concerns the culture in which they live: How are cultural meanings reinforced or reformulated through new modes of expression? Students read and discuss changing notions of literacy, they study new literacy practices through a research project, and they learn from one another through discussions about current events and personal experiences with new information and communication technologies.

Rather than having a fixed syllabus through which I guide the students systematically, I find that our syllabus is evolving continually. As Nancie Atwell (1987) writes in *In the Middle: Writing, Reading, and Learning With Adolescents*, the curriculum is not created in advance by me, but instead is "grounded in the logic of learning" (p. 3)—it unfolds as the students and I learn together about the new literacies. Students in the course learn about—and teach me about—topics as varied as cyberart, Internet radio, the digital divide in developing countries, privacy on the Web, censorship, virtual reality, emoticons, open source, collaboratories, online learning, visual literacy, copyright law and cultural values, e-mail etiquette, and representations of fairy tales in new media. We tie these diverse topics together by sharing the projects and examining the implications for literacy.

A good example of the way the curriculum unfolds through collaborative inquiry occurred in our discussions of computer-mediated communication. Books and articles abound to explain the different tools, such as e-mail, bulletin boards, instant messages, and video conferences, with analyses of the strengths and weaknesses of different technologies and studies of their use. But I often find that what I read falls short of explaining the on-the-ground experiences of my students and myself.

Instant Messaging: Re-Creating Self and Technology

In the spring semester of 2002, one student, Isaac Oates, developed a program called GradeAIM to allow users to upload their AOL Instant Messenger (AIM) buddy list (see Glossary) to a website at the National Center for Supercomputing Applications. The program can then display the social network implied by that list—which users are on the buddy list (one degree of separation), which are on the list of one of those "buddies" (two degrees of separation), and so on. For example, the figure shows that user 1,500 in the center has 10 others on his or her buddy list and that those buddies collectively have 70 additional buddies. Thus, user 1,500 is only two degrees of separation from 80 other AIM users.

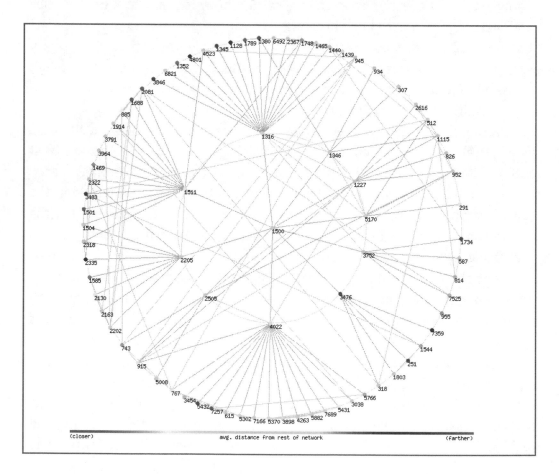

Another student, Omar Ashrafi, took on the marketing role for the study. Omar and Isaac surveyed users and spread the word about the program. I was impressed with the technical work they had done, but I was even more impressed with the response their program generated. Within a few days, over 1,000 users had come to the site, logged in, uploaded their buddy list, and explored the social network diagrams. After three weeks there were over 3,000 users. When another student discovered the site, he sent a mass e-mail to 42 other students telling them about it. Within 24 hours, 19 of those students also had signed up. These are remarkable numbers, belying the myth of uninvolved students. Soon there were requests from other campuses around the United States—requests that could not be accommodated due to limited Web server capacity.

What I saw through this project was not only that many students use AIM but also that there was an intense interest in seeing how one's use compared to others. Then there was a competition to see whose name was on the most buddy lists. It is interesting that, although there was a large variation at one degree of separation, by three or four degrees of separation most students were connected to the same number of others, and after six degrees, no new names appeared; every name on new buddy lists was already in the database. Through the social network diagrams and their thoughts about their connectedness to others, students came to see themselves in new ways.

But this story did not end with one project. I was curious about the fact that nearly every student used some form of instant messaging, though not necessarily AIM. Their enthusiasm surprised me, because I never saw much use for instant messaging, fearing perhaps the loss of control that it implies. Moreover, when I talked with faculty members, I found that many had never heard of it, those who had heard of it had little interest in trying it, and those who had tried it never wanted to use it again. There were a few exceptions of course, but on the whole, students were avid users and faculty members were avid nonusers. In contrast, every student and faculty member uses e-mail to communicate. This posed a challenge for the class as well as for me. We usually do not see such stark disparities in the use of new technologies.

Students talked about the various ways they used instant messaging. It was interesting to hear about the way international students use it to stay in contact with friends and family in their home countries. This leads to distinct preferences regarding instant message programs because of which writing script they support. One surprise was the key role instant messaging plays in doing homework.

A student "messages" another student to get details of an assignment or to discuss a problem. They coordinate their social time and their study time, arranging to meet at a certain point when enough has been done on the homework. It became clear that, for better or worse, instant messaging has become a key fixture in the university experience, and one about which many faculty members have little knowledge.

Faculty members were generally outspoken about their own potential use, saying things such as "I'm too busy!" or "I get too much e-mail as is; why would I want to get more electronic communication?" But that still left the question, Why "yes" for students and "no" for faculty? Why did instant messaging fit into the information ecology for students and not for their teachers, even though both groups are heavy computer users and both use the Web and e-mail extensively?

One clue came in a later class. A student related that he left his "away message" on even when he was at his computer using it. That way, he could see who was trying to contact him without having to reveal that he was there. Thus, he was screening calls, in a way analogous to the way many people use telephone answering machines. Further discussion revealed that most, if not all, the students in the class used away messages in a similar way. They had effectively reinterpreted a component of the instant messaging programs to meet their own social needs better, using the away message primarily for those times when they were actually there and often not when they were actually away. By using away messages in this way, students essentially turn a synchronous mode of communication (the "instant" in instant messaging) into an asynchronous mode. Thus, it begins to take on some of the characteristics of the asynchronous e-mail, which faculty do in fact use.

But there was more. One student admitted that she sometimes went systematically through her buddy list to read the away messages of all her friends. That way she could find out what they were doing, even though she realized that in many cases what they were doing was working at the computer while declaring that they were away. That also turned out to be a common practice, one that partially explains why there is such a disparity between student and faculty use.

Students in a later class session brought in Web links for spy programs, such as IMSPOT (http://www.imspot.com), which allow the user to see who is checking your away messages. As IMSPOT says about its "tracker," "This feature allows you to find out for once and for all who's viewing your profile and away messages while you're not looking. Is it a friend or family member or the new office secretary, or maybe it's that shy classmate?"

Thus, students are immersed in an evolving world of new technology development. Their use of away messages, their selection of tools, and the GradeAIM project show that they are not merely passive recipients of these technologies; rather they are active interpreters and reconstructors of it. That is not to say that they are not subject to the political, cultural, and commercial structuring of relations through these tools, but that the full story requires a consideration of their agency as well.

What this continuing saga says to me is that even a simple computer application, such as instant messaging, can play an intricate and fascinating role in people's lives. It is both a text for understanding, one with inexhaustible *"sources of possibilities of meaning*, rather than a passive object of investigation" (Linge, 1976, p. xix), and a text to be written anew. As a text it bears on students' use of other representational and communication media; on their language and cultural background; on the way they learn, work, and play; on their social relations; on their community; and on their sense of self. As instant messaging is interpreted and re-created, it contributes to the evolving meaning of literacy in their lives.

Where Are We Going?

The literature of science fiction provides us with vivid images of life in the future. To understand that new realm, we look for a computer like HAL from *2001: A Space Odyssey* (Clarke, 1999) to guide us as we work and play with robots, explore strange lands and times through holodecks, or transport our bodies on rocket ships. But as fanciful as these notions may be, they often pale in comparison with the latest news items about cloning, virtual reality, and microbots.

As much as writers try to go beyond the everyday reality, they must deal with the fact that we live in what cyberpunk author William Gibson calls "our increasingly science-fictional present" (Kim, 1996). One consequence is that the writings of classical science fiction writers, such as Robert Heinlein or Isaac Asimov, seem more of this world than in contrast to it. Even the more updated versions we see in Octavia Butler, Philip K. Dick, or Ursula K. LeGuin overlap with the news of the day. As Ray Bradbury says, "Science fiction itself has remained the same. We have caught up to it.... We're surrounded by cellular phones and fax machines and computers. We are a science-fiction generation" (Kim, 1996).

The tools many of us use every day outstrip what writers envisioned just a decade ago. Science fiction screenwriter Ron Shusett (*Total Recall, Alien*) laments, "We can't think far enough ahead any more" (Kim, 1996). The only saving condition for science fiction artists is that the new tools of hypertext, online discussion forums, multimedia authoring systems, retinal scanners, and virtual reality, which just a short while ago were the content of science fiction, are now available for them to use in *creating* science fiction. Thus, creators of movie and television content now regularly employ once fanciful tools.

Most of us hold contradictory feelings about these new technologies. On the one hand, we find that the excitement around new developments too often is revealed to be hyperbole. Moreover, the focus on technology alone takes us away from the important questions of life. As Thoreau (1971) once said,

> Our inventions are wont to be pretty toys, which distract our attention from serious things. They are but improved means to an unimproved end, an end which it was already but too easy to arrive at; as railroads lead to Boston or New York. We are in great haste to construct a magnetic telegraph from Maine to Texas; but Maine and Texas, it may be, have nothing important to communicate. (p. 52)

At the same time, we can easily be enthralled by the possibilities of new media. We know that Maine and Texas may not recognize what they have to communicate until they try it. We realize that taking a digital photo and sending it instantly to a faraway friend, building an online community of people with similar interests, and studying online from a distant university are just harbingers of what may be coming. Hyperbole soon slides into understatement. As Arthur C. Clarke says, "First our expectations of what occurs outrun what's actually happening, and then eventually what actually happens far exceeds our expectations" (Stix, 2001, p. 36).

What Will Prepare Us?

Educators today feel both the excitement of this emerging world and the challenge of preparing young people to live productively within it. They rightly wonder how to assess the changes they see in the new information age and how to decide what learning experiences can best prepare students for it. There are calls now for computer training as a core component of literacy and worries about issues such as the quality of website content and the need for new literacy skills. In this context, teachers worry about how they can teach the technical skills that are sometimes more foreign to them than they are to their students.

To answer the question of what today's students need to learn, we could ask those who thrive there. One candidate is Nathan Shedroff, who is currently creative director and a cofounder of vivid publishing, inc., an information products company that creates projects in both electronic and print media. In an interview with *internet.au* (1997), an Australian magazine about the Internet, Shedroff was asked what he wished he had learned more about in school to prepare himself for his current work. He replied,

> Few people are ever taught to create successful, satisfying experiences for others. Mostly, those folks are in the performing arts: dancers, comedians, storytellers, singers, actors, etc. I now wish I had more training in theater and performing arts to rely on...especially improvisational theater. That's like the highest form of interactivity. (pp. 40–41)

The contrast between improvisational theater and what many of us might have predicted Shedroff would say (how to program a computer? how to make webpages?) is striking.

Shedroff does not cite the need for more technical skills, even though he probably feels that need at times, but rather, a desire to be more fully human in his interactions with others. His work recalls Murnane and Levy's (1996) argument that the new basic skills are not only the *hard skills* of minimal reading, writing, and computation, but the *soft skills* such as the ability to communicate effectively both orally and in writing, and the ability to work productively with people from different backgrounds. Understanding the perspective of others; being able to work with complex, messy situations; and learning how to learn may become more crucial than ever.

Shedroff's words also take us back to John Dewey's (1938) *Experience and Education*, in which the author shows that the idea of education as preparation for life is self-contradictory. When we learn things or develop skills removed from their context of use, we too often find them sealed away in what Dewey calls a "water-tight compartment." Dewey writes,

> We always live at the time we live and not at some other time, and only by extracting at each present time the full meaning of each present experience are we prepared for doing the same thing in the future. (p. 49)

How then do we help learners as we all become immersed in a new information age? The answer may be neither to embrace the new information changes as unquestioned human advances nor to reject them as ephemeral and misguided. Instead, we need a way to engage critically with them—to understand the promises as well as the perils. Doing so would mean applying what Walter Kaufman (1977) calls "dialectical reading" (p. 59) to the evolving new media culture. This means that as we attempt to understand and engage with the changes before us, we neither embrace nor reject them, but rather enter into a kind of dialogue with them, asking what they mean and what they could be and how our interactions with them can lead to useful reflection on who we are.

The Technology Department and This Book

When John Elkins and Allan Luke asked me to serve as author and editor for the Technology department for the *Journal of Adolescent & Adult Literacy*, we conceived it as a space for dialogue about the unfolding of new literacies, not as a medium to deliver fixed conceptions of what these literacies are now or ought to be. The aim was to "increase dialogue about new communication and information technologies and explore what these media mean for literacy and literacy educators...to engage with these rapidly evolving literacy practices...[and] to understand what they imply for literacy education" (Bruce, 1998, p. 46). The department has examined various aspects of the new literacies and their implications for teachers and students. Any given month may focus on changing literacies, equity, censorship, globalization, language, or other issues that we need to rethink in light of our changing technological world.

We assumed that readers vary greatly in terms of how comfortable they feel with new technologies but that nearly all are aware that they pose new challenges and opportunities for becoming literate in today's world. Each column suggests something of the hypertextual, multimedia world we are entering. In addition to an Editor's Message, most columns have an Issue of the Month, a Data View (about new technologies), Interpretations, a Literacy Website of the Month, Websites to Visit, a Glossary, and other components, each with links to more information on the World Wide Web.

In the beginning I wrote most of the columns, but I soon realized that the department would be richer if I could bring in other perspectives. So, in the second year, I began to invite guest authors. The authors represented come from four different countries. Some are longtime colleagues, and some are new to the field. Several of them were students at the time of writing, including three undergraduates from the Literacy in the Information Age course mentioned earlier.

The columns themselves came to represent the new literacies they describe. Shortly after it appeared in print, each column was posted in *Reading Online* (http://www.readingonline.org) so that it could be realized as a hypertext and embedded in an online community. Many readers wrote with questions, comments, and suggestions. A common suggestion was that it would be useful to assemble the entire collection of Technology departments in a book so that the columns could be read easily as a unified set. Although the book could not claim to be a comprehensive, much less final, word on the subject, it would present multiple perspectives on a variety of topics in the area of the new literacies, all tied together by a vision of collaborative inquiry. Many readers felt that such a book would be a valuable introduction for the individual reader or a useful class text for courses in literacy, learning, communications, information technology, library science, Web design, or human computer interaction.

Following the decision to assemble the columns into a collection, we made several other decisions to make the book more useful than a simple reprinting would be. Authors were given the opportunity to update their columns, adding new insights or responding to changes in literacy practices. Some of the URLs were removed, both because they are less helpful in the print format than they are when live as in *Reading Online* and because many become obsolete in a short time. While the *Reading Online* columns were a monthly update, the book version needed to be more timeless. In addition, I departed from the chronological order in grouping the columns according to the larger questions they addressed and I added material, which I hoped would provide a useful context and not distort the authors' original ideas. In most cases, this material reflects the ongoing dialogue among the authors, the journal editors, and me, which did not make it into the column. Thus, the pieces that appear here are not identical to what was published in the journal. We kept the glossary each author had created with the corresponding column because some terms had special meanings in a particular column and readers may wish to use a column as a unified whole. At the same time, we thought it would be useful to offer a combined glossary at the end. For that, I tried to select or synthesize definitions that applied across the topics.

The columns in *Literacy in the Information Age* critique the way literacy practices are evolving as they simultaneously become ever more central in our lives.

They examine the changing nature of texts themselves as they are transmitted via oral, print, and electronic media (including online communities, websites, video, hypermedia, virtual reality, and other new technologies). As the first piece in this book argues, we often do not notice the technologies of literacy. But the means and the media by which people communicate are deeply embedded in our daily practices.

The columns also revisit enduring questions about the readers and writers of texts. The questions they ask build on traditions including reader response, folklore theory, writing studies, and human computer interaction. They employ a variety of research methods, including discourse and textual analysis, website analysis, interviews, and ethnography. Although acknowledging at the outset that the questions cannot be neatly categorized, I nevertheless grouped the columns into six broad areas:

1. Historical Perspective: How have literacy practices changed over time and responded to new technologies? What is the future of literacy?

2. Evolving Media Practices: What media are emerging in our literacy practices? How do technological, linguistic, political, and economic forces shape literacy practices today?

3. Personal Meanings: How is meaning constructed in both personal and social terms?

4. Ethical and Policy Issues: How are ethical and policy issues shaped by the changes in literacy?

5. Learning Opportunities: How can we understand and facilitate inquiry-based learning through new technologies?

6. Community: What role do the new literacies play in creating and maintaining community?

The columns provide tools for exploring these questions. Moreover, the authors are themselves engaged in creating as well as critiquing the new world we are entering. Through their studies of technology use and practice, they show us possibilities for both understanding our past and shaping our futures.

REFERENCES

Atwell, N. (1987). *In the middle: Writing, reading, and learning with adolescents*. Portsmouth, NH: Boynton Cook.

Bruce, B.C. (1998). New literacies. *Journal of Adolescent & Adult Literacy, 42*, 46–49.

Clarke, A.C. (1999). *2001: A space odyssey*. New York: New American Library.

Dewey, J. (1938). *Experience and education*. New York: Collier Books.

internet.au. (1997, February). Interview: vivid: strikingly bright. *internet.au, 16*, 40–41.

Kaufmann, W. (1977). The art of reading. In W. Kaufmann, *The future of the humanities* (pp. 47–83). New York: Thomas Y. Crowell.

Kim, A. (1996). Sci-fi invades Hollywood. *Entertainment Weekly*. Retrieved December 1, 2002, from http://www.ew.com/ew/features/archive/xfiles/scifi/251scifimain.html

Linge, D. (1976). Editor's introduction. In H-G. Gadamer, *Philosophical hermeneutics* (D. Linge, Ed. and Trans.) (pp. xi–lviii). Berkeley, CA: University of California Press.

Murnane, R.J., & Levy, F. (1996). *Teaching the new basic skills: Principles for educating children to thrive in a changing economy*. New York: Free Press.

Stix, G. (2001). 2001: A scorecard. *Scientific American, 284*(1), 36.

Thoreau, H.D. (1971). *Walden* (J.L. Shanley, Ed.). Princeton, NJ: Princeton University Press.

White, J. (2002, March 5). Six degrees of instant messaging. *The Daily Illini*. Retrieved March 5, 2002, from http://www.dailyillini.com/mar02/mar05/news/stories/news_story05.shtml

Historical Perspective

In his defense of general education against the purely technical, the psychologist and pragmatist philosopher William James wrote,

> You can give humanistic value to almost anything by teaching it historically. Geology, economics, mechanics, are humanities when taught with reference to the successive achievements of the geniuses to which these sciences owe their being. Not taught thus, literature remains grammar, art a catalogue, history a list of dates, and natural science a sheet of formulas and weights and measures. (1968, p. 312)

Today, we might say that without a historical consciousness, our understanding of the new media remains a list of software features. We risk being swept away by novelty and unable to critique what we see in terms of past experience.

This section contains an opening set of columns that raise historical questions, although they make no claim to providing thorough answers. "New Literacies" asks whether the transformation in literacy practices that some foresee is comparable to others we have experienced. "Constructing a Once-and-Future History of Learning Technologies" relates the story of a Web-based time line for literacy and learning technologies, one that welcomes the reader's contributions. "A Friendly, Welcoming Attitude Toward Change" addresses both positive and negative aspects of change and asks how we can prepare for an uncertain future.

REFERENCES

James, W. (1968). *Memories and studies* (pp. 312–314). New York: Greenwood.

Editor's Message

First, let me welcome readers to the inaugural column of the Technology department of the *Journal of Adolescent & Adult Literacy*. My hope for this department is that it will increase dialogue about new communication and information technologies and explore what these media mean for literacy and literacy educators. It's time for everyone in this field to engage with these rapidly evolving literacy practices—to embrace, reject, or work with them to understand what they imply for literacy education.

I imagine that *JAAL* readers vary greatly in terms of how comfortable they feel with new technologies but that nearly all of you are aware that they pose new challenges and opportunities for becoming literate in today's world. Most of us are just on the cusp; we see some of what is going on but find ourselves surprised again and again by new developments and often at a loss to keep up.

The Technology department will examine various aspects of the new literacies and their implications for teachers and students. Month by month it will focus on changing literacies, learning, equity, school and work, censorship, globalization, language, or other issues that we need to rethink in light of our changing technological world. I hope that readers will contribute website suggestions and questions to explore.

I want each column to suggest something of the hypertextual, multimedia world we are entering. In addition to my monthly message, most columns will have an Issue of the Month, a Data View (about new technologies), Interpretations, a Literacy Website of the Month, Websites to Visit, a Glossary, and other components, each with links to more information on the World Wide Web.

Original version published September 1998 in the *Journal of Adolescent & Adult Literacy*
©1998 International Reading Association

Will the Information Age Transform Literacy?

We don't notice the technologies of literacy because we treat our literacy technologies as natural and inevitable: How else could one write except with a pen and paper, or a typewriter? But when we look at literacy cross-culturally, or historically, it becomes difficult to ignore the means and the media by which people communicate. That we often conceive literacy without mentioning its technologies tells us mostly that these technologies are deeply embedded in our daily practices.

If we could go back in time, we would see the earliest human communities employ simple symbol systems. The nature of early literacy within those communities is closely tied to the available technologies of oral sounds, drums and flutes, gestures, facial expressions, petroglyphs, or the display of artifacts. As with the Internet today, there is a strong emphasis on visual images, icons, and brief sound segments. It is difficult to express certain ideas using these first media for literacy without the complex narrative structures that accompany later, more sophisticated oral language use.

Literacy transformations

primitive symbol systems
⟹ complex oral language
  ⟹ early writing
    ⟹ manuscript literacy
      ⟹ print literacy
        ➡ video literacy
          ⟹ digital/multimedia/hypertext literacy
          ⟹ virtual reality

Adapted from Bruce, B.C. (1997). Literacy technologies: What stance should we take? *Journal of Literacy Research, 29*(2), 289–309.

As societies move to more complex oral language, extended stories become possible. Later, early writing means that more ideas can be retained in permanent forms. At each stage (see Literacy transformations, above), new technologies afford new possibilities for communication and knowledge representation, making possible history as a field, formal schooling, the mercantile system, and many other changes. The technologies at each stage—devices, artifacts, methods of reproduction, distribution systems, and so on—evolve along with the changing conceptions of literacy and its role in social practices. In this way, the evolution of literacy is demarcated by a series of changes that are neither simply social, nor technical, but sociotechnical.

What can we say about the latest set of sociotechnical changes? Some would argue that we are about to embark on a communal journey into cyberspace, a world in which traditional conceptions of text will give way to virtual reality theater; that it will be a world where relations among people will be enhanced through their mediation by computers, and where global democracy will flourish as writers share their every thought through the universal hypertext. We could add that this cyberspace will mean prosperity for all as machines take over mundane work and embedded systems transform every object in our environment into intelligent companions.

Others counter that these changes will create a rigid class system as they reward the symbolic analyst elite and relegate everyone else to serving roles, or that relations between people will be replaced by relations with machines. But perhaps, as others claim, none of this is true; the cyberworld is merely another commercial blitz devised to make us purchase electronic gadgets and shop forever in a digital mall. Is the information age bringing, as Dickens might say, the "best of times" or is it bringing the "worst of times," or must we conclude from all the hyperbole that it is "so far like the present period" that we can do nothing but speak of it in contradictory superlatives?

It seems clear that technological changes neither determine nor are determined by social relations. What happens with new technologies depends in large part on how we interpret and respond to them, how we appropriate them into daily practices, and how we alter them to fit our needs. As a result we often overestimate the magnitude of changes in the near future. We expect transformations and find only "more of the same."

But as we become blasé about the latest gadgets, we find ourselves engaging in new practices made possible by the new technologies. These new ways of communicating, of relating to one another, and of accomplishing our daily lives create possibilities that go beyond what even the designers of the new technologies envisage. It is this yet to be designed world that we seek to understand.

Data

- The Internet now has more than 30 million hosts. See Network Wizards at http://www.nw.com.

- Traffic on the Internet has been doubling every 100 days. See The Emerging Digital Economy at http://www.ecommerce.gov.

- In the United States, 73% of white high school and college students have access to a home computer; only 32% of black students do. See Bridging the Digital Divide (1998) at http://www.2000.ogsm. vanderbilt.edu.

Interpretations

[C]omputers are, inevitably, culturally relative objects; unlike rocks and whales, they cannot be said to exist without people who possess culture, in which to recognize and use them. This is an important realization, because it brings us back to the mysterious thing called "meaning" after technocentrism has threatened to banish it. (p. 23, Jaron Lanier, "Moving Beyond Muzak," *Harper's*, *296*(1774), 22–24, March 1998)

Thus email is not the same one social practice and conception of giving and receiving meanings via digital text. Like "literacy," "email" is an umbrella term for a diverse and ever growing array of technological literacies. (p. 146, Colin Lankshear, *Changing Literacies*, Buckingham, UK: Open University Press)

Technology is making life easier and more convenient and enjoyable, and many of us healthier, wealthier, and wiser. But it is also affecting work, family, and the economy in unpredictable ways, introducing new forms of tension and distraction, and posing new threats to the cohesion of physical communities. (http://www.technorealism.org)

Over 60% of the citizens and 70% of the local businesses of Blacksburg, Virginia, USA, use the Internet on a regular basis. This is a result of a collaboration between the town, Virginia Tech, and Bell Atlantic to create one of the first electronic villages at http://www.bev.net.

Organizations

Some organizations based in the United States concerned with adolescent and adult literacy:

- International Reading Association, http://www.reading.org
- Literacy Volunteers of America, http://www.literacyvolunteers.org
- The National Council of Teachers of English, http://www.ncte.org
- National Center on Adult Literacy, http://www.literacyonline.org

Glossary

Cyberspace: as coined by science fiction writer William Gibson, a computer network in which users mentally traverse large data matrices; now commonly used to describe the Internet or the Web.

E-mail: a service that allows users to send and receive messages via computer and network; many services now support styled text, graphics, audio, or video.

Embedded systems: computer processors that work in appliances, cars, telephones, lights, and other devices; they are often invisible to the user and mean that nearly everyone is becoming a user of computer technologies, even without realizing it.

Host: a computer connected to the Internet with a registered name, such as http://www.reading.org. The term is used to refer to any single machine on the Internet, but a single machine can act as multiple systems, each with its own domain name and IP address, so the definition now typically includes virtual hosts as well.

Hypertext: a text in which "hot links" allow the reader to move to another text; these texts can be sounds, images, and video, as well as familiar printed texts. Hypertext blurs the line between author and reader, as each collaborates in the construction of the text to be read. It is the format for World Wide Web resources.

Internet: the global communications network that supports the World Wide Web and, increasingly, voice and video communications.

Sociotechnical analysis: an approach to the study of human activity that explicitly accounts for both social practices and the influence of material objects, such as artifacts, tools, and communications media.

continued

Glossary (cont.)

Virtual reality: systems that give the user the illusion of viewing or participating in a 3-D artificial world; current systems include 360-degree, 3-D visualization, surround sound, and even physical touch effects (haptic sensations).

World Wide Web (WWW): an Internet service based on hypertext links to organize and connect to Internet resources; as the Web begins to incorporate e-mail, telephone, recorded music and movies, radio, and television, it appears poised to become the all-encompassing communications media framework.

Constructing a Once-and-Future History of Learning Technologies

Editor's Message

When I think about learning technologies, I usually think of the latest device and what opportunities it affords for new modes of learning. So, the wireless portable device that a student could take on a visit to a museum fits my ideal, but not the stationary, messy, and dull chalkboard, despite the fact that it is, of course, a learning technology as well. I want the future to be fresh and unencumbered by the less than ideal realizations of the past.

However, as I think more about future possibilities, I realize that they are always shaped by present realities. We construct our stories of the future out of the materials of the present—the hopes and beliefs that nourish and limit our vision. For that vision to grow, we need to delve deeper into our past, for only there can we find the stuff to build a better future.

In the fall of 1999, I taught a course on the use of technologies for learning. We studied the World Wide Web, multimedia, communication and collaboration software, tutoring systems, virtual reality, and other new digital technologies. The more we became immersed in all these new developments, the more it seemed important to understand their antecedents and to evaluate them in the light of past successes and failures. In our effort to understand and build a better future, we found it increasingly valuable to turn to the past. Thus began our time line project. This month I explore what we are beginning to learn from this investigation of the past and future of learning technologies.

Original version published May 2001 in the *Journal of Adolescent & Adult Literacy*
©2001 International Reading Association

How We Built the Learning Technologies Time Line and What We Learned Doing It

The students involved in the time line project were a diverse and interesting group. There was an on-campus section of the course, which included both undergraduate and graduate students in computer science, education, and other fields. Some of the students held jobs in which they were developing or implementing learning technologies. For one student, the project work he completed in the course led directly to his obtaining a job in the French department to develop language-learning software. There was also an online section, consisting of students enrolled in Curriculum, Technology, and Educational Reform, a master's program for teachers, administrators, and technology coordinators interested in new learning technologies.

I knew the students possessed a collective resource of knowledge about the development of learning technologies and that they had the research skills to discover more through reading and personal contacts. But I could not anticipate how rich their collaboration on this history project would become or how much I would learn from it.

To get things started, I asked the students to construct a webpage for some event that they thought was significant, or simply interesting, in the history of learning technologies. I agreed to place those entries on a collective time line so that we could look for patterns among the events. You can see a small portion of the Learning Technologies Time Line (Middle Ages) we created below. Each underlined phrase is a hyperlink to a webpage, and each one was created by a different student.

600   "Arabic" Numerals developed by the Hindus

1453   The printing of the Bible with movable type by Gutenberg transforms society

1564   Graphite is discovered

1608   Hans Lipperhey's patent application for the telescope to the government of Zeeland

1635   Founding of Boston Latin, the first public school in the US

1651   John Dury invents the modern library

The first entries matched my expectations; they described technologies that had been designed explicitly for teaching and learning. For example, there was an entry for the development of the programming language Logo (Abelson & diSessa, 1981; Goldenberg & Feurzeig, 1987; Logo Foundation, 2000; Papert, 1980). Logo was important because it showed that even young children can understand and make use of sophisticated ideas in computing such as decomposing complex problems into simpler ones, thinking in terms of recursion, and representing data in arbitrarily complex structures. It was also an early example of the link between constructivist philosophy of learning and new technologies.

There were a couple of entries related to the even earlier PLATO system. PLATO was developed in the United States at the University of Illinois at Urbana-Champaign in the early 1960s, as one of the first computer-assisted instruction (CAI) systems (Bitzer, Lichtenberger, & Braunfeld, 1961). It eventually included thousands of course modules. Ten years before the Arpanet (forerunner of the Internet), 15 years before the personal computer, and 30 years before the Web, PLATO supported networked instruction using touch-sensitive screens, graphical interfaces, e-mail, and online chat spaces with multiple windows for multiple participants.

Examining these early developments helped us all to see current innovations in an appropriate historical perspective. In some cases, we saw that today's novelties were not so new after all; in others, we came to appreciate how much things had changed. Soon, there were entries for other key early systems, such as Scholar, HyperCard, and the graphing calculator. All the aforementioned might be considered tools designed explicitly for teaching. But before long there were other technologies that did not fit so neatly within the "learning technologies" label. Students saw that the Apple II computer was a major learning technology, even if it had other uses as well. The Web became an entry, as did technologies associated with it such as the Internet.

The activity opened up the question, What important learning technology might I describe? Once that happened, it was not long before one student decided to make the case that if the Apple II of 1977 were classified as a learning technology, then the Remington No. 2 typewriter of a century before should be too. Soon, we saw the pencil appearing on our time line, and then graphite; its discovery in 1564 made the pencil possible.

The time line stretched further and further into the past. I decided to ask my fall 2000 class to extend the time line. This time, I had a mix of students as well.

There were teachers again, also full-time doctoral students, and many were current or future librarians. They were enrolled in an online course on learning technologies offered through the Library Education Experimental Program (LEEP) http://www.lis.uiuc.edu/gslis/degrees/leep.html. Then, I asked the students in my course for undergraduates, called Literacy in the Information Age, to make their contributions. These students all added to the time line, bringing in the Rosetta Stone from 196 BCE and Ashurbanipal's Royal Library at Nineveh from 650 BCE. Today the time line goes back to 40,000 BCE, when cave paintings were first used as a means of communication.

One student asked whether we should not add the telescope, because it can be used to learn about the stars. Another added the stethoscope, which helped people learn about the human body. We now had tools for representing information, for communicating, for collecting and analyzing data—essentially a conception that includes all information and communications technologies. We also had organizations, such as the first public school in the United States, the first library, and the first university. Soon, the question arose, Is there anything that is not a learning technology? One student said, "Surely, we can't include the automobile!" But others pointed out that we use a car to get to class; we learn how to use a car; we learn about gasoline, construction materials, traffic laws, distance/rate/time, and many other things as we use cars. It became difficult to draw the line that clearly demarcated learning from nonlearning technologies. We began to see that it was the way we used a tool rather than its inherent properties that determined its capacity to support learning. Our conception began to move toward John Dewey's view of technology as a way to resolve a problem (Hickman, 1990).

I also asked the students to look ahead: What events will occur in the future history of learning technologies? Again, their creativity and resourcefulness surprised me. You can read now that virtual reality training becomes a requirement for all healthcare professionals in 2004; the Power Pencil, which stores the information that is written with it, appears in 2040, and holographic teaching comes in 2065. Entries such as this continue up to 3922.

As we looked at the time line as a whole, a number of characteristics stood out. I noticed first that events in the future often occur in years ending in zero. Note, for example, the interesting set of events proposed for 2010, as shown in another excerpt from the following time line. Again, each hyperlink (underlined) led to a webpage, and each page was created by a different student.

2010 The e-Trapper is introduced as the "all-in-one school tool"
The Internet is accessed entirely through wireless, handheld, pocket computers
The first widespread use of electronic textbooks in U.S. schools
House Co. starts production on the fully automated house for the consumer market
Children's Interactive Easy Reader Series debuts in book format
625 million homes now own DVD players

In contrast, past events happen all over the place. The placement of future events at decade and century boundaries correlates with a sense of their significance. In the past, every event is part of a long chain of developments so that it is difficult to identify the essential turning point. For the future, the opposite problem occurs. We have only essential events, and it is difficult to construct the chain of events in which that event should reside.

This situation leads to the somewhat paradoxical result that there is more disagreement about the past than about the future. When, for example, was the printing press invented? Should we mark the years 1453–1455 when Gutenberg printed the 42-line Bible? Or should it be the year he began work on it? Should we perhaps mark the year he formed a partnership with the wealthy burgher, Johann Fust, to build the press?

Alternatively, should we count the earlier printing done by others of less significant books or the much earlier printing in Korea or China, even if it did not involve movable type? Often there are conflicting claims, especially when we ask about "the first" of anything in an important sequence. Because we have not visited the future yet, our vision of it is shaped by literature and the broader literature of film, television, and Web genres. The past, of course, is also shaped by imaginative literatures as well as by documentary accounts. However, the literary accounts of the past are somewhat constrained to conform to documented happenings.

When events occur in the described construction of the future, they not only happen in isolation but also tend to have their effects all at once. Whereas the printing press required additional technologies of paper production and transportation to realize its power, such is not true of future devices. More often, just as in science fiction, they simply appear and work their wonders. Their work is little constrained by the social, cultural, and economic factors that play such an important role in the adoption of past technologies.

Nevertheless, the story of the future that we see in this time line does give us a visual aid for understanding the past and present uses of technologies for learning. We see there both the utopian and the dystopian visions of the technological world we are creating every day. In a small way, it may serve to inform scenario planning or future studies as applied to learning technologies.

Interpretations

A friend was cleaning out files in a library in Amherst, Massachusetts, when he came across a document that intrigued him. The document contained a list produced for a course taught in 1946. I was equally intrigued when he sent me a copy of the list. Gwladys Spencer was the instructor for the course, Library Science 54, which was taught at the University of Illinois Library School, Second Semester, 1946–1947. Much of the list, reproduced as is below, is unremarkable.

Types of Audio-Visual Materials and Equipment to Be Utilized by Libraries in the Educational Program
1. Blackboards and bulletin boards
2. Posters, cartoons, clippings
3. Dramatics: pantomimes, playlets, pageants, puppet shows, shadow plays
4. Trips, journeys, tours, visits
5. Models, objects, specimens
6. Charts: organization or flow, table, tree or stream
7. Graphs: area, bar, diagram, line, pictorial statistics
8. Maps: flat, relief, projected, electric, globe (celestial or terrestrial)
9. Microscopes
10. Microprojectors, reading machines; microfilms, microphotographs, microprint
11. Stereoscopes; hand, binocular, televiewers; stereographs, disc for televiewers
12. Flat pictures; photographs, prints, postcards, positive transparencies
13. Still pictures projectors and projected-opaque, filmslides, slides (glass, cellophane, ceramic, etc.)
14. Sound filmslides projectors; sound filmslides
15. Motion pictures projectors and projected: silent films, sound films
16. Sound recorders: transcriptions
17. Phonographs; disc, wire; recordings
18. Talking books
19. Radios, loudspeakers, public address systems, intercommunicating systems
20. Television

But several things struck me as I went through Spencer's list. One was that she included television in a course in 1946, showing that she had foresight about its eventual prominence as a communications medium. Another thing was that she included tools for investigation, such as microscopes, and "Models, objects, specimens." She clearly saw that audiovisual materials were more than simply devices for transmitting information. But more striking still are numbers 3 and 4 on her list. Among audiovisual materials and equipment, she included "pantomimes, playlets, pageants, puppet shows, shadow plays" and "trips, journeys, tours, visits." The presence of these says that she saw all the elements of her list as opportunities for enriching experiences, rather than simply as media for transmitting information.

Aside from the details of which tools she had available, the list tells me that Spencer had a broad view of how libraries could support learning and, more important, a vision of what learning could be. Today, we are excited about multimedia in education. But what we often mean is simply that a computer display can show students moving pictures with sound. Interactivity is an important additional component. But our vision of what that multimedia really means for learning needs to go beyond the technical features of the display to consider what students can do and how they can extract meaning from their own experiences.

Spencer saw that there were many tools and media that could enhance learning. She drew from traditional as well as emerging technologies to lay out a spectrum of possibilities for teaching and learning. Her list suggests an openness to diverse ways of learning and, moreover, a view of learners as active constructors of meaning.

Website of the Month

In 1996, the U.S. Public Broadcasting System produced a television special called *Triumph of the Nerds: The Rise of Accidental Empires*. According to PBS Online (http://www.pbs.org), the three-part show "zooms backwards on the information superhighway to show in vivid detail how youthful amateurs, hippies and self-proclaimed 'nerds' accidentally changed the world." The companion website http://www.pbs.org/nerds offers a variety of resources, such as a time line for the history of the personal computer, facts about some of the "nerds" featured on the television program, and the program transcript. You can also try out an interactive "pick the computer" game, which lets you test your nerd quotient.

> It's hard to believe that twenty years ago there were no personal computers, now it's the third largest industry in the world, somewhere between energy production and illegal drugs but the most amazing thing of all is that it happened by accident because

a bunch of disenfranchised nerds wanted to impress their friends. This is the story of how a handful of guys launched an industrial revolution. How they changed the culture of business, how they made history.

Robert X. Cringely, Part I of *Triumph of the Nerds*

How You Can Participate

The time line project exists on a public website: http://www.lis.uiuc.edu/~chip/ projects/timeline. Please come visit it to see some interesting student work and to learn a little about the history of learning technologies. I would be interested to hear what you see in the entries and what you learn from your exploration.

Beyond simply reading the time line entries, you might like to add one of your own. There is an online form at the end of the time line, which you may use to add an entry. You just need to give it a headline, a date, and a description, either as a URL or as text you send.

Glossary

Future studies: a form of inquiry in which futurists forecast a variety of alternative possible futures (see Dator, 1998). The goal is to help people invent and then move toward a preferred future. One approach to this is called scenario planning.

Learning technology: a tool or medium that helps learners construct new knowledge. It usually refers to a new information or communication technology such as visualization software, virtual reality, electronic bulletin board, simulation, tutorial, or interactive game. Depending on the use, practically any technology can be considered a learning technology.

The term *learning technology* is ambiguous in at least four ways. It can mean (1) the tool that helps one learn and thus enables *learning through* technology, (2) *learning how to use* technology, (3) *learning about* technology, or (4) a technology that itself learns. In (4) for example, genetic algorithms in effect learn how to perform more effectively in some environments based on feedback about their success and failure; thus, they are *technologies that learn*.

Logo: a programming language, essentially a version of the language Lisp, which was designed as a tool for learning. It is notable for its emphasis on modular design, extensibility, interactivity, and flexibility, all features that enhance its potential for learning. Wallace Feurzeig at Bolt Beranek and Newman led a team that created the first version of Logo in 1967. Seymour Papert, who had worked with Feurzeig and also with Jean Piaget in Geneva, led further developments of Logo at the Massachusetts Institute of Technology, Cambridge.

continued

Glossary (cont.)

Logo has been used across the curriculum, notably in mathematics, language, music, robotics, telecommunications, and science. The most popular Logo environments have involved the turtle, either as a robot that moves around on the floor or as an icon that moves about a computer screen and can be used to draw pictures.

Additional developments have included LogoWriter (adding word processing), LEGO Logo (connecting Logo to machines built out of LEGO bricks, motors, and sensors), MicroWorlds (adding drawing tools, a shape editor, and a melody maker), the Programmable Brick (with a computer inside it), and StarLogo (a massively parallel version of Logo in which thousands of turtles can carry on independent processes and interact with one another).

Scenario planning: "an approach to planning that starts from the assumption that, much as we try, we simply cannot predict or control the future. We can only imagine different ways in which the future might turn, stake out a course that makes sense today, and try to be flexible and alert when the unexpected inevitably occurs," according to the website http://www.marin.cc.ca.us/scenario. The site, Scenario Planning at College of Marin, provides a good introduction to scenario planning and shows its application to planning in the context of uncertain levels of state funding for California's community colleges.

REFERENCES

Abelson, H., & diSessa, A.A. (1981). *Turtle geometry: The computer as a medium for exploring mathematics*. Cambridge, MA: MIT Press.

Bitzer, D.L., Lichtenberger, W., & Braunfeld, P.G. (1961, October). *PLATO II: A multiple-student, computer controlled teaching device* (Rep. I-109). Champaign, IL: University of Illinois at Urbana-Champaign, Coordinated Science Laboratory.

Dator, J. (1998, November). The future lies behind! Thirty years of teaching futures studies. Introduction to the special issue on "Teaching Futures Studies at the University Level." *American Behavioral Scientist*. Retrieved from http://www.soc.hawaii.edu/future/dator/futures/behind.html

Goldenberg, E.P., & Feurzeig, W. (1987). *Exploring language with Logo*. Cambridge, MA: MIT Press.

Hickman, L.A. (1990). *John Dewey's pragmatic technology*. Bloomington, IN: Indiana University Press.

Logo Foundation. (2000). Website: el.www.media.mit.edu/logo-foundation

Papert, S. (1980). *Mindstorms: Children, computers, and powerful ideas*. New York: Basic.

OTHER SOURCES

Eisenstein, E. (1983). *The printing revolution in early modern Europe*. Cambridge, UK: Cambridge University Press.

Joy, B. (2000, April). Why the future doesn't need us. *Wired Archive, 8*. Retrieved from http://www.wired.com/wired/archive/8.04/joy.html

Nunberg, G. (1998, November/December). Will libraries survive? *The American Prospect Online*. www.prospect.org/archives/41/41nunb.html

A Friendly, Welcoming Attitude Toward Change

Editor's Message

After September 11, 2001, many people who had once celebrated change became all too familiar with its dark side. Most crushing, of course, was the loss of loved ones, but soon people around the world began to experience material losses of various kinds, divided communities and increased racism, the loss of civil liberties, and war, not to mention a diminished peace of mind.

Nearly everyone was affected by the declining economy, and many lost jobs, not only in New York City but around the world. The World Bank (2001) saw the economic downturn as "condemning as many as 10 million more people to live in poverty next year, and hampering the fight against childhood diseases and malnutrition." It further estimated that "an additional 20,000–40,000 children under 5 years old could die from the economic consequences of the September 11 attack as poverty worsens." Meanwhile, ideas such as torturing people suspected of terrorism to force them to talk became commonplace, and alliances with rogue nations and groups that abuse human rights were fully acceptable.

Change—which once associated itself with new clothes or the latest movie, with growth and improvement, and with enticing possibilities for the future—suddenly became a monster to be feared. People in the United States talked as if the once-hailed revolutions in computers and medicine had ended along with the destruction of the World Trade Center in New York. They wanted to turn back the clock on immigration or at least stop it. There was an understandable desire to bring everything to a halt and rewind to an earlier time.

Without dwelling on one of the most reported stories ever, it is fair to say that few people were happy about the changes wrought by the events of September 11. Even accepting or understanding these changes seemed impossible. It may still seem incomprehensible to speak of a friendly, welcoming attitude toward change. However, that is exactly what I would like to argue; such an attitude is necessary if we are to make sense of the world and our place in it. Moreover, it is the only way we can grow. This type of attitude applies not only to the catastrophic events, but also to the mundane experiences in our lives. It applies to the ways we teach and learn and to our efforts to understand new technologies.

Original version published April 2002 in the *Journal of Adolescent & Adult Literacy*
©2002 International Reading Association

Coping With and Welcoming Change

"Research," Charles F. Kettering said, "is a high hat word that scares a lot of people. It needn't. It is rather simple. Essentially, research is nothing but a state of mind—a friendly, welcoming attitude toward change" (Kettering Foundation, 2001, http://www.kettering.org).

Near the end of the fifth century BCE, the Greek philosopher Heraclitus pointed out, "You cannot step twice into the same river" (Fieser, 2001). He even went so far as to say that the one who steps is not the same person from one moment to the next. Heraclitus saw that unified things in the world inevitably break apart into a multiplicity of opposing phenomena. At the same time there is a way back to unity through harmony and peace. Phenomena in nature are constantly dividing and uniting in this way.

For Heraclitus, change was a fundamental constant in the way he conceived the world. If we accept his account it is not surprising that we see change as fundamental to our definition as human beings. We change along with the world around us, and who we become is determined by how we react to change. When a change occurs, it is often disruptive. Although change is rarely as disruptive as the events of September 11, any change can nevertheless upset the course of life. We know the world as it is, not as it might be. These perturbations can be purely destructive or they can be opportunities for growth.

It is no accident then that major theories of learning center around how an organism responds to disruption. For Piaget (1970/1972), the drive of the mind to assimilate new information periodically results in a condition of imbalance termed *disequilibrium* or *cognitive dissonance*. This conflict between expectations and experiences is essential for learning or development of cognitive structures. In Dewey's (1938) account, it is difficulty, especially a felt difficulty, that provides the raw material for learning. As we seek to overcome a difficulty, we are forced to modify our previous ways of thinking and acting. Similarly, Vygotsky's (1934/1962) zone of proximal development is that space in which an individual cannot succeed alone but can succeed with additional cultural mediation (e.g., artifacts, texts, and social structures). In each of these theories learning is essentially the trace of a successful response to change.

The processes of coping with the change that an individual undergoes are analogous to those that we see in disciplinary inquiry. In his well-known analysis of knowledge construction in science, Kuhn (1972) argued that normal science proceeds by working on problems within a paradigm or schema, much as an individual learns through small but generally expected changes. A revolution in science, meaning a shift in paradigm, occurs as the result of a crisis, something that cannot be assimilated (Piaget's term) into the dominant paradigm. Similarly, developments in educational practice can be viewed as paradigm shifts occurring in response to disequilibrating events. Hairston (1982) described this process in the field of composition that took place in the 1970s.

Coping With Change in Education

We see education today as a system that needs to respond to dramatic changes. These changes deriving from September 11 are set against a backdrop of economic, demographic, and technological developments in society at large. As we address them, we typically adopt one of many stances, spanning the spectrum from denial to celebration (see Glossary).

The most common stance toward change, and the one we nearly all adopt from time to time, is the utilitarian. Changes are seen instrumentally—as things to be analyzed and utilized. In the realm of new technologies most people emphasize the need for everyone to improve their skills. It is believed that if we learn how to control new technologies we can cope with change and make effective use of new tools. The clearest example of this approach is the development of standards for technology skills. These include defining the competencies needed to use a particular technology, specifying what students need to know to sign up for a subject of study or to graduate from a program, and articulating what teachers need to know or teach.

In the United States, official bodies such as the International Society for Technology in Education (ISTE) are concerned with accrediting teacher preparation programs and promoting appropriate technology use in education. They have developed guidelines for students, teachers, technology specialists, administrators, and programs (ISTE Accreditation and Standards Committee, 1996; National Educational Technology Standards Project, 1999). Individual states have developed similar standards, in many cases working from the ISTE and National Council for Accreditation of Teacher Education (NCATE) model. The ISTE and NCATE standards cover a broad area. In the case of foundations for all teachers there are standards for the following:

- Technology operations and concepts
- Planning and designing learning environments and experiences
- Teaching, learning, and the curriculum
- Assessment and evaluation
- Productivity and professional practice
- Social, ethical, legal, and human issues

These standards can be quite useful as a heuristic to promote dialogue about what is most important in teaching.

However, there are several problems that are quite familiar to anyone who has served on a standards committee. Sometimes, individual standards are far too specific (e.g., that people should know how to use a particular piece of software to do a given task). It is likely that the software in question is only one of many ways to accomplish a task, and would be superceded by the time the standards are actually implemented. On the other hand, a standard can be quite general, as in the ISTE/NCATE III. B: "Use technology to support learner-centered strategies that address the diverse needs of students." Representing what someone needs to know is difficult when circumstances vary and the type of knowledge needed is multifaceted.

Beyond the problem of representation is the underlying issue that the world is changing. We would like to prepare students and educators to cope well with the world they are about to enter, but as Dewey (1938) showed, the idea of education as preparation for life is self-contradictory. What one learns to satisfy a specific aim is too often compartmentalized—unavailable when one needs to react to a new situation. Learning how to learn is far more important than obtaining any specific skill or bit of knowledge.

Welcoming Change

If change is inevitable as Heraclitus said, if it is unpredictable as much of our recent experience tells us, and if it is traumatic as September 11 emphatically declared, we naturally seek some framework for response. The standards movement started with these premises, intending to provide us with tools to accommodate change.

Ultimately it is a reductionistic approach that attempts to categorize the modes of response, showing us only what we need to know and do.

Limitations of the standards and of other conventional process technologies—benchmarks, performance indicators, scope and sequence, and so on—are well known and perhaps best by those who work with them on a daily basis. Is there any alternative? How else might we think about a changing world and its implications for teaching and learning?

I suggested that Kettering's "welcoming attitude toward change" might be what is needed not just for research, as he says, but for response to any situation. But should we welcome all change? Aren't there times when we should say no either to disasters or to newness that undermines values we hold dear? That answer depends on what we mean by the word welcome.

If, by the word *welcome* we mean to accept without question or to embrace in all its dimensions, then the answer is clearly yes. We all need to develop the critical faculty that can help us look at something new and assess its strengths and limitations. However, there is another sense of welcome that Kettering probably intended. It is closer to the way one might interact with a visitor, for example, someone who has just moved to your neighborhood. In this second sense, welcoming means graciousness and openness to difference. There are several key aspects.

Listening. A welcoming attitude toward change requires listening and making the strange familiar. Rather than compartmentalizing experiences as good or bad it asks how meaning can be derived from the experience. Through listening, it attempts what Gadamer (1960/1994) called "fusing horizons," a process in which we stretch from our current understanding and our very personal history to understand the perspective of another.

Respect for diversity. Welcoming implies a respect for diversity. It recognizes that no one individual has the source of all knowledge and that every individual possesses knowledge no one else has. Thus, diversity becomes a resource for growth and not a problem to be overcome.

Humility. A welcoming attitude incorporates a strong dose of humility as well. Rather than emphasizing the accumulation of chunks of knowledge and skills, it assumes a continual incompleteness in knowledge and skills. It sees each situation as an opportunity to learn more. Thus, the teacher is a learner.

Growth through overcoming difficulties. In welcoming change, we seek to discover new connections and open new possibilities. When experiences are negative they still provide opportunities for growth, often more than positive ones do. Thus, the emphasis shifts from a model of things as they are to a dynamic one in which each experience brings with it the chance to grow. In the case of new technologies, a welcoming attitude would not include seeking mastery. Instead, the focus is on being open so that one is able to learn more easily.

(I would like to thank Ellen Knutson for pointing me to the Kettering Foundation's work and Christine Jenkins for discussions that enlightened my conception of change and inquiry.)

Other Views

For Gadamer (1960/1994), understanding can never be complete or total, but there can be partial understanding through which we can grow.

> [O]ne intends to understand the text itself. But this means that the interpreter's own thoughts too have gone into re-awakening the text's meaning. In this the interpreter's own horizon is decisive...[as] a possibility that one brings into play and puts at risk, and that helps one truly to make one's own what the text says. I have described this above as a "fusion of horizons." (p. 388)

Website of the Month

The Pew Research Center is an independent opinion research organization (sponsored by the Pew Charitable Trusts) that studies attitudes in the United States toward the press, politics, and public policy issues. It publishes widely cited research on the use of the Internet and other media by various groups, including adolescents (see http://www.pewinternet.org). Following September 11, the center tracked public attitudes about the events. Pew studies are an important resource for politicians, journalists, scholars, and public interest organizations. All the current survey results are made available free of charge on their website. The research program includes five principal areas of investigation.

- The People & The Press—explores public attitudes about the credibility, social value, and salience of the news media.
- The People, The Press & Politics—features a typology that divides the American electorate into distinct voting groups and identifies the basic values and attitudes that animate political behavior.

- The News Interest Index—measures on a regular basis how closely the public follows the major news stories and links this to views about politics and policy issues.

- America's Place in the World—a series of in-depth surveys and analyses of the public and opinion leaders on international policy in the post–Cold War era.

- Media Use—major surveys that measure the public's use of, and attitudes toward, the Internet and traditional news outlets.

Glossary

Stances Toward Change

I have argued that there were several classic stances concerning how new technologies should change education (Bruce, 1997). These stances apply to our attitude toward change in general.

Aesthetic: Others adopt an essentially aesthetic stance toward change. They believe change should be described and commented on but not fully engaged. This stance is similar to what Rosenblatt called the "aesthetic response" to reading.

Neutrality: Some say no specific stance toward change is needed, implicitly advocating a neutral stance. They fear the allure of today's fashion, stressing instead what they see as enduring values. Thus, they give little consideration to how events might alter their practices. In traumatic changes, it is often difficult to distinguish neutrality from denial.

Opposition: Others go beyond the neutral position to stand in active opposition to change. In many cases, their concern is that humanistic values will be subsumed by technocratic or economic forces. Kaufmann (1977) used the term *dogmatic* in a similar way in his discussion of the art of reading.

Skeptical: The pessimistic side of utilitarianism is practical skepticism. Proponents point to past unfulfilled promises and to the inertia of large systems as justification for their doubts.

Transactional: Dewey and Bentley's (1949) theory of transaction provided one more way to respond to change, whether that be in the form of new ideas in a text, a new technology, another person, or events in the world. In this theory, a transaction is the encounter of a person's unique, situated history with something new. Every transaction is different and holds the seeds of new meaning (see McDermott, 1981, p. x). A transactional stance means a welcoming attitude toward change, opening oneself to the significance inherent in such encounters.

continued

Glossary (cont.)

Transformational: In contrast to the oppositional position is the transformational one, especially when that stance conceives the transformation as positive. In extreme versions, we get what Kaufmann called the "exegetical response," a faith in the transformative powers of the new. The transformationalist argues that our task is to understand and guide the transformation.

Utilitarian: Some argue for a utilitarian stance (for Kaufmann, agnostic), saying that new tools or ideas need to be incorporated intelligently into practice. The utilitarian stance toward change is much like Rosenblatt's (1978) efferent stance in reading—a view of the text as a repository of information.

REFERENCES

Bruce, B.C. (1997). Literacy technologies: What stance should we take? *Journal of Literacy Research, 29,* 289–309.

Dewey, J. (1938). *Experience and education.* New York: Collier.

Dewey, J., & Bentley, A.F. (1949). *Knowing and the known.* Boston: Beacon.

Fieser, J. (Ed.). (2001). Heraclitus (535–475 BCE). The Internet encyclopedia of philosophy [Online]. Retrieved from http://www.utm.edu/research/iep/h/heraclit.htm

Gadamer, H.-G. (1994). *Truth and method* (J. Weinsheimer & D.G. Marshall, Trans.). New York: Continuum. (Original work published 1960)

Hairston, M. (1982). The winds of change: Thomas Kuhn and the revolution in the teaching of writing. *College Composition and Communication, 33,* 76–88.

International Society for Technology in Education Accreditation and Standards Committee. (1996, October). National standards for technology in teacher preparation. Retrieved from http://www.iste.org/standards/ncate

Kaufmann, W. (1977). The art of reading. In W. Kaufmann (Ed.), *The future of the humanities* (pp. 47–83). New York: Thomas Y. Crowell.

Kuhn, T.S. (1972). *The structure of scientific revolutions* (2nd ed.). Chicago: University of Chicago Press.

McDermott, J.J. (1981). *The philosophy of John Dewey.* Chicago: University of Chicago Press.

Piaget, J. (1972). *The principles of genetic epistemology* (W. Mays, Trans.). New York: Basic Books. (Original work published in 1970)

National Educational Technology Standards Project. (1999, November 18). National educational technology standards for students—connecting curriculum and technology. Eugene, OR: International Society for Technology in Education.

Rosenblatt, L.M. (1978). *The reader, the text, the poem: The transactional theory of the literary work.* Carbondale, IL: Southern Illinois University Press.

Vygotsky, L.S. (1962). *Thought and language* (E. Haufman & G. Vakar, Trans.). Cambridge, MA: MIT Press. (Original work published 1934)

World Bank. (2001, October 1). *Poverty to rise in wake of terrorist attacks in US: Millions more people condemned to poverty in 2002.* Retrieved from http://www.worldbank.org/developmentnews

Evolving Media Practices

Friedrich Nietzsche has been described as the first mechanized philosopher, the first to compose directly on a typewriter. He recognized that the new mode of production of text was implicated in his ideas and once wrote, or rather, typed, on the back of a postcard, "Our writing instruments contribute to our thoughts" (Kittler, 1990, p. 195). Nietzsche's observation has inspired much speculation about how the technology of writing shapes the content of writing, such as whether mechanized modes of text production lead to new ways of thinking about the human condition.

Today, we have many new technologies to inspire further speculation. Does hypertext lead to new ways of thinking, which are more network-like than linear or hierarchical? Do visual media imply following ideas through space rather than time, as in traditional narratives? How do new modes of collaboration across distance and time change our notions of authorship and the text? Does the sheer quantity of information alter the way we determine what is credible, novel, or true?

Although the columns here represent different perspectives and concerns, none of them adopts the popular media conception of new technologies as fully new and autonomous. Instead, they conceive "new media" as current events in a long evolution of literacy practices. Moreover, they reject the simple media effects model, in which the form or content of a text has easily predictable consequences. They recognize, as Nietzsche did, that our writing instruments make a difference. But they see the potential for people to be not merely tools of the new media, but active constructors of those media. As Feenberg writes, humans can choose to "relate to their environment actively as well as passively, selecting out that dimension of the world around them to which they adapt" (2002, p. 190).

The columns in this section explore a variety of dimensions of the relationship between media and literacy. "Mixing Old Technologies With New" examines the fact that we rarely throw away old practices entirely. Instead, we mix them in with what we are already doing, in the process transforming both the old and the new. In "Electronic Publication: Writing for the Screen," Mike Sharples reflects on his own experience as a writer who produces texts both online and on paper. "The Work of Art in the Age of Digital Reproduction" extends the discussion of new media to include the wide variety of visual arts now accessible through the Web and the new modes of creating art. In "Information Literacy: The Changing Library," Cushla Kapitzke asks how libraries are changing, becoming portals to the digital space, or "cybraries." The next column, "Digital Content: The Babel of Cyberspace," takes that question into literature, building on Jorge Luis Borges's fantastic visions. Then, "Searching the Web: New Domains for Inquiry" discusses the consequences for finding information in these new, vast information spaces. Bernhard Jungwirth was a student in the United States from Austria when he wrote "Information Overload: Threat or Opportunity?" He discusses there the contrasting views of information held in the United States and Europe. The last two columns explore the control of information. "Open Source: Everyone Becomes a Printer" discusses what it means when anyone can publish a text. Another student, Michael D. Brunelle, reports on his study of the free software movement in "Why Free Software Matters for Literacy Educators."

REFERENCES

Feenberg, A. (2002). *Transforming technology: A critical theory revisited*. Oxford, UK: Oxford University Press.

Kittler, F. (1990). The mechanized philosopher. In L.A. Rickels (Ed.), *Looking after Nietzsche* (pp. 195–207). Albany, NY: State University of New York Press.

Mixing Old Technologies With New

Editor's Message

In last month's Technology column I talked about the way literacy practices are changing along with new technologies. That picture of step-by-step changes is a convenient one, but it tells only part of the story. For one thing, the kind of literacy associated with one set of media for reading and writing does not go away when new media, such as the mass-produced book or the computer, become available. Instead of replacing one kind of literacy with another, we add to our repertoire.

But we don't just add either; we change the ways we enact literacy. In the realm of popular media, we see that television did not replace radio, although it did lead to changes in the ways that people used the earlier technology. Rather than sitting in front of the radio at home with family and friends, we took portable radios with us in the car, to the beach, or to work, and began wearing radio headsets. The content transformed along with the hardware, as radio drama and variety programs gave way to news and recorded music. In a similar way, we add to our ways of making and interpreting texts, and change the occasions for these practices. People still use quill pens and calligraphy brushes, although generally for aesthetic and symbolic rather than daily functional purposes.

Along with adding new technologies for literacy and changing the ways in which we use older technologies, we also create literacies that are hybrids of existing practices. We can see the great variety of these new literacies reflected in the electronic journals now coming online. Some of the periodicals appearing online look very much like their printed counterparts. Others add interactive features, more graphics, even video. Many have links to websites, and many become sites for collaboration through online discussion groups.

As these e-journals become more commonplace, they alter what the September JAAL editorial referred to as first-wave technologies (such as television), as well as the print-based technologies (such as newspapers) that preceded them. Each of these technologies undergoes changes as we develop our understanding of them and interact with them in new ways. We now see, for example, that newspapers not only cover the digital revolution, but that their format begins to take on characteristics of webpages, such as extensive use of graphics, cross-indexing, and even citations of URLs.

These multiple literacies make new demands on readers and writers and on those who are helping students to develop their literacy skills. Moreover, they challenge all of us to become aware that we are actively involved in shaping the very technologies we use.

Original version published October 1998 in the *Journal of Adolescent & Adult Literacy*
©1998 International Reading Association

Hybrid Literacies

It is no longer the case that we can easily separate the use of new technologies in literacy from standard practices. More often than not, literacy means combining a variety of new and old tools in creative ways; we have to develop hybrid practices that moot the question of whether to use new technologies at all.

I saw this variety in a course I taught recently for preservice teachers. In this course, every student created a set of webpages. Working with students in that process reminded me how much we are all caught between new and old literacies. For example, two students gave me their Web project on a floppy disk in an ordinary envelope. What they had written on the envelope appears in the figure.

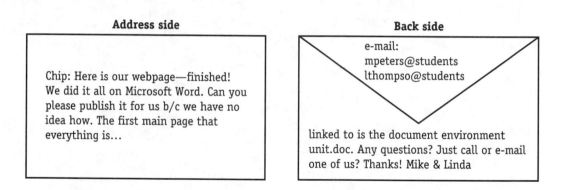

This text exemplifies the complex, changing, and hybridized literacies today's students need to learn. Physically, it consists of a standard envelope, but one that contains a magnetic disk. In spite of the impressive storage capacity of the disk, it turns out to be more effective to communicate using the blank paper of the envelope and a felt-tip pen. On the other hand, they ask for questions back via e-mail. They use hybrid morphemes, such as "b/c" for "because," drawing perhaps on e-mail discourse and webpages they have seen. Their text is created "all in Microsoft Word," but using the Hypertext Markup Language, or HTML, format appropriate for the Web. Mike and Linda are unconsciously creating a hybrid medium, one that combines paper and pen, floppy disk, and e-mail in a unique way.

They could have constructed a different hybrid, for instance, by e-mailing the files or their envelope message, or by requesting a response on paper.

Mike and Linda say this is their finished webpage, but of course the webpage isn't the envelope or even the disk, but information that won't be on the Web until it's posted on a server, and they have no idea how to do that. In fact, they know more than they claim, because they have created the documents for a fine website, using a word processor that supports hypertext. And they know that somehow the various files on the disk need to be transferred to a larger disk on the university Internet server. Although they are still learning, their knowledge is impressive enough to be daunting to some people.

As they are learning how to use these new technologies to accomplish a given task, Mike and Linda are doing something perhaps even more important. They use the Web as a way to represent themselves. In this case, their webpage becomes a portfolio that they use when seeking a teaching job. But the flexibility of the Web format makes it possible to portray many aspects of personal identity to the world. Many young people now have webpages proclaiming, "All About Me!" with links to pictures, friends, pets, favorite music, hobbies, and more. As a medium for these portrayals, the Web supports diverse, hybrid representations that express the diverse, hybrid character of societies and individuals today.

We see on the Web aspects of both old and new literacies intermingled and continually reconstructed. Even a technology as basic as e-mail developed in this way: About three decades ago, file transfer programs were developed to move large data files from one computer on the Arpanet to another. Early users realized that they needed to communicate with the person receiving the file at a distant site if they were to use the new technology effectively for transferring those files. Fortunately, they quickly saw that one kind of file they could transfer was a message to the other person. Moreover, they could send messages about any topic. Thus was e-mail invented out of file transfers. This process of appropriation of technology has made the history of technological change dynamic and difficult to predict. In a similar way, Mike and Linda are moving rapidly to become literate in new forms without abandoning the old. They appropriate certain practices, alter others, and blend them with both old and new needs to accomplish their purposes. In so doing, they become not just users of the new technologies, but active constructors of it.

Interpretations

Literacy has never been more central to work than it is today, and not just literacy, but "literacies," the multiple forms of literate practice that new technologies and new forms of social organization have brought about. The new literacies entail not only basic reading and writing but also "soft skills," such as the ability to use reading and writing to solve problems and to communicate complex information. Successful practice of this kind of literacy is part of "knowledge work."

> By the end of this century knowledge workers will make up a third or more of the work force in the United States—as large a proportion as manufacturing workers ever made up, except in wartime. (Peter Drucker, November 1994, "The Age of Social Transformation," *Atlantic Monthly*, p. 62)

> [E]mployers now look for hard and soft skills that applicants wouldn't have needed 20 years ago:
> - The ability to read and write at the ninth-grade level or higher
> - The ability to do math at the ninth-grade level or higher
> - The ability to solve semistructured problems where hypotheses must be formed and tested
> - The ability to work in groups with persons of various backgrounds
> - The ability to communicate effectively, both orally and in writing
> - The ability to use personal computers to carry out simple tasks like word processing (Richard Murnane & Frank Levy, 1996, *Teaching the New Basic Skills*, New York: Martin Kessler Books, pp. 31–32)

Website of the Month

NewJour, a comprehensive list of e-journals and other serial publications. In January 1998, NewJour added its 5,000th journal. The list's precursor was the Association of Research Libraries' directory of electronic journals, newsletters, and discussion groups, first published in 1991 by Ann Okerson.

Websites of the Month: E-Journals

Electronic journals concerned with adolescent and adult literacy:

- *Reading Online*, an electronic journal published by the International Reading Association. The audience is literacy educators interested in using the Internet for research, instruction, and communication. Features peer-reviewed interactive articles, reviews of print and nonprint materials, and ongoing professional dialogue about critical issues in literacy education.

- *Library Trends*, a quarterly journal that explores trends in library design and use. Each issue is devoted to a single theme from special libraries to emerging technologies. The site includes only abstracts and ordering information.

- *Computers and Composition* includes descriptions of computer-aided writing and reading instruction; personal accounts of teaching experiences; explorations of ethical, legal, and social issues around computers and writing; and discussions of how computers affect the form and content of written discourse, or the process by which it is produced and interpreted. There is both a print and an online version; the latter employs audio, video, and hypertext.

- *Teaching English as a Second or Foreign Language: An Electronic Journal*, a quarterly listserv journal on the teaching of English as a second or foreign language. It includes studies in ESL/EFL pedagogy, second language acquisition, language assessment, and applied socio- and psycholinguistics.

- The Virtual University Gazette, a monthly newsletter for distance learning professionals. It contains job announcements, updates on programs, and short articles on issues in technology-enhanced distance education, especially for adult learners.

Glossary

Arpanet: a network of computers designed to allow researchers to share expensive computer resources. It was created in 1969 at Bolt Beranek and Newman in Cambridge, Massachusetts, USA, and was the forerunner of the Internet, the infrastructure for the World Wide Web.

E-journal: a journal in electronic form. In some cases, an e-journal may appear as a World Wide Web page, with a URL; in others it is delivered by electronic mail, usually through a listserv.

First-wave technologies: communication/information technologies, such as radio, television, audio recording, video recording, cinema, and telephone, which operate primarily with analog representations of information. These technologies have been primarily used for one-way delivery of information, but there are many exceptions.

continued

Glossary (cont.)

Header: information included with an e-mail message such as who sent it, the date of sending, and the subject of the message. A full header can show the path that the message traveled, where an automatic reply will be sent, the message priority, and other features.

Hybrid literacy: a way of producing and interpreting texts that combines aspects of two or more sets of literate practices. For example, discussion on a moderated list may call for a unique blend of certain academic conventions for writing along with other conventions about friendly social interchange. The particular blend is in turn dependent on technological features such as how the listserv program displays messages and headers.

Listserv: an Internet service that allows a group of people to communicate via e-mail by sending mail to a single electronic address. Messages are forwarded to each person on a designated list and are often archived for future reference. Listserv communications vary greatly, including informal conversations, moderated list discussions, and formal publications, such as e-journals.

Moderated list: an electronic e-mail list with a moderator who may initiate and guide discussions, review messages for appropriateness, or issue periodic summaries.

Second-wave technologies: communication/information technologies, such as computers, the Internet, the World Wide Web, and digital video, which operate primarily with digital representations of information. These technologies present great opportunities for two-way communication.

Uniform Resource Locator (URL): an electronic address, typically one designating a computer file on the World Wide Web, such as http://www.reading.org. The URL system allows millions of computers, each containing thousands of files, to refer consistently to specific resources.

Electronic Publication: Writing for the Screen

Guest Author Mike Sharples

Editor's Message

I mentioned that from time to time this journal year I'd invite guest authors to write the *JAAL* Technology column. This month's guest, Mike Sharples, has worked for many years on innovative approaches in language and technology. He was a pioneer in creating environments for students to use computers to explore patterns in language through his Phrasebooks and Boxes programs. One thing I especially liked about this work was that Mike saw that language learning could be fun, and he built that perspective into his software. He has also been a leader in areas such as artificial intelligence, cognitive science, and computer support for collaborative writing.

Working, as he does, in the United Kingdom, Mike has a perspective on educational technology issues that will add to my view from the United States. When I asked him if he would be interested in writing this issue's column, I also told Mike that I would very much like to hear his latest views on electronic books. When he wrote back to me with his acceptance, he suggested the topic of paper versus electronic publication.

Online journals and e-books are beginning to appear as commercial products. In the Issue section Mike tackles questions such as What are the implications for reading and writing? Is it as easy to read from the screen as from a book? and Should we be writing for the screen rather than the page?

Original version published October 1999 in the *Journal of Adolescent & Adult Literacy*
©1999 International Reading Association

Writing the Dynabook

For most of us writing is painful. The longer it continues, the more agonizing it gets. With a long continuous work, such as a book or dissertation, you begin to lose direction and belief in your ability to perform. The text seems formless and divorced from reality, the audience becomes muffled and immaterial. All you hear is your own querulous voice doubting your ability to write and urging you to give up, until the pain vanishes in a lightheaded rush of revision and publication. F. Scott Fitzgerald captured this experience exactly when he wrote, "All good writing is swimming under water and holding your breath" (from an undated letter to Frances Scott Fitzgerald).

I have recently finished the equivalent of a long dive through a subterranean cave, having written a book for a general audience on the process of writing (Sharples, 1999). Throughout the two years it took to complete the book a question has been nagging at me, sapping my resolve to write, gloating at my writer's block. You find it so much easier to write online, it murmurs. You can type out 50 e-mail messages a day without effort. You enjoy creating webpages. Why put yourself through the agony of publishing a book?

I can easily dismiss the obvious answers. Academics rarely make good money from writing. Even with good textbook sales and above-average royalties, the rate of pay is about that of a jobbing gardener, and the work is far less healthy. Nor is being a published author necessarily the best way to achieve recognition and respect. A helpful (http://www.gwu.edu/~tip/, http://www.aber.ac.uk/media), thoughtful (http://www.eastgate.com/garden), or provocative (http://cogsci.rpi.edu) website can do more to boost a reputation than any number of worthy monographs.

So I wrote a book rather than a website, not for the reward it brings but for its intrinsic properties. A book can carry a story. The genre of popular science has succeeded by presenting difficult ideas as mystery stories, leading the reader on a narrative journey that gradually reveals clues about human abilities or the natural world. The codex book has evolved over many centuries as a medium for such intellectual storytelling, augmenting the linear text with a wealth of marginalia and illustration, from footnotes to pop-ups.

Until now, the best the computer industry has been able to offer to support narrative writing are cumbersome and expensive approximations to the printed book with flickering pages and jagged letters. But that is changing as, one by one, the advantages of a printed book over a computer are disappearing. Let me address the well-worn arguments.

- *You can't read a webpage in bed*. Yes, you can, and you don't need a light.

- *People can read text faster and more carefully from a printed page than a computer screen*. That may have been true when the screen glowed green and the text appeared as jagged lines of dots, but a detailed series of experiments with modern high-resolution "paper-like" screens (http://psych.utoronto.ca/~muter) showed that people can read short stories on screen with the same speed and comprehension as from a book.

- *You can trust a book*. The Anomalies Bibliography (http://anomalyinfo. com/biblio_t.htm) is a list of the best and worst books on the paranormal. Of the misleading or downright inaccurate books on that list, many of them bear the imprint of otherwise reputable publishers. The authority of a text comes not from printer's ink, but from the process of refereeing and criticism. Online refereed journals, such as the *Journal of Computer-Mediated Communication* (http://jcmc.huji.ac.il), are just as authoritative as paper ones.

I could continue, but comparing pages to computer screens, or books to websites, misses the point. The computer has flourished until now by imitating and then swallowing up earlier tools and media: the calculator, the typewriter, the spreadsheet. Soon it will devour the television. But it is also developing its own intrinsic character as a blender of interactive media, capable of merging text with images and of acting as a personal assistant, interpreter, guide, and teacher. The irony is that this genuinely new medium arose from a research project to design the perfect book.

One of the great untold stories of the computer age is Alan Kay's farsighted project to develop the Dynabook. In California, USA, at the Xerox Palo Alto Research Center in the 1970s, Kay led a group of talented researchers with a single vision: to design and build a multimedia computer the size and shape of an ordinary notebook.

To put this project in context, the smallest general-purpose computer in the early 1970s was about the size of a desk, and the word *multimedia* meant a slide-tape presentation. Kay and his team built a mock-up of the Dynabook out of wood, borrowed and developed novel ideas for interacting with the screen, constructed working interim Dynabooks, and devised a programming language that would merge the profusion of media into a symphony of interaction. After some 10 years of work, the Xerox company, eager to show some return on its investment, but unsure of how to market this radical new concept in computing, issued the Dynabook as a business computer named the Star. The business world could see little use for such a bizarre machine, and it flopped.

There the story would have ended, had not two young entrepreneurs from a newly successful company, Apple Computers, adopted the basic design of the Star for its new range of computers called the Lisa and later the Macintosh. The history of personal computing since that time can be seen as a struggle to realize the vision of the Dynabook. The wooden mock-up of the Xerox researchers bears an uncanny similarity to recent mininotebook computers such as the Sony VAIO SuperSlim Notebook. The interim Dynabooks with their high-resolution screens were the first desktop workstations. The method of interaction that the Xerox team devised—through a mouse, icons, menus, and multiple windows—evolved into the Windows interface. The team's object-oriented programming language, Smalltalk, was the forerunner of Java.

Yet, somewhere along this evolutionary trail the original purpose was lost. The Dynabook was to be a device for learners (the Xerox team was named the Learning Research Group), and its purpose was not to make office work more efficient but to augment the intellects of children and adults by means of a device for creating dynamic books: books that converse; books that weave together words, images, and sounds; books that enable children to become authors of music and animation.

A Dynabook is not simply a means of displaying print on a screen, but is a new medium with the power to (a) adapt to a reader's needs and interests; (b) remove the barriers between reading and writing; (c) share knowledge; and (d) create an interaction of words, sounds, and images.

After almost 30 years, the Dynabook hardware has arrived. In a press release issued in January 1999 the Fujitsu company announced the Stylistic 2300, a tablet computer the size, shape, and weight of a large-format book, with a new color "sunlight" display for reading outdoors, pen input, stereophonic sound, and a screen that can show full-motion video. It is, of course, promoted as a "paper-less mobile office." But it more than fulfills Alan Kay's emotive promise, written in the 1970s, that the Dynabook would have

> enough power to outrace your senses of sight and hearing, enough capacity to store for later retrieval thousands of page-equivalents of reference material, poems, letters, recipes, records, drawings, animations, musical scores, waveforms, dynamic simulations, and anything else you would like to remember and change. (Kay & Goldberg, 1977, p. 31)

Writing for this Dynabook will demand new skills to enable us to combine the narrative drive of text with the engagement of hypermedia. To do justice to the medium we shall have to learn new grammars of movie making (such as shots and transitions) and hypertext (with hyperlinks and trails). We shall either become, or work alongside, people who can choreograph interaction with the reader to offer multiple pathways, layers of information, simulated conversations, and animation. The four basic skills will be reading, writing, computation, and interaction design.

It will be some months or even years before Dynabooks are as affordable as, say, personal organizers or mobile phones, time enough just to begin the immense task of designing software that will enable authors to create the new dynamic literature; inventing ways to teach the skills of writing for dynamic books; and reconceptualizing writing as the blending of text, image, and interactivity.

Website of the Month

An imaginative attempt at creating a dynamic story on the Web is at http://www.nationalgeographic.com/egypt. It takes the form of an interactive edition of the February 1923 *National Geographic* magazine, giving an eyewitness account by Maynard Owen Williams of the discovery of Tutankhamen's tomb. The story is presented both as a simulated magazine and as a "silver screen" movie of the discovery. In one section, the same story is told from three viewpoints: Williams's official written account of the event, a series of photographs taken by Williams, and the letters that he sent to the editor of the *National Geographic*.

An article by Bart Marable about the making of the story appeared in the March 1999 *Web Techniques* magazine (pp. 18–23). In "Bringing Stories to Life Online," the designers of the website described how they evoked the feel of a 1920s magazine through a careful combination of color, layout, and typefont. The effect is, however, entirely spoiled by a large and gaudy banner at the foot of each screen advertising computer products. The site is a lesson for any aspiring Web author: Ensure that you keep full control over the screen presentation of your article.

Glossary

e-book and e-book reader: an e-book is a book presented in electronic form to be read primarily on a screen. It may provide interactivity through dynamic links, quizzes, or simulations. An e-book reader is a device, which may be in the form of a simulated book with two foldout screens, for viewing e-books.

Dynabook: the Dynabook was Alan Kay's vision of a "personal dynamic medium," a powerful personal computer that could be used by children and adults to explore and create words, music, sounds, and images and animations.

Planet eBook: a comprehensive and independent website exclusively focused on electronic books (eBooks) and eBook-related technologies (http://www.planetebook.com).

REFERENCES

Kay, A., & Goldberg, A. (1977, March). Personal dynamic media. *IEEE Computer, 10*(1), pp. 254–263.
Sharples, M. (1999). *How we write: Writing as creative design*. London: Routledge.

Guest Author

Sharples is Kodak/Royal Academy of Engineering Professor of Educational Technology at the University of Birmingham in the United Kingdom.

The Work of Art in the Age of Digital Reproduction

Editor's Message

The Web is filled with images—diagrams, drawings, photographs, computer animations, virtual reality, and, increasingly, streaming video. The ability of the Web to display all sorts of images in full color, often with moving or interactive aspects, is one of its great attributes and what makes it much more than simply a system for exchanging alphabetic text.

Oddly though, the proliferation of images, especially those we see on commercial sites and in the all-too-common banner and pop-up ads, obscures the capacity of the Web as a medium for sharing many other forms of art. Beneath the glitzy, commercial veneer the Web has become a major art medium: Serious students of art can examine art products across genres, cultures, and time; artists of all ages can present their work to larger audiences; all those interested in developing new forms of expression can experiment and extend the palette of possibilities; and anyone can explore art forms that are difficult to access otherwise.

Art on the Web can be a boon to teaching across the curriculum. There are many sites using art to offer new ways to approach the study of literature, history, culture, philosophy, and the sciences. Most important, these sites remind us of the importance of the aesthetic dimensions of learning.

This month's column investigates only a few of the ways that artists and appreciators of art are using the Web. How is the combination of digital media and new communication technologies changing the practices of making, understanding, and responding to art? It is impossible in a few pages to convey the richness and diversity of art online, but perhaps this brief tour can suggest another dimension of our expanding notion of literacy in the information age.

Original version published September 2000 in the *Journal of Adolescent & Adult Literacy*
©2000 International Reading Association

From Hand to Mechanical to Digital Reproductions of Art

At the time of writing this column, Walter Benjamin is getting much attention because of new critical studies and translations of his work. Much of that work is complex, fragmentary, and ultimately unfinished, perhaps not unlike the changing society he sought to understand. Nevertheless, his analysis of art and reproduction, written 65 years ago, is still relevant to discussions of Internet literacy.

In 1927 Benjamin began work on his famous Arcades project (Buck-Morss, 1991), in which he studied the social life of 19th-century Paris through its arcades (the prototype of today's shopping malls). The work eventually expanded to include the entire physical and historical "assemblage" of Paris from the catacombs to the Eiffel Tower. As he sought to understand the interplay of historical, political, aesthetic, and technological forces, he foreshadowed the "information ecologies" ideas of today (Nardi & O'Day, 1999).

Mechanical Reproduction of Art

One of Benjamin's most accessible and well-known essays is "The Work of Art in the Age of Mechanical Reproduction," written in 1935 (Benjamin, 1968). In that essay, he asked what happens to our experience of art, and to the artwork itself, when it becomes easy to reproduce it. He began with the argument that works of art were always reproducible. Students or apprentices learn how to replicate the work of their teachers, master artists and crafters reproduce their work for others, and third parties copy works for monetary gain or fame.

Nevertheless, the number of copies of a given work of art was always small. Moreover, it was usually possible to determine the authenticity and uniqueness of a given work. The painting by Leonardo da Vinci known as the *Mona Lisa* hangs in the Louvre Museum in Paris. Handmade copies or forgeries were easily detected. Furthermore, what the *Mona Lisa* has meant to generations of people has been closely tied to its unique physical positioning. Unfortunately, for many that has meant seeing it in a crowded room with dozens of people jostling for a glimpse.

Benjamin argued that the age of mechanical reproduction changed not only our aesthetic experience of art but also art's political functions, its commodity value, and the social relations constructed around it. He built on the work of the poet Paul Valéry, who earlier had written about the effects of lithography, photography, and other techniques in changing our relation to images. His words could be applied to the use of the Internet today:

> Just as water, gas, and electricity are brought into our houses from far off to satisfy our need in response to a minimal effort, so we shall be supplied with visual or auditory images, which will appear and disappear at a simple movement of the hand, hardly more than a sign. (Valéry, 1964, p. 226)

For Benjamin in 1935, the technologies of the phonograph, radio, and film only added to the prevalence of mechanical reproduction. The *Mona Lisa* could now be experienced at the cinema or on a postcard, each reproduction altering the future experience of the original.

New capacities for reproduction appeared with television and with advances in filmmaking and publishing. John Berger examined these in his work, which built on Benjamin's courses. *Ways of Seeing* (Berger, Blomberg, Fox, Dibb, & Hollis, 1972) was based on his British Broadcasting Corporation television series that expanded the ways of viewing and interpreting visual art. Through many examples, Berger showed that art both reflects and shapes our social world, that the contexts for viewing are critical, and that the expanded possibilities for reproduction have fundamentally altered the functions of visual learning.

Berger did not know about the Internet when he worked on this series and book, but his ideas extend easily into consideration of the new technologies. He would probably say that the new digital forms have vastly extended what art can mean, not simply by making art products available to wider audiences, but by spawning a diverse array of new ways of seeing.

Digital Reproduction

Today, the process of mechanical reproduction is expanded through electronic or digital reproduction. Benjamin's essay is not only reproduced in various print collections, including the paperbound Illuminations (1968), but also in multiple digital forms (see http://pixels.filmtv.ucla.edu/community/julian_scaff/ benjamin.html and http://Web.bentley.edu/empl/c/rcrooks/toolbox/common_ knowledge/general_communication/benjamin.html).

Each of these presents the same text, but in different formats and contexts that change its meaning. The images from *Ways of Seeing* are online, too. In contrast to those of the television series, they are easily accessible and can be viewed at leisure in any order. In contrast to those in the book, images are in color and can be viewed in various sizes or by focusing in on image details.

Digital reproduction brings several new elements to the process of diffusing art. First, people can reproduce art much more quickly than they could in the time of Valéry or Benjamin. Second, they can make many more copies, such that the *Mona Lisa* is reproduced on countless websites created by students, and then reproduced again by each visitor to the site as he or she calls up that webpage image. Taken together, the ability to reproduce images quickly and multiply leads to what U.S. Senator Charles Mathias called the "Era of Promiscuous Publication" (Post, 1996). In one reading of the future this will make copyright unenforceable. In another, it leads to technological restrictions on copying that could bring an end to the "Fair Use Doctrine," which permits individuals to make reasonable personal use of any image they have obtained legally.

A third element of digital reproduction is the capacity of the user, or viewer, to manipulate the work of art and thus control the context of viewing. Software allows users to adjust the image size and the resolution, to focus in on minute details, to extract portions of an image, to combine one image with another, and to surround the image with a new textual or visual context.

What do all these changes mean for the development of art? What are the implications for artists and students of art? How do they change the meaning of literacy in the information age? Jonathan Zittrain has said that discussions of technology always have two phases. First, we say "It's too early to tell" and soon after "It's too late to do anything about it." His solution to this is to focus on addressing the first before the second arrives (Allis, 2000).

Other Views

Our fine arts were developed, their types and uses were established, in times very different from the present, by men whose power of action upon things was insignificant in comparison with ours. But the amazing growth of our techniques, the adaptability and precision they have attained, the ideas and habits they are creating, make it a certainty that profound changes are impending in the ancient craft of the Beautiful. In all the arts there is a physical component that can no longer be considered or treated as it used to be, which cannot remain unaffected by our modern knowledge and power. For the last twenty years neither matter nor space nor time has been what it was from time immemorial. We must expect great innovations to transform the entire technique of the arts, thereby affecting artistic invention itself and perhaps even bringing about an amazing change in our very notion of art. (Valéry, 1964, p. 225)

Even the most perfect reproduction of a work of art is lacking in one element: its presence in time and space, its unique existence at the place where it happens to be. (Benjamin, 1968, p. 220)

[F]or the first time in world history, mechanical reproduction emancipates the work of art from its parasitical dependence on ritual. To an ever greater degree the work of art reproduced becomes the work of art designed for reproducibility. From a photographic negative, for example, one can make any number of prints; to ask for the "authentic" print makes no sense. But the instant the criterion of authenticity ceases to be applicable to artistic production, the total function of art is reversed. Instead of being based on ritual, it begins to be based on another practice—politics. (Benjamin, 1968, p. 224)

Website of the Month

Christopher Witcombe's site (http://witcombe.sbc.edu) is one of the best organized and most comprehensive resources providing pathways to art across the centuries, cultures, media, and genres. It relies on existing collections in various museums, galleries, television stations, journals, and other organizations throughout the world.

When you visit the site, you can find images of clay tablets with early writing from Mesopotamia. You can visit the caves of Elephanta, near Bombay, containing reliefs, sculptures, and a temple to the Hindu god Siva. These cave works date to the Silhara kings from 9 to 12 A.D. You can also see the "Lost Cities of the South" in the Public Broadcasting Service series on Africa narrated by Henry Louis Gates, Jr. Or you can visit Judy Chicago's The Dinner Party exhibition from 1974–1979.

Where You Can Find Art on the Web

Many other sites show Web art or talk about art. Open Directory alone lists 154,675 sites. Here are just a few starting points.

- The Heidelberg Project at http://www.heidelberg.org is an outdoor art environment in the middle of Detroit, Michigan, USA. Cars painted in polka dots, houses clothed in rainbows, and the outdoors turned into a sculpture garden become an unusual and beautiful urban environment. The environment also generates controversy, which you can read about at the site. The story of this site and its Web counterpart is a good illustration of how digital reproduction reshapes the political potential of art.

- The Web Gallery of Art at http://www.kfki.hu/~arthp/index.html is "a virtual museum and searchable database of European painting and sculpture of the Gothic, Renaissance, and Baroque periods (1200–1700), currently containing over 6,500 reproductions. Biographies, commentaries, guided tours are available" (according to the website).

- The Boston Cyberarts Festival at http://www.bostoncyberarts.org shows how the Web opens up new dimensions for art. The site "shows art in which the computer is integral to the art piece," including art that can only exist in the context of the Internet, art that is experienced as a navigable three-dimensional space, performance art, and sculpture and images conceived in relation to information technology. There is an online gallery featuring interactive exhibits by well-known "cyberworld" artists, such as Andy Deck and Mark Napier. Joseph Squier's "The Place," a classic piece of Web artwork, is presented there and at http://theplace.walkerart.org.

- Expression on the Web: A Continuum of Space Resources at http://www.SpaceArt.org is a site containing unusual works by artists who focus on images inspired by astronomy and space travel. There are also links to sites about astronauts and space in general.

- Clip Art sites, such as http://www.artclipart.com, provide extensive libraries of art that you can print out or use to make websites, brochures, and classroom newspapers.

- The Dia Center for the Arts in New York at http://www.diacenter.org has supported projects in many artistic media and created a site for interdisciplinary art and criticism. *Dia*, from the Greek word meaning "through," reflects the Dia Center's efforts to realize unusual art projects. The website is very well designed and presents a number of fascinating works with dynamic visual and auditory elements.

- Not for Ourselves Alone: The Story of Elizabeth Cady Stanton and Susan B. Anthony at http://www.pbs.org/stantonanthony is a site associated with a U.S. television documentary made by Ken Burns. The site allows viewers to follow events in the women's suffrage movement by seeing the photographs used in the documentary and by reading historic documents and essays.

- The International Museum of Collage, Assemblage and Construction (IMCAC) at http://ontologicalmuseum.org/museum/collage is a department of the Ontological Museum (Museo Ontologico) located in Cuernavaca, Morelos, Mexico, about one hour south of Mexico City. "The IMCAC is dedicated to the collection, study and exhibition of collage, assemblage, construction, montage, photo-montage, digital collage, and other constructive arts" (according to the website).

The Faces of Tomorrow project creates opportunities for young people to make and share art, and to create collective art pieces. It is a project of Boston Cyberarts, Inc., a nonprofit organization that organizes the Boston Cyberarts Festival mentioned earlier in this column. Since its debut at the 1999 festival, numerous arts programs, school groups, and afterschool programs have used this unique interdisciplinary project with middle school students.

As the site says, "Submit your face, your hopes and dreams, your curiosities and questions, your wonderings and speculations—in the form of a face." Young artists can become part of this collective art project by submitting an image created through drawing, photography, computer graphics, or any means that yields a digital image of the appropriate size (360 pixels square). Viewers can then call up individual images.

Glossary

Cyberart: a term used to denote art that uses, builds on, talks about, or in some other interesting way relates to the computer, Internet, or Web. See Rodney Chang's list of 72 propositions in his definition of *cyberart* (http://www.lastplace.com/page48.htm).

Image viewer: a program that allows the computer to display and control a visual image. There are many varieties. The major ones have plug-in versions that can be incorporated into a Web browser. Some simply display an image; others allow seamless panning and zooming on an image.

VRML art: art integrating audio and video for 3D digital imaging. Many different forms exist, making use of various "viewers" to display the art. The person experiencing the artwork can do so in a manner akin to exploring a real space, hence the "VR," or virtual

continued

Glossary (cont.)

reality, designator. Today, VRML art is included in many websites as a supplement to other content, not only as a separate art presentation. It is also being integrated with physical exhibitions of art in galleries and museums.

REFERENCES

Allis, S. (2000, March 26). Battle brews on rights to Web content. *Boston Sunday Globe*, pp. A1, A17.

Benjamin, W. (1968). The work of art in the age of mechanical reproduction. In H. Zohn (Trans.), *Illuminations: Essays and reflections* (pp. 217–252). New York: Schocken.

Berger, J., Blomberg, S., Fox, C., Dibb, M., & Hollis, R. (1972). *Ways of seeing*. London: British Broadcasting Company and Penguin Books.

Buck-Morss, S. (1991). *The dialectics of seeing: Walter Benjamin and the Arcades Project*. Cambridge, MA: MIT Press.

Nardi, B.A., & O'Day, V.L. (1999). *Information ecologies: Using technology with heart*. Cambridge, MA: MIT Press.

Post, D.G. (1996). New wine, old bottles: The case of the evanescent copy. Website based on article in *American Lawyer* (May 1995). Retrieved from http://www.cli.org/DPost/X0016_NEWWINE.html

Valéry, P. (1964). *Aesthetics* (R. Manheim, Trans.). New York: Pantheon.

Information Literacy: The Changing Library

Guest Author Cushla Kapitzke

Editor's Message

The new digital technologies are eliding the boundaries that used to exist between text and video, between school and society, between physical and virtual space. As they do, they also elide the lines we have drawn between student and teacher, learner and mentor, and in the case of schools between teacher and librarian. In the United States today, job categories such as "library media specialist" and "technology coordinator" are in rapid flux; the lines blur even as administrators and boards of education attempt to delineate them.

These changes are played out dramatically in libraries everywhere. Their role as repositories for printed information is significantly expanding. As that role enlarges, many questions arise: What will libraries become? What do students need to learn about navigating the new library space? How is the role of librarian changing? What do these new roles and capacities imply for the relation between teacher and librarian? What do they imply about new literacies?

For this month's column, guest author Cushla Kapitzke articulates key changes occurring around information literacy and raises issues that many are only beginning to consider. She also shows how technical and social changes cannot be separated.

Original version published February 2001 in the *Journal of Adolescent & Adult Literacy*
©2001 International Reading Association

Archive Fever: Libraries and "Cybraries" in New Times

Since the beginnings of recorded history, artifacts of symbolic memory have been collected and preserved in the physical space of libraries. The notion of having a secured place for information materials and knowledge resources is generally attributed to the Sumerians. Around six millennia ago, these inhabitants of small city-states in Mesopotamia combined pictorial signs with symbols to represent units of speech. This technology revolutionized communication, information, and education. Jacques Derrida (1996) claims that from the time humans discovered how to sustain meaning across time and space, they have suffered what he calls "archive fever," or the impulse to preserve an historical and cultural past through oral tradition and literate technologies. Archaeological evidence shows, for instance, that collections of Sumerian palace and temple libraries were cataloged, arranged in order, and supervised by trained personnel. This archive instinct continues to capture our imaginations as teachers, as print literates, and, for many of us, as cybernauts.

Libraries and museums are repositories for the printed, visual, and audio artifacts deemed memorable by society. Foucault (1986) called these disciplinary cultural spaces one of society's "heterotopic" sites because they are somewhat "other" to normal daily activity. As ordered places that users visit for short periods of time, they provide a distance, a space outside the everyday for engagement with other times, other histories, other identities, and other cultures. In this sense, they are places where, as kids, we would go to hear voices and possible worlds other than those of the schoolyard and community.

In schools, libraries are places where text, technology, and literacy converge in concentrated form. Like classrooms, libraries are private, exclusive places accessible only to student populations and those who are privy to their located languages and literacy practices. As archivist and custodian, the role of the librarian was to select, organize, mediate, and distribute society's symbolic materials. The Dewey Decimal Classification System (DDC) and Boolean logic are two examples of the tools and terms of "librarian-speak" that long have baffled and alienated many students and library patrons. Typical textual practices of libraries included searching the card catalog and "periodical indexes," locating materials via their "call numbers," skim reading, and note taking. These procedures and principles of print-based informational management, retrieval, and use remained largely unchanged for thousands of years, until two decades ago.

New Technologies and Libraries

Digitization and its two main derivatives, the Internet and hypertext, propelled information access and exchange into the era of cyberspace and the cyber library, or "cybrary." (For an example, see the homepage of the cybrary at the University of Queensland, http://www.library.uq.edu.au). Networked communications technologies have transformed not only the physical space of this time-honored learning place but also the literate and textual work that takes place in it. Milestones in the "technologization" of libraries include the automation of the catalog and the installation of OPACs, the introduction of electronic materials such as stand-alone CD-ROM indexes to which librarians only had access, the adoption of online information databases, and more recently the shift to library websites and Web-based catalogs (WebPacs). In the current transitional stage, digital or hybrid libraries integrate traditional and online services. Remote access means nevertheless that the necessity of going physically to a school or university library for informational materials is reduced or, in the case of virtual libraries, eliminated.

While still located in buildings, libraries are gradually transforming into dematerialized nodes of virtual, informational space that span oral, print, and digital cultures. The cybrary is an electronic gateway for clients located anywhere to access information located everywhere. Cybraries function as electronic "portals" to information services accessed just as easily from across Australia as across the counter or the campus. Without entering the premises or speaking to a member of staff, from any computer terminal with Internet access students are able to check if a book is on the shelf, request a resource, view their loans record, and peruse the list of new accessions. They can read their lecture notes, course reading lists, exam papers, and university handbooks. Postgraduate students and staff can request and receive journal articles via e-mail. The library homepage has become an entry point for subject-specific databases, full-text e-journals, free downloads of certain academic software, and information about online and face-to-face information skills training.

Cybraries and the New Literacies

What then has this transformation of the library meant for the work of students and teachers? In the process of researching a topic or preparing multimedia assignments for publication on the World Wide Web, students draw from a multiplicity of splintered literacies. They might, for example, start by researching their topic on the online catalog and the electronic databases to which the library subscribes. To locate and retrieve material from the Internet, they would need to understand and apply the differential uses and search protocols of the many subject directories, search engines, and meta-indexes available to them. If using webpage design or presentation applications for their assignments, students would need to download or print information, drag and drop text, insert backgrounds, create borders, and make hyperlinks to material in the document or to other files and websites. Students have the option of importing audio files of background music and interview material, or of inserting video clips and electronically scanned photos and images from other print materials.

These tasks assume technological competence in the creation and navigation of nested folders and directories and in the creation, saving, naming, and renaming of files. Depending on the software used, publishing a webpage requires network literacy to understand the local area network (LAN) and the procedures for transferring files back and forth to the server. Students also need socioethical competence in the codes of practice for using and publishing both print and electronic material. This includes knowledge of issues concerning copyright; plagiarism; the rights and responsibilities of system access and security; and standard social conventions regarding defamatory, obscene, or offensive material.

Literacy and Information Literacy

The technologization of language and text in the Information Age has generated many new theories and models for explaining and doing literate work. Visual literacy, digital literacy, media literacy, network literacy, critical literacy, and multiliteracies are some of them. The library profession's response to the proliferation of information was to reconfigure the library skills instruction programs of the 1960s into a research framework called "information literacy" (California Media & Library Educators Association, 1997). Most of the information science literature presents information literacy as an emerging approach rather than a fully defined, prescriptive model. Indeed, much of the literature bewails the slipperiness of the term and the lack of a universal definition with elaborated instructional goals and methods. Information literacy is variously understood as a process, a skill, or a competence. That information literacy should not be the domain of the teacher librarian alone and that training in it should be integrated across all subject areas are two points on which the profession agrees.

As used by librarians and teachers, information literacy consists of a hierarchy of information problem-solving skills that purportedly enable independent and effective learning. Most information literacy programs focus on tasks such as the creation and transmission of information, the construction and application of a search strategy, access to information (reference sources and periodical indexes), the structures of information (e.g., subject headings and the arrangement of database records), the physical organization of information (e.g., the DDC or Library of Congress Classification systems), and the evaluation of information. One leading model espouses information literacy as a process of steps: to define an information task or problem, to select appropriate resources, to solve the problem, to locate the resources in a collection, to read the materials, to synthesize the information, and to evaluate the product and the problem-solving process (Eisenberg, 1996).

Yet, that process and those strategies have been appraised and found wanting for learning and working in the information economies and cultures of New Times (Luke & Kapitzke, 2000). The ability to use and manipulate information is necessary, yes, but students need more than an understanding of the differences between data, information, and knowledge, and between fact and fiction. The non-linearity of hypertext sequencing is fast obliterating the conventional categories of knowledge and its hierarchical organization in, for example, the DDC. Furthermore, the ephemeral and hybrid nature of digital environments tends to elide differences between the real and virtual worlds, and therefore between factual and fictional ones. Information literacy derives from a print-based culture, and its logic as it currently stands maintains distinctions between, for instance, fiction and nonfiction, and between reading for pleasure and reading for information. These distinctions and their associated practices, such as the reading of novels in time reserved for silent, sustained reading (SSR), are becoming increasingly obsolete and discriminatory. For many youth today, particularly in advanced capitalist countries, reading is no longer performed alone with a book, but is a shared activity undertaken with and around a computer screen while engaged in conversation with others who are in the room, in cyberspace, or in both (Tapscott, 1998).

Libraries are affected not only by technological change but also by social and cultural change. Considering the pivotal role that the information literacy project plays in the educational enterprise, information literacy proponents should be mindful of the recent critical turn in educational theory and practice. This turn entails moving information literacy from the confines of the library to the arenas of language use and the social lives of youth, which in advanced economies comprise wall-to-wall multimodal information. It requires a sociology of information to account for the material and political bases of language and text use in libraries and their programs. As social practices, all literacies—including information literacy—are situated responses to specific political economies of educational contexts and classrooms (Luke, 2000). Because the discursive and material resources framing library practices vary within and across institutional sites, so do their learning outcomes. Selective traditions of information usage comprising combinations of canons, genres, literacy events, and social relations generate specific outcomes for certain social groups. Furthermore, those traditions of use confer differential identities, positions, functions, and powers to individuals in proportion to their mastery of the languages and discourses valorized by the literate economy in which they operate. Different libraries instantiate different regimes of rules, rationales, procedures, and practices for textual work, which in turn are socially and economically productive or counterproductive in terms of employment options and life chances for particular students.

Information literacy is not about analytic thinking or neutral cognitive processes but about improving student opportunity and capacity to design and forge lifeworlds in a range of text-based communities and economies (Cope & Kalantzis, 2000). It may be a process and a skill, but viewing it also as a socially constructed discourse and discipline opens a space for the possibility of social transformation through the interrogation and disruption of the discourses and economies that produce and reproduce it. Librarians, cybrarians, and teachers need therefore to shift their focus from a concern for a single, dominant theory of information literacy to the social and cultural construction of its pedagogies and, in turn, their variable political and discursive outcomes.

A Critical Information Literacy

This kind of critical information curriculum and pedagogy reframes conventional notions of text, knowledge, and authority, and in the process changes the traditional roles of students, teachers, and librarians. The library was the place students went to acquire a selective tradition of information use and its application to a curricular unit. By contrast, the cybrary must be both a place and a space not only for learning information but also for learning how to use information (i.e., the operational dimension of using online databases), for learning about information (i.e., the critical and political dimension), and for learning through information (i.e., the cultural dimension) (Lankshear, Snyder, & Green, 2000).

"Cybrarians," for example, can coordinate print and electronic resources between and among subject areas. With their expertise in the new information technologies and their knowledge of the collection, cybrarians might suggest texts that re-present a range of theoretical, ideological, and political perspectives on particular curricular issues. Take, for example, the topic of globalization. Rather than seek the facts or the truth about its negative or positive impacts, student reading and analysis could focus on the social construction of the discourses and practices of economic and cultural integration, which have costs and benefits, and advantages and drawbacks, in specific local and global contexts. In collaboration with the teacher, the cybrarian would furnish print and electronic texts produced by unionists, transnational corporations, indigenous peoples, feminists, environmentalists, and the World Trade Organization, all of which would present different and often conflicting versions of "reality." Opportunity to analyze how these positions are materialized in language and text would show students that the production of knowledge necessarily entails relations of power that are able to be contested and transformed. Considering the power of information networks to connect and disconnect, and to include and exclude (Castells, 1996), any pedagogy that ignores the political economy of information does a disservice to students, irrespective of whether they are part of and contributing to, or disconnected from, the electronic current of the Information Age.

A recent study in Australia (Meredyth, Russell, Blackwood, Thomas, & Wise, 1999) confirmed the digital divide along the same axes of gender, class, race, and geographic location that existed with print literacy. In the study, data were collected from 399 schools in all Australian states and territories. The total survey sample was 6,213 students from Years 6 and 7 and from Year 10, which is the final year of junior high school. The study reported that

- 85% of all students used computers outside schools;

- 50% used a computer outside school every day or almost every other day;

- a significant link existed between students' information technology skills, their confidence, their use of computers outside school, and the level of technology resources in homes;

- nearly all the students had more than half the basic information technology skills core to the operation of computers;

- 67% had all the basic information technology skills;

- more than half the students (65%) had a sound range of advanced information technology skills, including how to connect to the Web;

- more than half could use computers to create music or sound, and send an e-mail;

- 48% could create a multimedia presentation;

- 38% could make a website or homepage;

- indigenous students and those from small schools, especially in rural and isolated areas, were the most likely to lack basic skills;

- students who reported familiarity with the most complex uses of information technology were from independent schools and single-sex schools; and

- while the basic skills of girls were on a par with boys, boys had more advanced skills.

Other Views

Books constitute capital. A library book lasts as long as a house.... It is not, then, an article of mere consumption but fairly of capital, and often in the case of professional men setting out in life, it is their only capital. (Thomas Jefferson to James Madison, September 1821, http://www.ifla.org/I/humour/subj.htm)

Libraries are a kind of monumental writing, a writing and reading space in stone. (Jay D. Bolter, 1991, p. 101)

The archive is first the law of what can be said, the system of what governs the appearance of statements as unique events. But the archive is also that which determines that all these things said do not accumulate endlessly in an amorphous mass...it defines at the outset the system of its enunciability...[and] the system of its functioning. (Michel Foucault, 1972, p. 129)

Websites of the Month

http://www.edna.edu.au/EdNA/—EdNA Online: Education Network Australia—government-funded gateway for Australian educational resources.

http://www.hi.is/~anne/iasl.html—webpage for the International Association for School Librarianship.

http://www.infolit.org—National Forum on Information Literacy—a coalition of more than 75 education, business, and government organizations working to promote awareness of the need for information literacy and encouraging activities leading to its acquisition. It provides definitions of information literacy, descriptions of successful information literacy programs, and an extensive annotated compendium of linked websites.

Glossary

Boolean logic: a form of logic developed by the English mathematician George Boole that allows a database searcher to combine concepts in a keywords search using three commands or "operators": AND, OR, NOT.

Call number: a unique code displayed on the spine of library materials that represents the item in the library catalog and allows the user to locate the resource on the shelf.

Copyright: the exclusive legal right granted by a government to an author, editor, composer, playwright, publisher, or distributor to publish, produce, sell, or distribute a literary, musical, dramatic, or artistic work. Copyright law also governs the right to prepare derivative works, to reproduce a work or portions of it, and to display or perform a work in public.

Cybrary: an electronic gateway or portal for clients physically located anywhere to access information located everywhere.

Dewey Decimal Classification System (DDC): a system of classifying books and other works, was first published in 1876 by librarian Melvil Dewey, who divided human knowledge into 10 basic categories with subdivisions indicated by decimal notation.

Discourse: recurrent statements that constitute material and social relations of power.

Hybrid library: a library in which a significant proportion of the resources are available in digital format, as opposed to print or microform.

continued

Glossary (cont.)

Information science: a branch of knowledge that investigates the sources, development, dissemination, use, and management of information in all its forms.

Library of Congress Classification: a system of classifying books and other works devised by the Library of Congress in Washington, D.C., USA, which divides human knowledge into broad categories indicated by letters of the Roman alphabet, with further subdivisions indicated by decimal notation. Most research and academic libraries use Library of Congress Classification, whereas public and school libraries use the DDC.

Online catalog: a library catalog consisting of bibliographic records in digital format maintained on a dedicated computer that provides uninterrupted access via workstations that are in direct, continuous communication with the central computer during each transaction.

Online services: the branch of library services concerned with selecting and providing access to electronic resources such as online databases and CD-ROMs, including mediated searching, which is usually handled by an online services librarian.

Online Public Access Catalog (OPAC): a computer catalog of the materials in a library.

Virtual library: a "library without walls" in which the collection and resources are accessible only electronically and are not kept in paper, microform, or any tangible form.

WebPac: a public access online catalog with a graphical user interface (GUI) accessible via the World Wide Web, as opposed to a text-based catalog interface accessible via Telnet.

(Glossary adapted from Reitz, 2000)

REFERENCES

Bolter, J.D. (1991). *Writing space: The computer, hypertext, and the history of writing.* Hillsdale, NJ: Erlbaum.

California Media and Library Educators Association. (1997). *From library skills to information literacy: A handbook from the 21st century* (2nd ed.). Sacramento, CA: California School Library Association.

Castells, M. (1996). *The rise of the network society.* Oxford, UK: Blackwell.

Cope, B., & Kalantzis, M. (Eds). (2000). *Multiliteracies: Literacy learning and the design of social futures.* London: Routledge.

Derrida, J. (1996). *Archive fever: A Freudian impression.* Chicago: University of Chicago Press.

Eisenberg, M.B., & Berkowitz, R.E. (1996). *Information problem-solving: The big six skills approach to library and information skills instruction.* Norwood, NJ: Ablex.

Foucault, M. (1972). *The archaeology of knowledge and the discourse on language* (A.M. Sheridan Smith, Trans.). New York: Pantheon.

Foucault, M. (1986). Of other spaces. *Diacritics, 16,* 22–27.

Lankshear, C., Snyder, I., & Green, B. (2000). *Teachers and technoliteracy: Managing literacy, technology and learning in schools.* St. Leonards, NSW, Australia: Allen & Unwin.

Luke, A. (2000). Critical literacy in Australia: A matter of context and standpoint. *Journal of Adolescent & Adult Literacy, 43,* 448–461.

Luke, A., & Kapitzke, C. (2000). Literacies and libraries: Archives and cybraries. *Pedagogy, Culture & Society, 7,* 467–491.

Meredyth, D., Russell, N., Blackwood, L., Thomas, J., & Wise, P. (1999). *Real time: Computers, change and schooling. National sample study of the information technology skills of Australian school students.* Canberra, ACT, Australia: Australian Key Centre for Cultural and Media Policy.

Reitz, J.M. (2000). *ODLIS: Online Dictionary of Library and Information Science.* Retrieved July 22, 2000, from http://www.wcsu.ctstateu.edu/library/odlis.html

Tapscott, D. (1998). *Growing up digital: The rise of the Net generation.* New York: McGraw-Hill.

Guest Author

Kapitzke is a lecturer in the Middle Years of Schooling program at the School of Education, The University of Queensland, Australia.

Digital Content: The Babel of Cyberspace

Editor's Message

Anyone who is engaged in teaching people to read and write would be justified in questioning the relevance of the cyberworld to their concerns. This is especially so for those who teach adults, second language learners, or nontraditional learners. The basic issues of participation, engagement in learning, and fundamental skills stand out as priorities ahead of learning about complex new communication and information technologies, which in their promised form often seem to be perpetually just beyond the horizon.

Moreover, even if one grants the importance of the new technologies as learning resources or as occasions for developing critical job skills, their lack of availability often precludes their use. When they are available, they are often inaccessible because of lack of technical or administrative support, language barriers, and a host of other barriers.

Despite these legitimate reservations, it is increasingly obvious that those involved with literacy education can no longer conceive of their enterprise as separate from the realm of the new technologies. The most compelling reason may be that the distance between some learners and the technological world is itself a stark indicator of their exclusion from the dominant literacies of today. Each of the arguments about participation, engagement, skills, availability, accessibility, and so on, can be flipped to show that the cyberworld must not be ignored if we are to meet these learners' needs as literate citizens.

None of this really answers the "What do I do on Monday?" question, but it does say that we need to incorporate the opportunities and challenges of the new technologies into our discourse about teaching and learning. In this month's column I will take a fanciful journey into the Library imagined by Jorge Luis Borges and ask what it tells us about literacy resources today. Along the way, I will look at how digital libraries are growing and what they mean for literacy education.

Original version published April 1999 in the *Journal of Adolescent & Adult Literacy*
©1999 International Reading Association

What Kind of Library Is the World Wide Web?

> The universe (which others call the Library) is composed of an indefinite, perhaps an infinite, number of hexagonal galleries, with enormous ventilation shafts in the middle, encircled by very low railings.

Thus begins the fantastic tale written in 1941 by Jorge Luis Borges, called "La Biblioteca de Babel," or "The Library of Babel." The story was published in his collection Ficciones (Borges, 1962) and is available online at http://jubal.westnet.com/hyperdiscordia/library_of_babel.html.

You can learn more about Borges himself through the World Wide Web. There you can discover how he began writing when he was 6 years old, and that by age 9 he had published his translation of Oscar Wilde's "The Happy Prince" in a local newspaper. When he was 58, he was appointed to his dream job, the Director of the National Library of Argentina. But he was now almost totally blind, saying, "I speak of God's splendid irony in granting me at one time 800,000 books and darkness."

In "The Library of Babel" Borges envisions a world populated by books, much like his world, for he had led a life immersed in reading and writing. There is no Internet, and no computers exist like those of today, for his year is 1941, but his imagination moves far beyond such limitations. His books are held in a fantastic Library, whose architecture is like no existing library, but is nevertheless carefully and believably constructed. Each of the galleries within the Library is hexagonal with bookcases on four sides. The free sides lead to hallways from which one can reach additional galleries.

> There are five shelves for each of the hexagon's walls; each shelf contains thirty-five books of uniform format; each book is of four hundred and ten pages; each page, of forty lines, each line, of some eighty letters which are black in color.

These books contain all possible arrangements of the orthographic characters, punctuation, and spaces, leading some to assert "the formless and chaotic nature of almost all the books." It is assumed that

> the Library is total...[it includes] the minutely detailed history of the future, the archangels' autobiographies, the faithful catalogues of the Library, thousands and thousands of false catalogues...the translation of every book in all languages.

This totality of texts means that one can find anything in the Library, beautiful writing in every conceivable genre, information for every purpose, and guidance for every problem:

> When it was proclaimed that the Library contained all books, the first impression was one of extravagant happiness.

People saw that the Library could answer any question, no matter how arcane. If you wanted to know the annual catch of sea bream in Corsica, you could turn to the hexagon containing the book, http://www.netcorse.tm.fr/investir/corse/us_corse2.htm and learn that "in 1995, Corsica produced 900 tons of sea perch and sea bream." Of course, there was the nontrivial problem of finding that book in the first place.

> At that time it was also hoped that a clarification of humanity's basic mysteries— the origin of the Library and of time—might be found. It is verisimilar that these grave mysteries could be explained in words: if the language of philosophers is not sufficient, the multiform Library will have produced the unprecedented language required, with its vocabularies and grammars.

If you search the Web for "Library of Babel," you'll find hundreds of sites, an article by Dominic Gates in the October 1997 issue of the journal *PreText* at http://www.pretext.com/oct97/features/story1.htm being a good starting point.

> As was natural, this inordinate hope was followed by an excessive depression. The certitude that some shelf in some hexagon held precious books and that these precious books were inaccessible, seemed almost intolerable.

The Web today hides its precious treasures behind a greater mass of semi-precious or junk-grade texts. Moreover, it holds worse than useless works. As Borges would surely have surmised, it contains libelous portrayals, pornography, hate sites, and simple falsehoods. I once wanted to find the text for T.S. Eliot's "Little Gidding," especially the oft quoted,

> We shall not cease from exploration
> And the end of all our exploring
>
> Will be to arrive where we started
> And know the place for the first time.

Not only did I find many sites providing the text, but I also found many sites with the poem misquoted. As the Web grows, these misquotes may perpetuate as easily as the original text, providing us with a plethora of almost-Eliots wherever we look.

This phenomenon of nonsense growing faster than sense has led many to seek ways to clean up the Web. In the United States, the Communications Decency Act, whose key provisions were overturned by the Supreme Court on June 26, 1997 (http://www.aclu.org/court/renovacludec.html), was an attempt to criminalize the "knowing" transmission of "obscene or indecent" messages to minors through the Internet. Many people similarly want public libraries to restrict access to certain sites. There are a wide variety of software tools, such as CyberPatrol, CyberSitter, NetNanny, and A.D.L. HateFilter, to protect users from harmful sites. Schools have Internet policies to ensure that the Web is not used for inappropriate purposes. And teachers worry about the ratio of useless to useful information that students may encounter when surfing the Web.

> Others, inversely, believed that it was fundamental to eliminate useless works. They invaded the hexagons, showed credentials which were not always false, leafed through a volume with displeasure and condemned whole shelves: their hygienic, ascetic furor caused the senseless perdition of millions of books.

For better or worse the attempts to limit the Web appear to be futile. Restrictions of Web use in one country are quickly countered by the appearance of new websites in another. Attempts to monitor Web use are defeated by tools that allow anonymous use (see http://www.anonymizer.com). Replication and expansion of content proceeds much faster than any kind of control, whether rationalized by moral values or goals of content correctness. The Web remembers, because sites not only link to, but mirror each other, by copying content.

> [since the Library is total] there are always several hundred thousand imperfect facsimiles: works which differ only in a letter or a comma.

What does all this incredible content mean? Are we moving toward some global encyclopedia that accounts for everything or to an entropic doom of maximal disorder? Can we imagine that the Web itself holds the explanation of its own purpose and intrinsic worth?

> On some shelf in some hexagon (men reasoned) there must exist a book which is the formula and perfect compendium of all the rest.

Even if we cannot find that "perfect compendium," can we hope for a day when we know what is of value on the Web and what is not? That is unlikely, because the multifarious purposes of both Web readers and Web writers mean that even the apparently insignificant and the dubiously valid content may serve useful purposes.

> In truth, the Library includes all verbal structures, all variations permitted by the twenty-five orthographical symbols, but not a single example of absolute nonsense.

Whether one's interest is in sea bream production or in British poetry, in Argentinean libraries or in new recipes, the Web answers. Though it may not have the unimaginable extent of Borges' Library, it compensates by its capacity to grow, to create *de novo* a response to every conceivable query. Unlike an encyclopedia, it has no authoritative authors, no board of reviewers, no content policies, and no guarantee of stability from edition to edition. At the same time, it bears none of the limits of time and space that define conventional encyclopedias. Can such an unlimited enterprise yield any sense of order or meaning? Borges answers,

> Those who judge it to be limited postulate that in remote places the corridors and stairways and hexagons can conceivably come to an end—which is absurd. Those who imagine it to be without limit forget that the possible number of books does have such a limit. I venture to suggest this solution to the ancient problem: The Library is unlimited and cyclical. If an eternal traveler were to cross it in any direction, after centuries he would see that the same volumes were repeated in the same disorder (which, thus repeated, would be an order: the Order). My solitude is gladdened by this elegant hope.

Data

Conventional libraries are rapidly being converted into digital libraries (http://www.dlib.org), and the Web itself functions as a new medium for text creation. Thus, both as a repository for existing texts and as a global publishing house for new texts, the Web takes on characteristics of Borges's Library, though one hopes with that there is some more care behind each text than simply the exhaustive enumeration that Borges describes.

It is difficult to appreciate what the World Wide Web means without thinking of the sheer quantity of material it contains. Last year, Krishna Bharat and Andrei Broder published a study of the size of the Web and relative effectiveness of various Web search engines (http://decweb.ethz.ch/WWW7/1937/com1937.htm). They estimated that the Web as of March 1998 contained at least 275 million distinct, static pages. If we accept as a trend the annual doubling rate that many researchers have found, we could estimate that there are 550 million pages as of April 1999.

Taking Borges's 410-page book as a standard, and making a few simplifying assumptions about page size, we would get about 1.3 million volumes, more than 60% larger than the National Library of Argentina when Borges accepted his position as director there. Other estimates, which take into account the amount of information on each webpage, arrive at much larger figures. By most accounts, the Web is now comparable to the larger university and national libraries, though it may still be shy of the Library of Congress. However, that library (http://lcweb.loc.gov), along with many others, is rapidly entering its texts, photographs, movies, and sound recordings on the Web. It is thus clear that the Web will soon surpass any physical library in holdings, though critics may say it falls short in terms of comfortable chairs and musty smells.

Interpretations

Cyberspace, which exists in every country but also in none of them, appears to be a realm largely free of most laws. But there are two descriptive laws that have shaped its destiny.

One is the widely cited Moore's Law, proposed in 1965 by Gordon Moore (co-founder of Intel). This law holds that the computing power of a microchip will double every 18 months. The law has held up for nearly four decades. It has meant that computers have become smaller, hence faster, and cheaper. As the chips get smaller, more transistors can be stuffed into each chip, allowing new features to be added. The speed increases because the distance between the transistors is reduced. The accumulation of these quantitative changes has brought about qualitative changes in our lives.

As more transistors are packed into smaller and smaller spaces, microchip technology is approaching natural limits. At the size under development today, atomic layers can be counted and identified. Even Moore (1998) himself has said,

> So at some time in the next several generations, we really start to get to some fundamental limits. But not before we've gone through probably five more generations of

technology. If you extrapolate all those curves together...we run out of gas doing that in the year 2017.

The second law has an even more direct connection to the growth of the Web as a gigantic library. Metcalfe's Law, after Bob Metcalfe (founder of 3Com), states that the value of a network increases as more people use it.

> If you had the only telephone in the world, who would you call? Networks seem to grow more valuable to a user proportionately with the number of other users he or she can call. In a network with N users, each sees a value proportional to the N–1 others, so the total value of the network grows as N*(N–1), or as N squared for large N.

Just as is the case for Moore's Law, this law about networks has natural limits. Metcalfe (1995) himself has pointed out that once a critical mass is reached mere growth may not add much value. My telephone becomes valuable when most people I would like to talk with have one, but there's a lesser increase in value to add another 100 million people.

Website of the Month

The Human-Languages Page (http://www.ilovelanguages.com) is a comprehensive catalog of language-related Internet resources. There are directories for languages including Afrikaans, Akha, Akkadian, Albanian, Arabic, Aragonese, and Arberisht, to name just a few of the A's. If you go to the directory for Bahasa Indonesian for example, you'll find links to "20 Important Survival Phrases in Bahasa—with sound," "Linguistic odds-and-ends involving English and Indonesian—[such as] bilingual crossword puzzles, Indonesian tongue twisters, language riddles, and more," and an "index of Indonesian newspapers and magazines online."

The Human-Languages Page is a reminder of the diversity of human experience and the fact that, despite growing English dominance, by far most of the people in the world today communicate in languages other than, and often very different from, English. It also reminds us that the Web offers tremendous resources that can help any of us communicate with others. In particular, the language resources can be invaluable for anyone teaching someone whose original language is other than English.

Glossary

Digital library: a concept with varying definitions; the Association of Research Libraries (http://www.arl.org) has a definition (http://www.libnet.sh.cn/diglib/definition.htm) that suggests synonymy with "electronic library" or "virtual library"; a key elements is that the library uses new technologies to link diverse resources in a manner transparent to the user.

Dynamic (Web) page: a webpage that changes in response to user input, the time of day, or other variable information, a consequence being that it cannot be indexed easily by a Web search engine.

Metcalfe's Law: the value of a network for users is proportional to the square of the number of users.

Mirror site: a website that maintains a copy of another site so that the access load is distributed more evenly across the Internet, or users in a distant part of the world can have faster connections.

Moore's Law: the processing power on a microchip will double every 18 months.

Static (Web) page: a webpage that does not change and can thus be indexed by a Web search engine.

REFERENCES

Bharat, K., & Broder, A. (1998, April). A technique for measuring the relative size and overlap of public Web search engines. In *Proceedings of the 7th International World Wide Web Conference* (pp. 379–388). Brisbane, Australia: Elsevier Science.

Borges, J.L. (1962). *Ficciones* (A. Kerrigan, Ed.). New York: Grove.

Metcalfe, B. (1995, October 2). From the ether Metcalfe's Law: A network becomes more valuable as it reaches more users. *Infoworld, 17(40)*.

Moore, G. (1998, September 30). *An update on Moore's Law* (keynote address). San Francisco: Intel Developer Forum. Retrieved from http://developer.intel.com/design/idf/archive/sept97

Searching the Web: New Domains for Inquiry

Editor's Message

Many teachers today recognize the importance of online data sources for all kinds of research and writing projects. Some now permit students to include online sources in their work, and others go so far as to require the use of online sources.

There is a cornucopia of resources online. Reference tools include encyclopedias, dictionaries, and collections of quotes; libraries of poetry, short stories, images, and music; critical studies and research articles on every conceivable topic; information about authors and historical figures; government and public policy data; current events; and much, much more. Most teachers quickly see the problems that arise from such bounty. Issues of plagiarism, pornography, commercialism, and simple time wasting soon rear up regardless of the topic. When the cornucopia spills out 100,000 websites of dubious quality and relevance, it seems much less bounteous.

This month's Technology column addresses why it is important to think more critically about Web searching. Questions of quantity become important. As the Web grows rapidly, unpredictably, unevenly, and without the familiar monitors provided by textbook companies or district curriculum guides, how should we think about its use? For a start, how do the size of the Web and the quality of material on it affect searching? Given these issues, what are some good approaches to search the Web effectively? What tools are available and how can they be used?

These questions point to even more fundamental issues. Perhaps we need to move from a conception of searching the Web to find a piece of information to one in which a search is embedded in how we think. This leads to perhaps the most important question: How can searching become not only "looking up," but truly productive inquiring?

Original version published December 1999/January 2000 in the *Journal of Adolescent & Adult Literacy*
©1999–2000 International Reading Association

Searching Is the Journey, Not Just the Arrival

When students search the Web, it often seems that the problems are greater than the rewards. We seek ways to control those searches to avoid objectionable materials, plagiarism, or aimlessness, but in the process we may miss what is most valuable about the Web. Let us consider some questions about searches, which may help resolve this quandary.

Why Is It Important to Think Critically About Web Searching?

We tend to think first of Web searching as a simple process of looking up some item of information. For certain purposes, that conception is quite appropriate. For example, if I want to find general information about William Shakespeare, I type *Shakespeare* into my search engine. I get 660,000 webpages back, but among the top 10 is the Folger Shakespeare Library (http://www.folger.edu/Home_02B.html) in Washington, D.C. (administered by the Trustees of Amherst College), which has all sorts of interesting information, including lesson plans for teaching Shakespeare.

But, suppose I want to enter into the critical debates about Shakespearean authorship. Among the top 10 is the homepage of the Shakespeare Oxford Society (http://www.shakespeare-oxford.com). This group claims to be

> the second oldest continuously operating organization…involved in the…Shakespeare authorship debate. The purpose of the Society is to document and establish Edward de Vere, 17th Earl of Oxford (1550–1604), as the universally recognized author of the works of William Shakespeare.

I am inclined to believe their claim and am intrigued to examine their arguments. As I explore their website I am impressed by the care shown with their presentation, the detail of their documents, the source citations, and the opportunities for feedback. But, as a novice in this area I cannot be certain that this is the most credible starting point for my inquiry. Is this enterprise considered to be a fringe group? Are there more credible sources, perhaps even espousing the same argument?

Despite these concerns, I am relieved in some ways. Although the organization offers books and videos for sale through the site, these commercial aspects appear supportive of the generally academic mission. I don't see here troubling signs of racism or pornography that permeate the Web. My usual worry that the site may be superseded by a more recent one is allayed by the fact that their latest update is the date of my visit. Thus, although I do not know the authors or much about their domain of study, I find the site to be worth further investigation. If I can believe what I read there, I've found a timely resource with all sorts of useful information and links for further study.

What I have discovered here is a potentially useful source, but although I have spent some time examining it I still have doubts about how to interpret what I read there. When I return to the list of 660,000 documents that the search engine provided, I feel a bit overwhelmed. Will I have to spend this much time on every document and still not know what to make of it all? Will my students cope with this any better than I do?

I have discovered something else. For certain kinds of queries, my search is far from a simple "look-up." Instead, it appears to be part of the general process of inquiry, which is tentative and fallible. There is no absolute starting point nor any sure way to reach the end, assuming such a point exists. I need to muster all my resources for critical thinking to navigate the Web, but I may reap enormous benefits in the process.

How Does the Size of the Web Affect Searching?

The enormous size of the Web (see Data) is a mixed blessing. Hundreds of millions of pages hold forth the promise of having the text or images we seek, but the sheer volume of material gets in its own way. I recently searched for the U.S. Department of Commerce's report "Falling Through the Net," which is about the racial and income inequities in access to new information and communication technologies. My search engine offered up articles about World Cup soccer and the performance of an accomplished goalie defending her team's net. At other times I have found obsolete versions of material that exists elsewhere on the Web, but is unknown to the search engines. Very often I find it difficult to get past the many commercial sites that have engineered their webpages to appear first no matter how I specify a search query.

Given the number of webpages, it is surprising that one can find anything at all, much less do so in a matter of seconds. Improved search engines make that possible, especially when the user understands how the search engines work and puts some effort into selecting a good set of keywords.

How Does the Quality of Material on the Web Affect Searching?

I heard a teacher say recently that she discourages students from using the Web for research because the quality of material there is so poor. Although I would not abandon the Web because of its negative features, I can certainly sympathize. In fact, I can imagine that she might provide a list like the one below to support her point.

- Hate sites, pornography, violence, criminal activity, et cetera
  It is unfortunately the case that one cannot imagine any dark corner of human activity that is not now represented on the Web. Sites promoting substance abuse, suicide, bomb making, and racial hatred interleave with children's artwork, poetry, music, and images from the Hubble telescope.

- Commercialism
  Too many websites are created to sell something, not to provide valid and useful information. A recent estimate is that 83% of sites have primarily commercial content (Guernsey, 1999). Even in cases where the information is useful, the commercial assault is something to be avoided in schools and other learning environments.

- Incompleteness
  The Web pretends to a universality that it cannot support. It represents human knowledge, cultures, and values very unevenly, yet the hypertext medium suggests that everything is really there and equitably represented somehow.

- Authority
  The beauty of the Web is that anyone can make a website, for less than the cost of publishing a pamphlet. But a consequence of this is that there is no resort to any kind of recognized textual authority and no board of editors (as for a respected encyclopedia) who invite authors and vet articles for publication.

- Relevance
  There is so much material on the Web that the irrelevant far outweighs the relevant for any search.

- Timeliness

  The CNN Interactive website (http://www.cnn.com) is updated every few minutes. Other sites are created, posted on the Web, and never changed. Some sites, but not all, indicate when they were last updated, but it is usually difficult to determine whether the page you are viewing is the most recent in a series or just the one you happened upon. For Shakespeare, the timeliness issue may not be severe, but for many domains it is critical, yet unanswerable.

- Plagiarism

  When students (or anyone, for that matter) do find relevant information on the Web, it is all too easy to copy without attribution.

What Tools Are Available for Searching and How Can They Be Used?

Every technology arises out of the problems of previous technologies. This is a cycle we see operating with Web searches: The Web solves the problem of managing diverse, distributed sets of documents. That solution in turn makes it possible to post documents easily for all to read. This leads to a profusion of documents, many of which are poorly written and irrelevant for particular purposes. Search engines and search directories arise to solve the problem of managing the enormous quantity of material. Document designers then manipulate the pages that the search engines see so that their documents rank highest. Filters are developed to screen out unwanted material. Documents are designed to defeat the filters, and so on. A sampling of these tools are described in the Glossary.

What Are Some Good Approaches to Searching Effectively?

Much work is now underway to build better search engines, search directories, filters, jump sites, portals, and other technologies to enable more productive use of the Web. But what can an individual do to improve the experience of using the Web?

There are websites (of course!) devoted to this question. For example, Terry Gray has a useful review of some of the top search engines at http://www.daphne.palomar.edu/TGSEARCH and provides search tips specific to each engine. The Community Learning Network has information about many search engines and subject directories and a good set of FAQs about searching at http://www.cln.org/searching_home.html. Instead of going into great detail, I'll highlight three basic principles: (1) Understand how the Web and searches work, (2) select appropriate tools, and (3) use those tools effectively.

On the first point, it must be said that no one fully understands the Web, and even if a few did they would find their knowledge quickly dated as the technology and Web content evolved. Nevertheless, it helps to know some basic facts about how the Web functions and how search tools can help navigation.

For example, search engines do not go out and look at every webpage to answer a query. Many pages are hidden from the search engines behind organizational firewalls. Moreover, it would take far too long to examine every page as each query arises. Instead, the search engine builds a search index that enables fairly rapid searches. A consequence of this is that the user is not searching the Web, but the index, and is thus dependent on the quality of the index, its organizational scheme, and how recently it has been updated. Among other things, that means recent additions to the Web may not appear as the result of a search. A recent study (Lawrence & Giles, 1999) found that the best of the search engines finds only 16% of the relevant webpages, not counting those behind firewalls. These issues need to be understood when interpreting the results of a search.

The second point is that the choice of search engine or search directory is a major factor in how effective a search may be. For example, to find information about a book it may be more effective to search the database of an online bookseller than to search the entire Web. But, if the book is out of print it will not help to search the site of a bookseller offering only current titles.

Sites such as SearchIQ (Editor's message: This site is no longer available.) provide some information about the relative performance of different search tools, but there is no substitute for trying out different tools with the types of questions under investigation and then looking critically at the types of search results produced. It is also important to understand how a particular tool works and what assumptions it makes. A tool that aims to bring up frequently accessed sites may be appropriate if you plan to shop online and want to find popular commercial sites, but it is less appropriate if you want novel perspectives on understanding some issue of international relations.

Many people recommend metasearch engines such as Cyber411 at http://www.cyber411.com, which combines the results of 16 search engines. But, the larger number of hits may not offset the extra time that each search requires and the redundancy. This is particularly so because often if the desired sites do not appear in the first 10 items they might as well not appear at all.

The third point is to develop means for using these tools effectively. Each search engine has its own syntax for specifying Boolean expressions. Usually, a phrase in quotes means to find that phrase exactly as written. Thus, typing "best search engine" to AltaVista yields nearly 8,000 sites containing that phrase in quotes. Typing the three words *best search engine* without the quotes yields the same result, but typing *search engine best* produces 4.4 million webpages, the intersection of the 1.5 million webpages containing the term *search engine* and the 17.5 million containing the word *best*.

It is difficult to lay out general rules for doing searches because the approach depends on the problem being investigated. Perhaps one good general rule is this: If a search produces many irrelevant documents it is important to understand why that happened and not simply to decry the bloated Web world.

How Can Searching Become Not Only Looking Up, but Truly Productive Inquiring?

There are two problems with conceiving of Web searches as simply the looking up of information. The first is that we are often frustrated. The answers may be out there, but if we search inappropriately we get useless data. Most interesting questions require some effort ahead of time to be formulated well. It is worth giving a try to sites such as AskJeeves at http://www.askjeeves.com, but more often you will need to rethink the question in order to find the answers you seek.

The second problem is that the view of Web searching as simply finding information limits the key to its importance for education or other life activities. The joy and true value of the Web lie in the way it can open up our questions. We ask one thing, but the Web leads us to ask more questions and to become aware of how much we do not know. This suggests an alternative to the common practice of asking students to cite one library source and one online source for an essay. We could turn the Web's unruliness into a virtue. Instead, we might say, "Use the Web to find the answer to such-and-such question. Now, report on three things you learned that you had never imagined before you did that search."

The Web search engines are very important and useful resources, and they are playing a major role in the information age. However, they currently lack comprehensiveness and timeliness. The current state of search engines can be compared to a phone book that is updated irregularly and has most of the pages ripped out (Lawrence & Giles, 1999).

Data

Like many simple questions, this one turns out to be more complicated than it might at first appear. A good activity for students would be for them to define what they mean by the terms *big* and *Web* and then to search the Web for data or analyses to help them answer that question. Different approaches could lead to varying results, which in turn might call for justification of their strategies and critical thinking (see Murphy, 1998). There are a number of things we might count.

- Users
  The Internet surveys by the Nua company of Dublin, Ireland, estimate that 179 million people were Internet users as of June 1999. This is about 3% of the earth's population. More than half of those users are in the United States and Canada.

- Hosts
  The Domain Survey attempts to discover every host on the Internet by doing a complete search of the Domain Name System to find the name assigned to every possible Internet Provider (IP) address. It is sponsored by the Internet Software Consortium. They estimated in January 1999 that there were more than 43 million hosts on the Internet. The number of hosts had nearly doubled every year.

- Webpages
  A webpage can be anything from a few words to a site with video, interactive software, music files, or extensive text. Thus, when we say that there are so many pages on the Web, it is not quite the same as saying so many pages in a book. Still, if we knew how many webpages there were we would have some idea of the size of the Web, at least relative to what it has been.

  People have developed a variety of ways to gauge the Web's size in terms of pages. By comparing the pages returned by various search engines, Lawrence and Giles (1999) derived 800 million pages as a lower bound for the size of the (publicly accessible) Web as of February 1999 (see also Guernsey, 1999). This means the Web contains at least 800 million pages, probably somewhat more. They estimated further that these pages contain 6 terabytes of data versus the 20 terabytes of the entire U.S. Library of Congress. By the time of this issue, that lower bound on the size of the Web should have increased to well over a billion pages.

You can easily do an experiment yourself to get a rough measure of the Web's size. Go to AltaVista and search for the word *the*. You won't get any hits, because the search algorithm ignores common function words, but you will see the number of pages that the algorithm ignores. In July 1999, I found about 2 billion pages by this method. This is a rough measure because it excludes the pages that AltaVista doesn't know about, counts some pages with invalid links, and double-counts others. Nevertheless, it is a reasonable estimate not too far off from some more complex approaches.

- Hyperlinks
Members of the Clever Project (1999) estimate that roughly a million webpages are added every day. This is one rationale for their effort to develop algorithms for more sophisticated searching. These algorithms are based on studies of the interconnectivity of the Web, on how webpages have annotated connections to other pages. They estimate that there are more than a billion hyperlinks in the Web today, about one per page. If we take the higher estimate of webpages given above, then the number of hyperlinks must be considerably larger.

Win Treese has an Internet index newsletter at http://new-website.openmarket.com/intindex/index.cfm that regularly reports interesting items about the size and growth of the Web in the manner of *Harper's Index*. You can visit the site or become a subscriber to the index.

Comprehensive information about search engines, specialized search engines, and metasearch engines, as well as general information about searching and tips for searching are available at SearchIQ. This site provides independent reviews and rankings to inform the selection of search tools. Their reviews employ criteria such as overall relevancy of listings and organization by relevancy, ability to find sites for both broad and specific topics, comprehensiveness, lack of redundancy, logical grouping of listings, and speed.

Although the "IQ scores" that SearchIQ assigns are a novel feature of the site, I recommend looking more at their descriptions of the search engines and how they work. A low-scoring engine could easily be better for some purposes than the top-ranked engine.

Glossary

Authority: a website that is linked from many other pages (see Hub).

Boolean expression: an expression that evaluates to *true* or *false*; for example, used in a Web search, the expression *travel and France* is true for every webpage that contains both *travel* and *France*. Expressions that contain logical operators such as *and*, *or*, and *not* are Boolean, but all Web searches implicitly involve Boolean expressions.

Case sensitive: the property of paying attention to upper- and lowercase letters; each search engine has its own policy about this (e.g., is *White House* the same as *white house*?).

Domain name: a name that identifies the IP (Internet Protocol) address. For example, the domain name http://www.ed.gov represents a numerical address signifying a location in cyberspace. A domain name is the first part of the URL used to identify a webpage. Each host computer in the Domain Name System has a name, which allows computers using the World Wide Web to connect to the appropriate webpage.

Filter: a program that takes a list of documents and removes those that meet certain prespecified criteria; family filters are used to remove objectionable Web material, other filters are used to focus a search to retrieve the most relevant items, and any filter will occasionally let through unwanted items and screen out desirable ones.

Firewall: a network security system that allows a company, government, or other organization to keep its internal network files separate from the larger Internet community.

Host: a computer connected to the Internet with a registered name, such as http://www.reading.org. The term is used to refer to any single machine on the Internet, but a single machine can act as multiple systems, each with its own domain name and IP address, so the definition now typically includes virtual hosts as well.

Hub: a website with many links to other sites (see Authority).

Metasearch engine: a computer program, such as Dogpile, that collects the results from several search engines at once. This is especially valuable because no search engine indexes more than one sixth of the Web.

Ranking function: a means used by a search engine to order documents found in a search in terms of potential relevance, quality, or other criteria.

Search directory: a database that organizes documents according to categories and, usually, subcategories; it provides an alternative to general searching for finding particular items.

Search engine: a program that searches a database to locate all the documents that meet certain specifications given in search keys or a search query. It is commonly used to refer to programs for searching the Web. Most search engines return a list of webpages ordered by how well they match the specifications and by other heuristics, such as the number of sites that link to that page.

continued

Glossary (cont.)

Search index: a large database of document locations based on the words contained in each document; the index facilitates efficient, meaningful searches and is created by a program within the search engine.

Specialty search engine: a search engine that searches a limited database of documents, such as the telephone white pages; such an engine can be made more efficient for limited purposes and is more likely to return only the sorts of data that a user would want.

Spiders (search robots): a computer program sent out by a search engine to index documents on the Web to facilitate efficient search later on.

Terabyte: a trillion bytes of information, enough to represent a trillion characters; about 100 fairly large personal computer hard drives would be needed to hold this much information.

Webopedia: a good online glossary of computer terms.

REFERENCES

Guernsey, L. (1999, July 8). Seek—But on the Web, you might not find. *New York Times on the Web*. Retrieved from http://www.nytimes.com

Lawrence, S., & Giles, C.L. (1999). How big is the Web? How much of the Web do the search engines index? How up to date are the search engines? Retrieved from http://www.neci.nec.com/~lawrence/websize.html

Members of the Clever Project. (1999). Hypersearching the Web. *Scientific American, 280*(6), 54–60. Retrieved from http://www.sciam.com/1999/0699issue/0699raghavan.html

Murphy, J. (1998, July 5). It's not the size that counts, but how you measure it. *New York Times on the Web*. Retrieved from http://www.nytimes.com

Information Overload: Threat or Opportunity?

Guest Author Bernhard Jungwirth

Editor's Message

In his book *Information Anxiety* (1989), Richard Wurman claims that the weekday edition of *The New York Times* contains more information than the average person in 17th-century England was likely to come across in a lifetime. This personalizes the oft-cited estimate that more information has been produced in the last 30 years than in the previous 5,000. Statistics like these highlight the phenomenon of an information explosion and its consequence: information overload or information anxiety.

Vannevar Bush raised a similar alarm more than 50 years ago in his *Atlantic Monthly* article: "Thus far we seem to be worse off than ever before—for we can enormously extend the record, yet even in its present bulk we can hardly consult it."

How real is the phenomenon of information overload; how should we measure it; what are its causes; can anything be done about it; and if so, what? This month Bernhard Jungwirth takes on a set of complex issues that call for careful analysis of technology and new literacy practices. He shows how the questions are not just abstract problems for technology theorists, but are also practical issues for anyone who wants to become literate in today's world.

In keeping with the international character of this journal and with that of the Internet, this month's column has already traveled the world. Bernhard lives in Vienna, Austria; the journal editors are in Brisbane, Australia; and the International Reading Association headquarters are in the United States. The work cited comes from France, Germany, and the United States. In the process of creating this column, at least 50 e-mail messages were sent around the world.

Original version published February 2002 in the *Journal of Adolescent & Adult Literacy*
©2002 International Reading Association

Information Overload: Threat or Opportunity?

Direct access to uncountable relevant online sources, vast amounts of search results, and an increasing number of daily e-mails—these are all familiar experiences when we think of our work or the challenges students have to face. Do we really have to deal with an information overload, or are the developments in telecommunication just a great opportunity to become better informed? A more comprehensive sociotechnical, and even philosophical, perspective helps to reflect the significance of information overload in society and, therefore, in education.

In general, we have some sense of the increasing amount of information to which we are exposed. Many eye-catching numbers and comparisons help to confirm our assessment:

> Around 1,000 books are published internationally every day and the total of all printed knowledge doubles every 5 years.
> More information is estimated to have been produced in the last 30 years than in the previous 5,000. (*The Reuters Guide to Good Information Strategy*, 2000)

Threat or Opportunity?

More information—is it a threat or an opportunity? A way to begin this discussion may be to take an empirical view, although many statistical discrepancies offer room for interpretation. Such discrepancies include duplications (e.g., What is original and what is a copy? When should two pieces of information be considered as different and when as duplications?); compression and codes (e.g., a Word file is bigger than an ASCII file, even if it contains the same information); as well as data access (no data are available for many countries).

The size of the Internet—in particular of the World Wide Web—often illustrates the information overload in society today. However, to measure the Web we have to look at a major statistical problem, the so-called "invisible Web." It is made up of information stored in databases. Unlike pages on the visible Web, information in databases is generally inaccessible to the software spiders and crawlers that compile search engine indexes and determine the size of the Web (Sherman, 2001). This is a vital problem because information offered on the invisible Web tends to be qualitative (e.g., newspaper archives) and grows faster than the visible Web.

Bergman (2000) suggested that information available on the invisible Web is 400 to 550 times larger than that on the visible Web.

Due to these problems, valuable statistics are rather rare and often outdated. A widely recognized study is "Accessibility and Distribution of Information on the Web" (Lawrence & Giles, 1999). One of the major results of this study was that the publicly indexable Web contained an estimated 800 million pages as of February 1999, encompassing about 15 terabytes of information or about 6 terabytes of text after removing HTML tags, comments, and extra white space.

Differences Between the United States and Europe

Discussion about information overload brings up interesting differences between the United States and Europe concerning general public opinion and theoretical discourse. Europeans tend to be more skeptical and critical about technological innovations than Americans. *Wired* magazine talked about a new cultural war, U.S. exuberance against continental conservatism (Glenny, 2001). The early public perception of the Internet in Europe was highly associated with pornography or right-wing extremism, but the public opinions appear to have generated contrary theoretical opinions. Many U.S. thinkers are opposed to the public enthusiasm about technology, while theorists in Europe often counterbalance the widespread skepticism there.

Neil Postman is a famous technology critic in the United States and author of *Technopoly: The Surrender of Culture to Technology* (1993, Vintage). One of his basic assumptions is that uncontrolled growth of technology destroys the vital sources of our humanity. It creates a culture without moral foundation. As a consequence Postman named our society a "technopoly," where the primary—if not the only—goal of human labor and thought is efficiency, and where technical calculation is in all respects superior to human judgment. He added that one of the most ominous consequences of technopoly is the explosion of context-free information.

Postman also stated that technopoly flourishes in a milieu where the tie between information and human purpose has been severed (i.e., information appears indiscriminately, directed at no one in particular in enormous volume at high speeds, and it is disconnected from theory, meaning, or purpose). The "information glut" leads to the breakdown of a coherent cultural narrative, he argued. For without a meaningful context, information is not only useless but also potentially dangerous. In an analogy to the old saying that to a person with a hammer, everything looks like a nail, Postman said that to a person with a computer, everything looks like data. Postman defined this glut as a cultural "AIDS" (Anti-Information Deficiency Syndrome). The culture's immune system is not capable of filtering any more information.

When traditional information filters no longer work, Postman explained, we turn increasingly to experts, bureaucrats, and social scientists who (abetted by computers) control the flood of data. This might be expected when a technical solution is called for, but as human relations have become "technicalized" there are also experts in social, psychological, and moral affairs. The result is that we look for technical solutions to human problems. Postman judged this approach as incapable of answering the most fundamental human questions and barely useful in providing coherent direction to the solution of even mundane problems.

Paul Virilio, a French philosopher, represents a somber perspective similar to that of Postman. Virilio's theories stem from the basic consideration that speed is the determining factor and acceleration the driving force for development in society (Kloock, 1997).

Virilio recognized three eras of speed in history. The first is the transportation revolution in the 19th century; the second is the media-transmission revolution (based on the speed of light) in the 20th century; and the third revolution, which is still ahead of us, is transplantation.

The second revolution is relevant in the context of information overload. Communication based on electromagnetic media (e.g., radio, television, Internet) was, according to Virilio, the start of a new world order. Because electromagnetic signals are transmitted with the speed of light they are able to reach the highest possible speed. This implies that space and time are overcome and a real-time society is founded in which everything is everywhere at every time. Therefore human perception gets swamped, and as a consequence Virilio predicts a process of dehumanization. The disappearance of space and time can be understood as another description of information overload, or information bomb as Virilio also called it.

Bill McKibben, a U.S. author, wrote *The Age of Missing Information* (1992), in which he compared his experiences watching 93 television channels in 24 hours with spending a day in the mountains. McKibben concluded that we are living in the age of missing information, a time when the vital knowledge that humans have always possessed about who we are and where we live seems beyond our reach.

He lamented the loss of power found in unmediated experiences with nature and stated that the information explosion is drowning our senses and cutting us off from more fundamental information about our limitations and the limitations of the world around us. He judged mediated experiences of the world around us as a threat to the world itself. These are lessons that may be crucial to the planet's persistence as a green and diverse place and also to the happiness of its inhabitants—lessons that nature teaches but television cannot.

Richard S. Wurman stated that information has become the driving force of our lives, and the ominous threat of this ever-increasing pile of information demanding to be understood has made most of us anxious. This assumption has led Wurman to publish two books: *Information Anxiety* (1989) and *Information Anxiety2* (1989). He described information anxiety as a product of the ever-widening gap between what we understand and what we think we should understand. Information anxiety is a black hole between data and knowledge. It happens when information doesn't tell us what we want or need to know.

Interpreting the increasing amount of data as a threat is only one possibility. There is a broad variety of arguments opposed to that view—arguments that judge the environment of changing information as a new opportunity, or at least not necessarily as a threat.

Website of the Month

Lyman and Varian (2000) conducted the study "How Much Information?" and published the results on this website: http://www.sims.berkeley.edu/research/projects/how-much-info/index.html. It is one of the most comprehensive quantitative research approaches available and includes results such as this: The visible Web consisted of approximately 2.5 billion documents in October 2000, up from 1 billion pages at the beginning of the year 2000, with a rate of growth of 7.3 million pages per day. The study estimated that the total amount of information on the visible Web varied somewhere from 25 to 50 terabytes of information (HTML-included basis). Lyman and Varian also took e-mail into account. A white-collar worker receives about 40 e-mail messages in the office each day. Aggregately, there will be from 610 billion to 1,100 billion messages sent this year alone.

The study not only covers the Internet size but also represents an attempt to measure how much general information is produced in the world each year. Some significant numbers and insights are that the world produces between 1 and 2 exabytes of unique information per year, which is roughly 250 megabytes for every man, woman, and child on earth. An exabyte is a billion gigabytes. Printed documents of all kinds make up only .003% of the total. Magnetic storage is by far the largest medium for storing information, and it is the most rapidly growing, with shipped hard drive capacity doubling every year.

Lesk (1997) used a statistical approach to find out how much written information is produced in the world. Extrapolating from figures on paper production and the U.S. gross domestic product, he estimated 160 terabytes were produced each year. These are impressive numbers describing a sea of information. Will the growth of that sea create excessive demands on human culture as some have warned? Lyman and Varian (2000) concluded in their study,

> [I]t is clear that we are all drowning in a sea of information. The challenge is to learn to swim in that sea, rather than drown in it. Better understanding and better tools are desperately needed if we are to take full advantage of the ever-increasing supply of information.

Should the information age be characterized by the sense of drowning in a sea of information or by new opportunities arising from a better supply of information?

Other Views

There Has Always Been an Information Overload

Humans have dealt with a permanent information overload in every aspect of their lives and in every part of their history. Because humans are incapable of universal perception, what we perceive is inherently selective. Information overload affects every human's perception.

Historical examples support the view that information overload is not a new phenomenon. Ancient writers and writers in the Middle Ages produced so much data that there was a permanent threat of overfilled information storages, which led to the development of new information processing techniques (Giesecke, 1992). There were similar fears after the invention of the printing press. Concerns with information glut are the result of uncertainty during navigation of newly constructed information spaces, but they do not really depend on the particular amount of information.

Reduction of Complexity by Social Institutions and Cultural Techniques

Jelden (1997), a German philosopher, argued that in modern societies the reduction of complexity is helped by the division of labor and the selection criteria constituted by various institutions that filter information. Therefore, it is advisable not to lament an information glut but instead to be aware of how these new institutions develop.

Jelden used insurance agencies as an example of complexity-reducing institutions and argued that we are not able to live without these institutions. Technical tools may be less obvious examples in comparison with insurance agents, but they also reduce complexity. With the help of technical tools we are able to control electrical, chemical, and physical procedures we do not understand. Handling this lack of knowledge about things we do every day can be considered cultural techniques we have developed over generations. Without these cultural techniques and institutionalized selection criteria—and relying on individual natural ability—we would be unable to deal with even simple situations in daily life. That's why Anders (1961) talked about "The Outdatedness of Humans." The reduction of complexity by institutions can be seen as a substitute for human instinct.

History shows that wherever new opportunities for acting and thinking occurred, appropriate institutional procedures developed as well. For example, journalistic skills and rules for how to select information are now replaced by relevance criteria technically implemented in Internet search engines. It is as important now to reflect on selection criteria in these search engines as it was to be informed about journalists' work practices in order to judge information offered in newspapers. The politics of search engines are discussed by Introna and Nissenbaum (2000).

Jelden also pointed out that we should not be surprised that new filtering institutions are not completely reliable, nor have they ever been. One prerequisite of division of labor in a society is trust. Trust can never be based on knowledge (then it would not be trust anymore); it must be based on experience (Luhmann, 1979). We still have to create this experience in the information society.

Philosophical Dimension and Weltanschauung

Neil Postman's observation and prediction of a breakdown of coherent cultural narratives may be right. We are experiencing a less important role of homogeneous world views, and the big systems that explain the world—religion, science, and art—are losing their power. In many Western civilizations the major religions are losing their attraction as people find more individual substitutions. Even science, with an image of absolute reliability and exactness, has to admit that the absolute formulations of many laws are wrong (famous examples of paradigm shifts are Einstein's Theory of Relativity and Heisenberg's relations of uncertainty as opposed to classic physics), and at some point everything is based not on truth, but on basic assumptions. This rising pluralism and decline of concepts insisting on absolute truth can also be observed in the arts. Abstraction and ideas of postmodernism leave the artwork consumer with multifaceted options for interpretation.

How are these considerations related to information overload? The Austrian media philosopher Hartmann (1997) pointed out that hypermedia environments allow the desired recombination of decontextualized pieces of information. This matches the changes in the dimension of *weltanschauung* (a personal concept of the world). Hartmann stated that these additional opportunities and not the so-called flood of information are the actual result of new technologies.

Technical Extension

Human history is often viewed as a history of the extension of man. Explaining technology in relation to the human body has a philosophical tradition. Kapp, who published the first systematic philosophy of technology in Germany, looked at the human body as a basis for every invention. Technology for Kapp (1877) was an imitation of the body (e.g., the hammer is an imitation of the arm; optical devices rely on how an eye functions). Even Sigmund Freud described a human being as a "god of prosthesis."

This thinking leads to the idea of technology as a means of dealing with information overflow—technology as an extension of the brain. We can already observe the use of simple implementations. Imagine that the World Wide Web is printed out on paper, and you have to find a certain term manually. It would be almost impossible to succeed, but with the help of search engines it is comparatively easy.

Technology has been and will be a useful tool for managing information glut. Just mentioning buzzwords such as *artificial intelligence* and *information agents* gives the impression of further development. Not only pure technology but also design-related disciplines become more important. The growth of information architecture faces the challenge of increasing information. It deals with the design of organization and navigation systems to help people find and manage information more successfully (Rosenfeld, 1999).

Cognitive Adaptation

Adaptation to the requirements of the information glut could take place not only on the level of cultural techniques or technology, but also on a physiological level, at least in the long term. According to Rötzer (1999), researchers have discovered a brain area that is responsible for multitasking. Practice in using this area could certainly increase the ability to handle information overload.

How You Can Participate

Do you want to manage your information overload? Fox (1998) offers the following concrete advice.

- Do it now. The first rule for improving efficiency is to act on every item the first time you see it, hear it, or read it.
- Make the trash can your best friend.
- Keep a "not to do" list. What overwhelms many people is what they intend to do but never get around to doing.
- Set up organizing systems that work for you.
- Don't try to remember. Remembering, thinking, and worrying about future meetings and deadlines only distracts you from what you're doing now. It's better to have a good reminder system.
- Practice weekly planning—a week is the most practical unit of time to plan.
- Fill in the gaps in your Information Age skills. Most of us need to improve our ability to gather, access, process, and share information.

Glossary

The American Standard Code for Information Interchange (ASCII): the most common format for text files in computers and on the Internet. In an ASCII file, each alphabetic, numeric, or special character is represented with a 7-bit binary number (a string of seven 0s or 1s). There are 128 possible characters.

Einstein's Theory of Relativity: In 1905 Albert Einstein published his famous Special Theory of Relativity and overthrew common-sense assumptions about space and time. Relative to the observer, both are altered near the speed of light: Distances appear to stretch; clocks tick more slowly. Einstein's General Theory of Relativity is a separate theory about a very different topic—the effects of gravity.

Heisenberg's relations of uncertainty: Heisenberg formulated the relations of uncertainty concerning the simultaneous precise measurement of the position and velocity of microscopic particles and, consequently, the unpredictability of their behavior.

Invisible Web: This is the portion of the Web not accessible through Web search engines. It mainly consists of a broad variety of databases. Its content tends to be more qualitative and larger in comparison to the visible Web. Sometimes it is also called the deep Web.

Megabytes, gigabytes, terabytes, exabytes: A megabyte consists of 1,024 kilobytes, 1,024 megabytes are one gigabyte, and 1,024 gigabytes are one terabyte. One exabyte in turn is 1,024 times 1,024 terabytes. One terabyte is about the equivalent to the textual content of a million books. The number 1,024 is a result of the fact that computers use binaries (1,024 is 2 to the power of 10).

REFERENCES

Anders, G. (1961). *Die Antiquiertheit des Menschen. Über die Seele im Zeitalter der zweiten Industriellen Revolution* [The outdatedness of human beings. The soul in the age of the second Industrial Revolution]. München, Germany: C.H. Beck.

Bergman, M.K. (2000). *The deep web: Surfacing hidden values*. Retrieved from http://128.121.227.57/download/deepwebwhitepaper.pdf

Fox, J. (1998). *Conquering information anxiety. Relief from your data glut starts here*. Retrieved from http://www.ibt-pep.com/ciar.htm

Giesecke, M. (1992). *Sinnenwandel, Sprachwandel, Kulturwandel. Studien zur Vorgeschichte der Informationsgesellschaft* [Change of senses, change of language, change of culture. Studies about the previous history of the information society]. Frankfurt/Main, Germany: Suhrkamp.

Glenny, M. (2001). How Europe can stop worrying and learn to love the future. *Wired*, 9.02. Retrieved from http://www.wired.com/wired/archive/9.02/misha_pr.html

Hartmann, F. (1997). *Fetisch information* [Fetish information]. Retrieved from http://www.medienphilosophie.net/Essays/Information.htm

Introna, L.D., & Nissenbaum, H. (2000). *Why the politics of search engines matters*. Retrieved from http://www.princeton.edu/~helen/engine.html

Jelden, E. (1997). *Datenbombe Internet: oder: Wer teilt die Datenfluten* [Data bomb Internet—Or: Who divides the flood of information?]. Retrieved from http://www.heise.de/tp/deutsch/inhalt/co/2105/2.html

Kapp, E. (1877). *Grundlinien einer Philosophie der Technik* [Foundations of a philosophy of technology]. Braunschweig, Germany: G. Westermann.

Kloock, D. (1997). *Ästhetik der Geschwindigkeit* [Aesthetics of speed]. Paul Virilio. In D. Kloock & A. Spaar (Eds.), Medientheorien eine Einführung [Media theory—An introduction] (pp. 134–164). München, Germany: Wilhelm Fink.

Lawrence, S., & Giles, L. (1999). *Accessibility and distribution of information on the Web*. Retrieved from http://www.metrics.com

Lesk, M. (1997). *How much information is there in the world?* Retrieved from http://www.lesk.com/mlesk/ksg97/ksg.html

Luhmann, N. (1979). *Trust and power*. Chichester, UK: Wiley.

Lyman, P., & Varian, H.R. (2000). *How much information?* Retrieved from http://www.sims.berkeley.edu/research/projects/how-much-info/index.html

The Reuters guide to good information strategy. (1997). London: Reuters Ltd.

Rosenfeld, L. (1999). *Information architecture revealed!* Retrieved from http://webword.com/interviews/rosenfeld.html

Rötzer, F. (1999). *Schwimmen in der Informationsflut* [Swimming in the flood of information]. Retrieved from http://www.heise.de/tp/deutsch/inhalt/co/2865/1.html

Sherman, C. (2001). *The invisible Web*. Retrieved from http://web.archive.org/web/20010615155745/websearch.about.com/internet/websearch/library/weekly/aa061199.htm?once=true&

Guest Author

Jungwirth is a student at the University of Vienna.

Open Source: Everyone Becomes a Printer

Editor's Message

What is the Web? Is it a vast library, a repository of texts and images? Is it a shopping mall? Is it a site for collaboration among diverse people throughout the world? Is it the metatechnology that unites fax, e-mail, telephone, radio, television, video, and databases? It certainly carries aspects of each of these and more.

A key factor in what the Web means is the way we conceive of it and use it. This becomes evident when we consider debates such as that surrounding "open source." For many people the term was not even in their vocabulary until the antitrust suit by the U.S. government against Microsoft in 1999. There, we heard about alternatives to the nearly universal hold that Microsoft has over computer operating systems. One of the most important of those alternatives is open-source software development, such as that which has led to the Linux operating system.

The ideas about open source go well beyond the construction of computer operating systems. They relate to possible shifts in the way knowledge is produced and shared. Are we moving from a centralized model in which authorities produce texts and readers consume to one in which readers become partners in production as well? What does this mean for how we interpret texts and how we write? What does it mean for literacy development? This month I will examine some of the implications of open source for how we communicate and share knowledge.

Original version published May 2000 in the *Journal of Adolescent & Adult Literacy*
©2000 International Reading Association

From Open-Source Reading to Open-Source Writing

The invention of the printing press by Johannes Gutenberg in 15th-century Europe might seem at first to be a historical curiosity. There were earlier versions of printing in Europe, and several centuries before that in China. Initially, this invention meant only that certain texts, notably the Bible, could be produced more quickly and cheaply. In any case, not many people could read in Gutenberg's time, so the availability of texts affected only a small number of scholars in religious orders and in the few universities.

Thus, the printing press was neither especially useful in the beginning, nor even totally novel. But the combination of elements, including both the press and typography, which Gutenberg used in his "42-line Bible" project, made possible mass printing as we know it today. The possibility of wide dissemination of texts shook the foundations of the church by opening up sacred texts to multiple interpretations. It moved the Bible and other classical texts from the cathedral to the mass marketplace of ideas. Academic knowledge became the province of the masses, not the privilege of certain classes. The ability to represent knowledge in permanent, mobile forms made possible the development of modern science (Latour, 1988). These elements enabled the kind of mass literacy we see today. They are also at the heart of the Internet, including the claims for multimedia, hypertext, and global connectivity. Thus, the case is strong for classifying the invention of the printing press as one of the great events in modern history.

In the jargon of today, we could describe the printing press as a device that made possible "open-source" reading. Where before manuscripts were scarce and held behind locked doors, now they were widely available. Where before a text required a skilled decoder and interpreter, now anyone could acquire those skills and do the decoding and interpreting by themselves. Opening the source code facilitated the transformation of culture of the last four centuries, including both the positive and negative effects of that transformation.

Today, the term *open source* more commonly refers to a method of distributing software, not Bibles. Essentially, it means that programmers make available to all the actual text of their programs, the source code. Doing so means that they reveal its limitations, and also that they allow others to benefit by building upon it. Thus, there is both open-source writing as well as open-source reading. By doing this, the original programmer's work becomes much more widely disseminated. Its influence grows, not by being hoarded, but by being given away. The archetypal case is the development of the Linux operating system as an alternative to Windows.

Raymond (1998) applied the labels "bazaar model" to the open-source method for developing and distributing software and "cathedral model" to the more familiar, corporate-based method. He saw the Linux open-source community as "a great babbling bazaar of differing agendas and approaches...out of which a coherent and stable system could seemingly emerge only by a succession of miracles." Yet, he argued that, despite that babbling confusion, the open-source approach would lead to better designed, more useful software.

Recently, these ideas have been extended to scientific inquiry (Kiernan, 1999). As more and more scientists use computer programs to analyze data, many are also beginning to make their source code open. Some worry that their ideas may be stolen or their faulty methods exposed through this openness. But many see that sharing code can facilitate a new mode of collaboration through software. It also becomes a new mode of publication, often more informative and useful than the traditional journal article.

The open-source movement makes even broader claims, namely that it is more democratic and that it will revolutionize the way people communicate and work together in all realms (Bezroukov, 1999; Raymond, 1998, 1999). It also predicts a greater sharing of knowledge and with that a greater sharing of power. Through the bazaar called the Web, people who are geographically distributed can collaborate in making and distributing software, music, photographs, video, artwork, texts, and ideas without any central coordination.

As an example, we now see open-source, or bazaar, ideas percolating through the world of music with the advent of MP3 and other coding schemes. These allow anyone to distribute their own recordings (Samudrala, 1998) directly to listeners. An artist does not have to please the record company, but instead becomes one. People can now produce their own Internet radio as well, thus providing live broadcasts.

In all of these areas, open source has both its detractors and its proponents. Detractors argue that chaos can result, with everyone claiming authority. They see the need for consistency, quality control, and the protection of intellectual property rights. Proponents on the other hand argue that open source does essentially what the printing press did: It opens up participation to all the people.

Whatever the costs in messiness, they are far outweighed by the power of many and by extending democratic process.

The Greatest Invention?

Starting in 1981, the Reality Club has held meetings in the United States in Chinese restaurants, the New York Academy of Sciences, and various other venues in New York. More recently it has migrated to the Web, at the Edge Foundation (http://www.edge.org). This is a website designed as a forum for intelligent, thoughtful, and engaging exchange of ideas.

A couple of years ago a distinguished list of participants were asked, "What is the most important invention in the past two thousand years?" and "Why?" (Brockman, 1998). Their justifications—the answer to the "why" question—make the webpage (75 printed pages) well worth a visit. But it's still intriguing to know which invention tops the list.

There are several unexpected choices. Freeman Dyson, physicist and author of many works (including *From Eros to Gaia*, Pantheon, 1993) chooses hay as the most important "invention" of the last 2,000 years. He argues that civilization needed either a warm climate, such as in Mediterranean Greece, or some means for keeping horses alive through a cold winter by grazing. The "invention" of hay meant that in Europe, civilization could move north over the Alps, giving birth to Vienna, Paris, London, and Berlin.

But as one reads through the 100+ entries, it is apparent that one invention dominates the thinking of this group. Some try to think of alternatives to it; some look to future, unrealized effects of current technologies; and some simply acknowledge it. But few can easily dismiss the importance of the printing press. By vastly expanding the range of participation in literate activity, the printing press made possible the work in science and technology, which has led to other inventions, and has had an enormous impact on economic development, religion, art, and culture. At a fundamental level it has made universal literacy a realizable goal.

People or Machines?

In researching the open-source movement, I came across an article by Elinor Abreu (1999), in which she provided some good background on what's happening with the Open Directory Project (see Website of the Month), an example of the open-source idea applied to Web search directories. I thought the paragraph at the end was the most intriguing:

> "The most significant thing is it's really set off a revolution in terms of search engines," says Sullivan of Search Engine Watch. "In 1996, of the top six search engines, only Yahoo was human-powered. Today...four out of six are powered by humans."

So, the "revolution" is that we're replacing machines with humans! Regardless of the extent to which that happens, it is clear that open-source projects such as Open Directory do involve much larger numbers of people.

How You Can Participate

There are many ways you can participate in the open-source movement, short of developing components of the next operating system. One way I have found to be useful is the Open Directory Project mentioned above. For example, I edit a small corner of the Open Directory called "Literacy in the Information Age" at http://www.dmoz.org/Society/Issues/Education/Literacy/Literacy_in_the_Information_Age.

If you go to that website, you can see links to many additional sites organized into categories, such as Access, Computer Mediated Communication, Cyberspace Law, Information Media Literacy, Online Communities, and Quantitative Literacy. There is a link for you to "add URL." You can also send me suggestions for new categories. If you are more than casually interested, you can click on "become an editor" and volunteer to edit or coedit any of the more than 200,000 existing categories. You can also propose to create and edit an entirely new category.

It is also possible to import Open Directory or some portion of it into your own personal or school website. There is a free-use license that allows anyone to post on their site any portion of the Open Directory, with attribution.

Website of the Month

Open Directory is a community-produced search directory with organized, annotated links. The Open Directory Project (ODP) maintains the site, but thousands of editors manage specific categories. The search tree is downloaded regularly to Lycos, Hotbot, Netscape, and other major search engines.

The goal of the ODP is "to produce the most comprehensive directory of the web, by relying on a vast army of volunteer editors" (Open Directory Project, 2000). There are currently well over 1 million links, with about 100,000 being added every month.

For the volunteer editor, Open Directory offers several advantages. The ODP provides tools that make it much easier than building one's own webpage. ODP archives the site and manages its export to search engines and other sites. There are also software tools to help the editor check links and maintain consistency with other parts of the directory. The work one does in selecting and annotating links is not buried within one's personal or classroom page, but is immediately incorporated into a larger context. That context also provides the related links that one often needs.

Glossary

Bazaar model: a style of interaction, originally applied to software development, in which large numbers of people contribute, often without monetary compensation, to build some larger whole. Proponents accept and applaud diversity. They argue that people committed to a particular area will produce results whose value far offsets any problems due to lack of uniformity of overall structure. See *Cathedral model*.

Cathedral model: a style of interaction, originally applied to software development, in which a dedicated few work within a guiding structure. Proponents argue that the need for consistency and quality control outweighs the advantages of enlisting vast contingents of volunteers. See *Bazaar model*.

Linux operating system (http://www.linux.org): a version of the Unix operating system, which works with a variety of computers, including PCs, Macintoshes, and Amigas. As an operating system, it enables the user to invoke word processors, Web browsers, and other programs, as needed. In that sense, Linux is similar to Windows or MacOS. However, it is unusual in the way it has been created and in its cost. Linux development has been led by Linus Torvalds, but its continuing development occurs through an unusual collaborative arrangement in which programmers around the globe contribute pieces of the system. The software is free and represents the bazaar approach to software development.

MP3 (or MPEG3): a scheme for compressing audio signals without sacrificing sound quality. This allows a sound file to be small and easily transferred over the Internet. A musician could use MP3 to distribute a performance directly to a listener without need of a record company.

continued

> **Glossary (cont.)**
>
> **Open source:** a concept about how knowledge is constructed and shared, with implications for whether it is seen as intellectual property or collaborative inquiry. See the Open Directory category: http://www.dmoz.org/Computers/Open_Source

REFERENCES

Abreu, E. (1999, December 14). Netscape directory making a splash. In *The Industry Standard*. Retrieved from http://www.thestandard.com/article/display/0,1151,8187,00.html?nl=dnt

Bezroukov, N. (1999, December). A second look at the cathedral and the bazaar. In *First Monday*, 4(12). Retrieved from http://firstmonday.org/issues/issue4_12/bezroukov

Brockman, J. (Ed.). (1998). *What is the most important invention in the past two thousand years?* Retrieved from http://www.edge.org/discourse/invention.html

Kiernan, V. (1999, November 5). The "open-source movement" turns its eye to science. *The Chronicle of Higher Education*, A51–A52. Retrieved from http://chronicle.com/free/v46/i11/11a05101.htm

Latour, B. (1988). Drawing things together. In M. Lynch & S. Woolgar (Eds.), *Representation in scientific practice* (pp. 19–68). Cambridge, MA: MIT Press.

Open Directory Project. (2000). In *About the Open Directory Project*. Retrieved from http://www.dmoz.org/about.html

Raymond, E.S. (1998). The cathedral and the bazaar. In *First Monday*, 3(3). Retrieved from http://www.firstmonday.dk/issues/issue3_3/raymond

Raymond, E.S. (1999). *The cathedral and the bazaar: Musings on Linux and open source by an accidental revolutionary*. Sebastopol, CA: O'Reilly & Associates.

Samudrala, R. (1998, December 5). In *The future of music*. Retrieved from www.mp3.com/news/142.html

Why Free Software Matters for Literacy Educators

Guest Author Michael D. Brunelle

Editor's Message

A recurring theme in this column has been that the inside of the box matters. If we simply turn on a word processor, access a database, link to a network, or play a video with no concern for how and why it was put together, we can make ourselves and our students vulnerable. This point has been highlighted recently with the revelation that millions of computer users inadvertently open their files to any user of the Web through file sharing. The underlying means by which computers represent and transfer data have important implications regarding who has access to new technologies. Even the tools we use to edit documents and make presentations encode assumptions about texts we may not accept, but nevertheless adopt, when we use them uncritically.

One such technology is called "free software." This may sound like a bargain way to use computers, but free software can actually cost money. What makes it free is that the user can run the program for any purpose; study how it works; and adapt it, redistribute it, and release improvements. Free software (GNU Project, 2001) is closely related to "open source," though not exactly the same. Understanding what it means and its implications for access and use of new technologies is an important component of the new literacies. There are immediate practical implications for schools and other literacy centers, as well as individuals, in terms of both economics and control.

Original version published March 2002 in the *Journal of Adolescent & Adult Literacy*
©2002 International Reading Association

Developing New Literacies With Free Software

What sort of knowledge and experience is necessary for a person to be considered literate? Is literacy something to be achieved, or is it a continual process? As we struggle to understand and promote literacy in an increasingly "informated" world, we are faced with important choices about how we create and communicate. If our larger concepts of knowledge are constructed around the use of certain tools and techniques, we should consider the implications of the choices that we make when we teach and learn.

Context

When people turn on a computer, they expect to see a Microsoft logo. Because of the practical ubiquity of the software, there is tremendous pressure from companies, leaders, and what can often seem like society itself for every computer to run Microsoft Office, preferably on an Intel-powered, Windows-based machine. While many people may be more comfortable buying name-brand software or benefit from using exactly what everyone else uses, Microsoft does use its market position to penetrate other niches, slowly replacing programs from a diversity of sources with Microsoft equivalents and stifling competition (Wilcox, 2000). A typical organization is likely to be an almost exclusively Microsoft-driven enterprise, from servers to workstations to handheld devices.

Numerous problems are associated with relying on any homogenous network. The Internet works well, in part, because of its diversity and redundancy. Microsoft's success on the desktop would seem to increase the likelihood that organizations will choose Microsoft products for other services, such as Web and e-mail services. There are risks involved with relying on such a network. The software has several potential security vulnerabilities, and there have been several episodes in which malicious viruses and worms infiltrated Microsoft servers and e-mail clients because of these weaknesses. Despite such problems, and despite the budgetary demands of keeping commerical software up-to-date, most organizations do not consider alternatives, because computers should run Windows. Right?

Alternatives do exist, and always have—alternatives that can provide improved stability, reliability, flexibility, and cost-effectiveness, all while encouraging a broader commitment to help others. When AT&T changed the conditions of use for its Unix operating system, the Berkeley Software Distribution (BSD) project created a free version, available for anyone to use. In the past few years, the GNU/Linux operating system has emerged to present an increasingly real challenge to commercial software. Most of the servers that power the Internet today are run by free software or software based on open-source projects. One program that demonstrates the usefulness of free software is the Apache Web server, which accounts for over half of all Web servers. For a comparison of Web servers, see the Netcraft Web Server Survey (http://www.netcraft.com/survey).

Retrospective

When computers were still a new technology—a research tool—people and companies shared software for practical reasons. When hardware manufacturers sold products, they basically gave away the software, allowing access to the source code because its value was intrinsically linked to the hardware. It was in the interest of programmers and researchers to share software to control printers and other devices, exchange bug fixes and other useful bits of code, and generally be very open with their work because cooperation was the best way to make a computer do what they needed it to do. Most people learned to program because they needed to make the computer do something specific (e.g., analyze data, solve mathematical problems).

With the rise of the personal computer and numerous other industry developments, the technology market has changed considerably. Few computer users want or need to write their own software because software has become a product, taken for granted and often used for relatively simple tasks. There is no need to know how a printer driver works or how memory is managed by an operating system. This is certainly not an unwelcome development. Software should be easy to use and should meet the demands and needs of the users. But there are ramifications to the transformation of software into a commodity whose source code is no longer available to users.

The modern free-software movement exists for the simple reason that some programmers felt that the licenses imposed on users by companies selling software were too restrictive. Some people wanted to fix their own problems, some people were curious, and some people felt they were unfairly shut out of a process in which they had previously been intimately involved. Sometimes market failure is all that is necessary; operating systems like BSD and Linux rose in popularity and robustness because people wanted to use and experiment with Unix, but they were unable to pay the high licensing fees that AT&T was asking for its product or unable to forfeit certain rights in order to gain access to the source code.

Problems and Opportunities

Relying on Microsoft programs creates a user base that becomes ever more reliant on Microsoft products, trapping users in a cycle of dependence. While retraining people to use a new software environment can be costly, the long-term benefits can be great. Investment in free software is essentially an investment in human capital, rather than in a product doomed to be either replaced or discarded within five years. Because recurring upgrade costs are eliminated due to the free distribution of the software, actual cost is limited to maintenance and support functions performed by actual people. The money that would have been spent on software could be reinvested in training programs or other organizational initiatives. Rather than contracting with outside companies or training staff to remain dependent on commercial products, money could be spent on people that can help other people learn how to use software more effectively in their own jobs.

It would be difficult to make a direct correlation between using Linux and developing a more thorough understanding of what programs do, how the Internet works, and so forth, simply because the people that tend to use Linux are the people that have developed this sort of understanding anyway. However, it could be argued that learning to use computers with an open and flexible operating system like Linux offers people a more portable and flexible skill set and helps people break the cycle of consumption and dependence that ultimately reinforces a limited and limiting paradigm for information technology. Open-source software promotes computer literacy by allowing the user free access to the inner workings of the system.

Most computer users have a limited set of skills with only a few familiar applications (e.g., Word, Excel, or Outlook). Indeed, most people still learn how to use computers by repetitively using specific applications. Upcoming versions of free alternatives to these applications, such as Ximian's Evolution groupware program and the OpenOffice suite, are reaching a point at which the difference in quality and usability is not significant to the average user. The real difference is that these programs are free for anyone to update and support and cost nothing to purchase.

Significance

If free speech and free press are essential to the development of a general literacy, then free software can promote the development of computer literacy. Free software represents a different way of developing software, but the principles at the heart of the movement intertwine with a worldview not limited to computers. Free software allows people to fully participate in the processes that govern the way they work and play. Free software offers choice—not just between products, but a fundamental choice at the level of code.

Free software allows anyone access to the most basic elements of a program and permits their free modification. Free software offers a new model for engagement with knowledge—a surprising model, considering that society often seems to be dominated by corporations and other institutions that dehumanize some of the most important aspects of life. Free software can help put people back into the process by remaining as inclusive as possible.

The chaos of the Internet is always changing, always creating new patterns in data and lifestyles. Often, these patterns mirror the structures and institutions of the rest of the world: The same powers dominate, the same disparities remain, the same problems persist. On the Internet, however, the structures of the real world are even more susceptible to competition from people interacting in novel and distributed ways. Free software is one means for people to work cooperatively and build systems that encourage greater understanding and greater freedom, and we should strongly consider integrating this model with our educational programs.

Website of the Month

It has been said that no language is difficult to learn if it is the first one you hear. All the computers in the offices of the municipal government of Largo, Florida, USA, run free software (specifically, the K Desktop Environment on Linux terminals), and the municipal employees don't seem to mind not having Microsoft products on their desktops. One of the arguments against making the switch to free software is that average users won't be able to figure it out. This case study (http://newsforge.com/article.pl?sid=01/08/10/1441239) demonstrates how a well-designed system can save a lot of money in licensing costs and keep people working productively. The site also includes a discussion of the story.

Glossary

Berkeley Software Distribution (BSD): an offshoot of the ill-fated Unix development collaboration between the computer-science department of the University of California at Berkeley and AT&T. BSD Unix is the core of free operating systems like FreeBSD, NetBSD, and OpenBSD, as well as commercial operating systems such as Sun's Solaris and Apple's Mac OS X.

Free software: software is considered free if users can run the program for any purpose, study how the program works (by looking at the source code), adapt it to their needs (by modifying that source code), and freely redistribute modified or unmodified copies to anyone, all without having to ask or pay for permission.

GNU (GNU's Not Unix): a "Unix-workalike" development effort by the Free Software Foundation headed by Richard Stallman.

Linux: common name for GNU/Linux, an operating system based on the Linux kernel and the GNU tool set that has been the dominant open-source Unix-like operating system since 1996.

Unix: a multiuser, multitasking 32-bit operating system written in the computer programming language C and developed in the late 1960s at AT&T's Bell Labs; later development split between BSD variants and AT&T's own System V.

REFERENCES

DiBona, C., Ockman, S., & Stone, M. (Eds.). (1999). *Open sources: Voices from the open source revolution*. Sebastopol, CA: O'Reilly & Associates.

GNU Project. (2001). *The free software definition*. Retrieved from http://www.gnu.org/philosophy/free-sw.html

Wilcox, J. (2000, April 3). *Judge Thomas Penfield Jackson rules that Microsoft violated antitrust laws*. Retrieved from http://news.cnet.com/news/0-1003-200-1629387.html

OTHER RESOURCES

Lessig, L. (1999). *Code, and other laws of cyberspace*. New York: Basic Books.

Open Source Initiative. (2001). *The open source definition*. Retrieved from http://www.opensource.org/osd.html

Raymond, E.S. (1998). *The cathedral and the bazaar: Musings on Linux and open source by an accidental revolutionary*. Retrieved from http://www.tuxedo.org/~esr/writings/cathedral-bazaar/

Rosenberg, D.K. (2000). *Open source: The unauthorized white papers*. Foster City, CA: Hungry Minds.

Salon.com. (2001). *The free software project*. Retrieved from http://www.salon.com/tech/fsp/index.html

Wayner, P. (2000). *Free for all: How Linux and the free software movement undercut the hi-tech titans*. New York: Harperbusiness.

Young, R., & Goldman, W.R. (1999). *Under the radar: How Red Hat changed the software business— And took Microsoft by surprise*. Scottsdale, AZ: The Coriolis Group.

Guest Author

Brunelle is a graduate student in Library and Information Science at the University of Illinois, Champaign, Illinois, USA.

Personal Meanings

It is tempting to think of our relation to machines as being routine, mechanical, predictable, that is, machine-like. And writers such as Suzanne Damarin, Jacques Ellul, Martin Heidegger, Cheris Kramerae, Karl Marx, David Noble, Dale Spender, and others have warned of the dehumanization associated with technicizing our lives. But within societal trends that often reduce our human capacity, there is a wide range of responses to new technologies and assimilation of them into daily practices.

Through detailed interviews, Cynthia Selfe and Gail E. Hawisher (in press) have revealed remarkable stories of individuals' encounters with technology and the meaning it has in their lives. Likewise, many teachers see the diverse ways that students expand their creativity using new media. This section explores such issues of personal meaning, neither glorifying the technology nor discounting its potential, but rather, asking what can people construct it to be.

In "Seeing Ourselves in the Computer: How We Relate to Technologies," Punyashloke Mishra, Michael D. Nicholson, and Steven K. Wojcikiewicz develop a theory for response to technology, much as we might think of a theory of response to literature. They show that our relationship to technologies is personal in more ways than one. Gail E. Hawisher takes up another aspect of the personal in "Constructing Our Identities Through Online Images" as she explores how we present ourselves to others and how we construct an identity as we use online media. "Learning Through Expression" continues that theme, asking about the meaning of personal webpages for young people. Marcella J. Kehus then offers concrete tools to facilitate digital expression in "Opportunities for Teenagers to Share Their Writing Online."

REFERENCE

Selfe, C., & Hawisher, G. (in press). *Literate lives in the information age: Stories from the United States*. Mahwah, NJ: Erlbaum.

Seeing Ourselves in the Computer: How We Relate to Technologies

Guest Authors Punyashloke Mishra, Michael D. Nicholson, Steven K. Wojcikiewicz

Editor's Message

Readers of this journal are familiar with the idea of stance in reading. As Rosenblatt (1978) showed, our response to literature can involve an efferent stance, in which we seek information, or an aesthetic stance, in which we respond to the text as an artwork. Others have identified ways that individual readers develop their own stances toward a text, everything from resistance to the idea of reading to deep immersion in which one's own life is played out in a fictional narrative.

Although it is easy for us to see a novel or a poem as an artwork, and to imagine different stances one might take toward that work, it may be more difficult to envision a computer system in such a way. Our language leads us away from conceiving of the computer as worthy of a stance when we say "it's just a tool" or "it's only a bunch of 0s and 1s." But our stance toward a technology may be all the more powerful because we do not recognize it as such. When we think that we are simply operating a machine, we cannot see the many ways that our psychological processes shape how we use and interpret it.

This month we have a report on the research of Punyashloke Mishra, Michael Nicholson, and Steven Wojcikiewicz from Michigan State University, East Lansing, USA. They take seriously the idea that we need a theory of response to technology as much as we need one for response to literature. Their research is fascinating in what it reveals about technology, but is even more so in what it reveals about people and the way we interpret the world around us.

Original version published April 2001 in the *Journal of Adolescent & Adult Literacy*
©2001 International Reading Association

Does My Word Processor Have a Personality? Or Topffer's Law and the Design of Educational Technology

From the Golem to Frankenstein, from Isaac Asimov's robots to Rosie, the mechanical maid in *The Jetsons* (the old U.S. television cartoon show), people have been fascinated by the idea of human creations that become autonomous, sentient agents. Embodying human-like qualities (such as intelligence) in computers has been the driving force behind the field of Artificial Intelligence (AI). There has been a resurgence of interest in creating anthropomorphic and believable software "agents" through the use of natural-language processing, affective computing, and multimodal interfaces. We can see examples of this trend everywhere. There is the little "paper-clip assistant" that ships with Microsoft Office; companies like Extempo and Inago that offer interactive agents for "hire"; and Hagglezone, an online shopping website that lets you haggle with a software agent for the best price for anything from a lawnmower to a DVD player.

There are also products like MyPersonalTutor (2000, Microsoft), an early reading program that boasts of a social interface in the form of "the charming Professor P.T. Presto" who offers engaging "multimedia tutorials designed to help the child learn." Outside the realm of the personal computer are animatronic toys like Furby and My Real Baby, which are designed to show emotion and affect as well as to "learn" new behaviors and act in unpredictable ways. The key idea behind these products is that software agents (or artifacts) can be endowed to a greater or lesser degree with various elements of human personality that lead to more lifelike interactions with the user.

Most educators, social scientists, and humanists have been wary of the strong claims made for AI. It has been argued that computer personalities would lack the vitality and dynamism of human personalities. Software personalities would appear scripted, stiff, and unnatural. People would see through the charade and would ignore or maybe even resent human-like responses from a computer. In this column, we would like to argue that, contrary to these expectations, it appears that it is not difficult to imbue computers with human personalities. In fact, it may be impossible not to do so. Responding socially to computers and other interactive media is something we do naturally, and generating these responses may not be as much dependent on powerful AI algorithms as it is on explicit scripting of expressive features to convey appropriate social cues. Responding socially to computers, we believe, has significant implications for media literacy—especially in today's digital world.

To introduce our argument, we begin with a brief digression to Rodolphe Topffer (1799–1846), an artist, designer, and (last but not least) amateur psychologist. He was involved in the development of a new medium for expression and communication, just as we are today. As we shall see, his insights have a great deal to offer us, although our world is very different from his.

Introducing Topffer's Law

1999 was the 200th anniversary of Topffer's birth. Though his name is not widely known today, Topffer's legacy is all around us. He is, as it turns out, the father of the modern comic book. His greatest contribution was to combine visuals and text within a sequence of frames to build a story. By juxtaposing pictures and text and drawing them one frame at a time, Topffer brought both time and narrative into the picture. He also invented some of the comic genre's standard stylistic elements (such as narrowing the panels to speed up the action, or flashing quickly between characters). Here are just some examples of his legacy: Art Speigelman's *Maus*, the Pulitzer Prize-winning Holocaust memoir-in-comics; Superman and Batman comic books; and Sunday morning newspaper cartoon sections.

Topffer, however, saw his work with picture stories as a simple hobby, devoid of any significant artistic merit, something he did "mainly to brighten his evening hours" (Wiese, 1965, p. x). He believed that his most significant and lasting contribution would be to the psychology of art and caricature, something to which he devoted many of his final years. Long before psychological laboratories and controlled experiments, Topffer began a series of systematic experiments on the art of caricature. The results of this work are presented in a slim volume titled *Essay on Physiognomy* and published a year before his death.

The success of the picture book, Topffer argued, came from one thing, and one thing only—a knowledge of physiognomics and human expression. The picture-book artist must create convincing personalities with readable characters and expressions. During his experiments, which involved drawing hundreds of caricatures of human faces, Topffer came to realize that creating convincing personalities was not difficult. He found that it was impossible *not* to do so. This led him to frame a law, which Gombrich (1972) eponymously called Topffer's Law: Any human face, however poorly and childishly drawn, possesses necessarily, by the mere fact of existing, some perfectly definite expression. In other words, any squiggle that we can interpret as a face will have a distinct individual personality. As the art critic Gombrich said,

> The most astonishing fact about these clues of expression is surely that they may transform almost any shape into the semblance of a living being. Discover expression in the staring eye or gaping jaw of a lifeless form, and what might be called "Topffer's Law" will come into operation—it will not be classed just as a face but will acquire a definite character and expression, will be endowed with life, with a presence. (p. 289)

Modern science bears out Topffer's psychological insight. It seems that humans have an instinctive ability to see faces everywhere. Be it the front grille and headlights of a car or the three holes of a wall socket, faces are all around us. Scientists who study the brain have argued for a specific module in the brain that is "tuned" to recognize faces. There are people with damage to specific regions of the brain (or with congenital brain deficits) who *cannot* recognize faces, a deficit called prosopagnosia or face-blindness.

Topffer's Law, interesting though it may be, has remained a curiosity with limited relevance outside the psychology and art of caricature. However, we would like to argue that Topffer's Law holds true for more than just squiggles on paper, and that it may allow us to understand some recent research findings on people's psychological responses to interactive media—computers. Personality is not something inherent in face-like sketches or in wall sockets; it is something we read into the world around us. We are meaning-making, pattern-seeking creatures, and it seems that just as we read personality into squiggles of ink on paper we read personalities into all kinds of interactive artifacts, such as word processors and ATM machines. This may seem a bit strange at first glance—a word processor with a personality!

Topffer's Law and Interactive Media

Over the past decade there has been some fascinating research to indicate that people often respond to computers (and other media) as they would to real people and events—as if the computer were an autonomous agent with feelings and thoughts. People seem to follow all kinds of social rules when interacting with computers, however bizarre or silly this may seem. This line of research was first conducted by the Social Responses to Computing Technologies group at Stanford University (Stanford, California, USA), led by Clifford Nass and Byron Reeves (see Reeves & Nass, 1996). Over the past year, we at Michigan State University have been extending this line of research. This research indicates that people are polite to machines (Nass, Moon, & Carney, 1996), read gender and personalities into them (Nass, Moon, & Green, 1996), are flattered by them (Fogg & Nass, 1996), and treat them as teammates (Nass, Fogg, & Moon, 1996). People stereotype computers as being native or nonnative speakers and, even more strangely, they rate the nonnative computer as less competent than a native one (Alvarez-Torres & Mishra, 2000; Alvarez-Torres, Mishra, & Zhao, in press).

People are flattered by computers that praise them and rate computers that flatter them as being "better" and more "user friendly" than ones that criticize them, even when they are told that this flattery has no basis (Fogg & Nass, 1996). People read personality characteristics, such as dominant or submissive traits, into computer tutorials (Moon & Nass, 1996), and there is some evidence that they prefer interacting with the submissive computer, though it seems that they learn more from the dominant one (Mishra, Tan, & Zhao, 2000). It is easy for people to form a social contract with a computer—when they perceive that the computer has treated them unfairly they punish it (Ferdig & Mishra, 2000).

Though space limitations prohibit us from offering details of these studies, we offer one example. Consider the common-sense idea (and one that is supported by research in social psychology) that any person, for example one of the authors, would be more willing to reveal personal information about himself to another person if that person were to reveal some personal detail to him. For instance, if you were to ask Punya to tell you the greatest disappointment in his life, he would reveal more to you if, prior to asking, you were to reveal something that has disappointed you. Strangely enough, it appears that people apply this "social rule" even when interacting with computers.

In a study conducted by Moon (2000), participants were interviewed by a computer on a variety of topics, and their responses were telling. In one condition they were asked questions about something personal, for example: "What has been your biggest disappointment in life?" In another condition they were asked the same question prefaced by the following:

> This computer has been configured to run at speeds up to 266 MHz. But 90% of computer users don't use applications that require these speeds. So this computer rarely gets used to its full potential. What has been your biggest disappointment in life?

Notice that nowhere does the computer describe itself in first-person terms or indicate that it has emotions, feelings, or attitudes. Despite that, people were significantly more willing to reveal personal information in the second condition than in the first. Essentially, people were applying the social rule of "disclosure begets disclosure" to a computer; they were responding to the computer just as they would respond to another person.

Do any of the study participants seriously believe that a 266 MHz computer can feel disappointed? Or, as the findings of the other studies indicate, do they think that a computer can have personality, gender, and ethnicity? None of the participants in our studies (and the studies conducted at Stanford) claimed to do so when directly asked about it. What is fascinating, though, is that what the participants said did not match what they did. This "intentional stance" (Dennet, 1987) appears to be unconscious, instinctual, and independent of age, experience, and expertise (Reeves & Nass, 1996; Turkle, 1984; Weizenbaum, 1976). It is important to note that these counterintuitive effects are achieved not by designing some fancy agent-based, AI-driven, high-tech computer program that requires a couple of million dollars to develop, but rather with the simplest of text or voice-driven interfaces.

The evidence suggests that generating personality in a piece of software is not difficult. As Topffer realized with respect to his caricatures, it may be impossible to prevent personality from kicking in. Thus, we can extend Topffer's Law into the digital age and argue (a) that almost all interfaces, however badly developed, have personality; and (b) that personality can be generated through the subtlest of cues (these could be the manner in which text messages are phrased or the layout, as well as the use of images and other media). Of course, the use of anthropomorphic agents, such as those described earlier, will only enhance this effect.

Implications for Media Literacy

Literacies and technologies have always been intricately connected. New technologies, with their new constraints and affordances, reveal new ideas of what constitutes literacy. We believe that Topffer's Law (in the new and expansive version we present here) has a lot to contribute to our understanding of media literacy, especially with respect to the new interactive media.

A key aspect of literacy is becoming a sensitive and critical user of media. Advocates of agent-based anthropomorphic technologies often talk of how wonderful these new tools will be (Baylor, 1999). However, there is a darker side to these tools to which we must become sensitive. It is clear that this reading of agency into interactive media is something that can be used against us as information consumers. Advocates of media literacy have often argued for awareness of how information is presented and for sensitivity to techniques that could be used by partisan groups and individuals to manipulate our responses. The ability to instantiate stereotypes, to enhance certain social behaviors over others, can be used to manipulate us for good and for ill. That we are often unaware of these effects makes them even more insidious.

The website for NetSage claims to have a "radical approach to managing online relationships." Its creators label it "Social Intelligence" and argue that "it changes customer behavior." Most children's software uses anthropomorphic agents to involve and motivate children. There is some evidence (Turkle, 1984) that children are more susceptible to these social media than adults are, though this is an area that needs much more research. A greater awareness of Topffer's Law will allow us to recognize these manipulative techniques and thus become smarter in how we deal with these new technologies.

Media literacy is not just about becoming smarter media users, but is also about becoming creative, flexible media creators. We believe that if Topffer's Law holds true it has implications for how we train the next generation of educational technology designers. Though the findings we describe here have been applied in a variety of settings, from the development of voice-mail systems to the design of productivity software (Nass, 1997), they have not had much impact on theory, research, and design related to educational technology. There are two main reasons for this. First, the study of psychological responses to media is an extremely new area of research. Second, this research has not focused on issues of learning. Reeves and Nass (1996), the premier researchers in this domain, said their goal was rather straightforward:

> We are interested in making technologies more "likeable." And just as "liking" leads to various secondary consequences in interpersonal relationships (e.g., trust, sustained friendship, etc.), we suspect that it also leads to various consequences in human-computer interactions (e.g., increased likelihood of purchase, use, productivity, etc.). (p. 138)

Educators have to consider more than just creating a "likeable" computer personality. They have to consider issues of student cognition, affect, and pedagogy as well.

Research in educational technology can focus on harnessing this natural reaction to interactive media to our advantage. These findings emphasize the importance of the social relationship that can develop between a computer and the learner. For instance, research shows that indiscriminate flattery gives users a better feeling toward the computer program (Fogg & Nass, 1996). Flattering users, irrespective of context, may make sense for commercial software producers, but its application to educational technology is problematic. It may give learners a false sense of accomplishment, which may do more harm than good in the long run. Research on student attribution indicates that, in certain contexts, teacher praise may have a negative impact on student self-efficacy (Meyer et al., 1979). The research on stereotypical behavior toward gender and nativeness raises many complex questions for the designer. It would be unacceptable to use a male or native-speaker voice as a narrator in educational software just because research indicates that such a tutor is perceived as more authoritative and knowledgeable. An educator's goal is as much to undermine the insidious effect of such stereotyping as it is to teach content.

Thus, designers of educational software tools have to go beyond the purely cognitive aspects of working with computers and factor in the social and psychological aspects as well. This makes our task far more challenging, bringing as it does an immense domain of social and personality psychology to bear on educational technology. For instance, consider the design of software characters and personalities, a domain that educational technologists do not know much about.

The idea of designing characters is a complicated one, and, as one designer of interactive media said, "Character creation is a black art. No one ever wrote a book on how to be good at it" (White, 2000). In this we can learn from the true experts, the people who create interactive characters for a living: people in theater. Designers of interactive media, especially those who work at the forefront of new media, are sensitive to this. As Nathan Shedroff, a designer of interactive websites, said,

> Few people are ever taught to create successful, satisfying experiences for others. Mostly, these folks are in the performing arts: dancers, comedians, storytellers, singers, actors, etc. I now wish I had more training in theater and performing arts to rely on...especially in improvisational theater. That's like the highest form of interactivity. (quoted in Bruce, 1997, p. 291)

Final Thoughts

Two hundred years after Rodolphe Topffer's birth, in March 1999, the Swiss Post Office released a series of six stamps honoring his comic art. Carrying images from his picture books, these stamps are a welcome honor, given to Topffer for developing an art form that is so important today. Ironically, as we have seen, these picture books were not something he felt were his greatest contribution; they were, in his mind, whimsical and effervescent. Of far greater value, in his opinion, was what came out of his work on the picture books—his musings on the nature of caricature and the language of physiognomy. It seems particularly appropriate that this work (which has been neglected for so long) is once again offering insights and perspectives to a new generation of artists and designers as they begin to understand and develop a new medium. As one of his early admirers, the poet and scientist Wolfgang Goethe, said, Topffer (and Topffer's Law) might indeed, in the future, "produce things beyond all conception."

Website of the Month

Just Think Foundation (http://www.justthink.org) is a media-literacy website committed to educating children, especially at-risk children, about how to comprehend what is being said in media and how to create media messages in various forms. The site consists of reports of projects completed; information for parents and teachers, including lesson plans and recent news events; and a list of resources on media literacy for inquiring minds. However, you will not find much there about issues raised in this column (such as reacting socially to interactive media). Issues of the psychology of human-computer interactions and of attributing personality to media have important implications for the creation and presentation of media; thus far they have not received the degree of attention, we believe, they deserve.

Some Other Sites of Special Interest

Affective Computing (http://www.media.mit.edu/affect). This is a website at Massachusetts Institute of Technology. Led by Rosalind Picard, the affective computing group focuses on creating personal computational systems endowed with the ability to sense, recognize, and understand human emotions, together with the skills to respond in an intelligent, sensitive, and respectful manner toward the user and his or her emotions.

Botspot (http://www.botspot.com). The term *bot* is abbreviated from *robot* and is a piece of software that runs automatically. Bots have been developed for a variety of purposes, and you can find an extensive list of them at Botspot as well as latest news on bot technology. Be sure to try out some of the "chatter-bots" that can be accessed from this site.

Extempo (http://www.extempo.com) and Inago (http://inago.com). These two develop software agents for hire. As the first site claims, "Extempo enables businesses to automate real-time customer care over the Internet through the personalized services of smart, interactive agents." Go to these websites to chat with software agents such as Erin, the virtual bartender.

irobot (http://www.irobot.com). This company produces robots for the consumer market. Their latest is My Real Baby, a product they describe as an "interactive, robotic, artificially-intelligent, emotionally-responsive baby doll." This is among the first of a new breed of interactive toys.

Glossary

Intentional stance: Dennet (1987) argued that when we characterize a system, either natural or artificial, in terms of beliefs and desires, we adopt "the intentional stance." In this column we use the term somewhat differently to categorize how people respond to interactive media as if it were a psychological being or actor. There is increasing evidence that this intentional stance appears to be an unconscious response, independent of age and expertise.

Interactive agents: semi-autonomous, proactive, and adaptive computer programs. Agents do not necessarily have human-like qualities (such as language-processing abilities and so on). However the development of human-like agents (with beliefs, intentions, knowledge, and even emotions) is a growing area of research.

Physiognomy: the art of studying outward appearance (such as facial features and expression) in order to discover temperament, character, and personality.

Topffer's Law: as defined by Gombrich (1972) and based on work by Rodolphe Topffer: Any human face, however poorly drawn, possesses necessarily, by the mere fact of existing, some perfectly definite expression and character. In the present context, we extend Topffer's Law to include the perception of personality and character in interactive artifacts (such as animatronic toys or computer software), however poorly they may be designed.

REFERENCES

Alvarez-Torres, M.J., & Mishra, P. (2000, April). *Computers with accents: Stereotypes, credibility and learning*. Paper presented at the annual meeting of the American Educational Research Association, New Orleans, LA.

Alvarez-Torres, M., Mishra, P., & Zhao, Y. (2001). Judging a book by its cover: Stereotypical responses to interactive media and its effect on the recall of text information. *Journal of Educational Media and Hypermedia, 10*(2), 161–183.

Baylor, A. (1999). Intelligent agents as cognitive tools for education. *Educational Technology, 39*(2), 36–40.

Bruce, B.C. (1997). Literacy technologies: What stance should we take? *Journal of Literacy Research, 29*, 289–309.

Dennett, D. (1987). *The intentional stance*. Cambridge, MA: MIT Press.

Ferdig, R.E., & Mishra, P. (2000). *Emotional responses to computers: Experiences in unfairness and spite*. Paper presented at the annual meeting of the American Educational Research Association, New Orleans, LA.

Fogg, B.J., & Nass, C. (1996). *Silicon sycophants: The effects of computers that flatter*. Paper presented to the annual meeting of the International Communication Association, Chicago.

Gombrich, E.H. (1972). *Art and illusion: A study in the psychology of pictorial representation*. London: Phaidon Press.

Meyer, W., Bachmann, M., Biermann, V., Hempelmann, P., Ploger, F., & Spiller, H. (1979). The informational value of evaluative behavior: Influence of praise and blame on perceptions of ability. *Journal of Educational Psychology, 71*, 259–268.

Mishra, P., Tan. S., & Zhao, Y. (2000). *Dominant and submissive computer programs? What does this mean for the learning experience?* Paper presented at the annual meeting of the American Educational Research Association, New Orleans, LA.

Moon, Y. (2000). Intimate exchanges: Using computers to elicit self-disclosure from consumers. *Journal of Consumer Research, 26*, 324–340.

Moon, Y., & Nass, C.I. (1996). How real are computer personalities? Psychological responses to personality types in human-computer interaction. *Communication Research, 23*(6), 651–674.

Nass, C.I. (1997). Interviewed by Rob Killheffer. *Omni Magazine*. Retrieved November 17, 2000, from http://www.omnimag.com/archives/chats/br050297.html

Nass, C.I., Fogg, B.J., & Moon, Y. (1996). Can computers be teammates? *International Journal of Human-Computer Studies, 45*, 669–678.

Nass, C.I., Moon, Y., & Carney, P. (1996). *Are respondents polite to computers? Social desirability and direct responses to computers*. Paper presented at the annual meeting of the International Communication Association, Chicago.

Nass, C.I., Moon, Y., & Green, N. (1996). *How powerful are gender stereotypes? An experimental demonstration*. Paper presented at the annual meeting of the International Communication Association, Chicago.

Reeves, B., & Nass, C.I. (1996). *The media equation: How people treat computers, television, and new media as real people and places*. Cambridge, UK: Cambridge University Press/CSLI.

Rosenblatt, L.M. (1978). *The reader, the text, the poem: The transactional theory of the literary work*. Carbondale, IL: Southern Illinois University Press.

Turkle, S. (1984). *The second self: Computers and the human spirit*. New York: Simon & Schuster.

Weizenbaum, J. (1976). *Computer power and human reason*. San Francisco: Freeman.

White, P. (2000). Interviewed by *Newmedia* magazine. Retrieved July 12, 2000, from http://www.newmedia.com

Wiese, E. (1965). *Enter the comics*. Lincoln, NE: University of Nebraska Press.

Guest Authors

Mishra teaches at the College of Education, Michigan State University, East Lansing. Nicholson (Department of School Psychology) and Wojcikiewicz (Department of Educational Psychology) are doctoral students at the same university. The research discussed in this column is partially funded by grants from the Dean's Technology Fund and The Joe and Lucy Bates Byers Faculty Research Fellowship.

Constructing Our Identities Through Online Images

Guest Author Gail E. Hawisher

Editor's Message

The Web has raised curious contradictions about personal identity. On one side we see an increasing depersonalization: Online courses now substitute e-mail for face-to-face meetings. The computerized form letter is the genre of choice in business. People work so much in isolation that the computer begins to replace all personal interaction and becomes an addiction. You can visit Dr. Maressa Hecht Orzack's site at http://www.computeraddiction.com to see how far you, or "your friend," has gone along the path to Internet Addictive Disorder.

On the other side, e-mail, Web rings (see http://www.webring.com), online photo albums, and other new media forms bring people together. Families and old friends stay connected by sharing pictures, video, and writing through the Internet. People of all ages now create images of themselves through their websites and their e-mail signatures (see "Seeing Ourselves in the Computer: How We Relate to Technologies," December 1998). Many people, especially in Japan, even put their diaries on the Web, sharing their daily events and their most personal thoughts with the global community.

Questions about how new technologies reshape our relations with one another and our own identities do not yield simple answers. As we use these technologies, we start with familiar goals—to learn, to share, to commiserate, to have fun—but we accomplish these goals in new ways. Moreover, as we adopt new practices, or ways of communicating and representing ourselves, we begin to change as well. If we want to know what these new practices mean for us and for literacy education, we need to look more closely at how people actually use the new media and what they mean to them.

In this month's column, we are fortunate to have Gail E. Hawisher discuss issues related to women's use of new communication technologies and, in particular, how women use personal images to connect with one another. Gail is known internationally for her work in writing studies, computers and composition, and literacy studies.

Original version published March 2000 in the *Journal of Adolescent & Adult Literacy*
©2000 International Reading Association

An Online Picture Is Worth 1,000 Words

For the past few years, I've been engaged in research that looks at the online lives of women and the visual dimensions of the World Wide Web. My abiding interest lies in how the new technologies—and, in this case, the Web—change what we're about as writers and as teachers of writing. Most recently this research has taken the form of looking at how women, in and out of academe, represent themselves visually on the Web and how others represent them in this new medium. Here I'd like to bring together at least two aspects of this research, explore how women use and get used visually in electronic settings, and then turn to issues of the visual in our own teaching lives.

To begin, most published discussions have paid little attention to what happens when the mostly verbal context of electronic discourse is transformed into the visually rich space of the Web. Until recently those of us in literacy and technology studies have understandably focused almost exclusively on the textual. But the heightened possibilities for self-representation brought about by the Web suggest that a simple transfer of arguments about online verbal lives—with their emphasis on egalitarianism—is inadequate as a strategy for exploring visual representations.

To give you some background, I should note that five years ago when Patricia Sullivan and I began studying the online lives of 30 academic women in writing studies, visual authoring on the Web was still in its infancy (see Hawisher & Sullivan, 1998). As part of that study, however, we created a listserv— women@waytoofast—and discussed the many issues women encounter online, including the construction—or not—of images of ourselves. The chapter we authored in connection with the study (see Hawisher & Selfe, 1999, pp. 268–291) was primarily concerned with verbal online experiences the women encountered, but here I'd like to turn to visual considerations that grew out of that study.

As part of the women@waytoofast discussion, in the time just preceding the Thanksgiving holiday in the United States, some of the women began representing themselves visually and then talked of dress and appearance. It all started with one of the women noting how much trouble she had remembering people online and then writing,

```
      XXX
      X X
     XXX  X XXXX
      X XX    XX  /
      X         XXXX
    X             X
    X             X
      X           X
      XX   XX
         | |
         | |
         //
```

Well, it wouldn't have to be realistic photos or even faces. Pick an image. I know that this involves even more rhetorical choices, but I know that I'm not the only person in the world who isn't very word-oriented and something visual to hang a message on would help me a lot and others too I think. Why do electronic lists have to be so tyrannically verbal and linear? That's a pretty dorky bird I managed to construct above.

Less than an hour later, another added:

In Marge Piercy's *He, She, It* an older woman cruises the information networks giving herself a sexy young identity. Here's mine. The curly hair is accurate at regular intervals when the perms are new. (I'm not getting older, just better.)

```
    (%%%%)
  (%%%% %%%%)
   (%%% %%%)
    (%% * * %%)
    (%% : %%)
    (%    %)
    (%    %)
```

And still another began to theorize about the opportunities online visuals might hold for women:

Re-imaging/imagining ourselves through technology seems like an empowering concept. Very connected to Foucault's technology of the self, gaining access to technology to change how we "appear" to the world, to revise those Virtual Valerie porn images to something that more accurately represents our lives in the material realm. Besides if Madonna can re-create herself every so often and get dubbed a feminist, why can't we?

Hope everyone has a relaxing holiday.

```
)))//////(((
)))//////(((
))) * * (((
))) ^ (((
))) o (((
))) (((
```

But there were still others who regarded the capability of representing ourselves online very seriously and not without important consequences. Another of the women wrote:

Hi everyone,

The very idea of choosing a face to accompany my online words horrifies me. Should I choose an "authentic" image, one that shows my age and deviations from standard female beauty markers? Or does the electronic medium license me to alter my image? License? Does it *mandate* that I alter my image....

In creating a face to accompany my words, how would I deal with the very diverse audience of the net—remembering that I might want to retain a professional image for the job search and in addition construct a fanciful image for other lists or create some feminist symbol-face for this list? Will my female face get more or less respect if I make it nice looking, smiling? Does nice looking reinforce the nice training that I want to shed, or does it indicate my insistence on new and nice rules? Or should I make a face very much at odds with my words (mean face/nice words or nice face/mean words) in order to subvert stereotyping?

Ah so many rhetorical decisions if we add visual rhetoric. And gender issues become heightened, I think, rather than lessened.

And almost as an afterthought she added:

Is anyone here making homepages? I have enough trouble with words.

For some, the "faces," "picts," or "e-art," as the women called them, were fun and foregrounded woman@waytoofast as a safe place in which to play—an e-space where they might risk seeming foolish. Yet they immediately connected the personal and playful aspects of e-space with the serious, professional, and scholarly. E-art was used as a platform for self-representation and for self-critique at the same time that it moved the discussion into areas of how one represents oneself in e-space, in one's department, as a job candidate, or as an untenured faculty member.

Largely as a result of this study and the women's thoughtful responses, Patricia Sullivan and I turned from e-art to visual representation on the Web. The Web with its graphical interface makes possible the "imaging" or "re-imaging" that some of the women on waytoofast desired and may indeed allow us to represent one of our many selves more graphically to the rest of the online world. Alan Purves (1998) has written that the coming of print destroyed the importance of the image and made it suspect, but that today it has returned and is shaping the ways in which the new literate world operates.

Gunther Kress has argued that the landscape of the 1990s is "irrefutably multisemiotic" and that "the visual mode in particular has already taken a central position in many regions of this landscape" (in Hawisher & Selfe, 1999, p. 69). The Web underscores the importance of the visual to the extent that it firmly folds the visual into communication processes. That is, it allows Web authors simultaneously to construct and to broadcast themselves visually with an ease and speed that hasn't been possible before.

Yet despite the promise of the Web for visual images that resist categorization, last year when I again searched the waytoofast homepages, I found few homepages of the women@waytoofast. And when I did find homepages, there were few that seemed to be staking out new subject positions for themselves—for the most part, we seemed to be going about the same old academic business as usual, featuring our academic accomplishments, our teaching, and sometimes something about our personal selves. At the following websites you can find fairly typical representations of what we saw. Cynthia Selfe's "look" for the department includes a pleasant photo of herself with links to her online curriculum vitae, which tells her viewers about her education, scholarship, teaching, and all those related categories that show up on academics' hardcopy credentials. (See http://www.hu.mtu.edu/~cyselfe.) My own departmental homepage "look" also bears a strong resemblance to those in other academic departments and features the pleasant smiling image, along with links to my scholarly areas of interest and recent publications. (See http://www.english.uiuc.edu/facpages/Hawisher.htm.)

Although there was some variation in the kinds of homepages the waytoofast women constructed, most of them exhibited a professional look that seems to cut across our institutions. A few of the women included childhood pictures to give a somewhat narrative representation of themselves, others included no pictures, but with artwork and color they managed to create an inviting personal image of themselves. See, for example, Nancy Kaplan's homepage at http://raven.ubalt.edu/staff/kaplan. Her homepage includes the requisite professional information—her affiliation, publications—but also includes sites that she likes and that she calls "worth the whistle." She closes her webpages with a metaphor of the kitchen and cooking, but not before she has introduced personal information, under Nancy Kaplan, in the very first reference to herself at the site.

Nancy Kaplan—born quite a few years ago and then some time later educated at the University of Michigan and Cornell—considers the really important things to be everything that's absent from her official homepage:
   Her children, Eva and Erica (a small bit of whose artwork can be found in the story about one of the many citizens of E/Street, a WEBaltimore Community). Her friend, partner, lover Stuart. And their three cats—Athena (the portly), Lilith (the

paranoid), and Vyvyan (the playful). I won't embarrass any of us, least of all Athena, with the family portraits.

Unlike my homepage and Cynthia Selfe's, created by someone other than us (using snapshots taken or collected to advertise our departments), Nancy's homepage is homegrown, so to speak, created to show students her interests but also to broadcast her persona to anyone on the Web who might come across her homepage.

Of course, there are other images of women on the Web that the women themselves did not create—that were posted to the Web not to advertise their departments or professional credentials but to sell the wares of society. Let me shift focus for a moment to mention another image of women that I found at the commercial enterprise of Victoria's Secret back in 1996. These pictures surprised me not so much for their content but for the fact that they were maintained by Jake, a student at Georgia Institute of Technology. When the website was accessed, you saw a lingerie-clad woman not so different from those we see in fashion magazines, only this time gazing directly out at us from the screen rather than a page. At the time you could also order the clothes pictured there through Jake, who included his own e-mail address and working 800 phone number.

These images are the same kind that bombard us daily in the popular media and, more recently, in the catalogs that have taken over snail mail. In writing of the growing use of the visual, Gunther Kress (in Hawisher & Selfe, 1999) noted that

> The body is coming to be used as a medium of representation and communication: even a brief look at a contemporary rock video will illustrate this clearly enough, and so do the industries of aerobics, jogging, roller-blading, and the televisual entertainments developed out of these. (p. 69)

He might well have added the World Wide Web. He went on to argue that

> These changes are not in themselves new: the body has been used in many cultures and in many periods as a medium of communication.... The point is...that after a period of some two-to-three hundred years of the dominance of writing as *the* means of communication and representation, there is now, yet again, a deep shift taking place in this system. (p. 69)

But, as Kress would readily admit, not all uses of representations of the body are the same. The Victoria's Secret online bodies tend to emphasize current objectified representations of "femaleness" and serve to reproduce the age-old stereotypical relations between the sexes.

Another of the women in the waytoofast study, Kitty Locker, also has a website where she chooses to represent herself more as a teacher or resource person, pointing her students (and whoever else might access her pages) to sites on the Web that she finds information-worthy and wants to share with others. (See http://www.cohums.ohio-state.edu/english/People/Locker.1/kolhome.htm.) Although her page doesn't disrupt conventional notions of femaleness, it did lead me to a group of websites in which women's homepages begin to challenge the culture's dominant narratives as to what it means to be female.

Thinking about how women in fields other than writing might represent themselves, I pursued one resource on Locker's page, "Women and the Web," and came to "Babes on the Web." Ostensibly, Rob Toups's "Babes on the Web" would seem to support the stereotypical representations of women. An interesting aspect of these webpages, however, is that although Toups constructed his homepage, replete with an image of himself with cigar and rifle, he didn't construct the pages of the women to which his links lead. Despite being among the 400+ "babes" he advertises, the women themselves created the personas that emerge from their pages. I should note that Kitty Locker probably did not intend for viewers to access Babes on the Web from her website. But because we can't necessarily control the content of all the links we insert, no Web creator is ever completely sure as to where his or her links might lead.

Among the 400+ women linked at Toups's site is Eve Andersson, who greets us with a headshot that strikes a traditional pose, smiling and affable, but with green face, red hair, and antennae, all enhanced by a constant stream of soft murmurings of the numbers in the expansion of pi, namely, 3.14159.... She calls herself the "famous" Eve Astrid Andersson. Although the green face and antennae signal deviations from a professional demeanor, Eve populates her space with displays of her academic credentials and work experience. The viewer learns that she graduated from Cal Tech, moved to Berkeley as a graduate student in the Department of Mechanical Engineering, and was formerly an employee of Creative Internet Design, a Web consulting agency in Pasadena, California. Interwoven in her "credentializing" are fables, personal information, games, creative writing, artwork, photos of herself and family, and spoofs of her lived experiences. Through it all, she visually represents herself as an athlete, lab technician in workout clothes, traveler, jailbird, wine taster, thinker, 20-something with-it chick—all working to challenge stereotypical images of a 20-something woman engineer. An alien, who was yellow as a baby, Eve entertains viewers with stories of her growth to her adult green state. The mixture of cartoons with colorized photos (and "real" ones) lends a childlike whimsy to the life of a young woman who also depicts herself as a devotee of pi.

When placed alongside the professional and institutional homepages, Eve Andersson and other women on the Web seem to stake out multiple subject positions for themselves. They "doctor" photos, use cartoons, animate quirky representations of themselves, and in general play with the visual in ways that blur the boundaries between physical and virtual selves. It's a cyborgian move in that they're using the technology to capture representations of themselves while at the same time adding and changing bodily features. In displaying their ears, calves, and sometimes tattoos, they celebrate their own writings of their bodies. In contrast, the professional women presented earlier are ostensibly valued for their minds and knowledge—their bodies are extraneous and potentially damaging to their success.

With these images, then, we begin to see how some in and out of the field of writing studies represent themselves on the Web and how they are represented. We see women pictured in online advertising in ways that seem familiar to us—as objects to be ogled and stimulated, commodities to be sold and bought. But we also see examples of the possibilities the new media begin to provide women for activism—for forging new social arrangements by creating a visual discourse that startles and disturbs. In claiming this cyborg territory as their own, the 20-something women on the Web—Laurel Gilbert and Crystal Kile (1996) told us that "grrrls have attitude, girls don't"—clothe themselves in "attitude" and, as Donna Haraway (1991) aptly stated, commit their cyborg selves to "partiality, irony, intimacy, and perversity" (p. 151).

Let me now turn briefly to our work as teachers in online classroom settings and tell a story on myself. A few years ago, with a digital camera, I began taking pictures of my students and featured them in a graphical conference program I was using at the time and also in the pages of class websites. Most of the students seemed to enjoy the representations and would regularly remind me that they hadn't yet had their pictures taken or posted. For several semesters, then, I organized my classes in this way, extending class discussion online and enhancing it, I thought, with the visual representations. I did this in both graduate and undergraduate classes until one of the undergraduates, a young African American woman, complained about her picture and asked me to take it again, which I did. Although I noticed that the second picture wasn't any better, the student didn't complain, but I began wondering about this picture taking I was doing and realized that invariably my African American students tended not to look like themselves in the pictures; often they looked older and their features were flattened. What I didn't know and what I've subsequently learned is that most processes of photographic reproduction have been "optimized" for European faces. Our photographic processes emphasize the kinds of contrast that you can achieve with pale faces; they are not set up to catch the kinds of contrast that dark faces comprise (Winston, 1996). In other words, color palettes on computers tend to be optimized for light faces and exhibit a much greater range of lighter colors (and pinks and reds) than of the kinds of colors found in darker faces.

What conclusions can we begin to draw from these snippets of the pictorial presented here? First, there is the group of academic women on waytoofast who think that at times the visual might help in online communication. Some of them, however, disagree and argue that images present all sorts of problems we have not yet adequately considered.

Second, there is the huge growth of the World Wide Web on which we can represent ourselves pictorially although only a few women in the study fully availed themselves of the capability. And some who initially included pictures don't now. Perhaps they have decided to eschew the visual, retreating in an age when stalking and harassment have become all too familiar.

Third, we see some women representing themselves online—with the visual and the verbal—in creative, rhetorically effective ways. Eve Andersson and many other 20-something women, whose websites I studied for this research, make the visual work for them.

Fourth, we see women being represented through online advertising in ways that seem familiar to us, but the visual immediacy of the Web tends to transform the viewing experience, startling us (or at least me) with its vividness and energy. Finally, you see me as teacher, incorporating computer technology into my class in unthinking ways. In representing the students visually, I unwittingly made computer technology work to emphasize my place in the world at the expense of someone else's.

Perhaps the most obvious conclusion to be drawn from these examples is that the electronic world, and even our "unelectronic" world, is packed full of images that we view and interpret daily and which, in turn, exert a tremendous influence over us. When we become objects on the Web and have no say in how we're being represented, the outcome is predictable—we end up reproducing old identities and re-create traditional narratives with new technologies.

Certainly this world of images, on the Web and otherwise, argues for our own—and our students'—greater critical awareness of the workings of the visual. Increasingly, as teachers, we are expected to use the visual as an adjunct to our teaching, and I would argue that few of us are able either to interpret or construct images with sufficient understanding of what we perceive or convey with our own designs. Few of us are as expert as the 20-something Eve Andersson and her self-representation as a green-faced devotee of pi; few construct so personable a site as Nancy Kaplan's "kitchen."

I end with a quotation from Susan Leigh Star, sociologist, poet, feminist. In an unpublished manuscript, *From Hestia to Homepage: Feminism and the Concept of Home in Cyberspace*, she notes that "we have known for a long time that home can be a safe haven—or the most dangerous place a woman can be (statistically it is the most likely place for a woman to meet a violent death)." Let us hope that our "homes" in cyberspace can contribute to our students' and our own positive sense of home—without inviting the dangers, without creating misrepresentations. Let us make sure that the online pictures we produce work to convey the 1,000 words we wish to send. If we neglect tending to the visual in our professional work and our teaching lives, we are likely to wake up one morning to find that we live primarily in a world not only of the sound byte but also of the quick take.

Website of the Month

The Media Foundation, a nonprofit organization, manages the Adbusters site, sponsors the Canadian Adbusters magazine, and supports PowerShift, an advocacy advertising agency. The foundation describes itself as "a global network of artists, writers, students, educators and entrepreneurs who want to launch the new social activist movement of the information age." Included at the site are "spoof ads," such as the visual representation of a sneaker-making Indonesian woman "being all that she can be" while running barefoot with a baby in her arms. Other visually compelling ads include "Joe Chemo," lying in a coffin, and another, a picture of "Baby McFry" outfitted with a crown of french-fried potatoes and bib featuring an *M* in the shape of arches. There are also "uncommercials" such as the one that features a pig draped over North America, reminding viewers that the average

North American consumes 5 times more than a Mexican, 10 times more than someone in China, and 30 times more than a person in India. Overall, the website invites viewers to take seriously visual commercial representations and to question their impact on our daily lives.

Listservs

Some listservs in writing studies and literacy and technology:

- ACW-L (Alliance for Computers and Writing)—provides a discussion list for members of the Alliance for Computers and Writing and anyone interested in issues concerning literacy and technology.
- NCTE-talk—provides a discussion list on English teaching at all levels. The website also includes several other lists sponsored by the National Council of Teachers of English. Contact person: Eric Crump. If you access the website, select Teacher Talk in the sidebar.
- WAC-L (Writing Across the Curriculum)—provides a discussion list for all teachers interested in issues related to Writing Across the Curricum and classroom practices.

Glossary

The American Standard Code for Information Interchange (ASCII): refers to information that can be transmitted easily from one environment to another because it is without control characters particular to specific software and hardware. It includes few characters from languages other than English.

Cyborg: usually refers to a being that is half machine, half living entity. Donna Haraway wrote that "a cyborg is a cybernetic organism, a hybrid of machine and organism, a creature of social reality as well as a creature of fiction" (1991, p. 149).

E-art: electronic art, used here to indicate ASCII pictorial representations.

Egalitarianism: refers to equality for human beings across different social settings. When applied to electronic environments, the term is used to argue that a lack of social context cues in online discourse results automatically in nonhierarchical structures across gender, race, sexual orientation, and a host of our other differences. In other words, because paralinguistic cues (e.g., appearance, facial expressions, and tone of voice) are absent online, what is said supposedly becomes more important than who says it.

continued

Glossary (cont.)

Listserv: software that enables receipt of e-mail submissions and the redistribution of the messages to individual e-mail accounts. The term today has been generalized to refer to the electronic discussion group itself, such as WAC-L, a list or listserv on writing across the curriculum.

Multisemiotic: several modes, including the visual, aural, and written, are all part of the society's meaning-making apparatus. With the rise of electronic communication technologies, increasingly our senses are assaulted with sound, images, and even smells that conspire to gain our attention.

Picts: a term used here to refer to the ASCII representations women created on the listserv women@waytoofast.

Quick take: a photograph or image that may misrepresent the person or event being captured digitally or on film. Sound bytes and quick takes are often stripped of the context necessary for adequately understanding what's at hand.

Semiotics: a theory of signs aimed at studying how images and other kinds of social discourse are produced, interpreted, and come to "mean."

Visual discourse: pictorial representation of language in action.

REFERENCES

Gilbert, L., & Kile, C. (1996). *Surfer grrrls: Look, Ethel! An Internet guide for us*. Seattle, WA: Seal Press.

Haraway, D.J. (1991). *Simians, cyborgs, and women: The reinvention of nature*. New York: Routledge.

Hawisher, G.E., & Selfe, C.L. (1999). *Passions, pedagogies, and 21st century technologies*. Logan, UT, and Urbana, IL: Utah State University Press and The National Council of Teachers of English.

Hawisher, G.E., & Sullivan, P. (1998). Women on the networks: Searching for e-spaces of their own. In S. Jarratt & L. Worsham (Eds.), *In other words: Feminism and composition* (pp. 172–197). New York: Modern Languages Association.

Purves, A.C. (1998). *The Web of text and the Web of God: An essay on the third information revolution*. New York: Guilford

Winston, B. (1996). *Technologies of seeing: Photography, cinematography and television*. London: British Film Institute.

SUGGESTIONS FOR FURTHER READING

Adler, K., & Pointon, M. (Eds.). (1993). *The body imaged: The human form and visual culture since the Renaissance*. Cambridge, UK: Cambridge University Press.

Balsamo, A. (1996). *Technologies of the gendered body: Reading cyborg women*. Durham, NC: Duke University Press.

Berger, J. (1972). *Ways of seeing*. London: Penguin.

Dibbell, J. (1993). A rape in cyberspace, or how an evil clown, a Haitian trickster spirit, two wizards, and a cast of dozens turned a database into a society. *The Village Voice, 21*, 36–42.

Eldred, J.C., & Hawisher, G.E. (1995). Researching electronic networks. *Written Communication, 12*(3), 330–359.

Gill, M.S. (1994, January). Terror on-line. *Vogue*, 163–166, 195.

Hawisher, G.E. (1992). Electronic meetings of the minds: Research, electronic conferences, and composition studies. In G.E. Hawisher & P. LeBlanc (Eds.), *Re-imagining computers and composition: Teaching and research in the virtual age* (pp. 81–101). Portsmouth, NH: Boynton/Cook.

Kaplan, N., & Farrell, E. (1997). Weavers of Webs: A portrait of young women on the net. In G.E. Hawisher & C.L. Selfe (Eds.), *Literacy, technology, and society: Confronting the issues* (pp. 424–440). Upper Saddle River, NJ: Prentice Hall.

Kress, G., & Van Leeuwen, T. (1996). *Reading images: The grammar of visual design*. London: Routledge.

Star, S.L. (Ed.). (1995). *The cultures of computing*. Cambridge, MA: Blackwell.

Guest Author

Hawisher directs the Center for Writing Studies at the University of Illinois, Urbana-Champaign, USA.

Learning Through Expression

Editor's Message

About 15 years ago I spent some time in Alaska working with Andee Rubin, Carol Barnhart, and teachers in village schools. We wanted to see whether a computer system with word processing, e-mail, a database, a writing planner, and other tools could be used to help students improve their reading and writing. I remember presenting this program (Quill) to the local school board in the tiny village of Shungnak one evening.

When the chair of the board asked us what the program could do, I explained that their students could learn about people all around the world by communicating through e-mail. Electronic communication would open up vast opportunities to learn about the world and other cultures. The chair listened thoughtfully, paused to reflect, and then asked, "That is good, but can our children also use these tools to tell the rest of the world about themselves?" He was intrigued to think about using computers and networking to learn about the world, but even more so to imagine students using the same tools to teach the world about themselves.

This desire to teach about oneself, as well as to learn and to express one's ideas, feelings, and values, is at the heart of the computer experience for many adolescents. They do this through chat rooms, which for many have replaced the telephone as a means of daily communication; through e-mail; and through multiuser games now percolating through the Internet.

The diversity and richness of adolescent life is also portrayed through personal webpages. This month, the Portraying Yourself on the Web section offers a small compendium of examples of this means of self-expression. You can easily find many more such pages. One way is to search the Web using as the search keys "about me" and "years old." You'll discover an incredibly rich set of pages, each one revealing and impressive in its own way.

Original version published December 1998 in the *Journal of Adolescent & Adult Literacy*
©1998 International Reading Association

Expression as a Path to Learning

What are the best resources for learning? In *The School and Society*, Dewey (1915/1956) characterized the "impulses" of the child as the true resources of the school. These include the impulses to communicate, construct, inquire, and express oneself. The impulse to communicate derives from the human need to participate in social worlds, to ask questions, to share, and to gain new knowledge. The importance of the many functions of language to learning is reflected in the centrality of language to nearly all models of teaching. The impulse to inquire is the desire to understand the physical, biological, and social worlds around us. It, too, is fundamental to the learning process. Dewey also saw that young people have the need to construct, or make things, and to have effects on the world around them. Finally, he identified the need to express oneself, through language, visual arts, and music. Although these impulses are separately named, they actually constitute different aspects of the unified whole of the learner's purposes. There is no implication that they should be separated out in schooling or be practiced and acquired in isolation.

Dewey suggested that however else we might conceive curriculum, we cannot ignore the fact that for learners the curriculum begins with their background, abilities, interests, and prior experience. These elements are realized through the learner's impulses, which in turn provide the inescapable foundation for learning. The recognition that these impulses are the fundamental resources for learning— as opposed to computers, books, videos, labs, worksheets, or scope and sequence plans—does not imply that they are all of learning. Dewey, in particular, wrote at length about how education must recognize the needs of society and the collective accumulation of knowledge, not simply respond to the child. Nevertheless, Dewey saw that in the bringing together of child and society, the interests of the child were often neglected. If we could instead attend to these interests, we might gain a deeper understanding of the learning process and of the role new technologies can play in education.

Using new communication and information technologies, teachers and students are discovering more ways to communicate with others, to make things, to learn about the world, and to express themselves. Their discoveries point to exciting possibilities for learning today and in the new century. Thus, these new tools expand the range of possibilities for students to learn through communication, inquiry, construction, and expression.

Despite their great potential, there is now ample evidence that the existence of new media for learning does not in and of itself lead to better teaching and learning. If anything, the new media may simply amplify existing approaches to teaching. Thus, we need to look closely at how new media are actually used.

In a 1997 study of some of the most advanced technologies for learning (those supported by the U.S. National Science Foundation), Jim Levin and I found that many new systems do provide rich environments for communication and inquiry, reflecting attention to two of the impulses Dewey identified. There was less opportunity for construction, a consequence perhaps of many systems emphasizing the rich digital content now available on the Web. There was even less support for personal expression, consistent with the assumption in many curricula that art and personal expression are somehow less central to learning, and can be neatly parceled out from learning content and skills.

Although some would argue that we need to parcel out the impulses, I see the power of the Web and other new media in the support of more integrated learning. In fact, without much explicit effort on the part of curriculum or technology designers, students are using the new technologies to do exactly the kind of integrated learning through communication, inquiry, construction, and expression that Dewey envisioned. The personal webpages included in the next section and those referred to in the Website of the Month represent but a few examples of how students are telling the world about themselves. In the process they are learning new technical skills, practicing language use, and enhancing their understanding of many topics.

Portraying Yourself on the Web

The Web has provided a new medium for personal expression. Young people, and those not so young, are using the richly intertextual, multimedia canvas not just to learn, but to teach the world about themselves.

The excerpts below give just a glimpse of a few webpages. They don't include the background music, the photographs, the video segments, the rich graphics, or the imaginative use of fonts and backgrounds. In order to see those, you need to search the Web itself. (Youngsters' names have been changed and e-mail addresses omitted to protect privacy. Students' typographical and grammatical errors have not been altered.)

- All about me

  Hi. Thanks for visiting my home page! My name is Hilary. I'm 13 years old and I live in Tasmania, Australia. I go to college in Launceston and I have many friends that I hang out with on the weekend and at school. My favourite type of food is Italian, especially lasagne. I love animals and have a horse. I think Hanson are just the best and I like Savage Garden. My favourite subjects at school are Maths and Design and Technology. I like pistol shooting and I'm a member at George Town Pistol Club. I also love getting E-mail.

- Hello, my name is Max but you can call me MATSU

  As you see I'm a big NBA fan. So, now something about me. I'm 15 years old, my birthday is on the 20th of April. I live in Estonia, which is a small country in Europe. My hobbys are as you already know basketball and my second big hobby is computers. I've worked with computers since I was 12 or 13 years old. That would be all for now, if you would like to know something about me send me an e-mail.

- Welcome to the Horrible Page of Mall Rat Madam

  Hello all and welcome to the sorry little place I call home on the World Wide Web. This page isn't going to be really spectacular, in fact it will probably suck. I am just making it to let people have a glimpse of my world. On this page you can learn about what I like, what I hate, why I am the way I am, and not much more. So hang on to your booties, here is my page

- About me...

  Ok, let's see. I am 14 years old and from one of the largest states in the USA, Texas. I am about 5'4" and weigh 107 pounds. I am a tanned, brown eyed, brunette. I have a nice smile with straight teeth, which is good because I love to laugh and smile.

- My name is Tom and I am 13 years old

  Detailed summary:

  I was born in Santa Monica in 1983. My name is Tom. I have lived in California, for 13 years. Like the sand through the hour glass, so are the years of my life. I like to do a lot of different things. Some of my interests are playing sports, playing my electrical guitar, talking on the phone, and watching TV. Some of the sports I play are: soccer, bike riding, roller blading, tennis, basketball, football, and skying. I spend lots of time with my friends but my work always comes first. My favorite subjects at school are Programming, Science, Social Studies, Literature (mythology), and Physcial Fitness. My political views are astray right now with all the negative publicity that the presedential candidates are throwing at each other.

- General description

  What you are going to see here is little bit of information about me and my family. I'm 17 years old, I was born in Guatemala. I was born on November 5, 1979. I'm short with black hair.... We are 7 members in my family, which are Mom and Dad, two sisters and two brothers. My sisters are 16 years old and 12 years old. My brothers are 6 years old and 1 year.... My goals is to graduate from High School and go to college. I will be majoring in Nursing. To help many people that are sick and they need help.

- JOHANNA

  Ik ben dus Johanna. Dit is de eerste keer dat ik een HTML pagina maak hieronder ga ik iets ver tellen over mezelf in het Nederlands, en in het Engels. Eerst ga ik wat over mezelf in het Nederlands vertellen. Ik ben Johanna. Ik ben dertien jaar, en zit op het Zernike college in Haren. Mijn hobby's zijn: schaatsen, tennissen, vissen, taekwondo, ping-pongen... Now I'm going to tell you something about me in Englisch. I am Johanna. I am 13 years old, en go to a school called "Zernike college." I go to school in Haren (in the north of Holland). My hobby's are....

Interpretations

The First World Wide Web Personal Home Page Survey was conducted among authors of personal homepages on computers in Pennsylvania, USA. Among the findings were these:

- The most common reason cited for writing a personal webpage is "means of self expression" (49% of the sample). Other common reasons were "to learn/practice HTML" (48%) and "to distribute information to friends/people I know/people I meet" (43%). Less popular reasons were "to distribute information to people I don't know with similar interests" (34%) or "to distribute information about myself to professional contact or potential contact or potential employers" (24%). Apparently, many webpage writers view the Web as a place to express themselves and to connect with those they already know.

- Nearly all (91%) of webpage authors say they present themselves accurately in their webpages. But only 78% feel that others are presented accurately. Those under 20 years old were more likely (64%) to report that they present themselves very accurately than were older Web authors (36%).

- Only 14% of personal webpage authors were women. Other surveys have found that 34% of Internet and Web users are women.

Website of the Month

Every year, the creators of the competition ThinkQuest (Advanced Network & Services of Armonk, New York, USA) organize an international competition for students ages 12 to 19 to use the Internet as an interactive, collaborative teaching and learning tool. Students work in teams to create webpages on topics in arts and literature, history, math, science and technology, social science, sports and health, and other categories.

A 1997 winner was *To Kill a Mockingbird, Then and Now*. It was developed on the 35th anniversary of the film based on Harper Lee's book. The site has a variety of learning activities focused on issues of gender, class, and race, which are illustrated by short clips from the film. As the student authors of the webpage say,

> The teaching of *To Kill a Mockingbird* offers a tremendous opportunity for teachers to help students communicate on several major issues that they must deal with in life but seldom have the chance to discuss. The very issues and terms that make the book a challenge to teach are in fact opportunities to "heal" wounds and scars that have long remained unaddressed.

The instructional activities also encourage students to look closely at the film and the novel as art forms, considering how they were made and how they affect viewers and readers.

Glossary

Hypertext Markup Language (HTML): a language for writing webpages. The first webpages had to be written directly in this language, with an expression such as the following to indicate a hyperlink: "<A HREF="http://io.advanced.org/thinkquest/">ThinkQuest</A>." In this case, were the above link active, the reader of the webpage would see only ThinkQuest. When he or she clicked on that word, the Web browser would automatically connect to the Web server (see glossary entries, below) containing the ThinkQuest site.

continued

Glossary (cont.)

Search engine: a program that searches a database to locate all the documents that meet certain specifications given in search keys or a search query. It is commonly used to refer to programs for searching the Web. Most search engines return a list of webpages ordered by how well they match the specifications and by other heuristics, such as the number of sites that link to that page.

Search key: a string of text used to guide a search engine (see previous glossary entry) to find webpages. The keys can include phrases as well as individual words or parts of words. Users can specify keys that must be present in the webpage as well as those that must not be present and with some search engines, use Boolean operators (AND, OR).

[Web] browser: a computer program that allows the user to explore the World Wide Web by interpreting documents written in HTML or other hypertext languages.

[Web] client: a computer that allows the user to connect to a server program in order to retrieve (download) or post (upload) Web documents.

[Web] server: a program running on a host computer that maintains Web documents accessible via a Web browser.

REFERENCES

Bruce, B.C., & Levin, J.A. (1997). Educational technology: Media for inquiry, communication, construction, and expression. *Journal of Educational Computing Research, 17*(1), 79–102. Retrieved from http://www.ed.uiuc.edu/facstaff/chip/taxonomy

Dewey, J. (1956). *The school and society*. Chicago: University of Chicago Press. (Original work published 1915)

Opportunities for Teenagers to Share Their Writing Online

Guest Author Marcella J. Kehus

Editor's Message

As inexpensive personal computers began entering schools in the early 1980s, the use of word processors for learning to write soon became one of the most widely used applications. The new tool offered many advantages over traditional pencil and paper.

- With convenient editing features, students did not have to copy over in order to make changes in their writing.
- These features also supported free writing and various ways of exploring and manipulating texts.
- Printers made the writing easier for others to read, thus expanding the possibilities for writing to real audiences.
- Multiple copies of writing for classmates, parents, and portfolios could be produced easily.
- The use of keyboards, although at times a barrier, was also an aid to students who were learning to spell and compose.
- Associated tools such as spell checkers and formatting programs helped many students focus more on the content of their writing, or the purposes they were trying to achieve.

The advent of the Web a decade later extended these advantages. It was now possible to share writing with much wider audiences and to link it with the writing of others. New tools for graphic design and interactivity further enhanced what students could do.

Today, most teachers know that the combination of word processing with the Web holds a great potential for student writers. Many are finding ways to overcome the initial barriers of finding equipment and beginning to integrate these new tools into writing across the curriculum. But as with any technology, there are unanticipated consequences of their use. Issues of access, privacy, plagiarism, commercialism, cost, and community arise in new guises and usually before most of us are ready.

In this month's column, Marcella Kehus shares her experiences with helping students write for audiences not only beyond the teacher, but beyond the classroom, the school, and the geographical community. Marcella is a teacher and doctoral candidate in Reading and Language Arts at Oakland University in Rochester, Michigan. Her work with TeenLit.com (see Website of the Month), one of the best sites for teen writers, and her study of its use are all-too-rare examples of what we must do if we are to understand more about the meaning of new technologies for developing literacy.

Original version published October 2000 in the *Journal of Adolescent & Adult Literacy*
©2000 International Reading Association

Working With Teen Writers Online: Policies, Procedures, and Possibilities

I became interested in the issues of policies, procedures, and possibilities of on-line communities through my experiences as one of the creators and hosts of TeenLit.com. The roots of TeenLit.com stem from two colliding ideas I had a few years back. First, I have always believed that publication was the key motivator and application for teaching students to write, but I was continually frustrated by the scarcity of real publishing opportunities for my students. Second, as I was doing some Web publishing outside of my teaching responsibilities, I was struck by the relative ease, immediacy, and low cost of publishing on the World Wide Web and even more impressed with the potential and growing audience for reading work published there. And so, toward the end of 1999, with this idea, a few hundred dollars, and a teacher friend of mine as partner, TeenLit.com was born on the World Wide Web. And since its very inception, TeenLit.com has been concerned with two primary purposes: (1) providing an authentic purpose and audience for teens' writing and (2) providing a forum for a community of such adolescent writers to form and thrive.

For example, in an initial study of TeenLit.com (Kehus, 1999), I provided an online bulletin board for visitors to post messages about the published writing or even drafts of their own. As you can see from the Figure, activity on the site has been high, and increasing fairly steadily between its start in the first week in January 1999, with 89 visits, to the last week of July 1999, with 754 visits. On average today, we have approximately 1,500 visitors a week to the site (based on weekly average of unique visits from 4/16/00 to 5/13/00). Postings to the Web are detailed in Tables 1 and 2. Table 1 summarizes the formal genres of writing published on the site, while Table 2 shows the distribution of postings to the discussion board.

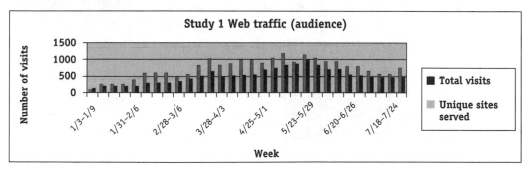

Table 1: Purpose of Published Writing on TeenLit.com

Category	Percentage of Published Writing (*N*=103)
Teen writers—poetry	82
Teen writers—short story	10
Teen writers—essay	6
Teen writers—book reviews	1
Teens cool links	< 1
Teacher resources	< 1
Teacher links	< 1
Not listed—add a new category	< 1

Table 2: Purpose of Teen Writers' Discussion Bulletin Board Postings

Category	Percentage of Total Postings (*N*=99)
Feedback to writing published on TeenLit.com	30
Other—miscellaneous	14
Not selected	14
Random thoughts	13
Draft—want feedback	9
Ideas	7
Book talk	5
Teacher comments	4.5
Publishing opportunities	2.5
Contests	0
TeenLit.com website	0

It's clear that we've accomplished our initial goal with TeenLit.com. Our visitors are active in posting original writings, comments to other members, and so forth that serve a broad audience of adolescent writers and readers. However, whether or not we can say we have an actual community of writers is open to doubt. I believe the lack of a feeling of community can be traced to four key reasons:

1. Our site is public and anonymous. Because of this, visitors were able to post any kind of message without regard to factors such as taste, amount of personal information included, and so forth. Thus, there were the occasional inappropriate postings (rude, personal info, or dangerous).

2. TeenLit.com is unbounded and dynamic with an indeterminate audience. That is, because any visitor could post and read messages here, the population of this community has no known bounds and is ever changing. Someone about to post a message, then, is not clear who the audience is. A visitor posting a message for a particular author has no guarantee that this author will read the message, while it is certain that many others can.

3. Giving feedback to other writings was the most popular type of posting (30%), yet less than 10% of the published writings have drawn any feedback, and many postings (35%) have had no replies.

4. The site's broad, public, anonymous nature prevents making connections or building relationships.

Building on these lessons, I am currently studying a subset of TeenLit authors who have elected to join a smaller, private online community known as eWeb. Because this group will be a private and identifiable group of voluntary involved authors from TeenLit, empowered by a number of Web-based technologies, I continue to examine the development and possibilities of such an online community.

From my first study, as well as my current work, I have learned a great deal. In this column, I share some of the lessons I've learned about publishing on the Web, working with adolescents online, and attempting to establish community. For, indeed, the World Wide Web is murky water, especially when dealing with minors, and we have had to be continually responsive in our policymaking within this website. The Web is constantly changing and broaching new frontiers, and so some of this information will be outdated quickly. Because I believe that students' work on the Web is both powerful yet problematic, I hope to guide you through some of our lessons. I'll begin with the broadest forms of public policy regarding content rating, children's online privacy, and copyright.

Policies From the Outside

Content rating. Before censorship advocates push for government regulation, the Web publishing community has voluntarily created and used its own content-rating system. This system provides for hidden code in the header of pages that browsers read to determine the appropriateness of a site given the user's (or his or her parent's) guidelines. Website administrators are responsible for registering their site with either one or both of the two emerging regulatory sites, RSACi (http://www.icra.org) or SafeSurf (http://www.safesurf.com), and for placing the appropriate codes on their webpages. Using a standard known as PICS (Platform for Internet Content Selection), both of these sites currently have volunteers rate their sites' content in violence, nudity, sex, and profane language. SafeSurf has added categories for intolerance, homosexual/heterosexual themes, gambling, and glorifying drug use. With these ratings in place, parents, schools, and other concerned individuals can set up Web browsers to view content that meets their specific standards, in alliance with PICS. This can be done with independent software or directly from within the most recent editions of Internet Explorer and Netscape Navigator.

Children's Online Privacy Protection Act (COPPA, at http://www.ftc.gov/ reports/privacy3, or http://www.idg.net). Issues of privacy on the Internet are hot topics today, and nowhere are they more alarming than when soliciting information from minors. Thus, the U.S. government, specifically the Federal Trade Commission, has enacted COPPA. This Act is being implemented with a "sliding scale" that will gradually become more strict over the next two years as technology and webmasters work to catch up with its demands. In final form, the latest version of this Act requires written verifiable parental consent before anyone on the Internet can get information from a child under the age of 13 in such situations as joining an e-mail list, submitting a form, or posting to a bulletin board. Thus, our site requires participants to be 13 years of age or older, and we attempt to verify this by asking this question of age before allowing any submission, posting, or addition to the mailing list.

Copyright (http://lcWeb.loc.gov/copyright/circs/circ1.html). As with any text, as soon as someone puts his or her work in writing, that text is copyrighted to the author. However, plagiarism on the Internet is as easy as copying and pasting, so copyright(s) of the author(s) need to be made clear and foreboding. Although one can still register a copyright for further proof and protection, regulations now allow the use of the © symbol along with the year of first publication and the author's first and last name without formal registration. On TeenLit.com, our privacy policy clearly explains that authors retain all copyright (allowing us to publish online once) and may revoke this privilege from us and have their writing removed from the site at any time. On a few occasions, outsiders have wanted to use our students' writing for various purposes, such as publication in an anthology, use in a class, and even use on statewide testing. When these persons contact our site, we simply work as the intermediary, passing their requests on to authors, yet maintaining authors' privacy by not sharing their e-mail addresses, full names, or other contact information. Ultimately, the authors, as holders of copyright of their own writing, make the decision and follow through on such requests. (See http://www.teenlit.com/policy.htm.)

Policy From the Inside

Though the above topics are broad and affect everyone publishing on the World Wide Web, I have found other principles equally important in maintaining an ethically responsible site for adolescents that strives for a sense of community. These principles are summarized below.

Monitor live bulletin boards or other interactive forums. Such space leaves opportunities for flaming, spamming, privacy breaches, stalking, and more if not monitored and edited for violations daily.

Protect privacy of all members. I suggest that students never give out their last names, e-mail or webpage addresses, or other personal information. In fact, published writers are known only by their first name, grade, location, and the "About the Author" text they provide on our site.

Link responsibly. Though it is said that you can get anywhere on the Web within six clicks, visit and be selective about the sites you provide links to in terms of appropriateness. Though we have found it impossible to regularly monitor our links after initially approving them, providing a policy and contact information for "links gone bad" wherever links are provided will enable your visitors to be proactive in helping you remove inappropriate links. For example, after initially being teen writing sites, at least three legitimate sites were converted to pornographic sites using the same site address. We do not know whether this happened due to the initial domain name expiring, being bought out, or more devious means, but we do know that we would have still been sending innocent teens to those sites if our members had not immediately notified us of the change. The World Wide Web is ever-changing; working on the Web is a commitment to keeping up with its fluidity and being responsible for its impact.

Provide opt-out options. If you allow members to publish and join, you should also allow them to "unpublish" and "unjoin."

Be up front. Reveal any affiliates (companies you link to for profit), as well as your use of cookies, IP addresses, and mailing lists.

Other Views

[Virtual Communities are] "social aggregations that emerge from the Net when enough people carry on those public discussions long enough, with sufficient human feeling, to form webs of personal relationships in cyberspace." (Rheingold, 1993, p. 5)

"The Net seems to provide a vehicle to explore the self and for children to establish themselves as independent, self-governing individuals." (Tapscott, 1998, p. 56)

"There is something about writing for the unseen audience out there at the other end of the line that inspires students not only to write more but to produce better writing. I also believe connecting kids with other kids around the country through an electronic network helps break down cultural, ethnic, and economic barriers." (Hunt, 1996, p. 231)

How You Can Participate

While teachers are certainly encouraged to send their students to TeenLit.com, we do not accept whole-class submissions. We do, however, allow up to one submission per author per genre per month, so send your very best writers. I also encourage teachers to promote the online publishing of their students' work—given the above cautions, of course. Toward that end, I offer the following considerations.

- *Design pages with a WYSIWYG editor* (see Glossary). For individual pages, the editors that come with Netscape Navigator (Composer) or Internet Explorer (Front Page Express) work just fine. To create and maintain a whole site, full programs such as Microsoft Front Page or Adobe GoLive work well.

- *Find a place to post your pages.* This might mean on your school's Web space (follow their Acceptable Use Policy), on free space (put up with space restrictions and annoying ads), or getting your own domain name (US$70 for two years) and hosting (about US$20 per month).

- *Enlist students.* As soon and as much as possible, enlist students to contribute content, design, and other ideas and to do the actual work. Student ownership is key.

- *Promote usability*. Keep the user interface simple, self-explanatory, and very explicit.

- *Try to attract visitors*. Submit to search engines and arrange for mutual links.

- *Aim to build an online community*. Provide as much interaction and communication between members as possible. Keep content fresh. Allow for relationships and identities to be established. Be open to suggestions and meeting your members' needs.

- *Seek advice*. Here is some advice from Kimberly Siedlik, our site's editor (to whom I am eternally grateful for reading through all the submissions, judging, responding, and doing work that I could never do alone).

  a) Publishing criteria: Establish and make visible on the site a clear set of criteria against which all submissions will be judged. Make sure the criteria are able to cover a variety of age groups and genres and that they include the privacy and rating issues discussed previously.

  b) Have a submissions editor: Although some of our 8th-grade writers are as competent and mature as some of our 12th-grade writers, you should make allowances for age and ability differences. Given the global possibilities of the World Wide Web, consider that some of your submissions may come from countries where English is a second language.

  c) Consider your audience: Keep the site interesting for your readers by varying the authors (by age) and the genres that you post. Also consider making a policy against class or group submissions. This will prevent your site from becoming heavy in one type of writing, such as 9th-grade personal essays, and will stop your inbox being flooded.

  d) Revision: In my experience, the more personal and detailed the feedback I give a writer, the more likely the writer is to revise and even resubmit. To aid in this time-consuming process, I have recruited the help of some of our teen participants to give advice and feedback to struggling writers. Remember to keep copies of all submissions so that you will them to compare against revisions.

Website of the Month

TeenLit.com (http://www.teenlit.com) is a private not-for-profit website currently funded and administered by two secondary teachers in southeastern Michigan. In addition, TeenLit.com has been generously supported over the last two years (2001–2002) by grants from The McCarthey Dressman Education Foundation (http://www.mccartheydressman.org). The purpose of TeenLit.com is to promote teen literacy by providing a forum for teen writers to publish and discuss their writing, review and discuss books they read, and to provide a resource for their teachers. TeenLit.com is also a research site for these teachers to investigate the efficacy of the World Wide Web in facilitating teen literacy in the above-mentioned ways by examining the interchanges that occur through this venue.

Places That Publish Secondary Student Writing Online

I Love Poetry (http://www.ilovepoetry.com). Online publishing of poetry along with articles, bulletin boards, and chat rooms for poets.

Ayn Rand Institute Essay contest (http://www.aynrand.org/contests). Annual contest for students in grades 9 to college; be sure to request the Teacher's Contest Kit.

The Diary Project (http://www.diaryproject.com). This site "encourages teens to write about their day-to-day experiences growing up." Diary entries are posted by the most recent data as well as sorted by topic, and all are submitted online by teens.

Eve Magazine (http://www.evemag.com). Eve aims to "provide a sanctuary of depth and intelligence" for girls that other magazines don't seem to offer. They also accept submissions for sections such as PowerChick, Rant Wall, Junk Drawer, Boy's Eye View, and Poetry Hive.

Poesie.com (http://poesie.com). Along with claiming a great deal of inter-activity, this site lets the writer publish after merely registering, and, possibly, even get feedback. A commendable model, though it lacks any editorial controls or monitoring.

Potato Hill Poetry (http://www.potatohill.com). This site "wishes to ignite a passion for poetry in schools across the country" though we find its contest most promising.

Teen Ink (http://www.teenink.com). With a strong history of print publishing of teen writing, TeenInk has made a nice transition to the Web.

Use Your Voice (http://www.useyourvoice.com). Invited contributions here include categories such as monologues, poetry, quotes, and life. This site boasts to be the only one, "dedicated to, run by, read by, and completely written by teens."

Word Forge (http://www.artsforge.com/wordforge.html). This site adds a twist by focusing on online writing collaborations.

Glossary

Affiliate (or reseller, or VAR, Value Added Reseller): An affiliate links to another site for profit. For example, TeenLit.com links to Amazon.com with a special code that tracks visitors so that TeenLit makes a commission on any purchases they make there.

Acceptable Use Policy (AUP): the policy of a company, school district, or owners of computer networks that explicitly states what is and is not acceptable, including, for instance, how and when computers might be used for personal use, what sort of sites can and cannot be viewed, what sorts of e-mail are allowed, and what specifically may be posted on a website.

Cookie: a small file placed on the user's computer by a website that allows it to track and remember visitors. Cookies must be enabled and can be disabled on your browser. They are relatively harmless in that they can't damage or even access your system and do not contain high-stakes information (such as credit card numbers), but they are a way of tracking and thus infringing on your privacy.

Flaming: any derogatory message sent online, either posted to a message board or e-mailed. A particularly harsh flame might include a deluge of such messages.

IP address: every time you log on to the Internet, your Internet Service Provider (ISP) assigns you a unique IP address number that allows your computer to communicate with others (usually servers) to browse the Web and exchange e-mail. Your IP address can make you vulnerable to hackers as this is their way into an unprotected computer, but those most vulnerable are computers that are continually linked to the Internet with the same IP address, such as ones using cable modems or servers.

continued

> **Glossary (cont.)**
>
> **Opt-out:** Most reputable companies using e-mail lists usually give directions somewhere in their e-mail and/or on their site to allow you to remove yourself from such lists. This is known as the opt-out or option to get out.
>
> **Platform for Internet Content Selection** (PICS): This was developed as a common symbol system of rating content, specifically to allow control over what sorts of Web content a browser is allowed to view, mostly by parents controlling their children's Web viewing.
>
> **WYSIWYG** (pronounce wizzywig): What You See Is What You Get is the slang-term title for software, in this case webpage creation software, that is very user friendly and straight-forward.

REFERENCES

Christian, S. (1997). *Exchanging lives: Middle school writers online*. Urbana, IL: National Council of Teachers of English.

Edgar, C., & Wood, S. (Ed.). (1996). *The nearness of you: Students and teachers writing on-line*. New York: Teachers and Writers Collaborative.

Howard, T., & Benson, C. (Ed.). (1999). *Electronic networks: Crossing boundaries/creating communities*. Portsmouth, NH: Boynton/Cook.

Jones, S. (Ed.). (1999). *Doing Internet research: Critical issues and methods for examining the net*. Thousand Oaks, CA: Sage.

Kehus, M. (1999, December). *An online discourse community of adolescent writers*. Paper presented at the annual meeting of the National Reading Conference, Orlando, FL.

Rheingold, H. (1993). *The virtual community: Homesteading on the electronic frontier*. Reading, MA: Addison-Wesley.

Tapscott, D. (1998). *Growing up digital: The rise of the net generation*. New York: McGraw-Hill.

Guest Author

Kehus is a secondary English teacher and doctoral candidate in reading and language arts at Oakland University in Rochester, Michigan, USA.

Ethical and Policy Issues

Teachers today are becoming familiar with the host of ethical issues arising from the use of new information and communication technologies: Their students can go to the Web to find customized essays for assignments as well as pornography and hate sites. Through online chat spaces they can connect with pedophiles or hurt others by spreading lies or racial slurs. Some students are learning about destructive hacking, in which they can destroy websites, examine personal data, or steal credit card information.

The student who has illegally downloaded copyrighted music or movies now represents the norm. Others have distributed software for bypassing the copy protection on DVDs. In realms such as these, the definitions of *legal* and *ethical* are actively debated and by no means simple to resolve.

At the same time, others are using new media to address social justice concerns. Many are involved with groups such as the Independent Media Center (http://www.indymedia.org), which presents an alternative to corporate-controlled media. Others have established support groups for people who encounter discrimination on the basis of race, gender, physical ability or appearance, language, or culture. Many students have become involved with groups such as Computer Professionals for Social Responsibility (http://www.cpsr.org), which promotes democracy and accountability in public decisions about information technology. Countless others are using e-mail, the Web, digital video, and other new technologies as part of efforts to combat hunger, build affordable housing, fight racial discrimination, support international human rights, and otherwise organize political action.

In addition to addressing personal ethics, we need to examine public policies in this arena. Additional issues become salient then, such as what meaningful access is and how to achieve it, or how to assess the consequences of the adoption of new technologies.

In "Teaching and Learning: Whose Computer Is It?" Yong Zhao, Sophia Hueyshan Tan, and Punyashloke Mishra ask what can happen if we think of the computer, not as the teacher's machine, but as the student's, or the child's, in an outside-of-school role. Their column pushes us to consider what the function and role of the computer ought to be. "Access Points on the Digital River" extends the question of where and how a student might use a computer to ask what are the conditions increasing access in the world today. "Challenges for the Evaluation of New Information and Communication Technologies" looks at the need for better evaluations of the use of new technologies and also the challenges inherent in analyzing the new media. "Educational Reform: How Does Technology Affect Educational Change?" continues that theme, looking especially at how new technologies fit within existing social and political structures.

All this points to what Larry Hickman calls *responsible technology* (1990). This is not a particular type of technology, nor even a feature of technology. Instead, it is a commitment to design, distribute, implement, and interpret technologies with the understanding that they reflect our histories and shape our futures. It is to see technologies as arising from situations teeming with values (Kohn, 1997) and to call for a critical engagement with both their antecedents and their consequences. Further, it is to see ourselves as both part and parcel of the technologies we create.

REFERENCES

Hickman, L. (1990). *John Dewey's pragmatic technology*. Bloomington, IN: Indiana University Press.
Kohn, A. (1997). How not to teach values: A critical look at character education. *Phi Delta Kappan, 78*(6), 428–439.

Teaching and Learning: Whose Computer Is It?

Guest Authors Yong Zhao, Sophia Hueyshan Tan, Punyashloke Mishra

Editor's Message

When we invite young people to use new technologies, they often take them in directions we never anticipated. This uncertainty is what makes new tools and media fascinating and frightening. In the United States, groups as diverse as Computer Professionals for Social Responsibility, the Motley Fool investment advisory, and the Church of Scientology recognize this in their use of the phrase, "the good, the bad, and the Internet."

One consequence of uncertainty is that people become cautious. We see this in the tendency to use new technologies first in ways that replicate old practices. Thus, early television sets looked the way radios looked, and our computer desktops look like the desktops they purportedly replace. Another consequence is that we seek to retain control—to ensure that we decide whether, where, when, and how the new technology is employed.

In the classroom, these tendencies can mean that teachers often see the computer as a tool to help them do their work, and they are uneasy about what students might do with it. As a result, students are limited in the range of things they can do with new technologies. There is nothing wrong with taking advantage of the ways that technology can aid teaching, but a focus on teaching per se can limit what learning can occur. This month, Yong Zhao, Sophia Hueyshan Tan, and Punyashloke Mishra of Michigan State University tell us about an innovative program that opens up possibilities for young people as the primary users of the computer.

Original version published December 2000 in the *Journal of Adolescent & Adult Literacy*
©2000 International Reading Association

Going Beyond the Teacher's Machine

We are problem solvers. Every day we face many problems: some trivial, some significant, some familiar, some novel. For solutions to them we look to ourselves, other people, and new technologies. When presented with a new technology, we immediately ask what problem it might solve or whether the technology might become a problem itself. Teachers and students have different lives and different problems, although they spend a significant portion of their lives together in the same place. As a result they have different reactions to new technologies. They conjure up different images of what problems technology might help them solve and what problems it might cause.

Consequently, teachers and students have different attitudes toward computers. They put them to different uses. Teachers see, and are often advised to see, the computer as a tool to help them teach better—to make their presentation more attractive and effective, to manage their students more efficiently, and to communicate with parents more easily. Computers are believed to have the potential to alleviate teacher headaches such as outdated curriculum materials, hard-to-explain concepts, students' uneven intellectual and social development, lack of time for professional interactions with colleagues and experts, and uninterested students.

Students, on the other hand, see the computer as a solution to a different set of problems: making and keeping friends, managing boredom, and dealing with school and family. Thus kids use computers to play games, chat with old friends and make new ones, design websites, build robots, discover the latest cool songs, and send pictures to their grandparents (Cole, 1996; Nardi & O'Day, 1999; Resnick & Rusk, 1996).

Educational technology has often been about solving teachers' problems with technology. Although the ultimate goal is to enhance student learning, which is paradoxically the teacher's problem, technology has always been viewed as a tool to help teachers teach better. Students have had little say over where computers are placed, how and when they are used, or what should be on them. Concerns over students' needs are only indirectly and peripherally related to decisions about computers in schools. Regularly computers are found in secure labs, in the classroom corner, or on the teacher's desk. The teacher strictly manages student access to them. The teacher decides when, where, and how they are used. Computers in some sense have been consecrated as only the teacher's machine.

The view of the computer as the teacher's machine has resulted in some undesirable practices—practices that move us away from our intended goals, which fueled the generous investment in school technologies. First, drill-and-practice programs are still by far the most common in classrooms. Applications (e.g, Powerpoint) that help them do presentations are the most popular among teachers. Further, we routinely find teachers having students compose and revise their writings with paper and pencil instead of a word processor. Only when the writing is complete are students allowed to type and print it. The idea is to improve appearance rather than use the computer to assist writing, in the way it is used in the real world. The same is true with teachers' practice of scanning students' drawings and printing them out so that students can take them home to show their parents.

The last example is perhaps most troubling. Schools have spent lots of money and energy getting wired to the Internet so that everyone can enjoy the benefits of this wonderful information and communications technology. Then, right after school staff get the Internet connected, they start spending money and energy trying to restrict access to it. They build firewalls. They install filter software such as CyberSitter (http://www.cybersitter.com) and SurfWatch (http://www1.surfwatch.com). They develop elaborate Internet user policies. They require students and parents to sign Internet access agreements akin to the ones signed prior to a major surgery. After all this, few teachers actually engage students in any Internet-based communication activities such as chat or e-mail (Becker, 1999). Most schools do not give students individual e-mail access. Online chat is strictly prohibited. FTP and Web publishing are generally not allowed on school servers. Many websites are blocked, and in essence the Internet is reduced to a reference book for the teacher.

The teacher-centered configurations and practices of technology teach students to be serious about the computer too. It ceases to be an object of fascination and imagination. It is reduced to a tool—the teacher's tool. It is something students have to learn to improve their grades, something they have to put up with to please their teacher. Much of what students do with the computer is well structured and supervised, such as very low-level keyboarding or simple restricted Web searches. It is not too far a stretch to say that many students may have a richer experience with computers in a local electronics store than in school.

Alternatively we could view the computer as the student's machine—one that students can use to solve their problems and that can help them do things better—a machine each student can play with (Garner, Zhao, & Gillingham, 2000). For the past three years we have been developing a program that attempts to realize this view. In the following sections we describe the program and report what happened when technology was seen as the children's machine.

The Program: KLICK!

In the spring of 1998, a group of educational technology researchers and middle school teachers and administrators in the United States got together at Michigan State University in East Lansing to work on a grant proposal that would eventually lead to funding for an after-school program in 10 middle schools in Michigan. The program, later to be called Kids Learning In Computer Klubhouses (http://www.klick.org), or KLICK!, was designed as an after-school program to serve mostly middle school students. These clubhouses would be operated by and within local schools with support from the College of Education at Michigan State University. These clubhouses would follow a common set of principles and offer a series of common activities. While operated by local schools, these clubhouses would work together as a consortium. Students within the clubhouses would be involved in voluntary, authentic, and engaging activities. These activities, supported by computational media, would provide participating students personally meaningful experiences and result in authentic products useful to them or the community at large (Zhao, Mishra, & Girod, 2000).

Although the spirit of what makes a clubhouse is hard to define or outline, we identified three key factors for making a clubhouse a clubhouse. The first and perhaps most important of these is the freedom to choose what to do and when and how to do it. Bruner (1996) has argued for

> building school culture that operates as mutual communities of learners.... Let these schools be a place for the praxis (rather than the proclamation) of cultural mutuality—which means an increase in the awareness that children have of what they are doing, how they are doing it, and why. (pp. 81–82)

Schools, as we know them, are far from Bruner's conceptualization. But we want KLICK!, an after-school program, *not* to just be an extension of the traditional school day. Students in KLICK! should be free to decide how and when they want to use whatever technological tool(s) they need to achieve their goals.

Adults in KLICK! are not there to determine the nature and scope of the students' activities. Instead they are there to offer support, point out possibilities, and maintain a free and safe environment for all participants. To ensure true choices in learning opportunities, we emphasized the importance of networking and community beyond the immediate physical boundaries. We wanted KLICK! participants to be able to engage in activities requiring resources and expertise that may not be available within a local site or school. This is significant given that many of our sites are either in rural or inner-city areas—locations where resources and expertise may not be easily available. Moreover, our goal was to develop a KLICK! community wider than the local site (or local community) and to use the capabilities of current networking technologies to help us achieve this.

A second important property of a KLICK! clubhouse is that it produce "works" or *oeuvres*, as the French cultural psychologist Ignace Meyerson called them. As Bruner explained it, *oeuvres* can be grand, such as arts and sciences of a culture, as well as minor, such as a school team's winning a soccer game. "Oeuvres are often touchingly local, modest, yet equally identity-bestowing" (Bruner, 1996, p. 22). KLICK! encourages students to produce both personally meaningful works as well as products that are useful for their community. Through a consortium arrangement, we hope that KLICK! participants can develop a better sense of "localness" and identity in their works because they now belong to a larger community with more potential collaborators, competitors, and audiences.

The third and final important property of a clubhouse is collaboration. In a learning community, especially one that encourages personalized learning activities, collaboration is especially important. It not only provides the necessary venues for participants to access one another's skills to complete their works, but also introduces the opportunity for students to recognize and respect others as valuable sources of knowledge.

What Happens When Computers Are Made the Children's Machine?

> We have all known for years that if you treat people, young kids included, as responsible, contributing parties to the group, as having a job to do, they will grow into it—some better than others, obviously, but all benefit. (Bruner, 1996, p. 77)

Bruner was right. In the two years since KLICK! opened in January 1999, KLICK! kids, or KLICKers as they call themselves, have used their "own machine" to do some wonderful things for themselves, for their teachers, for their schools, and for their community. Their "mucking around" at the computer has resulted in dramatic changes in attitudes toward the school, impressive gains in technology proficiency, and amazingly meaningful and practical works.

Looking at what KLICKers did helped us better understand what problems kids care about and what kind of things they want the computer to help them with. It also revealed (a) how difficult it is to truly make the computer the children's machine in the current school setting and (b) the tension between the two views of how computers should be used in schools.

Living online: Exploring identities. The most popular activity at all KLICK! sites is online communication, IRC, Instant Messenger, the Palace (http://www.thepalace.com), and e-mail. KLICK! provides each participant with an e-mail account, access to a set of KLICK! text-based chat rooms as well as a graphical chat environment (the Palace). Every day hundreds of students come to the 10 clubhouses to participate in some kind of online communication activities. They "talk" with their friends from the same school, other KLICK! schools, KLICK! central office staff, and whomever they find interesting. Of particular interest is the KLICK! Reporter project (Garner, Tan, & Zhao, 2000).

The KLICK! Reporter project was created with the online project-based workshop model in mind. The original goal was to help improve students' writing by engaging them in authentic projects. Two or three students from each of the KLICK! sites were asked to serve as reporters who would contribute to the weekly Password Express, an electronic newsletter of KLICK! A graduate research assistant served as the project coordinator. Each week the reporters were to meet online and discuss what they might write. The coordinator hosted these meetings and provided guidance.

By standards of prescribed goals, the project has failed miserably. Students did not do what the adults wanted them to do, which was to write, design, and publish. However most reporters continued to show up for the chat meetings and to have frequent e-mail communications with the coordinator and one another. Site coordinators have regularly praised this activity because the students like it. Many reporters have also expressed great appreciation for this activity and the coordinator. Further, a closer look at what the reporters did during and after the online meetings shows that the kids were learning something very important: living online.

This project revealed an interesting tension between the two perspectives. The project is assessed to be a failure by the "teachers' machine" standards because the reporters are not writing in the traditional sense. However, from the "children's machine" perspective, they are learning quite a lot: complex graphical user interfaces, multiple and fluid identities, social consequences in virtual communities, and multimedia and multimodal communication tools. Moreover they enjoy being a part of this community. Here are some more examples of what students enjoyed doing in KLICK!

Webbing for the community: Playing with design and multimedia. Developing websites in local communities is another major KLICK! activity. KLICK! students have developed more than 50 websites for local businesses, community service organizations, and schools. For example, a student in Baldwin (a small rural community in western Michigan) developed and maintains the website for the local emergency service and his parents' dry-cleaning business. A group of students in the same school developed and maintain the website for the local chamber of commerce. A student in Armada (a rural community in eastern Michigan) developed websites for the local hardware store. Students in the clubhouse in De Tour Village (a small rural community in Michigan's Upper Peninsula) developed a website for the community's centennial celebration.

Being helpful to others: Offering services to the community. Works are not only tangible products, they also include externalized experiences and activities. In Brethren Middle School, KLICK! students have participated in the "Adopt-a-Teacher" program, which offers teachers technical and research assistance by KLICK! members. In Cass City, KLICK! participants served as assistants to community members who came to use the computers. In Detroit, students have been trouble-shooting computers and the network in the school. For that purpose, the students have developed a database of information they collected about all the school computers. In Baldwin, students have been offering computer instruction to senior citizens.

Who I am and what I like: Expressing yourself. KLICKers have spent lots of time finding ways to express themselves. Melinda (pseudonyms are used for all students) developed a photo essay on the Web about a nearby cement factory that attracted her curiosity every time she and her mother passed it. Sarah has been writing and publishing a novel about the Dragonites on the KLICK! website. Browsing through KLICKers' personal homepages you can find elaborate creative sites about Pokémon, the National Hockey League, medieval weapons, pet care, and other things in which kids are interested. KLICKers also have developed antismoking digital videos, antidrug animation movies, and interesting three-dimensional animations of things they care about.

Closing Comments

Technology, particularly the computer and the Internet, not only provides solutions to existing problems, it changes the problems we have to solve every day. It also creates more problems that demand new solutions. In other words, technology innovations not only improve the means but also change the ends. The definition of *literacy*, for example, has already gone through many changes due to technological changes, and we expect more in the future (Labbo, 1999). The computer not only makes it easier to transmit text and mix different media, but it also requires us to be able to read and write hypertext and multimedia documents. The Internet has already made virtual communities common places where millions of people interact with one another every day. The ability to participate in these communities is much more than just being able to type and read. It also includes being able to manage multiple identities and deal with multiple information sources.

Children, through active use of technology to solve problems, are in a sense practicing and learning the new literacy brought upon them by new technologies. Their mucking around with new technologies is actually a way to participate in the future. Unfortunately, due to the prevalent view of the computer as the teacher's machine, any computer use that does not directly lead to improved learning of the traditional subject matters is considered irrelevant. As a result, adults often ignore or trivialize children's interaction with computers, viewing it as mindless or fruitless mucking around. Worse yet, some adults see kids playing with computers as a dangerous criminal act that must be prohibited. We hope that KLICK! and other similar projects, such as the Fifth Dimension and the MIT Media

Lab Computer Clubhouses (Resnick & Rusk, 1996), provide a counter argument—playing with computers is necessary and can lead to good things. (The Table illustrates some differences between the two uses of the computer.)

The Teacher's Machine vs. the Student's Machine

	The Teacher's Machine	**The Student's Machine**
Tasks	Used to create drill-and-practice tasks Used to present content	Used to create artifacts (including word documents, graphics, animation, music, art)
Software	Mainly presentation software	A variety of software (including games, simulations, applications, digital videos, communication-related software) Even presentation software is not necessarily used as presentation software (e.g., Powerpoint used to simulate animation)
Purpose	Used mainly for the product (e.g., write and edit on paper then type final draft on computer) Students work for teachers	Used for both process and product (e.g., type, edit, create, communicate, collaborate, and publish on computer) Students work for themselves, their peers, and their communities
Display	Products are displayed on paper (e.g., show parents print-outs)	Products are displayed in different media (e.g., show parents on paper, on computer, and on the Web)
Internet	Restrict access to Internet Internet is used as a reference book	Explore various facets of Internet Internet is used as the Internet, as a medium for communication, inquiry, construction, and expression
Terms	Used on teachers' terms (teachers decide when, where, and how)	Used on students' terms (students decide)

How You Can Participate

The current KLICK! sites are funded through a grant from the U.S. Department of Education. Recently we received funding to expand KLICK! to a total of 20 schools in Michigan. KLICK! has started to accept new schools from around the United States, and schools can apply for grants from the Department of Education's 21st Century Community Learning Centers program or use its existing facilities to establish KLICK! sites. Please visit the KLICK! website for more information.

Website of the Month

The KLICK! page (http://www.klick.org) has information about the KLICK! consortium, sample activities, and students' products.

Other Sites of Interest

The Computer Clubhouse Network (http://computerclubhouse.org) provides information about an effort similar to KLICK! Originally developed by the Computer Museum in collaboration with the Massachusetts Institute of Technology Media Lab (http://www.media.mit.edu), it is another after-school program for youth. Unlike KLICK! the Computer Clubhouse is located in nonschool community-based agencies.

The afterschool.gov website (http://afterschool.gov) is a site developed and maintained by several U.S. federal agencies to provide information about after-school programs. The 21st Century Community Learning Centers site (http://www.ed.gov/21stcclc), maintained by the U.S. Department of Education, provides information about this grant program.

Glossary

File Transfer Protocol (FTP): the most widely used way of moving files from one computer to another over a network. There is a set of commands in FTP for making and changing directories, and for transferring, copying, moving, and deleting files. Formerly, all FTP connections were text based, but graphical applications are now available that make FTP commands as easy as dragging and dropping. Numerous FTP clients exist for a number of platforms. Common FTP clients include Fetch (Macintosh) and ws_ftp (Windows).

Internet Relay Chat (IRC): a system of clients and servers allowing people all over the world to communicate via typed messages. IRC allows multiple users to converse in real time on different "channels." Channels vary in traffic and content. IRC clients are available for nearly all platforms.

Instant Messenger: a type of software that enables instant messaging, a type of communications service that lets one user create a private chat room with another individual. Typically, the instant messaging system alerts the user whenever somebody on his or her private list is online. The user can then initiate a chat session with that person. AOL Instant Messenger (AIM) was the first instant messaging system to become popular on the Internet.

continued

Glossary (cont.)

Oeuvre: The French cultural psychologist Ignace Meyerson used the plural *oeuvres* to refer to artifacts, activities, and events of a culture that bear its identity. In *The Culture of Education*, Bruner (1996) applied the term in an educational context to refer to authentic products and events of schools.

REFERENCES

Becker, H.J. (1999). Internet use by teachers (http://www.crito.uci.edu/TLC/FINDINGS/internet-use). Irvine, CA: Center for Research on Information Technology and Organizations, University of California at Irvine.

Bruner, J. (1996). *The culture of education.* Cambridge, MA: Harvard University Press.

Cole, M. (1996). *Cultural psychology: A once and future discipline.* Cambridge, MA: Harvard University Press.

Garner, R., Tan, S., & Zhao, Y. (2000). Why write? *Computers in Human Behavior, 16,* 339–347.

Garner, R., Zhao, Y., & Gillingham, M. (2000). After 3 p.m. *Computers in Human Behavior, 16,* 223–226.

Labbo, L.D. (1999). *Toward a vision of the future role of technology in literacy education.* Paper presented at the Forum on Technology in Education: Envisioning the Future, Washington, DC.

Nardi, B.A., & O'Day, V.L. (1999). *Information ecologies: Using technology with heart.* Cambridge, MA: MIT Press.

Resnick, M., & Rusk, N. (1996). The Computer Clubhouse: Preparing for life in a digital world. *IBM Systems Journal, 35*(3 & 4), 431–440.

Zhao, Y., Mishra, P., & Girod, M. (2000). A clubhouse is a clubhouse is a clubhouse. *Computers in Human Behavior, 16,* 287–300.

Guest Authors

Zhao is an associate professor of educational psychology with interests in children's use of computers, teacher adoption of technology, technology diffusions in schools, and Web-based learning environments. He also directs the Center for Teaching and Technology. He is the founding director of Kids Learning in Computer Klubhouses (KLICK!), a consortium of technology-rich after-school programs. Tan is a graduate student at Michigan State University and Mishra teaches at the same university.

Access Points
on the Digital River

Editor's Message

All the talk about the digital age, new literacies, dot-coms, and the new information economy amounts to little for those who have no access to the new tools and media. And for those of us who have some access, our experience of new technologies depends crucially on the amount and types of access we do have. In previous Technology columns ("*How Worldwide Is the Web?*" February 1999; "Communities for the New Century," February 2000; "Open Source: Everyone Becomes a Printer," May 2000), we have looked at access in various ways, but there is still much more to be said. You'll find some questions about access that deserve serious attention in this column's How You Can Participate section.

In this column I consider directly three of the things that people need to make meaningful access a reality:

1. having access to the tools,
2. having the ability to use those tools, and
3. having an access point—the connections to a social network providing the necessary knowledge to use the tools.

As a way to get into a complicated set of issues, I'll start by thinking about an older technology and about how I gain access to and through it to valuable experiences.

Original version published November 2000 in the *Journal of Adolescent & Adult Literacy*
©2000 International Reading Association

What Makes Meaningful Access a Reality?

Although the rivers in most of the northern hemisphere are now growing colder and even beginning to freeze, my thoughts are back in the warming spring when nearby rivers flowed quickly with spring runoff. I am traveling solo in a wood-and-canvas canoe down a swiftly flowing stream. That I'm able to do this at all is due to the fortunate circumstance that I have an old but sturdy canoe and a strong paddle. But many other things make this possible.

When I go to the river, I need the physical ability to paddle. I may need a special type of paddle for a particular type of canoe or for certain abilities/disabilities. I also need to look for a place to put the canoe in the river. Although in some sense I might be able to put the canoe in anywhere, in practice I need to drive my car close enough to be able to carry the canoe to the bank easily. The bank cannot be too steep or too covered with brush. Perhaps most important, the entry point can't be in someone's backyard, unless public entry is permitted there.

The place where I "put in" is called an access point. But the actual access point is much more than physical. It is also a certain level of knowledge. Although I can learn by doing, I benefit from teachers and others who provide ongoing support. I'm also helped by maps, guidebooks, weather forecasts, and tips from locals. I need my health and the time to get away. The list goes on and on, but thinking even a little about it makes me aware of how much my "solitary" adventure depends on a network of relationships. These involve family, friends, finances, laws, knowledge, things, places, and institutions. I need my canoe and my ability to use it, but my real access point is a community.

Finding a Digital Canoe

Anyone who wants to enter the swiftly flowing digital age requires a comparable network of support. That some of us are unaware of this reflects the fact that strong networks become invisible when they function well. It is only when the network breaks that we begin to understand how it really operates. This recalls Heidegger's (1962) example of the hammer with a broken handle, in which the hammer's function becomes most evident when it fails. Our understanding of the network of support changes qualitatively when its taken-for-granted operation is disrupted.

While some young people have become dot-com millionaires, many more have been left behind. This has led to increasing concern about the growing digital divide between rich and poor and between black and white ("Communities for the New Century," *JAAL*, February 2000; Hoffman & Novak, in press) and to a natural response to find ways to make computer resources accessible to all.

For some, the solution seems simple: Just find a way to provide computers to everyone. Whereas at one time such a solution was fantastic, today it is quite imaginable—at least in developed countries. Many worthwhile programs are now underway to make computing resources available in libraries, community centers, churches, and other venues. There are also programs to provide low-cost new computers or reconditioned computers donated by companies as they upgrade their equipment (see National Computer Recycling Programs at http://www.microweb.com/pepsite/Recycle/National.html).

The digital divide between countries is even greater than that within countries (*JAAL* Technology department, February 1999; May 1999). Nevertheless, fascinating programs are underway to provide access to new technologies and to explore what they can mean in the most impoverished settings. For example, consider physicist Sugata Mitra's work to help the poor in India enter the information age (Judge, 2000).

There was a wall separating Mitra's research center in New Delhi from a garbage-filled empty lot used by the poor. In early 1999, Mitra embedded a computer in that wall and gave it a high-speed connection to the Internet. Anyone passing by could play with it, but there was no manual, no trainer, and no accommodation for the fact that few in the community spoke the English language used on the computer. In this so-called hole-in-the-wall experiment, Mitra found that many children, ages 6 to 12, were able to use the computer to browse the Web, download music files, and draw pictures. Although there was no keyboard, the children even learned to write using a Paint program and the "character map" inside Microsoft Word. When asked "How do you know so much about computers?" one boy said, "What's a computer?" The children had no formal knowledge, yet they could still enjoy and benefit from the access the experiment afforded.

Programs such as the one in India clearly help many people, but just as having a canoe is a necessary—although far from sufficient—ingredient for canoeing, having a computer is only part of what most people need to have meaningful access (Coyle, 1994). In Mitra's experiment, few adults even attempted to use the computer, and even the most advanced children would "plateau out" in what they were able to do.

Being Able to Paddle

In order to canoe, I need not only the boat, but also the ability to use it. I need to know how to paddle, but also to have equipment that accords with my physical ability. A small child, for example, can paddle a canoe, but only with a small paddle and a special seat that allows him or her to reach the water.

The situation with computers is similar. After experiencing some eye problems, I found that formerly accessible information on the computer screen was too hard for me to read. But by using a larger monitor and adjusting the font size, I learned that I could restore my access. Many people require even larger adjustments. For example, if you have a text-only browser, you cannot see the images that appear on webpages. But if the Web designer has used ALT text (Flavell, 1994–2000), you may be able to obtain substitute textual information that accomplishes most of the function of the image.

Current technologies provide many other ways to enhance access, and yet, paradoxically, each advance may also increase the gap between haves and have nots. For example, the ASCII code made computers easier for everyone because it made it possible to use digits and letters. Yet, by favoring English over other languages, it may have facilitated the dominance of English-speaking countries in the information industry. The fact that Japan has done quite well with computers using ASCII should remind us that these technical features never determine success or failure by themselves, but they certainly play a role in how we use and think about technologies. (The sites and sources listed later in the Website of the Month and References sections provide a good introduction to the many issues involved in making computers physically accessible to all.)

Access Points for the Digital River

If I have a canoe, and I'm physically able to use it, I still can't go canoeing unless I have a way to get it into a river. "Putting in" may appear to be a physical process of moving the canoe from dry land to water, but prior to that it means finding my place in a network of social relationships. I need to learn how to canoe, partly on my own, but also through interactions with others. I have to learn the location of the physical access point through reading, using maps, talking with others, or exploring. I have to negotiate the permission to put in. I have to learn all the critical information about the river, such as where the waterfall is or where I can "take out." All of these things reflect both types of knowledge and relationships with many people.

In a similar way, I need more than a computer to have access to the real meaning of the new information age. I need to connect myself and that computer to a network of people, organizations, software, and information programs. Some of that connection depends on financial resources, some on the vagaries of personal circumstances—where I work or go to school, who my friends happen to be. Other aspects depend on the support of employers, teachers, parents, and others who set out to help me learn. I may need encouragement to try new things. Thus, my access point for my cyberjourney is only in part the number I dial to reach the Internet provider. More crucial are the connections I make to all the people who help me develop the knowledge I need.

A Successful Launch

My successful launch, then, depends on at least three things: (1) finding my canoe—the computer, the Internet link, data, and software; (2) being able to paddle—having the tools such that factors like language and physical ability are no barrier; and (3) finding an access point—having the network of social relationships and knowledge that make my journey possible.

Other Views

Physicist Stephen W. Hawking is one of the most famous people whose work has been enabled by assistive technologies. Despite having Amyotrophic Lateral Sclerosis (Lou Gehrig's disease), he is able to maintain a highly productive career and has inspired many. On his website he describes how this works:

> I communicate with a computer system.... The screen is mounted on the arm of the wheel chair where I can see it.... A cursor moves across the upper part of the screen. I can stop it by pressing a switch in my hand. This switch is my only interface with the computer. In this way I can select words, which are printed on the lower part of the screen. When I have built up a sentence, I can send it to a speech synthesiz-er...though it gives me an accent that has been described variously as Scandinavian, American or Scottish.... I can also give lectures. I write the lecture beforehand, and

save it on disk.... It works quite well, and I can try out the lecture, and polish it, before I give it.

Perhaps the most fundamental requirement for access is the desire to have it. We sometimes assume that computer or Internet access is all to the good, but there are many valid reasons why some people might choose not to launch their computers. R.W. Burniske (2000) reminded us of this in a defense of computer illiteracy:

> Our present climate, which indoctrinates many educators through the gospel of the technology "thought collective," makes it virtually impossible for students to "not learn" technical computing skills. Yet, as we experiment with new learning environments shouldn't we consider potentially harmful effects? What if the embrace of "computer literacy"—particularly an impoverished form emphasizing technical skills while neglecting ethical concerns—should marginalize more robust forms of human literacy? In light of such possibilities, perhaps the "creative maladjustment" that perpetuates computer illiteracy will prove to be a virtue, providing an essential counter-balance to de-humanizing forces.

Website of the Month

The GirlTECH site (http://math.rice.edu/~lanius/club/girls.html), maintained by Cynthia Lanius, provides an excellent set of resources aimed at helping more girls enter technical careers, especially in computer science. On the first page, there is a list of 10 tips for getting girls interested in computers. Although these tips are to help girls specifically, most are useful for anyone who needs additional access to the digital world. Here is a sampling of site topics: ways to work together; good role models; encouragement; opportunities to see benefits; physical access.

Some Other Sites of Special Interest

Matching Person and Technology (MPT) Assessment Process (http://members.aol.com/IMPT97/mptdesc.html). Marcia J. Scherer, Director of the Institute for Matching Person and Technology, provides this site, which describes the MPT process. There are various self-report checklists that take into account the environments in which the person uses the technology, the individual's characteristics and preferences, and the technology's functions and features.

http://lrs.ed.uiuc.edu/access. Michelle Hinn has developed this excellent compendium of links to access issues "dedicated to the dissemination of information pertaining to the universal accessibility of Web-based course materials, particularly for persons with disabilities."

Center for Applied Special Technology: Universal Design for Learning (http://www.cast.org/udl). CAST has a number of resources, including its widely used "Bobby" for checking webpages for accessibility.

Digital Divide (http://www.pbs.org/digitaldivide). This Public Broadcasting System website includes video samples from a television series on the digital divide as well as interactive components on educational technology, gender, race, and computers in the workplace.

The Adaptive Technology Resource Centre (http://www.utoronto.ca/atrc). This University of Toronto center offers an excellent collection of information and links on technologies to improve access.

Girl Geeks (http://www.girlgeeks.org). This site has surveys on attitudes toward computer use as well as many links and helpful information on women and computing.

Parents, Educators, and Children's Software Publishers (PEP) (http://microweb.com/pepsite/Recycle/National.html). This site provides well-annotated links on U.S. computer recycling programs.

Stephen W. Hawking's Webpages (http://www.hawking.org.uk). Hawking's personal site includes not only interesting scientific and biographical materials, but also information about his own use of adaptive technologies.

How You Can Participate

This month's Technology column only touches the surface of the whole access issue. I'd like to pose here a few questions that deserve further consideration:

- Is more access a good thing? (See, for example, http://www.computer addiction.com.)
- How are changes in technology (e.g., the shift from desktop computers to handheld devices) changing the access landscape?

- What is the role of gender in access to information technology? (See the surveys at the Girl Geeks website.)

- How does access interact with privacy?

- How are people differentially enabled or disabled by new information technologies? That is, are there ways that one person benefits by increased access at the expense of others?

Glossary

Alternative text for images (ALT text): a term used in webpage design, referring to the use of text to convey information to a user of the webpage, primarily when the image is not being displayed. This can be useful for a blind reader who can still understand the webpage content with a speech synthesizer. But it is also helpful to a user who has a text-only browser, such as Lynx, or for one who has set the browser not to load images (as might be done with a slow Internet connection). Nearly everyone who has looked into the issue of webpage accessibility strongly recommends the use of ALT text. For example, the following HTML code <a href=next.html> <img src="downarrow.gif" alt="more"></a> might be used on a webpage to indicate a link to additional information in the file "next.html." Assume here that the image represented in the file "downarrow.gif" shows a down-pointing arrow to a sighted reader who is using an appropriate browser, while the word *more* provides comparable information to other users.

Unfortunately, most editing programs for webpages do not treat ALT text as the norm, but rather as the exception. So, authors of webpages need to remember to include the text alternative. In addition, they need to think about the function of the image. In the example above, both a down-pointing arrow and the word *more* or *next* would indicate to most users that additional information could be found by clicking on the hyperlink. Sometimes, the designer simply says something like "link" or "image17" that turns out worse than no ALT text at all.

The American Standard Code for Information Interchange (ASCII): a code for computers, which was developed in the days of teletype machines. It allows programmers to represent familiar symbols in terms of numbers, on virtually all computers. Using eight bits, ASCII can represent 128 characters, including upper- and lowercase letters, numbers, punctuation, and other symbols. ASCII significantly expands access to computers. It makes possible the use of familiar characters, such as the letter *a* instead of a string of binary symbols, such as "1100001."

But ASCII also defines classes of users in terms of ease of access. Because it is limited to representing characters in use in the American alphabet, it cannot fully represent the characters in the major European languages (e.g., Spanish tilde, French cedilla, German umlaut) much less ideographic languages such as Chinese. U.S. users can represent the dollar

continued

Glossary (cont.)

sign (36), but there is no representation for the British pound. Nevertheless, ASCII is the primary code used on the Internet and in many software packages. Thus, it enables, but differentially enables, access to the tools of the new information age.

Unicode: The Unicode Standard specifies the representation of text in software. It works in principle as ASCII does, but by using 16 bits a programmer can represent 128 times as many characters. Unicode can represent European alphabetic scripts, Middle Eastern right-to-left scripts, and scripts of Asia, as well as punctuation marks and mathematical and technical symbols. It provides codes for diacritics, such as the Spanish tilde (ñ). There are currently codes for 49,194 characters. With Unicode it is possible to provide a unique number for every character, regardless of computing platform or program. The code is currently supported in many operating systems, all modern browsers, and many other products.

    The Unicode Consortium is a nonprofit organization founded to develop and promote this standard. Membership includes organizations and individuals in the computer and information processing industry throughout the world.

REFERENCES

Burniske, R.W. (2000, May 24). In defense of computer illiteracy: The virtues of "not learning." *TCR Online*, Doc. No. 10526. Retrieved from http://www.tcrecord.org

Coyle, K. (1994, October 8). *Access: Not just wires*. Paper presented at the annual meeting of the Computer Professionals for Social Responsibility, San Diego, CA. Retrieved from http://www.kcoyle.net/njw.html

Flavell, A. (1994–2000). Use of ALT texts in IMGs [website]. http://ppewww.ph.gla.ac.uk/~flavell/alt/alt-text.html

Heidegger, M. (1962). *Being and time* (R. Macguirre, Trans.). New York: Harper & Row.

Hoffman, D., & Novak, T. (in press). The growing digital divide: Implications for an open research agenda. In B. Kahin & E. Brynjolffson (Eds.), *Understanding the digital economy: Data, tools and research*. Cambridge, MA: MIT Press. Retrieved from http://ecommerce.vanderbilt.edu

Judge, P. (Ed.). (2000, March 2). A lesson in computer literacy from India's poorest kids. *Business Week Online*. Retrieved from www.businessweek.com/bwdaily/dnflash/mar2000/nf00302b.htm

OTHER SOURCES

Anson, D.K. (1997). *Alternative computer access: A guide to selection*. Philadelphia: F.A. Davis.

Bain, B.K., & Leger, D. (1997). *Assistive technology: An interdisciplinary approach*. New York: Churchill Livingston.

Burniske, R.W. (2000). *Literacy in the cyberage: Composing ourselves online*. Andover, MA: Skylight.

Cook, A.M., & Hussey, S.M. (1995). *Assistive technology: Principles and practice.* St. Louis, MO: Mosby.

Galvin, J.C., & Scherer, M.J. (1996). *Evaluating, selecting and using appropriate assistive technology.* Gaithersburg, MD: Aspen.

Kohl, H. (1994). *"I won't learn from you" and other thoughts on maladjustment.* New York: New Press.

Shade, L.R. (1993, August 17–19). *Gender issues in computer networking.* Paper presented at Community Networking: The International Free-Net Conference, Carleton University, Ottawa, ON, Canada. Retrieved from http://www.vcn.bc.ca/sig/comm-nets/shade.html

Challenges for the Evaluation of New Information and Communication Technologies

Editor's Message

How can we be sure that all the new computers and networks appearing in classrooms around the world will really make a difference for learners? Do we know for certain that the money and time invested in them makes a difference? What criteria should we use and how can we measure success? These questions raise additional questions about differences in the way we use technologies. For every success story, there are other stories about problems or unanticipated negative effects. Why do we so often discover that new technologies remain underused or misused?

Journal articles or newspaper accounts sometimes describe in great detail one classroom in which marvelous learning occurred through the use of some new system, but they usually fail to mention the teachers who merely rewrote their current methods in a new medium without any substantive effect on students' learning. Such reports rarely talk about the larger number who knew about the system but failed to use it, and they never discuss the many who were not interested enough to learn anything about it at all.

Few of us are professional evaluators, but we are all affected by the public arguments made for and against different technologies and their uses. These arguments rely on more or less formal methods of evaluating what happens when these technologies are used. We need to understand what can be concluded about technology use and what the limits of current methods might be. We are also often called on to interpret specific results, such as that the use of technology within a particular literacy program led to improved learning. We need to understand how to think of such results in larger contexts and to interpret them for ourselves and others.

In this month's column I will consider various aspects of issues related to evaluation, access, and literacy learning.

Original version published March 1999 in the *Journal of Adolescent & Adult Literacy*
©1999 International Reading Association

Evaluation of Communication and Information Technologies in Education

The potential of new information and communication technologies for teaching and learning was recognized early. Programmed instruction as well as the programming language Logo were developed more than 30 years ago, and the earliest applications of time-sharing operating systems included teaching. Almost immediately, people began to ask whether the new tools would lead to better, more effective, or more efficient education.

Evaluating the New Information Technologies (Johnston, 1984) made clear why this quite reasonable question would not be so easy to answer. More recent books (Baker & O'Neil, 1994; Roblyer, Castine, & King, 1988) have shown both positive and negative effects, as well as the difficulty of framing that question in a straightforward way. The debate continues in reports available on the Web, such as "Technology Counts '98," published last fall as a special report by *Education Week*.

In this month's Issue section, I will explore some reasons why information and communication technologies are difficult to evaluate and why these difficulties do not deter us from using the technologies in spite of the lack of solid evaluations.

Ten Reasons Why Information Technologies Require New Evaluation Approaches

Differences among adopters. Designers of new educational programs know that early adopters of new technology have different experiences than later adopters. The early ones tend to be more adventuresome, more knowledgeable about the area, and often receive more support than those who adopt later. This phenomenon achieves its maximum effect with new technologies. The first users are typically computer science experts relative to those who adopt later, and their patterns of use are strikingly different. This means that evaluations have to be understood with respect to the community of users and cannot be assumed to refer to the technology per se.

Scale effects. Often, when an older technology has been employed in an educational setting its effects can be viewed independently of its use in other settings. The use of a chalkboard in one class is affected only indirectly by its use in another class. But information technologies are often also communication technologies, which connect across settings and produce network effects. Their operation depends directly on what happens elsewhere. For example, an e-mail discussion group operates very differently with 10 members versus 1,000. Thus, how an innovation scales up becomes critical. Scalability is a factor for any educational innovation, but it can rarely be ignored when we look at information technologies.

Geography. As use scales up, the new media reshape geography through spatially dispersed contexts of use and variations in implementation. A school program involving collaborative data acquisition and analysis may in its very definition be an international program. Looking at other classrooms involved in the program is not just a matter of increasing sample size, but one of observing a single but geographically dispersed context of use.

Media as systems. New information and communication technologies must be understood, not merely as discrete tools but as components of complex systems. The computer on my desk is in some ways akin to a copy machine or a typewriter, but when we consider the variety of software that can alter its mode of operation or transform it into an Internet machine, we see it is but one cog in a gigantic system. Thus, it is not trivial to identify what is being evaluated when we evaluate its use.

Rapid change. Another issue is the newness and changeability of the technology. I have found in a variety of projects to develop technology-based learning that we were tinkering with the software throughout in a way we did not do with text materials. Once something was completed it was usually obsolete because of changes in the companion technologies. This meant we were effectively engaged in perpetual formative evaluation (Bruce & Rubin, 1993). There are few educational programs involving information technologies that remain unchanged for long, often not even until the evaluation report appears.

Trail of use. Despite the ability of information technologies to store massive amounts of data, crucial user information is often unavailable. Many programs do not keep, or they lose, important parts of student work. Electronic files become unreadable with changes in the technology. Students delete files whose corresponding paper version might have been saved. The impermanence of technology use is a challenge for both teachers and evaluators.

Re-creation of the technology. Yet another issue is appropriation of the technology within social practices. Despite the apparent fixedness of technology, it can actually be more malleable in use than a paper-based curriculum. That has led some researchers to turn to situated evaluation approaches.

New roles for teachers and students. New modes of teaching and learning come packaged with new technologies. In fact, many new tools are promoted precisely because they change the role of teacher from disseminator of information to a facilitator in the construction of meaning. They also raise fundamental issues about whether they are being used as tools to help students learn other things, or as phenomena to be understood on their own. These and other issues about roles, curricula, and purposes for learning add to the complexity of evaluating new technologies.

Technical characteristics. There is also a difficult issue of technical characteristics of the technology: features of an interface, the quality of a simulation, or the design of a hypertext. Virtually all programs in education involve materials or technologies of some sort, but new information technologies raise the level of complexity a notch or two and require new evaluation methods.

Access. Finally, one of the most important issues is access to technology. New information technologies entail significant investments not only in equipment, but also in training, support, and changes in traditional practices. Moreover, there is much evidence that technologies reify social stratification, as in the English language dominance of the World Wide Web. Rather than reducing inequities in education, as most of us hope will happen, these technologies may create and solidify inequities as never before. The attribution of goodness to some new approach must therefore be tempered with careful consideration of its accessibility.

The Case for Situated Studies

In a 1949 book, *Knowing and the Known*, Dewey and Bentley articulated the idea of transaction, which was later applied by Louise Rosenblatt to develop a theory of the reader's response to literature. Transactions provide one way to think about this problem. Rather than conceptualizing the technology as a discrete object that acts on people, they would want to understand the way the technology participates in an organic relationship with living social practices. Transaction moves us away from questions such as What are the effects of the technology? toward questions such as What processes are occurring in the social system in which this technology participates?

Examination of the unique uses that technology fosters leads the evaluator to more situated studies. One result of such studies of how technologies affect literacy education has been to show how realizations of technologies vary tremendously depending on the teacher's goals, students' previous experiences with computers, the available support, and the organization's policies with respect to assessment and curriculum. One teacher may use a word processor to create practice lessons on punctuation, while another may develop a yearlong theme study that relies on extensive student writing and revision for publication. These great differences suggest that the teacher's creative role is vital to the successful use of new technologies. It is much more important to understand how people use technologies than simply to measure their effectiveness across broad averages of use.

Another result of situated studies of new technologies has been to show clearly how technologies rarely produce simple, one-step changes. Instead, changes occur over long periods, as teachers and students develop enlarged understandings of what the technologies can do. Both need time to integrate new tools into existing teaching and learning practices.

This research has also shown that the richness of the new technologies—the access to vast resources on the World Wide Web, the powerful new media, the interactivity—can sometimes lead to a focus on content or methods in teaching, with less attention to individual learners, thus manifesting Dewey's map in place of the territory. Simply using computers or connecting to the network does not ensure that teaching is easier and more effective or that students will be automatically well prepared to live in the 21st century. Instead, making good use of new technologies increases the demands on teachers, at least initially. Educators face major challenges to use these technologies effectively to expand the possibilities for learning.

Making Decisions in the Face of Uncertainty

These considerations about the complexity of technology may reassure the evaluator, but they do not help the literacy educator trying to make decisions about whether and how to use new technologies. How do we decide what to do? Is technological literacy an essential part of literacy now? Have new technologies become essential tools for learning? How can we think about the apparent conflicts between the classroom and the workplace, between learning for today's needs versus tomorrow's, between using the technologies of today and those likely to appear in the future?

A situated perspective does not tell us whether learning to program in Basic was a good use of student time in the 1980s, but it does suggest that the conventional view of schooling as merely preparation for something else is inadequate. It leads us to think of technologies as integral parts of what we do as literate beings, rather than as isolated tools that are employed to fix problems or as magical devices that can replace good teaching. A deeper understanding of these issues could lead us to rethink how we use technologies to promote literacy and to more informed, yet never easy, decision making.

Data

None of the questions about effectiveness of technologies makes sense if those technologies are unavailable. The great discrepancy in personal income within and between countries means that people effectively live in very different technological worlds. Some of this can be seen in the 1998 edition of the Human Development Report from the United Nations:

Inequalities in consumption are stark. Globally, the 20% of the world's people in the highest-income countries account for 86% of total private consumption expenditures; the poorest 20% a minuscule 1.3%. More specifically, the richest fifth:

- consume 45% of all meat and fish (the poorest fifth, 5%)
- consume 58% of total energy (the poorest fifth, less than 4%)
- have 74% of all telephone lines (the poorest fifth, 1.5%)
- consume 84% of all paper (the poorest fifth, 1.1%)
- own 87% of the world's vehicle fleet (the poorest fifth, less than 1%)

Among other things, it is evident that for the more than a billion people worldwide who have no telephone, Internet access is unattainable. Less glaring discrepancies operate even within affluent countries to mean that students in different communities have divergent opportunities to learn through or about the new technologies.

Interpretations

Steve Ehrmann has pointed out that there are always two ways to look at any educational innovation. One is to consider its uniform impact—that is, to assume that the educator is trying to shape learning in the same way for all learners.

The second is to examine the unique uses that emerge when we assume that all learners actively interpret and make use of the resource in their own way.

These two perspectives, both important for almost any evaluation, are particularly important when technology is in use. Most instructional uses of information technology are meant to be empowering—i.e., to create fresh choices for instructors and learners. When students communicate more, when they work on projects, when they collaborate, the diversity of potential outcomes for learners increases. Any evaluation which uses only the uniform impact perspective will miss some of the most important consequences of this type of innovation.
(From S.C. Ehrmann, *How (not) to evaluate a grant-funded technology project*. Paper presented at the National Endowment for the Humanities, Washington, DC, April 29, 1997.)

Website of the Month

Bobby (http://www.cast.org) was created at CAST (Center for Applied Special Technology), a not-for-profit organization whose mission is to expand opportunities for people with disabilities through innovative uses of computer technology. It is a Web-based public service that analyzes webpages for their accessibility to people with disabilities and for their compatibility with various browsers. Bobby follows the guidelines of the W3C Webpage Accessibility Initiative at http://www.w3.org/WAI/GL. A website that passes the Bobby test may then display the approved icon. Bobby has links to thousands of websites, and over 3 million webpages are tested for addition each month. The Bobby program follows the CAST principles that "universal design for learning" should provide multiple representations of content, multiple options for expression and control, and multiple options for engagement and motivation. It checks to make sure, for example, that the website

- provides alternative text for all images,
- provides transcripts for all audio files,
- provides a description and a caption for video information,
- does not use color as the sole means of conveying important information,
- nests headings properly,

- provides a mechanism to allow users to freeze movement or update, and
- uses the LANG attribute to identify the language of the text.

Adhering to these guidelines makes it more likely that the website will be usable by people with visual or hearing impairments; by those with older or less expensive equipment; by those who speak other languages; and, as the term "universal design" implies, by anyone.

Glossary

Alternative text for images (ALT text): the inclusion of text that describes what is in an image so that a user who cannot see clearly can at least read about the image, often using a large font or a speech generator.

Formative evaluation: evaluation applied to a program under development in order to find ways to improve it; widely employed for technology-based programs because of the rapid technological changes.

Frames: technique for webpage design that allows information to be displayed and manipulated in different portions of the screen; while useful, it makes webpages inaccessible to those whose browsers cannot process the frames and also makes it impossible to bookmark specific subsections of the site.

Network effects: the phenomenon that the effects of a particular technology may depend on how it is interconnected with other devices, and how those effects depend on the structure, size, and operating characteristics of the network.

Situated evaluation: an approach to evaluation of technology use that assumes the technology is not set a priori, but comes into being through use.

Situated studies: a research method that explicitly incorporates an analysis of the context in which literacy is practiced or learning occurs.

Summative evaluation: evaluation applied to judge the overall effect of a developed program; most suitable for the uniform impacts perspective on a learning program.

Technocentrism: a way of thinking about the use of technology that attributes all important changes to the technology itself.

Transaction: a phenomenon in which mind and reality, or a "knowing" and the "known," are conceived as a unified entity.

Webpage accessibility: the degree to which the content of a webpage is available to people in different groups, such as those who speak a language other than the author or who have a low-speed network connection.

REFERENCES

Baker, E.L., & O'Neil, H.F. (1994). *Technology assessment in education and training*. Hillsdale, NJ: Erlbaum.

Bruce, B.C., & Rubin, A.D. (1993). *Electronic quills: A situated evaluation of using computers for writing in classrooms*. Hillsdale, NJ: Erlbaum.

Dewey, J., & Bentley, A.F. (1949). *Knowing and the known*. Boston: Beacon.

Johnston, J. (Ed.). (1984). *Evaluating the new information technologies*. Washington, DC: Jossey-Bass.

Roblyer, M.D., Castine, W.H., & King, F.J. (1988). *Assessing the impact of computer-based instruction: A review of the literature*. New York: Haworth.

Educational Reform: How Does Technology Affect Educational Change?

Editor's Message

As we start off the 1999–2000 volume of the *Journal of Adolescent & Adult Literacy*, we are likely to experience a continuing vigorous discussion about the year 2000 problem. Whatever the ultimate resolution, a safe forecast is that many in computer circles will be devoted to talking about this issue, if not to actually fixing it.

In case you live in a cabin in the woods, comfortably oblivious to all modern communications media, the year 2000 problem (also called the Y2K bug) refers to a class of computer malfunctions that will affect computers and all sorts of other devices with embedded processors when the year changes from 1999 to 2000. The general difficulty is that many computer programs take shortcuts, such as storing years by the last two digits—99 instead of 1999, to take a pertinent example. The year 2000 is then interpreted as 1900, meaning that calculations based on subtracting one year from another can go seriously awry. The nature of the problem is captured concisely by Steven C. Meyer at http://quotes.prolix.nu: "It would be just like programmers to shorten 'the year 2000 problem' to 'Y2K'—exactly the kind of thinking that created this situation in the first place."

When we consider the interdependencies of modern life, it is clear that completely fixing our own computers does not protect us from other parts of the modern system breaking down. Tony Blair, Prime Minister of Great Britain, has said, "The Millennium Bug is one of the most serious problems facing not only British business but the global economy today. Its impact cannot be underestimated" (Rosencrantz, 1999).

There is already much written about the year 2000 problem, including websites such as the United Kingdom's Action 2000 site, which is counting down the seconds to January 1, 2000; many books, which are smugly Y2K compliant; and even a website of editorial cartoons about Y2K. Accordingly, this month's Technology column will not dwell on the topic. Nevertheless, Y2K is a timely focus to keep in mind as we explore the question of how technology relates to educational reform, whether it is seen as a key to bring about reform or as a reason to reform education in the first place.

In this column, we will look at the relation of technology to educational reform. Will new technologies bring about improvements in the overall state of literacy? Will they demand changes in what literacy means? How well can we anticipate what these changes will be?

Original version published September 1999 in the *Journal of Adolescent & Adult Literacy*
©1999 International Reading Association

Technology and Educational Reform

In his annual State of American Education speech, U.S. Secretary of Education Richard Riley echoed a sentiment central to the educational reform agenda when he asserted that "How we learn is changing and technology is very much at the heart of this transformation." The tangibility of this view is evident by the inclusion among the seven initiatives for U.S. education the challenge: "Every classroom will be connected to the Internet by the year 2000 and all students will be technologically literate."

Many educators see technology as central to education reform. Some emphasize the need to teach students new technological skills. Others argue that new technologies can transform education by offering new tools to support inquiry throughout the curriculum. Finally, many see the need to teach about the impact of new technologies on business, health care, science, media, education, and everyday life.

This is an exciting time, and the prospect of improved education for all students is one that deserves more attention. But, as every teacher who has worked to bring technology into education has learned, the simple addition of new devices has little chance of producing real change. Moreover, we are now seeing the unanticipated effects of new technologies, ways in which they do both more and less than we had hoped.

One reason that educational reform through technology is difficult is that reform of any large system is an uncertain enterprise. Not only is it uncertain, but also our expectations about how change can occur are often unrealistic. We often expect that a technology will accomplish a particular task, assuming that the main issue is simply to obtain it and learn how to use it. This presumption of simple, linear change is evident in the discussions about wiring up the schools. But there are many reasons why change does not occur in straightforward ways.

Latent functions. The sociologist Robert Merton (1957) distinguished an important feature of technologies and how they affect social systems: "The distinction between manifest and latent functions was devised to preclude the inadvertent confusion, often found in the sociological literature, between conscious *motivations* for social behavior and its *objective consequences*" (p. 60). Merton's distinction can be applied to examine how a new technology, introduced to accomplish one purpose, has functions inherent in its design that bring about other changes. For example, the introduction of a word processor in a classroom has the manifest function of making it easier to edit documents. But its attractiveness as a device can lead students to "mill about" as they await their turn to use it. This milling about can in turn lead to increased social interaction and to more reading of one another's drafts (Bruce, Michaels, & Watson-Gegeo, 1985).

Revenge effects. A general aspect of the introduction of any new technology are the consequences that no one could have anticipated, the latent functions that no one saw. One such category includes what Edward Tenner (1996) called "revenge effects." These occur when a technology entails system changes we never anticipated or wanted; for example, the new office suite software that requires you to buy a new computer just to run it, or to seek technical help you did not need with the previous version. "Revenge effects mean in the end that we will move ahead but must always look back because reality is indeed gaining on us" (p. 354).

There are also reverse revenge effects when a technological change brings with it benefits we never imagined. This can happen with an abandoned technology, which had values we never recognized until the newer model appeared. For example, carpal tunnel syndrome, a repetitive stress injury of the wrist and forearm, is a revenge effect of the office computer, one that may become prevalent in schools when computers become more commonplace. This syndrome was a rare occurrence with the manual typewriter. As Tenner (1996) has said, "In retrospect, the key-pounding, carriage-returning, paper-feeding chores required by the old manual-style typewriters had the reverse revenge effect of reducing the likelihood of carpal tunnel syndrome. Unfortunately the light touch and blazing speed of computer keyboard entry often turned out to cause unexpected pain" (p. 12).

Cascade effects. The various effects, side effects, and unanticipated effects of the introduction of a new technology become part of the system of use of that technology. As the system changes, its reaction to the new technology alters further. There are then effects of the effects, which lead to more massive but even less predictable changes.

This can be seen in terms of a problem recently recognized in the U.S. space program. This is an unpredicted, but literal, example of a cascade. As the United States has launched more and more satellites, space probes, and human space missions, with all their rockets and boosters, the amount of debris in space has grown rapidly. Collisions are becoming increasingly frequent, and each collision adds to the number of objects able to participate in future collisions. The fragmentation of one spacecraft can then generate debris that can destroy other spacecraft. The accumulation of debris in an orbit, and the potential cascade effect, then endangers use of that orbit for any future space missions.

Tom Malone and Kevin Crowston (1993) discussed another kind of cascade with the introduction of trains and automobiles. They talked about a "first order" effect as people simply substituted train travel for horse-drawn carriage rides. This led to a "second order" effect: The overall amount of travel increased when it could be done more cheaply and conveniently. Finally, there were "third order" effects as people began to live in suburbs and shopping malls developed.

Invisibility. Ironically, as new technologies become incorporated into our daily practices in significant ways, they tend to become less, not more, noticeable. Soon, we cease thinking of them as technologies at all. To some extent, this has happened with the telephone, although we are continually reminded that it is a new technology when we see offers of mobile phones, answering machines, and other enhancements.

A striking example of the invisibility effect was given by Henry Petroski (1989) in his book, *The Pencil*. Referring to the meticulous list Henry David Thoreau made prior to his adventure in the woods, he said,

> But there is one object that Thoreau neglected to mention, one that he most certainly carried himself. For without this object Thoreau could not...[sketch] the fleeting fauna...label his blotting paper pressing leaves...record the measurements he made...write home...[or] make his list. Without a pencil Thoreau would have been lost in the Maine woods. (pp. 3–4)

As new technologies become incorporated in education we may similarly forget that they are there. Already, many people do not consider the word processor to be a new technology, like the Web, but merely an ordinary tool needed to accomplish daily work.

The problem of scale. In an article titled "Reforming the Wannabe Reformers: Why Education Reforms Almost Always End Up Making Things Worse," Stanley Pogrow (1996) argues that "education reforms almost always fail because they are usually based on combinations of a number of myths" (p. 658). One of these myths relates to scale. When a demonstration or model project is carried out in one classroom or one school, there are a number of conditions that contribute to its success. People are more forgiving of problems, because the new program is considered to be experimental; extra attention is devoted by administrators and the public, because of the novelty; the teachers involved are volunteers, eager to try something new; extra resources are used, before the imperative to become cost effective; and developers are directly involved in making sure the program works. These conditions rarely persist when the successful innovation is expanded to a large scale. Thus we have what Pogrow called the "biggest myth of all! [that anyone] can understand large-scale change by understanding what happens on a very small scale" (p. 659).

Cathedral versus bazaar. In a widely cited article, Eric Raymond (1998) discusses how software development has proceeded by one of two predominant models, the cathedral or the bazaar. He described the highly successful (and free) Linux operating system, which has been developed by a loosely organized confederation of programmers throughout the world:

> No quiet, reverent cathedral-building here—rather, the Linux community seemed to resemble a great babbling bazaar of differing agendas and approaches (aptly symbolized by the Linux archive sites, who'd take submissions from anyone) out of which a coherent and stable system could seemingly emerge only by a succession of miracles.

This bazaar approach is effectively what much of the Web has become: people who are geographically distributed collaborating in the creation and distribution of software, music, artwork, texts, and ideas without any central coordination. To the extent that this process continues, the notion of a given information or communication technology having a fixed referent will become an anachronism. Instead of talking about whether a given technology brought about reform, we will have to speak of our immersion in an ongoing, distributed process of change.

Websites of the Month

One of the best sources of thinking about the Internet and its social implications is *First Monday* at http://www.firstmonday.dk. I used several articles there in doing research for this column and recommend it for readings that take a serious look at current Internet developments, but are neither overly technical nor abstract. It has published articles on the politics affecting the Internet, the economics of new technologies, development of new software and hardware (such as the MP3 music protocol), Internet use in specific communities, and the implications of the Internet for reading and writing in various settings. The website contains all the back issues. In addition, there is a monthly electronic-mail posting that describes the articles in each new issue, along with hyperlinks to each of them.

First Monday is also one of the first peer-reviewed journals on the World Wide Web, starting in May 1996. Today, the NewJour archive lists thousands of electronic journals and newsletters. That is but a small fraction of all such e-journals, although only a few are peer reviewed with a continuous publication history.

Other Views: How Technologies Affect Us

As Richard Cox has pointed out, if nothing else has changed in the information age, the amount of talk about it has increased. Much of this writing uses technology as a focal point to revisit core issues of human value.

> Anyone who may be annoyed, as I often am, with the struggle to keep current with the technical support needed to play in the Information Age, can also be fatigued with reading to understand what it is they are participating in. An unintended consequence of the modern computer or information revolution is the revolution in publishing about the revolution. (Cox, 1998)

> In the film [Fritz Lang's *Metropolis*], Rotwang is a mad scientist who creates a robot he hopes he can love, a robot with both mechanical and human attributes. But the robot quickly gets out of control because she has no soul, no heart, she doesn't care. The point of the film is that technology without heart will be debased. Our own creations, Rotwang's children and grandchildren, can get it right, if we choose. (FM Interviews, 1996)

> [A]cross disciplines, authors affirming some version of technological determinism tend to adopt a macro perspective, while those denying technological determinism tend to adopt a micro perspective. This pattern...explains how and where machines are permitted to make history. (Misa, 1994, p. 118)

Glossary

Cascade effect: a series of effects of an initial perturbation of a social system. This happens, for example, when a new technology is introduced and practices shift to accommodate it. Then, there are effects of that initial change, which lead to even less predictable changes. This is one reason that it is often said that people overestimate the short-term impact of innovations, but underestimate the long-term effects.

In a school, we might observe small initial changes with the introduction of Web browsing. Students would spend some time doing a new activity. But, over time, teachers might see how students could use the Web for research, and later for publishing. As these new uses develop, the entire ecology of reading and writing could shift to a new center of activity.

continued

Glossary (cont.)

Latent function: a function of a new technology that becomes apparent only through practice. For example, complex computer technology may lead to greater collaboration as people are forced to help one another in order to use it at all. That collaboration might be considered desirable or might not, but it was not a conscious motivation of the system designers.

Legacy system: a computer system that was developed long ago, but still has value today. Typically, the organization has invested considerable resources in its development or in collecting data in a particular form for use with the system.

As conditions change, these systems risk losing some of their capabilities, or, in the case of the Y2K problem, begin to produce errors they never did in the past. A large amount of software and hardware development is devoted to maintaining and updating legacy applications, or to designing new products that can work with existing applications or import data from them.

Linux operating system (http://www.linux.org): a version of the Unix operating system, which works with a variety of computers, including PCs, Macintoshes, and Amigas. As an operating system, it enables the user to invoke word processors, Web browsers, and other programs, as needed. In that sense, Linux is similar to Windows or MacOS. However, it is unusual in the way it has been created and in its cost. Linux development has been led by Linus Torvalds, but its continuing development occurs through an unusual collaborative arrangement in which programmers around the globe contribute pieces of the system. The software is free and represents the bazaar approach to software development.

Manifest function: the purpose built into the design of a new technology or inherent in the reasons for its adoption. These are the expected or desired functions of the innovation, which may or may not be realized.

Revenge effect: an effect of using a new technology, which we never anticipated or wanted. This occurs when we use a new tool to accomplish one purpose without realizing how it would affect other aspects of our lives. For example, the introduction of gypsy moths to the United States was intended to make silk production a reality, yet led to massive destruction of hardwood trees in the Northeast. This is more than a simple side effect that would have been anticipated and conceived as part of the bargain in adopting the innovation.

Reverse revenge effect: a revenge effect that appears with an older technology. This can be positive, as when we realize a benefit that was invisible until the new technology took it away. The benefits of a high-fiber diet are one example: As technology to refine foods became more commonplace, we created health problems that earlier food technologies had not created without our recognizing it.

continued

Glossary (cont.)

Y2K problem: a class of problems related to how computers represent and manipulate dates, which became apparent in the move from 1999 to 2000. The most common cause of this is that many programs written to minimize data storage used only the last two digits of the year, thus "05" means "1905." On January 1, 2000, some users of computers encountered difficulties because the programs were not able to distinguish 1900 from 2000. There are a variety of similar problems, such as programs that use "99" to indicate missing data, but also use two digits to represent a year.

REFERENCES

Bruce, B., Michaels, S., & Watson-Gegeo, K. (1985). How computers can change the writing process. *Language Arts*, 62, 143–149.

Cox, R.J. (1998, May 4). Drawing sea serpents: The publishing wars on personal computing and the information age. *First Monday*, 3(5). Retrieved from http://www.firstmonday.dk/issues/issue3_5/cox

FM Interviews. (1996, May 6). Spreadsheet anthropologist Apple researcher Bonnie Nardi observes digital villagers at work. *First Monday*, 1(1). Retrieved from http://www.firstmonday.dk/issues/issue1/nardi/index.html

Malone, T.W., & Crowston, K. (1994, March). The interdisciplinary study of coordination. *ACM Computing Surveys*, 26(1), 87–119. Retrieved from http://ccs.mit.edu/papers/CCSWP157.html

Merton, R.K. (1957). *Social theory and social structure*. Glencoe, IL: Free Press.

Misa, T.J. (1994). Retrieving sociotechnical change from technological determinism. In M.R. Smith & L. Marx (Eds.), *Does technology drive history? The dilemma of technological determinism* (pp. 115–142). Cambridge, MA: MIT Press.

Nardi, B.A., & O'Day, V.L. (1999). *Information ecologies*. Cambridge, MA: MIT Press.

Petroski, H. (1989). *The pencil: A history of design and circumstance*. New York: Knopf.

Pogrow, S. (1996). Reforming the wannabe reformers: Why education reforms almost always end up making things worse. *Phi Delta Kappan*, 77(10), 656–663.

Raymond, E.S. (1998). The cathedral and the bazaar. *First Monday*, 3(3). Retrieved from http://www.firstmonday.dk/issues/issue3_3/raymond

Riley, R.W. (1999, February 16). *New challenges, a new resolve: Moving American education into the 21st century*. The Sixth Annual State of American Education Speech, Long Beach, CA. Retrieved from http://www.ed.gov

Rosencrantz, I. (1999, January 7). A year from now we may live in a different world. *The American Reporter*, 5. Retrieved from http://www.american-reporter.com

Tenner, E. (1996). *Why things bite back: Technology and the revenge of unintended consequences*. New York: Random House.

Learning Opportunities

New technologies provide opportunities to learn new things and to learn in new ways. In addition, they pose a challenge: Even if they were to have no value as learning tools, it is clearly important to learn how to use them and how to analyze them critically.

This section explores various ways that new technologies are transforming our literacy practices, and conversely, that learners are transforming those same technologies. We are embedded in a situation, as John Dewey might say: The idea of a complete understanding of that situation is not just difficult, but incoherent, because we ourselves are part of it. As we experience and reflect, our knowledge of the situation changes, because the situation itself changes when we do. In such a context, Dewey called for local experimentation and social mobilization as the mechanisms for change. Thus, the problem is not one of articulating a vision of the essence of technology, nor of specifying its costs and benefits for learning, but of engaging in the process of growth.

These ideas are developed a bit further in the column "Dewey and Technology." Then, in "Using the Web to Support Inquiry-Based Literacy Development," Ann P. Bishop and I extend those thoughts in terms of practical attempts to foster learning and community-building. Kevin M. Leander pursues similar themes in his column about online writing labs, "Laboratories for Writing." Jamie Myers and Richard Beach look at hypertext and the way it may support the development of critical thinking in "Hypermedia Authoring as Critical Literacy." In "Computer Mediation for Learning and Play," William E. Blanton, Melanie W. Greene, and Michael Cole look at learning in its multiple arenas outside the formal classroom, in particular, the activities of the Fifth Dimension. The idea of learning in nontraditional ways is continued in the discussion of distance learning in "Education Online: Learning Anywhere, Any Time." Umesh Thakkar, Maureen P. Hogan, Jo Williamson, and I then look at how technologies of remote instrumentation and the Web connect learners to people and resources beyond the classroom in "Extending Literacy Through

Participation in New Technologies." Finally, D. Michelle Hinn, Kevin M. Leander, and I tell the story of a simulated junior high school and how it was used in a teacher education course in "Case Studies of a Virtual School."

Dewey and Technology

Editor's Message

As we think about the changes that the 21st century may bring in educational practices, it's natural to consider the roles that new information and communication technologies may play. Typically, we identify three kinds of reasons for their use.

One reason often cited is that economic success in information age society appears to demand new skills and new ways of making meaning; thus, there is the need to learn (to use) the new technologies, just as we need to learn language. For many parents, and teachers, too, this appears as the overriding goal for incorporating technologies into learning.

A second reason is that these new technologies promise ways to transform education by offering vast resources for learning and new tools to support inquiry throughout the curriculum; thus, we see the opportunity to learn through new technologies. This is analogous to the argument that once we have learned to read we can read to learn.

A third reason is that intelligent participation in the coming era requires an understanding of the ways that these new technologies are transforming industry, health care, science, language, international relations, and everyday life. Thus, we see the need to learn about new technologies and the ways they permeate life, just as we need to learn about language and its role in social life. The field of social informatics, and programs on science, technology, and society highlight this goal.

In short, there is a parallel to Michael Halliday's (1978) analysis of the function of language: We need to learn technology, to learn through technology, and to learn about technology.

As we delve deeper into the question of technologies for education, many seek to understand characteristics and implications of new technologies—computational visualization, remote instrumentation, intelligent agents, MOOs and MUDs, collaboratories, telementoring, image processing, virtual reality theaters, embedded systems, speech recognition/generation, intelligent tutors, digital video, wearable computers, and so on. This future-oriented strategy is a necessary component of assessing what capabilities the new technologies afford.

However, there is a past-oriented strategy that may be equally revealing about the shape of future educational practices. This month's issue calls for a reexamination of foundational ideas in education that may provide insights for efforts to expand and transform education in the coming information age.

Original version published November 1998 in the *Journal of Adolescent & Adult Literacy*
©1998 International Reading Association

Technology and Dewey's Conception of Learning

Although John Dewey wrote in the late 19th and early 20th century, not the much talked about 21st, his thoughts seem increasingly prescient. As John McDermott (1981) wrote,

> [H]is work maintains a creative vitality...the paradox is that Dewey achieved this vitality, not by having written for the future, but rather by writing out of his own present experience...he believed that ordinary experience is seeded with surprises and possibilities for enhancement, if we but allow it to bathe over us in its own terms. (p. x)

This vitality is seen in the fact that many people working to construct technologies for learning now cite Dewey, primarily in terms of his advocacy of learning by doing. They propose models for learning based on immersion in practices of the larger society. This approach would certainly find some support in the progressive education movement that developed from some of Dewey's ideas, but his contribution to the construction of 21st-century education may go much deeper.

Learning by doing. To see this, we first have to understand what Dewey does not say. He wrote little about technologies per se, which may be one reason that his work appears to some to have little relevance to current discussions about 21st-century education. In fact, he did not even have much to say about the dominant educational technology of his day: the book. Despite his being a great scholar and the author of many texts, one has to search to find references in Dewey to books as educational tools.

The references to books in Dewey are implicitly negative. For example, in a discussion of subject matter (1956), which may be taken as a proxy for books, he says, "The map is not a substitute for personal experience. The map does not take the place of the actual journey" (p. 20). In other words, personal experience is at the center of education, not subject matter. There is a role for subject matter: It is to aid in the development of experience and to aid the learner in extracting deeper meaning from future experiences.

What would Dewey have thought about the World Wide Web? Some researchers argue that the new interactive and collaborative learning models delivered through the Web and other media contrast with the inadequate models of the past that Dewey clearly opposed. Thus, they see a neat equation of

Dewey = learning by doing = constructivism = interconnected, interactive webs of new technologies = 21st-century education = good

standing in opposition to

textbook based = subject-matter driven = stultified teaching of the past = bad

Problems with this simple model. As appealing as this opposition might be, it suffers from three problems. The first is that Dewey might well have applied his critique of book learning to all the new technologies now being proposed as mechanisms for transforming teaching and learning. Dewey would have asked whether ordinary experience had been eliminated as the foundation for learning and, if so, whether the result could be anything but hollow. If, as he claims, education is the search for the structure of experience, then even the most exciting technological interaction might have little meaning in the student's lived experience.

The second problem is that the opposition trivializes Dewey's philosophy and thereby misses the insights that his work does provide for thinking about new technologies and education and, more broadly, for technologies and social change.

The third problem is that without specifying the relations among subject matter, media, activity, meaning construction, and experience, the simple opposition obscures what may truly be transformative about the introduction of new technologies for learning.

Technology and learning. There are a number of questions related to technologies and learning, which Dewey's work may help us answer. Let us consider just one of these this month: Why should we use new technologies for learning? Judging from the statements of U.S. leaders, school administrators, corporate sponsors, and parents' groups, this is a nonquestion. The only concern is quantity: How fast can we get as much technology as possible into the schools and the workplaces? How quickly can we wire all the schools? How soon can we make everyone technologically literate?

Challenging us to reflect on what we do, Dewey would ask us to pause to think more about how learning through technology serves as a point in the development of experience. In what ways is the experience afforded by interaction with a computer a substitute for other modes of learning? Does it bear the same relation that the map does to the territory, in which case it may be a feeble abstraction for direct, lived experience? Or, does it provide new avenues for experience and the means to access previously inaccessible realms? Perhaps computer interaction serves best as a means to reflect on, analyze, and extend other experiences? The point here is not that there are simple answers to these questions, but that serious consideration of them may enlarge our understanding of how we may best make use of new technologies and make sense of their impact on students.

Dewey would certainly value learning about new technologies, especially if that were through participation in authentic social practices that use those technologies. Just as in his lab school students learned about raising sheep, shearing them, spinning wool, making cloth and clothes, students today might learn about the many ways that technologies enter into the work and life of society at large. But that learning would have to include critical understanding that continually asks questions such as these: How do these technologies change the nature of language and knowledge? What are the economic consequences, both good and bad, of their use? What do we gain and what do we lose as we move inexorably into the information age?

Finally, Dewey would certainly value learning technology, if it means that students become more capable of participating in society and it enlarges the scope of their abilities to communicate. On the other hand, he might question learning technology if that were conceived merely as preparatory to later life.

Later, we'll look at additional questions that Dewey may help us examine: Why do we so often discover that new technologies remain underused, misused, and unused? What are the best resources for learning? Where do new technologies fit in the social world of schooling? How can we think about the apparent conflicts between the classroom and the workplace, between learning for today's needs versus tomorrow's, between using the technologies of today and those likely to appear in the future?

Website of the Month

Last summer, the American Museum of Natural History in New York selected the first annual Young Naturalist Awards (http://www.amnh.org/science). The Museum created these awards "to recognize excellence in biology, earth science, astronomy and cultural studies in students from grades 7–12." The competition is administered by the Alliance for Young Artists and Writers, Inc., a nonprofit division of Scholastic.

This year, the awards were based on reports students wrote about a walk through a natural area in their community, an object in their home or classroom, or a species that most people would consider to be a pest. Excerpts from their reports appeared in the June *Natural History* magazine, but to see the full reports with all the photographs and drawings you need to go to the Web. These Web publications and the biodiversity site are good examples of enhancing learning through use of new technologies.

Websites of the Month: Organizations

Some centers based in the United States concerned with technologies for learning resources:

- Center for Innovative Learning Technologies (http://www.cilt.org). This is an alliance of industry, research, schools, and others "to stimulate the development and implementation of important technology-enabled solutions to critical problems in K–14 science, math, and technology learning."

- Center for Lifelong Learning and Design, at the University of Colorado at Boulder (http://www.cs.colorado.edu/~l3d). The goal is "to establish, both by theoretical work and by building prototype systems, the scientific foundations for the construction of intelligent systems that serve as amplifiers of human capabilities (e.g., to expand human memory, augment human reasoning, and facilitate human communication)."

- Center for Social Informatics, at Indiana University (http://www-slis.lib.indiana.edu/CSI). The CSI conducts research into information technology and social change.

Addendum

To: chip@uiuc.edu
From: Allan Luke
Date: November 1998
Subject: Technology and Dewey's conception of learning

Really enjoyed the Issue section planned for the November technology column—and it got me thinking about where Dewey's work would stand in relation to the new technologies. You're right—there's a tendency to reduce Dewey to "learning by doing" and then assume that the various constructivist approaches forwarded now fit this. One of the things that gets left out is a recognition of Dewey as a pivotal social philosopher and critic (and, at times, exponent) of industrial society.

Two things struck me about your piece—first your mention of Halliday and Dewey together. Both are focused on intellectual technologies as tools for solving problems. The most memorable Dewey I read as an undergraduate was *Art as Experience* (1935a)—where he argues that art and technology are tools for the solution of social and intellectual problems. He defines problems as organism/environment disequilibria, where there are active disruptions of the relationships between people, communities, and their ecological and social environments. This was a cornerstone of his approach to teaching and learning, and it matches well the approach of Paulo Freire (1970) and others working on critical literacy: that teaching and learning need to be problem based; that it requires an analysis of one's social, cultural, and economic environments; and that it is goal directed toward change and transformation.

So I agree with your point about the "use of new technologies" rather than the technologies themselves being absolutely focal. If we wanted to second-guess what Dewey would say about the new technologies—it strikes me that he would argue that their value depends on the kinds of problems that they're applied to, and to what ends. (While Halliday would focus on the effects of the technologies on our intellectual practices, processes, and semiotic/linguistic systems; see Halliday & Martin, 1996.)

Second, you also reminded me recently that Dewey would have focused our attention on the relationships between three key elements: the new technologies, what Dewey called "older institutions and habits" (especially those of schooling), and, to use his words, "capitalist economies." Check out this quote (Dewey, 1935b):

> The conflict is between institutions and habits originating in the pre-scientific and pre-technological age and the new forces generated by science and technology. The application of science, to a considerable degree, even its own growth, has been conditioned by the system to which the name of capitalism is given, a rough designation of a complex of political and legal arrangements centering about a particular mode of economic relations. (p. 75)

So what I'd add is that Dewey would certainly refocus us on the uses of technologies, and on their uses for social problem solving. But he'd also focus us on the economics of the new technologies. It seems to me that teachers and students need to be talking and thinking about these questions: Who is getting access? Which communities of teachers and learners are getting excluded and silenced? and Whose industrial, commercial, and corporate interests are being advanced by the proliferation of these technologies?

I'm not a Luddite (otherwise I wouldn't be on e-mail so much), but it seems to me that we might be repeating some mistakes we made with print literacy if we rush headlong into teaching and learning programs without building in a critical literacy perspective from day one. Could we call it "critical technological awareness," following Norman Fairclough's (1992) "critical language awareness"?

Glossary

Idealization: the set of practices originally envisioned for a technology, rather than the realized practices. This is analogous to an intended, as opposed to an enacted, curriculum.

Realization: the set of practices associated with actual use of a technology. These may differ markedly from the idealization represented in documentation, a curriculum unit, or a teachers' guide.

Situated evaluation: an approach to evaluation of technology use that assumes the technology is not set a priori, but comes into being through use.

Situated studies: a research method that explicitly incorporates an analysis of the context in which literacy is practiced or learning occurs. It is particularly appropriate for investigations of the use of new technologies, because users typically find diverse ways to realize their potentials. In fact, to the extent that new technologies for learning truly empower students and teachers, we would expect that they would be used in unexpected ways.

Social informatics: the study of how information technologies are used in social contexts, how that use leads to social changes, and, conversely, how social practices influence that use.

Technocentrism: a way of thinking about the use of technology that attributes all important changes to the technology itself. ·

Transaction: a phenomenon in which mind and reality, or a "knowing" and the "known," are conceived as a unified entity; from Dewey and Bentley's (1949) *Knowing and the Known*.

REFERENCES

Dewey, J. (1935a). *Art as experience*. New York: Minton, Balch.

Dewey, J. (1935b). *Liberalism and social action*. New York: Minton, Balch.

Dewey, J. (1956). *The child and the curriculum & The school and society*. Chicago: University of Chicago Press. (Original works published 1902 and 1915)

Dewey, J., & Bentley, A.F. (1949). *Knowing and the known*. Boston: Beacon.

Fairclough, N. (Ed.). (1992). *Critical language awareness*. London: Longman.

Freire, P. (1970). *Pedagogy of the oppressed*. New York: Continuum.

Halliday, M.A.K. (1978). *Language as a social semiotic: The social interpretation of language and meaning*. Baltimore: University Park Press.

Halliday, M.A.K., & Martin, J.R. (1996). *Writing science*. London: Taylor & Francis.

McDermott, J.J. (1981). *The philosophy of John Dewey*. Chicago: University of Chicago Press.

Using the Web to Support Inquiry-Based Literacy Development

Guest Coauthor Ann Peterson Bishop

Editor's Message

A theme throughout the four years of my (Chip's) tenure with the *JAAL* Technology department has been the importance of an inquiry approach to understanding literacy, learning, and technology. This month, Ann Bishop and I, as two participants in a growing community of inquiry, share some of what we have learned about facilitating inquiry-based learning in the classroom; in independent studies; in libraries, museums, and communities; and in all the arenas of life in which people attempt to make sense of experience and grow.

In 1868, Charles Sanders Peirce proposed the idea of communities of inquiry to account for the way that people construct knowledge in collaboration with others. He argued that what is real depends on the decision of the community. When we consider how an invariant curriculum ill suits a changing world, his idea seems even more relevant now than when he first articulated it. In order to foster such a community, we have employed Web-based communication and knowledge-building tools such as the Inquiry Page (http://inquiry.uiuc.edu).

With the tools on this website, visitors can create modifiable representations of ongoing stages of inquiry that we call Inquiry Units. For example, teachers can represent the initial stages of inquiry in a unit, which is then continued by students as a spinoff. This process blurs the line between curriculum development and student work and between teacher and student in a way that is more productive for future work and learning. The Web-linked Inquiry Units thus provide a tangible form of a community of inquiry as well as insights for future development of Web-based resources.

Portions of this column were adapted from a talk I presented at ROCMELIA 2001, the Fifth International Conference on Multimedia Language Instruction at the National Taiwan University in Taipei, Taiwan, and published in the conference proceedings (Chuang, Y.S., Wang, Y.S., & Wang, P.L. [Eds.]. [2001]. Taipei: Crane).

Original version published May 2002 in the *Journal of Adolescent & Adult Literacy*
©2002 International Reading Association

Issue

How Can We Support Inquiry-Based Learning?

Our students encounter rapidly changing technologies and information resources, as well as the need to understand a complex global society. Yet the traditional modes of learning are often inadequate for coping with these changes or building on the students' diverse and rich personal backgrounds. Moreover, these modes are poor models for the collaborative inquiry and reflective practice (Schön, 1983) that people need as they engage with others in their roles as students, citizens, and productive members of society.

Traditional curricula in most countries have emphasized a delivery of content approach. Knowledge is assumed to exist or be encoded within texts. The role of the teacher is to manage the delivery of this knowledge, and the role of the learner is to absorb as much as possible. More specifically, students are expected to master certain basic learning skills such as solving problems, remembering textbooks, following directions, working alone, and "covering" the curriculum.

Whether such a predetermined curriculum and approach to learning were ever fully adequate is debatable. But in today's rapidly changing world it is clear that they are not. Students need to learn much more than textbook knowledge. Instead, they need to be able to examine complex situations and define the solvable problems within them. They need to work with multiple sources and media—not just a textbook. They need to become active learners, to collaborate, and to understand the perspectives of others. In short, they need to learn how to learn, and they must ask (find problems), investigate (multiple sources/media), create (engage actively in learning), discuss (collaborate and debate), and reflect to do that.

Thus, there is a shift from a transmission-oriented pedagogy to a more open, inquiry-based mode of teaching and learning. The value of inquiry-based learning is now widely recognized (Bruce & Davidson, 1996; Minstrel & Van Zee, 2000; Short et al., 1996; Wells, 2001). For example, the Carnegie Foundation's Boyer Commission on Educating Undergraduates in the Research University (1998) has set a priority on making research-based learning the standard. The main goal of the American Association for the Advancement of Science's Project 2061 is science literacy for all high school graduates. By this the group means the development of the broad, critical perspective and habits of the mind that come through scientific inquiry.

Diversity of Learners and Disciplines of Study

All learning begins with the learner. What children know and what they want to learn are not just constraints on what can be taught; they are the very foundation for learning. For this reason, Dewey's (1956) description of the four primary interests of the learner are still apropos: *inquiry*, or investigation—the natural desire to learn; *communication*—the propensity to enter into social relationships; *construction*—the delight in creating things; and *expression*, or reflection—the desire to extract meaning from experience. Dewey saw these as the natural resources—the uninvested capital on which the active growth of the child depends. As Dewey recognized, schooling is not only about the individual, but also about the intersection of the child's interests with those of the society. The disciplines we study in school represent centuries of collective thought as well as the interests of the larger community in maintaining itself by communicating its knowledge and values to the next generation.

Newcomers to a field of inquiry are often frustrated by the gap between their ordinary experience and the codified knowledge of a discipline of study. In the field of education, for example, many have trouble connecting what they know of their own learning processes, or the experiences from their own teaching, with the canonical articles and theories they are given in university courses. Dewey argued that this gap widens when we reify disciplinary knowledge, viewing it as static and constructing it as different in kind from the knowledge we gain through daily living. If instead we could see the disciplines represented as the ongoing processes of a community of inquiry, then the conflict between personal, situated knowledge and historically constituted, communal knowledge would become a problem of integrating and not of choosing one over the other.

Learning as Process

A key idea for inquiry learning is that there is a cycle or spiral of inquiry. Do not think of knowledge as static and the learner as an empty vessel whose job it is to absorb as much as possible of that predefined material. Instead, view the learner as an inquirer, learning through work on meaningful problems in real situations. The Figure below places the primary interests of the learner in the framework of a cycle of inquiry (Bruce & Davidson, 1996). For any question or problem, a learner should think of asking, investigating, creating, discussing, and reflecting as means for its resolution.

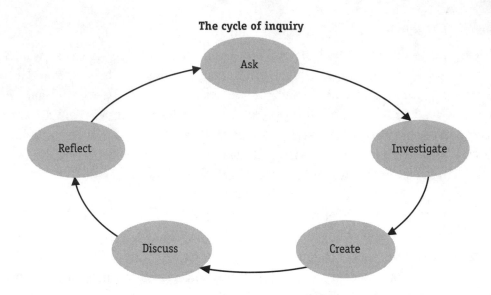

The cycle of inquiry

Communities of Inquiry

In language learning there are many efforts aimed at creating curricula that put the learner first. These models also emphasize the essential nature of participation in a community of inquiry. For example, Berghoff, Egawa, Harste, and Hoonan (2000) asked what schools would look like if they operated on the assumption that literacy involves a full range of interpretive abilities—not only the capacity to use language. Their work assumed that learners who make meaning draw from different dimensions of knowing—different forms of expression, different kinds of ideas, and different cultural frameworks. By recognizing and honoring these differences in the classroom, the school can create a richer way to explore the path to knowledge.

Short, Harste, and Burke (1995) talked similarly about creating classrooms for authors and inquirers where reading and writing are integral to processes of learning about oneself and the surrounding world. Short et al. (1996) showed how an integrated curriculum emerges from a view of learning and language united through inquiry processes. There have also been models (Wells, 2001; Wells & Chang-Wells, 1992) that show how the inquiry process reveals deep connections among classroom activity, learning, and language. Bruce and Easley (2000) talked about the need for communities of inquiry to support teachers as they attempt to foster more inquiry in the classroom.

It is crucial to recognize that a successful community of inquiry is not one in which everyone is the same, but instead is one that accommodates plurality and difference. Clark (1994), for example, considered different ways this accommodation can occur. In some cases, it compartmentalizes differences or establishes a hierarchy of one set of values and ideas over others. It can exclude, as well as include, people and ideas. Clark argued that we should focus on maintaining equitable relations first and then consider collective tasks.

> [This] renders the progress of expertise in a community secondary to a relational and epistemological practice of confronting differences so that its participants can come to understand how the beliefs and purposes of others can call their own into question. With this as its primary practice, the project of maintaining community can accommodate both equality and difference. (p. 74)

Differences among participants in the inquiry community can thus have different consequences, depending on how they are addressed. Productive work emerges when differences are not subsumed to a larger order but are understood through a hermeneutic process. A challenge for the inquiry community is to maintain a focus without denying individual experiences, perceptions, and values.

Research Questions

Some of the research questions that emerge from an inquiry perspective on learning are these:

- How do we connect subcommunities and disciplines but still recognize the diversity of each learner?
- How do we promote the process of inquiry at all levels for all participants?
- What tools and procedures best support a community of inquiry?

We are addressing these questions in the context of a project we have developed (and a set of tools we are now using and studying) called the Inquiry Page.

Collections Policy

The project has followed an unusual path with regard to building and managing content on the Inquiry Page. We can describe what is going on with the collection of material on the site from either "publishing" or library "collection development" perspectives. In publishing material online, many other educational sites have review committees, selection procedures, and rankings to separate the good from the bad. Libraries typically assess the needs of their intended community of users and develop criteria to govern their identification and acquisition of material to meet their users' needs. There's certainly a value to both website publishing and library approaches to building collections of useful material. With the Inquiry Page, we're working on mechanisms to add to what others have done in the realm of setting collection policy.

Inquiry Units contributed by Inquiry Page members make up one of the site's core collections. These units represent a variety of document types, such as syllabus modules, student assignments, project proposals, and records of personal and informal research. We've taken the position that no Inquiry Unit is ever really finished and unambiguously good. A very good unit might need to be adapted to fit particular students or local resources whereas an incomplete unit might be very useful for some purposes or when complemented by a text or other activities. We also see value in being able to share inquiries in progress, whether they are about a science question, a community problem, or a way of teaching.

Inquiry Page policies tend not to dictate or exclude users and creators of Inquiry Units. We support the ability of people to identify, evaluate, and modify units to suit their own situation. We use tags such as Public/Private, Ready to Use/Not Ready to Use and keywords as a way to indicate the status of a unit. Also, unit authors can easily put in their own text to describe a unit's status. For example, we could say in the Background section, "This unit is under development" or "We're trying to put together some good resources for a unit, but it's not ready for classroom use without some additional effort." Because development of the Inquiry Page proceeds through use, we don't want to prescribe or predetermine how it is used, but we do want to learn through the diversity of its uses.

Design and Evaluation

The Inquiry Page develops through a process of *participatory design*. Users contribute to all the various resources on the site, but more importantly they are its designers—through e-mail, electronic bulletin board discussions, and workshops. Participants in this process include K–12 teachers, museum educators, librarians, university students and faculty, and others engaged in various lifelong and informal learning activities. The site encourages a process of inquiry about teaching and learning and about how technology can best support it.

The Inquiry Page aims to respond to human needs by democratic and equitable processes. The users develop the site through creation of content, contributions to the interface, and evaluations—often simply by discussing its usefulness within the inquiry community and what works or does not in the context of their own settings. Workshops on the Inquiry Page—in a wide variety of settings, from academic conferences to small, local settings of potential use—are one focused evaluation activity that serves design through use quite well. Such workshops offer a window on use, and that helps anchor further design of inquiry-based learning technologies (social and digital) in authentic experiences while stimulating creative extensions.

Studies of the Inquiry Page use *situated evaluation* to take into account that actual use is an interaction between specific, local circumstances and the introduction of new tools and ideas.

> [Situated evaluation is a] new framework for understanding innovation and change. This framework has several key ingredients: It emphasizes contrastive analysis and seeks to explore differences in use. It assumes that the object of study is neither the innovation alone nor its effects, but rather, the realization of the innovation—the innovation-in-use. Finally, it produces hypotheses supported by detailed analyses of actual practices. These hypotheses make possible informed plans for use and change of innovations. (Bruce & Rubin, 1993, p. 215)

These evaluations tend to be formative and forward-looking, with the goal of improving future practice. Current interactive tools on the site for evaluation include a feedback form with automatic posting of feedback results. Inquiry participants also use methods such as case studies and participant observation to assess site use as a whole and to evaluate whether Inquiry Units meet specific needs. Results of these evaluations feed back into the site design and are also represented in articles about the project. Consider several examples.

- When a group of women in the community decided to use the site to take control of their health needs and to obtain better information, they noted that the emphasis on grade levels and school subjects was not appropriate for their community-action project. We found a way to change the presentation of the units so that grade levels and school subjects were not so prominent. We are also now working on a type of style sheet to allow customization for other projects.

- We conducted workshops for Missouri Botanical Gardens' users, who told us they wanted to include multiple website links in their units. This led to the idea of having live URLs. After we added that feature, other users asked for full HTML support. Today the site can be used by anyone, but users who know HTML can add functionality to their own units.

- Initial groups of middle school teachers who used the site realized that their students could be users and unit creators as well. They wanted a way to initiate a unit and then have students continue the investigation. This led to the idea of spinoffs, in which one user can build on the work of another. Since then, other users have considerably expanded the range of uses for spinoffs.
- As the units came to be used more in courses, instructors began to ask for a *comment* feature. That was added, and now other students as well as the teacher can add comments to one another's units.

Examples such as these are common in the development of any new website, but they have been even more evident for the Inquiry Page because of its assumption that user knowledge is necessary to create a useful site.

Melding the Learner and the Discipline

Much work on new media for education represents a melding of the learner and the discipline framed by inquiry-based learning. It does that in part because, as a relatively new field of study, it does not privilege a limited or static conception of its key ideas or even of its own boundaries. New educational media's communal knowledge bears a complex relationship with individuals in the community, but it does not stand apart and promote rigid hierarchies of knowledge. The social relations in the community tend to be supportive and constructive. People see themselves valued for their own experiences and perspectives even if they are new to the community. Old-timers find that their own inquiries remain fresh because of this openness.

Our object of study has been how new information and communication technologies promote the very same processes in contexts of teaching and learning, the workplace, and other social realms. In the case of the Inquiry Page, we see a similar dual role for inquiry. That is, the project is devoted to fostering collaborative inquiry among students, teachers, and community members. To do that, it offers Web-based tools, face-to-face meetings, research, and evaluation. At the same time, there is no recipe for either inquiry learning or for how to support it. Thus, the project itself exemplifies the very processes it seeks to support.

Website of the Month

The Inquiry Page (http://inquiry.uiuc.edu) is simultaneously a website, a community of learners, and a research project. It emphasizes how teachers weave a learner's interests with those of the curriculum by supporting teachers as they share their successes and their collective expertise. The website serves approximately one million page views per year. In addition, there are weekly meetings for site users and a wide range of workshops and conferences. The site is also the locus for research, promoting the idea that even its own structures and beliefs need continual reexamination.

The Inquiry Page supports teachers and learners of all ages and curricular areas. It is a website for collaborative curriculum development through the creation of Inquiry Units. These units become starting points for inquiry through which students are encouraged to ask questions, investigate, create, discuss, and reflect. The Inquiry Page is used to

- present problems for researchers,
- demonstrate how research results can be used,
- support the integration of knowledge across a community of inquiry,
- provide a means for all students to collaborate and learn from one another,
- support development of an active digital library,
- document the learning process, and
- articulate lesson plans that are more open-ended and student centered.

Teachers are also learners in this process—about phenomena in general and the processes of teaching and learning. They inquire through their access to resources on teaching and learning, including quotes about inquiry teaching, articles, project links, curriculum units, and content resources; they communicate with other teachers through various online communication media; they construct their own versions of curricula using the online Inquiry Unit generator; and they reflect on teaching and learning experiences as they share both literal and textual photos of their classrooms through these units.

A key concept throughout is that the processes of creating, using, and critiquing the site and the resources within it should exemplify the open-ended aspects of inquiry and social participation that the site encourages. We hope that participants will learn about the tools and the development process as they construct resources they can take away with them. Moreover, we invite them to join in the collaborative process of developing the Inquiry Page.

How You Can Participate

A major activity of the Inquiry Page is to foster the online creation of Inquiry Units by teachers (or students). Each unit starts with a guiding Question and provides a space for activities of Investigation, Creation, Discussion, and Reflection. These activities are often conceived as part of the inquiry cycle and give structure to some important aspects of inquiry that might be supported in a successful learning environment. In order to create a unit, the user must fill out a Web-based form that leads to an XML-formatted data structure. When the unit is called up again by the same or another user, a dynamic HTML file is generated.

Inquiry often leads to new ideas, results, theories, and questions, which can be communicated with others. This communication is central to the inquiry process. To facilitate it, Inquiry Units are indexed by user-generated keywords, grade level, subject area, or partner projects. In addition, users can indicate whether the unit is public or private, ready to use or not ready to use, open to comments or not open to comments, and whether their e-mail address is to be shown on the unit. These tags can be used by other users as they search for units. Once a unit is located, it can be used as is or the user can do a spinoff to modify the unit to fit specific purposes. Students can "spinoff" a copy of the teacher's unit to describe a course module or assignment, thus using the curriculum Inquiry Unit as a starting place for their own work.

Inquiry Units are being used in a variety of ways in teaching and learning about language arts. They are created by teachers for classroom activities that span educational levels from prekindergarten to graduate school. Students create Inquiry Units to fulfill course requirements or pursue extracurricular goals. Librarians create units to facilitate the use of educational resources by both teachers and students. Community members create units that help them achieve their personal goals as they pursue learning outside the classroom context.

Presented below is a sample of Inquiry Units that represent the range of educational activities tied to language arts in a variety of use settings.

What are the processes and consequences of electronic publication?
Chip Bruce

This unit serves as one section of a syllabus for an undergraduate course in new literacies. It presents students with readings associated with one week of the course.

What directions do children's interests take in story reading as inquiry?
Sylvia Steiner, Linda Chu

Two kindergarten teachers present the lesson plans they used over two months as they developed inquiry-based activities revolving around the well-known children's book *The Phantom Tollbooth* (2000) by Norton Juster.

What does hatching chicks have to do with language arts?
Pat Brown

Language arts activities—charting and graphing, spelling and writing, and receptive and productive language activities—associated with a chicken-egg hatching program are described in this unit.

Poetry as play
Sharon Comstock

A librarian created this unit to describe how she used the concept of exploratory play with children in grades 3–5 to guide them in the production of their own book of poetry.

What library and information services are provided for librarians serving the Latino community? How can we present these in the form of a website to librarians and other information professionals?
Yanira Vegerano and Heather Booth

In this unit, two graduate students in library and information science describe and present a website they created called *A Librarian's Guide to Latino Services*. The website includes resources, from a brief description of the sociocultural basis of Latino heritage to a bilingual dictionary of computer terms to lists of award-winning multicultural children's books—intended to help librarians create a library environment that better serves the Latino community.

Create your personal SisterNet spiritual health plan
Arlene Anderson
With this unit, a local community member, participating in a workshop on computer use as part of a spiritual health seminar for the general public, learned about relevant Web resources in the context of writing a personal spiritual health plan.

What we find intriguing is how Inquiry Units play a role in helping people cross boundaries that can hamper inquiry-based learning in practice. For example, Vegerano and Booth's unit demonstrates the movement of learners to teachers; the many comments attached to their unit by practicing librarians demonstrates that what was a learning experience for them resulted in a product that librarians in the field found immediately useful. We see that boundary spanned in another direction by Steiner and Chu. Their unit makes explicit their efforts to learn about inquiry-based pedagogy as they implemented inquiry-based activities in their kindergarten classroom. It also blurs the boundary between educational genres because it integrates a lesson plan with sustained reflection on it. We also see boundaries crossed between academic disciplines (science and language arts in Brown's unit), and between professions (teachers and librarians in Comstock's unit). Finally, the boundary between reading and writing in new media is crossed in Anderson's unit.

Glossary

The Inquiry Page contains a variety of resources. These have evolved through interactions with different user communities, each seeking different ways to represent ideas about inquiry and curriculum. The following defined resources can be found at the Inquiry Page.

Evaluating inquiry instruction: a webpage linked to articles, presentations, and other resources regarding the special issues of evaluating inquiry-based learning.

Inquiry in action: a section in which teachers can show what inquiry looks like in their classrooms or where researchers can show their own processes of inquiry. It includes photos, video, text descriptions, and links to Inquiry Units.

Inquiry partners: a growing collection of partner projects, courses, and schools.

Inquiry resources: a dynamic incorporation (using Digital Windmill) of the Open Directory category Reference, Education, Learning Theories, and Inquiry-Based Learning. This category is edited by the Inquiry Page development group.

continued

> **Glossary (cont.)**
>
> **Inquiry Page:** a Web resource containing a database of units for inquiry-based instruction across grade levels and subjects.
>
> **Quote of the day:** a collection of writings on teaching and learning with a special emphasis on those that expand our conception of what learning can be.

REFERENCES

Berghoff, B., Egawa, K.A., Harste, J.C., & Hoonan, B.T. (2000). *Beyond reading and writing: Inquiry, curriculum, and multiple ways of knowing.* Urbana, IL: National Council of Teachers of English.

Boyer Commission on Educating Undergraduates in the Research University. (1998). *Reinventing undergraduate education: A blueprint for America's research universities.* Retrieved from http://notes.cc.sunysb.edu/Pres/boyer.nsf

Bruce, B.C., & Davidson, J. (1996). An inquiry model for literacy across the curriculum. *Journal of Curriculum Studies, 28,* 281–300.

Bruce, B.C., & Easley, J.A., Jr. (2000). Emerging communities of practice: Collaboration and communication in action research. *Educational Action Research, 8,* 243–259.

Bruce, B.C., & Rubin, A.D. (1993). *Electronic quills: A situated evaluation of using computers for writing in classrooms.* Hillsdale, NJ: Erlbaum.

Clark, G. (1994). Rescuing the discourse of community. *College Composition and Communication, 45,* 61–74.

Dewey, J. (1956). *The child and the curriculum & The school and society.* Chicago: University of Chicago Press. (Original works published 1902 and 1915)

Minstrell, J., & Van Zee, E.H. (Eds.). (2000). *Inquiring into inquiry learning and teaching in science.* Washington, DC: American Association for the Advancement of Science.

Peirce, C.S. (1868). Some consequences of four incapacities claimed for man. *Journal of Speculative Philosophy, 2,* 140–157. Retrieved from http://www.peirce.org/writings/p27.html

Schön, D.A. (1983). *The reflective practitioner: How professionals think in action.* New York: Basic Books.

Short, K.G., Harste, J.C., Burke, C. (1995). *Creating classrooms for authors and inquirers* (2nd ed.). Portsmouth, NH: Heinemann.

Short, K.G., Schroeder, J., Laird, J., Kauffman, G., Ferguson, M.J., & Crawford, K.M. (1996). *Learning together through inquiry: From Columbus to integrated curriculum.* Portland, ME: Stenhouse.

Wells, G. (2001). *Dialogic inquiry.* New York: Cambridge University Press.

Wells, G., & Chang-Wells, G.L. (1992). *Constructing knowledge together: Classrooms as centers of inquiry and literacy.* Portsmouth, NH: Heinemann.

Guest Coauthor

Bishop teaches in the Graduate School of Library & Information Science at the University of Illinois at Urbana-Champaign.

Laboratories for Writing

Guest Author Kevin M. Leander

Editor's Message

In the age of the Internet, it is easy to equate technology with surfing the Web, but there are many other forms of technology, even specifically of digital electronic technologies, that play important roles in the development and practices of literacy. One of these is the online writing center. Some versions of online writing centers are akin to the online chat rooms to which many teenagers devote much of their after-school time.

Online, real-time, or synchronous communication has a long tradition in computer systems for education, going back at least to the PLATO system in the 1960s. But, in its earliest manifestations, online communication, whether real-time (as in an online chat) or asynchronous (like e-mail), was not considered directly educational. It was a fun part of the system to be used after the real learning had been accomplished. Today, however, both of these forms are seeing wide use as legitimate media for learning.

Proponents of online writing centers find value in the enthusiasm of participants and the fact that participation in the center means extensive reading and writing. Many instructors see great benefits in the writing and reading exhibited in the centers, yet others question their value or highlight problems. These diverse views suggest that we need to explore more deeply to discover exactly what happens online.

In our investigation of technology and literacy this month, we are led by Kevin Leander, a former secondary school English teacher now teaching at a university in the United States. Kevin has done in-depth studies of literacy in high school and college settings. His research has revealed the complex interplay of technologies, physical space, discourse, and social interaction in everyday learning settings.

Original version published April 2000 in the *Journal of Adolescent & Adult Literacy*
©2000 International Reading Association

Relocating Literacy, Rewriting Space

Feminist geographer Linda McDowell (1997) suggested that it might be more productive to think of our contemporary relations to localized place as "reterritorialized" rather than "deterritorialized." For example, rather than imagining in cyberspace that we have been somehow stripped clean of our local relations to physical place, it may be more productive to ask how relations to cyberspaces and physical places have been renegotiated and rearranged. How might we describe these new place-like ensembles? Still more important for our purposes, how do we understand literate practices "situated" within them? To address the issue of place and literate practices I focus here on the development of online writing centers (often called OWLs, for Online Writing Laboratories). In their multiple relations to cyberspaces and physical places, as well as to institutional and cultural practices, online writing centers offer a unique opportunity to consider the complex knot of place and practice.

Although researchers have raised a myriad of issues regarding the management of consultants, schedules, network technologies, and student papers in the development of online writing centers (e.g., Harris & Pemberton, 1995; Healy, 1995), the concerns voiced in this column are somewhat different. Here, I'll consider online writing centers as a particular case, in order to make some initial observations about the codevelopments of place and literate practices with the developments of new online technologies. What does the development of online writing centers show us about the creation of "new" spaces for literacy? Here are some interpretations.

The Proliferation of the Online Writing Center

As of mid-September 1999, there were 278 online writing centers linked to the National Writing Centers Association website at http://departments.colgate.edu/diw/NWCA.html. This site catalogues primarily centers based in the United States and chiefly those associated with higher education. The proliferation of online writing centers is noteworthy when we consider how they, like the persons and courses of study they serve, are deeply connected with the construction of institutional identity. One can imagine, for instance, that the production of many fewer, yet superior, online writing centers as collaborations across universities, schools, and writing groups of various sorts might be a better use of institutional resources and cyberspace.

If the institutional import of having one's own online writing center presence were lessened, perhaps the State University of New York (SUNY) Albany's online writing center and that of Broome Community College (Binghamton, New York) at http://www.sunybroome.edu/~writecenter would be "de-centered" in cyberspace and share an online writing center, rather than being two of nine online writing centers in the SUNY system. Yet, the current development of online writing centers appears to be deeply tied up with the felt need for "presencing" oneself and one's institution on the Web (as well as with hybrid relations to material centers, discussed later). For institutional visibility, an online writing center is arguably more important than its offline counterpart.

The proliferation of online writing centers should not necessarily be taken as an indication of a vast degree of diversity among them. While I will attempt to highlight their diversity, at the same time I am struck by how the online writing center has become stabilized or durable as a cultural form. In what might be called the "genrification" of the online writing center, a set of common characteristics across writing centers has developed rapidly. Most online writing centers, for instance, have information about their offline counterparts' basic services (e.g., location, scheduling, staffing); most include links to general writing resources such as the Hypertext Webster Gateway for accessing various online dictionaries, *Roget's Thesaurus*, or the *Columbia Guide to Online Style*; many contain "handouts" of various sorts related to writing and grammar problems and issues; and a growing number include e-mail links that permit students to submit their papers for online tutoring.

Like personal or university homepages, the online writing center is a text subject to a powerful centripetal pull to become like many others in form, function, and content. This "genrification" also operates, of course, at the level of hyperlinked resources. As a high value is often placed on writing centers with the largest number of student handouts, these centers and their handouts become constructed as more central centers to other more peripheral centers that develop in (linked) relation to them. Nevertheless, it is still possible for student writers to connect to 70 different grammar hotlines by e-mail or telephone across the United States.

Hybrid Relations of Online and Offline Writing Centers

Within the online writing center based at Salt Lake Community College, Redwood Campus (Salt Lake City, Utah), there is a webcam that peers into the space of the physical, offline writing center at the same institution. When I clicked on the webcam, I was a voyeur of room AD 218 and able to watch the back of one student writing at a table; get a silent side profile of two other students talking at another table in the distance; and see someone come from off camera, stage left to stage right, to retrieve something from a filing cabinet. Around the periphery of this cam-view are hyperlinked resources on the webpage. Some resources are based on local activity, such as a schedule of writing advisors at three locations on campus, and many are more distant. I followed a link, for example, to the National Writing Project, where I learned of an online conference with writer and teacher Donald Murray. SLCC's webcam as an online entree to an offline world, and its textual positioning with respect to a large array of more local and distant activity, is a good metaphor of the hybridization of the writing center across online and offline spaces.

Such hybrid relations are ubiquitous. At the Colorado State University Writing Center (Fort Collins), for instance, a student needing guidance on research may select links to the CSU's Morgan Library, where in mid-September of 1999 a librarian offered a face-to-face workshop in Room 165 on Finding Full Text Articles Fast; he or she may likewise consult an online guide to Using the Library of Congress. It is tempting to consider these hybrid relations as unidirectional, where the online writing center is based on and extends its offline referent.

Yet, returning to the example of the webcam at Salt Lake Community College, consider how the presence of an online camera constructs the writing space and activity of the students within the center. How are writing, having conferences, and drafting shaped when they are made more or less visible to a dispersed Internet public? As a more mundane example, how are writing handouts developed when they are produced for mass audiences via online distribution, rather than for more local ones? Finally, how might face-to-face tutoring relations develop when tutors are also working in online communication and hybridizing their practices across this activity?

There has been a certain amount of anxiety within the online writing center literature over the threat of physical writing centers being taken over by online centers for reasons of institutional efficiency (e.g., Stuart Blythe's piece in the first issue of *Kairos*, an online journal for "teachers of writing in webbed environments"). While such anxiety may be warranted, particularly when we consider the market-driven motivations of much of distance education, when we view it from the perspective of the locations writers themselves select, we end up with a form of development that is much more complex than replacement. For instance, the Dakota State University Online Writing Lab (Madison, South Dakota) started as an online center alone, with no offline counterpart, with the expressed purpose of better serving students in remote locations. Although a physical writing center does not yet exist at DSU, writing consultants often meet face to face with formerly online students on campus (E. Johnson, personal communication, September 13, 1999). A similar relation was evident in a distance writing-tutoring project between graduate students at the University of Arkansas at Little Rock and the Oak Ridge Campus of Roane State Community College in Tennessee. Although none of the community college students in the project used the writing center prior to the distance project, following it many of them repositioned themselves in the school's physical writing center for study, including online and offline work on its computers.

Relation of the Online Writing Center to the Classroom

What kinds of relations are being shaped with respect to the classroom in online writing centers? What ought such relations to be? We might expect that "decentering" the writing center in cyberspace might make it more inviting to students reluctant to enter an offline, physical space. Conversations within the center might be less directly implicated in institutional hierarchy, as the institution might be backgrounded within these conversations and spaces. Could writing theorist Stephen North's early student-centered vision of the physical writing center be even better realized online: "In short, we are not here to serve, supplement, back up, complement, reinforce, or otherwise be defined by any external curriculum" (in Healy, 1995, p. 185)? Might the movement into cyberspace make the writing center somewhat more of a "semiautonomous space" (Healy, 1995; Kali & Trimbur, 1987) with respect to the institution, classrooms, and the curriculum? If so, toward what end?

The relation of the offline or online writing center to its institutional home is a pivotal issue for its development. A commonplace positioning of the "center" is between the student and the classroom. The space of the center permits the student to move toward some better formulation of an "ideal text" (Knoblauch

& Brannon, 1984), mediating for the respective professor and course. However, if the writing center is to provide some kind of leadership in writing practices and theory, if it serves a purpose of helping students not only to engage in disciplinary discourses but also to critique those discourses, and if the center connects students to conversations about writing that extend well beyond particular institutional course structures, then something akin to a more semiautonomous space makes sense. Perhaps at issue is not merely the value of autonomy or agency, but the way in which such autonomy is imagined.

As a construct, the semiautonomy of the writing center space and its practices need not be imagined as a semipermeable barrier between the student and the "external curriculum," but as "de-centering" from the institution through powerful connections to other sociocultural spaces and practices extending well beyond it. The center space in this relation has been conceived by Eric Crump as a "technoprovacateur" whose role is to facilitate student participation in increasingly broad literate networks (with a large dash of fun), rather than simply to permit passage to a designated classroom space.

In sum, while it seems like a good thing for the online writing center to have a link that leads a student to the criteria for making a Disease Education Poster in Microbiology 300, at the same time it is worrisome to imagine that online writing centers could construct themselves as mere clearinghouses for writing assignments constructed by faculty, high-tech mediators of the student dorm space and the classroom space.

To get an indication of how current online writing centers are expanding space and practice, consider the meanings of writing within them. Across the vast array of online writing centers, one generally finds that they are primarily engaged with the relatively narrow line of generic practices associated with academic literacies: argumentation and research, a regular but small stream of personal essays, résumés, cover letters, and the like, and a still smaller trickle of creative writing. Of course, none of this should come as a surprise, and we may well argue that online writing centers would be remiss not to support students with what J. Paul Johnson dubs traditional academic "papertext" or "a technological-epistemological product which locates the writer as a rational, stable subject and presents the text as a coherent, printed totality" (see http://english.ttu.edu/Kairos/1.1/owls/johnson.html). The significant mainstay of writing centers has been to offer sound advice about academic prose with a personal touch:

A thesis statement is one of the greatest unifying aspects of a paper. It should act as mortar, holding together the various bricks of a paper, summarizing the main point of the paper "in a nutshell," and pointing toward the paper's development. Often a thesis statement will be expressed in a sentence or two; be sure to check with your professor for any particular requirements in your class—some professors prefer a more subtle approach! (See http://writing.richmond.edu/~writing/wweb/thesis.html).

Yet how would writing be conceived, and the writing space of the online center be transformed, if as Johnson suggests we were to disrupt the notion "that the proscenium classroom is the only valid context for writing"? What if online writing centers became academic leaders as spaces for the advancement of multiliteracies (New London Group, 1996)? Consider this shift as represented in the publication procedures for the online *Journal of Computer Mediated Communication* at http://www.ascusc.org/jcmc/submiss.html:

Articles submitted may be of any length. Articles may be written in any format. Articles may contain any combination of text, tables, graphics, animation, or audio component. JCMC editors will make every possible effort to accommodate presentation formats.

Were even *some* writing conceived closer to this formulation of representation, imagine the potential transformations of space and practice both within the online writing center (in terms of resources, expertise, archived media files, technical tools, electronic spaces) and with respect to the cultural networks in which the online center participates.

Other Views

Transforming Space and Practice in Online Writing Centers

Teaching research and reflections are beginning to suggest ways in which the online environment changes the relation between the writer and the writing consultant. For example, drawing from an extended example of interactions with a student, David Coogan discusses the potential for the online conference to "break down the barriers between academic writing and conference talk" and, hence, "turn papers into acts of communication." "E-mail communication," writes Coogan, "doesn't try to deconstruct a text, it tries to latch on—to connect to a text." Of course, the pedagogic practice of making connections through response, thus using the student text as a turn at talk in a larger conversation, is not restricted to online communication. At the same time, the practice of dialogue afforded by e-mail computer programs and by social use suggests how the online space supports a dialogic, open relation to the writer's text as it is put into circulation.

Still more intriguing relations of space and practice, though, are attempts at weakening the one-tutor-one-writer model of writing center practice and attempts to convert one-on-one dialogues into "multilogues" and to unbound their respective spaces. In this regard, of particular interest are the online writing spaces being developed at the University of Missouri-Columbia. The Online Writery at http://web.missouri.edu/~writery contains within it differently structured cyberspaces for writing and response, including a Writery Café, which is dubbed by the site as a "conversation coffeehouse for writers," an "open environment in which to discuss writing in any form." Technically speaking, the Writery Café is just a simple archived newsgroup, which permits writers to post, for example, papers, questions, quips, or comments. After participating as a lurker in the Café for two weeks, I became fascinated with how the space destabilized tutor/tutee or consultant/student relations. An official staff member of the space was linked as a resource, but was weakly present within the list, where participants from wide geographical spaces (e.g., Australia, the United Kingdom, the United States) shifted roles between sharing writing, apologizing for being late to respond, prompting each other to write more prose and less poetry, setting up contests for the list, and so on. Submitted pieces would often result in a long string of responses from the distributed group; amid this conversation the respective authors would offer response to other pieces of writing as part of the multilogue. (For a more expansive version of the Writery Café with many writing resources, check out http://trace.ntu.ac.uk for the trAce Online Writing Community.)

A similar widely distributed participant base, and a dynamic of shifting writer/respondent roles, is also evident in the Online Writery's forums, which use HyperNews and permit users to post texts and comments without leaving a common Web space. Notably, the topics of the three forums for threaded posting and discussion are Poetry, Fiction, and an H(tml) HELP Forum. An HTML help forum appears a deliberate movement to include Web-based representation as a form of literacy (rather than simply a new medium for the "papertext"), and learning about technology as a significant aspect of the writing process. The forum reflects how literacy space, representation form, and tutoring practice relations may develop in dynamic relation to one another.

How Accessible Are Online Writing Centers?

One argument for the development of online writing centers is that they greatly expand accessibility. The online construction "deterritorializes" the spatial and temporal dynamics of the writing center, permitting writers access any time, anywhere. Demonstration projects have also made evident how writing centers and associated tutoring programs can bring together consultants and writers who would otherwise not interact, such as graduate students at the University of Arkansas at Little Rock and community college students at Roane State Community College, Oak Ridge, Tennessee. (See Jordan-Henley, J., & Maid, B.M. [1995]. Tutoring in cyberspace: Student impact and college/university collaboration. *Computers and Composition, 12*, 211–218.)

Yet, despite these possibilities, we still need to raise important questions about how access is constructed within cyberspace. As with any Internet resource, online writing centers are implicated in a number of equity issues with respect to access. Yet there are also more specific access issues of concern with these literacy resources. In particular, how do online writing centers structure access for nonnative speakers of English who represent a large part of their clientele? Although many English as a Second Language (ESL) students may be able to use resources developed for native English speakers, others will not. Suzan Moody's review of ESL resource and access issues at eight large online writing centers revealed that the greatest number of resources concerned English grammar. Only half the centers provided information for ESL students on how to write essays. Although some of the resources on writing and grammar are written for students of limited English proficiency, Moody urges that more explanatory material and models of writing need to be developed that pay special attention, among other issues, to simple explanation, vocabulary choice, and accessible sentence constructions. Such development is all the more critical for nonnative speakers of English when we consider the many proxemic, embodied, and other subtle verbal and nonverbal forms of communication that are either absent or reconfigured within computer-mediated communication.

Website of the Month

Lingua MOO (http://lingua.utdallas.edu) is an Internet-based learning, research, and collaboration environment developed by Cynthia Haynes and Jan Rune at the University of Texas, Dallas. Unlike most of the online writing center media discussed earlier, a MOO is a synchronous learning environment, where people interact in real time, representing themselves as characters in a shared virtual space. Advocates of synchronous participation often point to the enhanced sense of community building in sharing real time (and space).

Moreover, within the MOO, participants not only are able to move among online spaces, they also are able to create such spaces themselves. As programs, MOOs permit users to construct virtual "rooms" for interaction, rooms that also store and post various texts and objects. Thus, unlike the offline or online writing center that invites students into an already stable space, the MOO is a malleable set of space/text relations. Lingua MOO describes itself, in this regard, as a "new archi/TEXTural community...where writing IS the landscape." The MOO is a powerful resource for exploring the complex dynamics of literacy, place, and identity.

The Lingua MOO homepage contains a host of links to resources and educational projects related to MOOs, but most important is a gateway to the Lingua MOO environment, where visitors can log in and participate as guests. Of particular technical interest at Lingua MOO is a new interface recently developed. Unlike Telnet-type systems and the demands that they place on users to memorize a host of commands, the new enCore Xpress MOO interface is a movement toward a point-and-click mode of interaction, opening up MOO-based interaction for a broader range of participants and uses.

Glossary

Deterritorialized: stripped from a relation to local place.

Forum: an online discussion group, sometimes called a newsgroup or a conference. Web-based forums are often archived so that participants can follow and post to past and current threads.

MOO: an acronym for MUD, Object Oriented. A MUD is a Multiple-User Dimension (also Domain, Dungeon, or Dialogue), a computer database that permits multiple users to log in by Telnet and interact in real time. In MOOs, users can also create, manipulate, and move among virtual objects (including rooms).

Reterritorialized: a dynamic and complex relation to developing spaces.

Telnet: a program that allows a personal computer to link to another computer, via the Internet or other network. Telnet has a history of being used for connecting smaller

continued

> **Glossary (cont.)**
>
> machines to larger mainframe computers, but is currently used to remotely access and control computer servers of all size via the Internet.
>
> **Webcam:** a digital camera for transmitting real-time digital images (usually at speeds much slower than video) over the Internet.

REFERENCES

Harris, M., & Pemberton, M. (1995). Online writing labs (OWLs): A taxonomy of options and issues. *Computers and Composition, 12*, 145–159.

Healy, D. (1995). From place to space: Perceptual and administrative issues in the online writing center. *Computers and Composition, 12*, 183–193.

Kali, H., & Trimbur, J. (1987). The politics of peer tutoring. *Writing Program Administration, 11*(1–2), 5–12.

Knoblauch, C.H., & Brannon, L. (1984). *Rhetorical traditions and the teaching of writing.* Portsmouth, NH: Boynton/Cook.

McDowell, L. (Ed.). (1997). *Undoing place? A geographical reader.* New York: Arnold.

New London Group. (1996). A pedagogy of multiliteracies: Designing social futures. *Harvard Educational Review, 66*(1), 60–92.

Pegg, B. (1998). UnfURLed: 20 writing center sites to visit on the information highway. In E.H. Hobson (Ed.), *Wiring the writing center* (pp. 197–215). Logan, UT: Utah State University Press.

Guest Author

Leander teaches language and literacy courses in the Department of Teaching and Learning at Vanderbilt University in Nashville, Tennessee, USA.

Hypermedia Authoring as Critical Literacy

Guest Authors Jamie Myers, Richard Beach

Editor's Message

In his *Critique of Pure Reason* (1929, Palgrave; http://www.arts.cuhk.edu.hk/Philosophy/Kant/cpr), Immanuel Kant showed how it can be that all our knowledge begins with experience, yet in order to make sense of those experiences we must know other things first. He focused especially on the fact that we frame experiences in space and time but cannot derive the ideas of space and time out of experience. His analysis provided the foundation for the constructivist educational theories of Jean Piaget, Lev Vygotsky, and John Dewey.

Kant's conception of how an individual constructs knowledge out of internal representations has since been extended to models of how the individual makes use of socially constructed representations. A fundamental idea in this work is that the ways we represent knowledge shape what it is possible to know and what we need to know. We are both empowered by our representations and limited by them. In today's realm of learning technologies, we would say that representations provide both affordances and constraints for sense-making.

This is why the new representational means of digital technologies can be so important. Although we cannot go beyond our human capacities in terms of space and time, we can use new media to engender experiences that enlarge the possibilities for making meaning. Hypertext is one such medium that has expanded those possibilities, and now, with hypermedia, the expansion continues.

In this month's column, Jamie Myers and Rick Beach ask how hypermedia can foster critical literacy. They emphasize the social aspects of inquiry afforded by the new media. Drawing from their new book (Beach & Myers, 2001), they examine how new tools enhance the possibilities for six major dimensions of inquiry-based learning. They use examples from language arts classrooms to show that critical awareness and engagement are called for in the new literacy and in turn are fostered by immersion in new forms of representation.

Original version published March 2001 in the *Journal of Adolescent & Adult Literacy*
©2001 International Reading Association

How Hypermedia Fosters Critical Literacy

Hypermedia combines hypertext (texts linked together by multilinear nodes) and multimedia (e.g., photos, video, art, audio, text) to produce an interactive media experience for participants. Because hypertext allows participants to choose optional paths through multimedia, participants can construct and respond to hypermedia interactively. Literacy instruction has recently been enabled and broadened enormously through the rapidly developing array of technological tools used to create hypermedia. Our representations of the world are viewed electronically as quickly as we move whole paragraphs to change the flow of words and the position of graphics. Discussion groups and live chat rooms provide wide-open spaces for the negotiation of subjectivities and the construction of our possible identities. The image, the animation, video, and music spill in and out of our desktop computers contributing to the expanding intertext we create to name ourselves, others, and the world. It will be just as critical in the next 10 years, as it has been in the last 10, to constantly remind ourselves that the power of technology is generated within our cultural uses of these tools and not simply determined by the nature of the tools themselves.

That said, we cautiously set out in this column to highlight some pedagogical frameworks in which we believe students have used hypermedia tools such as Storyspace™, HyperStudio™, HyperCard™, and various Web authoring programs to generate a practice of critical literacy (McKillop & Myers, 1999; Myers, Hammett, & McKillop, 1998). Our underlying assumption is that our uses of representational tools to signify and negotiate meanings are embedded in larger socially constructed literacy practices in which our symbolic activity helps us to (a) achieve the culturally valued purposes of a community and (b) negotiate the opposing values of multiple communities.

How we speak, dress, gesture, listen to music, and use texts from print to video provide the symbolic tools through which we interact and interpret one another and the world. Our ongoing symbolic interactions and activity within a community, or what we refer to as a social world, not only result in our implicit acquisition of the symbolic tools needed to keep the community going, but also construct the ideology of possible identities, relationships, and values realized within that community. Hypermedia authoring for critical literacy pushes this one layer further when students create hypermedia texts to explicitly reflect on how symbolic interactions construct community and ideology.

The hypermedia practices we highlight, therefore, evidence the use of technology in which authors use symbolic tools to name, critique, and negotiate the underlying ideologies constructed and often contested through symbolic interaction within or between multiple social worlds. As Edelsky (1999) noted,

> Studying systems—how they work and to what end—focusing on systems of influence, systems of culture, systems of gender relations...being critical means questioning against the frame of system, seeing individuals as always within systems, as perpetuating or resisting systems. Being noncritical...means seeing individuals as outside of...[and] separate from systems and therefore separate from culture and history. (p. 28)

Because acts of critical literacy are embedded in larger cultural practices that circumscribe how and why we create and use texts, we must pay particular attention to the pedagogical frameworks in classrooms in which we ask students to author hypermedia as critical literacy.

Critical Inquiry Into Social Worlds

The first pedagogical frame for hypermedia construction asks students to look into how words, symbols, and actions construct our social worlds as systems. Our book (Beach & Myers, 2001) more fully describes the curricular framework we advocate for English language arts classrooms. Briefly, this inquiry-oriented curriculum involves six recursive inquiry strategies that are involved in hypermedia productions.

1. *Immersing*—entering into the activities of a social world, experiencing the social world as a participant, or observing a social world. Students may use hypermedia software to collect and link images and texts (e.g., those of adolescent females scanned from teen magazines and ads).

2. *Identifying*—defining concerns, issues, and dilemmas that arise in a social world, or from conflict across multiple social worlds. In identifying various intertextual patterns evident in the images of adolescent females, students identify the issue of how these magazines portray females to achieve the purposes of the beauty-industry system.

3. *Contextualizing*—explaining how the activities, symbols, and texts used in one or more social worlds produce the components of a social world—purposes, roles, rules, beliefs, and traditions operating in a system. By pulling images and texts out of their original context and recontextualizing them in a new hypermedia context, students become more aware of how the magazine images of adolescent females reflect an ideology of commercialism and consumerism in which their possible identities, relationships, and values are positioned.

4. *Representing*—using symbolic tools to create a text that represents a lived social world or responds to a represented social world. Students use hypermedia to represent their own beliefs or to explain how texts are used to represent worlds to achieve certain purposes. They juxtapose pictures and video from their own lives that resist and oppose other commercialized images of females.

5. *Critiquing*—analyzing how a representation of a social world privileges particular values and beliefs; analyzing how particular literacy practices within a social world promote certain meanings while marginalizing other possibilities. In hypermedia projects this is most often accomplished by setting contesting texts in juxtaposition to create a critique of opposing values and identities.

6. *Transforming*—revising one's meanings for the components of a social world, changing one's actions and words within a social world to construct more desirable identities, relationships, and values. Through hypermedia authoring students both identify and experience how symbolic interactions and texts construct the ideologies of their social worlds, thus generating the power within them to use words, symbols, texts, and actions with others in alternative ways that seek to transform problematic social worlds.

Ninth graders at State College High School used a range of hypermedia tools to inquire into various social worlds in which they were members (http://www.ed.psu.edu/k-12/socialworlds). Three of the projects introduced students to specific hypermedia software while the fourth involved students videotaping themselves playing computer video games. Across the projects, as students analyzed multimedia texts and created new texts to represent their ideas about a social world, they engaged in a critique of the values constructed within a social world.

One student examined the social world of peer groups in the high school. She took many digital photos of groups in action during the school day. Using Adobe Photoshop™ she edited these images to grayscale and colorized specific objects that signified group belonging or exclusion. Through her final photo essay, projected through the computer, she represented the complexity of peer group relationships:

> My favorite picture is one of a group of girls standing together in the bathroom. Every girl in there is from a different group, and yet the girls all mingle and talk. This is one of the best examples of an objective group because, although I know this sounds odd, no one is judged in the bathroom.

By highlighting how our uses of specific symbols in particular spaces construct our social relationships, this student's project generates the possibility of transforming the symbolic interactions that construct future peer relationships beyond the bathroom.

Several of the ninth graders used the software Adobe Premiere™ to author QuickTime movies from still images, video clips, and music. By juxtaposing a series of images set to specific types of music and song lyrics, the final hypermedia product focused on a value, identity, or relationship significant within a social world. One of the boys used scenes from the movie *Days of Thunder* (1990; Tony Scott, Director) and clips from the song "The Distance" by Cake to represent how a "romantic interest will drive an athlete to perform better than he has before and strive to be the best. On the other hand, if the athlete is in a troubled relationship...performance will suffer notably." While there is much to the ideology underlying competitive sports left unexamined in this hypermedia project, the intent to reveal an underlying value, and the analytical processes engaged to construct the hypermedia representation of this value, initiated the practice of a critical literacy.

Students also used SoundEdit 16™ software to isolate lyrics in popular songs in order to explain how the words represented significant experiences in social worlds. By far the most popular with the ninth graders was the critique of how songs represented the various aspects of relationships and identity within the social world of romance. One girl used popular music to represent how "people care for other people by their words and actions" in various romantic relationships.

Because she believed that romance meant many different things, she used the power of sound editing to juxtapose short clips from popular songs to explore how "within each relationship some kind of conflict occurs" and how "people might change the aspects of this social world by doing something different in a romance." The critical literacy practice initiated through this technology tool is one that teachers often struggle with when they ask students to specifically explain why they like or do not like a song, movie, or text. Here, the student was able to isolate specific meaningful excerpts and, in juxtaposing them with other clips, explicitly identify the words and actions that promote particular underlying values, forms of relationship, and possible identities.

The ability to digitize video from handheld cameras gives students an important tool for analyzing interactions and activity in a social world. When two boys examined their own video game playing, they noted how particular behaviors were constructed, "such as attitude change, relationship depletion (for short periods of time) and anger and/or celebration." Here is an important instance of how students can engage in a critique of their own use of a highly popular technology tool by using another technology tool to capture, analyze, and represent their critique. The students noted how the different video games constructed feelings of success and power as they escaped the pressures of outside social worlds— particularly school and family worlds.

Important to the construction of a critical consciousness is how these technology tools allowed students to focus on specific symbolic actions and words and to explicate how our uses of texts construct the ideologies underlying social worlds. With this awareness comes the hope of greater consciousness and agency in interpreting and authoring texts and, thus, the ability to transform future social worlds to achieve higher levels of social justice and equity.

Critical Response to Literature

Students also use hypermedia to construct critical responses to literature (Landow, 1997; McKillop & Myers, 1999). Technology tools allow readers to connect to the text a vast array of multimedia life experiences that become relevant through their response to the text. They may construct their own hypertext versions of texts, including thematic/lexical annotations or intertextual links or paths/trails to related texts, themes, topics, biographical information, or historical contexts. Although much of talk or writing about texts focuses simply on response to a text, hypermedia invites students to explain their textual experience within the larger cultural and ideological contexts that shape their interpretations. For example, in studying Daniel Defoe's *Robinson Crusoe* students used hypermedia to post alternative versions of the story that reversed the master/servant roles of Crusoe and Friday, along with background cultural information about Western imperialism (Soetaert & Mottart, 1999).

Students have used QuickTime videos to interrogate or challenge implied ideological stances evoked by literary texts. In response to Ray Bradbury's *Fahrenheit 451*, two teachers had small groups create QuickTime videos about a significant theme in the novel: individuality, knowledge as power, censorship, utopia, or thought control. Using the software Avid Cinema™, 15 groups of students extended these ideas into images, movies, music, and words drawn from their own everyday lives. Their movies (http://www.ed.psu.edu/k-12/fahrenheit) became opportunities to express their own ideologies as they layered personally significant experiences with popular culture onto the literary experience of the novel while simultaneously reinterpreting the potential meanings of the texts in reference to it. The small-group structure also forced the students to continually negotiate the potential meanings for (a) each text used in their video and (b) the meaning constructed across the sequence of juxtaposed clips.

In these hypermedia productions, the concrete portrayals of experience in sound, music, or video clips play an important role in fostering critical analysis. Employing particular graphic material invites students to go beyond easy generalities about an issue to grapple with the everyday realities portrayed in the clips. As Halio (1996) notes, "the more particular and specific writers are when they construct possible worlds, the more general and applicable the meanings of these texts become" (p. 345). She cites the examples of students portraying the effects of television violence on children:

> Those who added sounds of children playing violent kicking games after watching the Power Rangers, or playing peaceful creative games prior to watching television, were able to move beyond generalities into specifics. Rather than standing off from the scene and observing clinically, the authors moved into their texts, orchestrating effects—talking about particular children and particular television shows. (p. 345)

Students have also used sound and music as ironic or contradictory comments against the official meanings associated with the image or text. In a literature-of-wars project in Browning's (2000) class, students opened the project on the literature of war with Jimi Hendrix's version of "The Star Spangled Banner." Ironic juxtapositions were generated often in an extensive class response to William Shakespeare's *Romeo and Juliet* (http://www.ed.psu.edu/k-12/culture/rj). Songs such as "Some Enchanted Evening" sung by Frank Sinatra and "Come to My Window" by Melissa Etheridge became the soundtracks for digital images of the students enacting the masked ball and a video clip of Romeo climbing to Juliet's balcony. The greatest irony was generated when two additional soundtracks were offered for Juliet's funeral scene, creating two entirely new moods for the visual experience of the event.

Constructing these intertextual and intercontextual links between texts and cultural contexts leads students beyond the text to examine how they are being positioned in a media culture to adopt certain ideological stances. (For additional examples of critical hypermedia in response to literature, see http://www.ed.psu.edu/k-12/culture.) They must then grapple with the question, What must a reader believe or value to have this response to the text? Answering this question leads them to critique the underlying ideologies that frame the interpretation of a text. Creating alternative anti-imperialist versions of Robinson Crusoe leads them to entertain tensions between contesting ideologies rather than the textual artifact alone.

Going beyond illustrations to interrogations. Students often initially use hypermedia simply to annotate or graphically illustrate a text. For example, in response to E. Annie Proulx's *The Shipping News*, a class of central Pennsylvania undergraduates in English education formed small groups and also built websites in response to the novel (http://www.ed.psu.edu/k-12/shippingnews). These students responded to more traditional literary aspects such as character, theme, and style. In webpages about the main character Quoyle, students connected his circumstances, motivations, and development to other characters in other stories, movies, and music. Other students responded to themes of death and romance, connecting other multimedia texts that offered similar perspectives. Many students responded to the language used in the novel and created sites to focus on knots and other stylistic elements, making connections to similar texts. However, although these students generated an interesting intertextual array of texts for interpreting the novel, their juxtapositions did not seem to intentionally attempt to expose problematic representations or contest underlying ideologies between the text and their own lives.

In contrast, in responding to the same novel, a group of university students in Newfoundland, Canada, constructed a hypermedia website (http://lord.educ.mun.ca/educ4142) that represented a more critical interrogation of the text (Hammett & Barrell, 1999). On the basis of instruction about ideological stances evoked by texts, many of the students resisted the portrayals of their home, Newfoundland, in the novel and, working through this response, created websites full of images and text that read against depictions in the novel. The hypermedia representational tools provided an opportunity for students to explore their own identities and communities and to juxtapose images and texts based in ideologies that contested those attributed to Proulx through her text.

One reason that the Newfoundland students adopted a more critical stance than the Pennsylvania students was that they framed their representing and contextualizing in terms of the issue of Proulx's misrepresentation of their own cultural world. When critical literacy practices emerge from authoring hypermedia in response to literature, the exposure, exploration, and juxtaposition of one's own life experiences to offer contrasting meanings is always present (Myers, Hammett, & McKillop, 2000).

Knowledge Construction in the Classroom Through Hypermedia

In this pedagogical frame, students author hypermedia to construct knowledge about the world or alternative perspectives about different phenomena.

Poetic devices knowledge base. McKillop (McKillop & Myers, 1999) taught seventh graders to use StorySpace™ to build hypermedia knowledge bases in which students combined original poems, images, and QuickTime movies (using Adobe Premiere) to explain the various literacy devices used in poetry. While the analysis of the multimedia pages and hypertext links found many media connections functioning as simple iconic illustrations of ideas in poems (e.g., the picture of a bird because the poem mentions a bird), some instances of critical thinking occurred when students juxtaposed texts to generate contested meanings. One of the best examples involves the juxtaposition of a student's poem originally titled "The Springs" with an excerpt of a nature video of a bear catching and eating fish. By changing the title of the poem to "The Crying Fish" the student intentionally sought to resist the intended meaning of the nature video by making the bear's actions problematic.

Cultural literacy practices. Graduate students at WooSong University, South Korea, authored websites based on their inquiries into cultural literacy practices (http://www.ed.psu.edu/k-12/koreanliteracies). Various small groups explicated how cultural identities, relationships, and values were constructed through symbolic interactions with particular texts. The students examined how the issue of Korean reunification is represented by media texts in juxtaposition to personal opinions; how the use of hand phones and the advertising of cellular services constructs particular values, relationships, and identities; and how texts construct such a high value for Picachu among Korean children. The influx of Japanese animation, environmental water issues, pressures to be a sports hero, and the use of children's literature in schools are among other knowledge bases constructed about Korean literacy practices.

Teen issues. Thirty small groups of ninth graders published a website (http://www.ed.psu.edu/k-12/teenissues) about teen issues around four main themes: fitting in, family and friends, romance, and out in the world. Each small group published webpages with essays and a QuickTime video to explore several aspects of their life experience as teenagers.

American history/culture. Patterson's (2000) middle school students at Portland Middle School, Portland, Michigan, used Storyspace™ to construct hypertexts based on research on U.S. history and culture (http://angelfire.com/mi/patter/america.html). In a joint project with students in Ghana, Africa, the African students wrote the first part of a story about a slave captured in Africa, and the Portland students completed the story with the slave's experience in America. Students then created hypertext narratives with links to information about slavery. Others created biographical webs for Sitting Bull and for Sacagawea—the Native American who accompanied the Lewis and Clark expedition—again with links to historical events. Some students used Native American poetry to create poetry webs with links to information about Native American history and culture. As Patterson noted (http://www.npatterson.net/mid.html), working with Storyspace™ shifted students away from simply rehashing information about persons to understanding people and events as shaped by historical and cultural forces.

Other Views

Hypermedia/Hypertexts

We have illustrated several instances in which hypermedia authoring generates what we define as a form of critical literacy. We are less sanguine about the degree to which students will adopt a critical stance in responding to hypermedia/hypertexts produced by others. Students may be so mesmerized or overwhelmed by navigating the many options and paths in these texts that they may focus more on structural cues for activating links than on critically responding to texts (Douglas, 2000; Goldman & Rakestraw, 2000). They may choose only links consistent with their own beliefs and attitudes, mitigating any potential tension between their own and the text's ideological stances. This role of reader as active constructor of texts raised the question for Landow (1997), who asked "WHO controls the text?" (p. 267). In their critique of uses of hypermedia in the classroom, Palumbo and Prater (1993) argued that the creation of alternative links/pathways makes for highly disorienting experiences with users becoming "lost in hyperspace" through "cognitive overload, user disorientation, superficial browsing, and disinterest" (p. 67). Landow (1997) took a different perspective, perceiving the role of disorientation as "pleasurable, even exciting" (p. 117).

In the midst of this debate between advocates of print versus hypermedia, Ryan (1999) was wary of the "either/or" essentializing of oppositions between print texts (e.g., linear, ordered, sequential, having authorial authority and predetermined meaning, hierarchical, logical) and electronic texts (e.g., spatial, decentered, bottom-up, playful, fluid, interactive). She noted that these features can also be applied to both electronic and print text. She expressed concern that hypertext theory has too often resorted to an "End of the Book" rhetoric that doomed to extinction the pleasures and modes of thinking associated with the print medium. This rhetoric has done more to turn off amateurs of literature than to promote electronic textuality (p. 104).

Theorists have also raised questions about how hypermedia expropriates and refashions traditional media. Bolter and Grusin (2000) examined the ways in which new digitalized hypermedia refashion or "re-mediate" more traditional forms of media-television, film, radio, or print texts, creating hybrid mixtures of the old and the new. (See http://www.lcc.gatech.edu/%7Ebolter/remediation/book.html for a summary and video clip about their book.) For example, in the United States a Cable News Network webpage refashions on-the-spot television news coverage by continually updating information, simultaneously providing information on alternative topics, and even engaging users through polling. At the same time, the old media draw from the new media to keep their audiences. Film incorporates computer digitizing to create virtual realities; television news includes computer read-outs and graphics and refers viewers to its own webpages.

A central element of the new digital hypermedia is "hypermediacy," which Bolter and Grusin (2000) defined as a fascination with the media form itself and its immediacy of presentation that evokes an immediate, emotional response. Hypermediacy equates this emotional experience as highly mediated by hypermedia with a sense of reality, raising interesting questions about reality (or virtual reality) and truth.

In an essay about the pedagogical implications of this shift toward hypermedia, Bolter (1998) argued that hypermedia challenges the traditional emphasis in literacy instruction on understanding or producing unified coherent texts based on a definitive single perspective. Drawing from Landow, he called for an alternative focus on teaching a "rhetoric of expectations and arrivals" (p. 10) that helps students understand where certain links may take them and how they should respond to their destination. Given the important role of graphic representations in hypermedia, he posited the need for often marginalized art and video-production instruction to help students respond critically to images.

These portrayals of a hypermedia world suggest the need for major changes in literacy instruction to provide students with a range of tools for interrogating their social worlds. The three pedagogical frames described in this column illustrate how hypermedia authoring invites students to connect their media-rich everyday lives to the print-dominant texts of school learning and, in doing so, to negotiate fuller meanings for all texts in terms of the possible identities, relationships, and values promoted within the literacy/mediacy experience. As students use hypermedia authoring tools to focus and juxtapose particular words, images, symbols, and sounds, they can generate critiques of the ideologies that define their contested meanings and shared social lives. Within such a critical literacy practice, hypermedia authoring constructs the critical consciousness and agency required to transform the texts of our lived and represented world.

Website of the Month

A primary tool employed to construct hypermedia and hypertexts is Storyspace™ (Bolter, Smith, & Joyce, 1990) published by Eastgate. The Eastgate webpage (http://www.eastgate.com) describes various uses of Storyspace™ in the writing classroom as a tool for constructing hypertexts. Storyspace™ allows students to develop and link multimedia material within windows that can include or be embedded in other hierarchical windows. Students can continually view their work from linear, hierarchical, tree, or network perspectives that serve as a tool for defining and revising their intertextual links.

Readers of hypertexts created with Storyspace™ can keep track of the lexia or pages they have visited using the Roadmap feature. Storyspace™ has been easy for middle school and high school students to learn, equally appealing for college students and teachers, and it provides better dynamic organization with a more Web-like presentation than software like Hyperstudio™. Projects can be exported to HTML files for Web publishing. (The PC version of the software, however, does not handle QuickTime video or sound-file embedding as well as the Macintosh version does.) The Eastgate webpage also contains numerous links (under "Courses") to largely college course syllabi describing various uses of hypermedia and hypertext in the classroom.

Glossary

Hypermedia: a combination of hypertext and multimedia that creates interactive experiences with media.

Hypertexts: texts linked together with various navigational tools so that users can select a range of different paths or trails.

Lexia: the different pages linked together in hypertext, triggered by clicking on words or buttons.

Multimedia: music, sound, images, artwork, graphics, or video, for example, incorporated into hypermedia.

REFERENCES

Beach, R., & Myers, J. (2001). *Inquiry-based English instruction: Engaging students in life and literature*. New York: Teachers College Press.

Bolter, J.D. (1998). Hypertext and the question of visual literacy. In D. Reinking, M. McKenna, L. Labbo, & R. Kieffer (Eds.), *Literacy and technology: Transformations in a post-typographic world* (pp. 3–14). Mahwah, NJ: Erlbaum.

Bolter, J.D., & Grusin, R. (2000). *Re-mediation: Understanding new media*. Boston: MIT Press.

Bolter, J.D., Smith, J., & Joyce, M. (1990). *Storyspace*. Cambridge, MA: Eastgate.

Browning, T. (2000). Hypermedia design in the English classroom. In D. Hickey & D. Reiss (Eds.), *Learning literature in an era of change: Innovations in teaching* (pp. 137–151). Sterling, VA: Stylus.

Douglas, J.Y. (2000). *The end of books—Or books without end: Reading interactive narratives*. Ann Arbor, MI: University of Michigan Press.

Edelsky, C. (1999). On critical whole language practices: Why, what, and a bit of how. In C. Edelsky (Ed.), *Making justice our project: Teachers working toward critical whole language practice* (pp. 7–36). Urbana, IL: National Council of Teachers of English.

Goldman, S.R., & Rakestraw, J.A., Jr. (2000). Structural aspects of constructing meaning from text. In M.L. Kamil, P. Mosenthal, P.D Pearson, & R. Barr (Eds.), *Handbook of reading research* (Vol. 3, pp. 311–335). Mahwah, NJ: Erlbaum.

Halio, M.P. (1996). Multimedia narration: Constructing possible worlds. *Computers and Composition, 13*(3), 343–352.

Hammett, R., & Barrell, B. (1999). Resistance and re-representation as reflection. *English Education, 31*(3), 248–254.

Landow, G.P. (1997). *Hypertext 2.0: The convergence of contemporary critical theory and technology*. Baltimore: Johns Hopkins Press.

McKillop, A.M., & Myers, J. (1999). The pedagogical and electronic contexts of composing in hypermedia. In S. DeWitt & K. Strasma (Eds.), *Contexts, intertexts, and hypertexts* (pp. 65–116). Cresskill, NJ: Hampton Press.

Myers, J., Hammett, R., & McKillop, A.M. (1998). Opportunities for critical literacy and pedagogy in student-authored hypermedia. In D. Reinking, M. McKenna, L. Labbo, & R. Kieffer (Eds.), *Literacy and technology: Transformations in a post-typographic world* (pp. 63–78). Mahwah, NJ: Erlbaum.

Myers, J., Hammett, R., & McKillop, A.M. (2000). Connecting, exploring, and exposing the self in hypermedia projects. In M. Gallego & S. Hollingsworth (Eds.), *What counts as literacy: Challenging the school standard* (pp. 85–105). New York: Teachers College Press.

Palumbo, D., & Prater, D. (1993). The role of hypermedia in synthesis writing. *Computers and Composition, 9*(2), 59–70.

Patterson, N. (2000). Weaving a narrative: From teens to string to hypertext. *Voices From the Middle, 7*(3), 41–47.

Ryan, M. (1999). Cyberspace, virtuality, and the text. In M. Ryan (Ed.), *Cyberspace textuality: Computer technology and literary theory* (pp. 78–107). Bloomington, IN: Indiana University Press.

Soetaert, R., & Mottart, A. (1999). Communicating complexity: Content, interaction and media in teaching literature. In M. Kooy, T. Janssen, & K. Watson (Eds.), *Fiction, literature, and media* (pp. 51–59). Amsterdam: Amsterdam University Press.

Guest Authors

Myers teaches English Education in the Department of Curriculum and Instruction at Pennsylvania State University, University Park, USA. Beach teaches English Education in the Department of Curriculum and Instruction at the University of Minnesota in Minneapolis.

Computer Mediation for Learning and Play

Guest Authors William E. Blanton, Melanie W. Greene, Michael Cole

Editor's Message

About 20 years ago, I was fortunate to become acquainted with some people at the Laboratory of Comparative Human Cognition (LCHC), a research unit at The Rockefeller University in New York City. This group, led by Mike Cole, was concerned with a broad range of issues in the general areas of communication, collaboration, activity, literacy, meaning making, and social justice. Soon, I began participating in an e-mail discussion group known as xlchc—the laboratory as extended through computer mediation. This was an early example of the power of the new medium, not only for informational exchanges, but also for building and maintaining a scholarly community.

Later, the LCHC moved to the University of California at San Diego. The electronic discussion forums, now a family of e-mail groups, moved as well, or perhaps I should say, they continued and grew in their cyber homes. Members of the LCHC used the new media not only for their own interactions, but also for their explorations of how learning environments could be enhanced. Eva Ekeblad gives a rich account of this history in her article "Contact, Community and Multilogue: Electronic Communication in the Practice of Scholarship" at http://hem.fyristorg.com/evaek.

A major element of the LCHC work has been the Fifth Dimension, a distributed literacy consortium of after-school enrichment programs. I asked Mike whether some of those working with the Fifth Dimension would share their experiences in a Technology column, and Bill Blanton, Melanie Greene, and Mike agreed to give an account of their work. To get them started, I just asked a few questions. As you'll see, they had plenty of answers.

Original version published November 1999 (updated March 2000) in the *Journal of Adolescent & Adult Literacy*
©1999–2000 International Reading Association

The Fifth Dimension—A Construction Zone for Literacies

Why Might the Fifth Dimension Be a Valuable Intervention in Middle School Settings?

This is an ideal question to begin our discussion. According to the *NAEP 1998 Reading Report Card for the Nation and the States* (Donahue, Voelkl, Campbell, & Mazzeo, 1999), reading achievement has increased for U.S. children in grades 4 and 8 over the last four years. However, closer examination reveals that the increase is limited to subgroups of children. The data show that although 62% and 74% of fourth and eighth graders, respectively, have mastered the knowledge and skills prerequisite for proficient grade-level performance, only 31% and 33% have mastered knowledge and skills necessary for analysis and application in subject matter. Less than 10% of children at these grade levels performed at the advanced level. On another front, many middle grade schools seem to be falling short of meeting the social and emotional needs of young adolescents (Carnegie Council on Adolescent Development, 1989). An often suggested intervention is extracurricular programs, before and after school, that provide remediation or enrichment, supervision, individual attention, and peer interaction. A premier example of such interventions is the Fifth Dimension.

What Is the Fifth Dimension?

As you have probably heard, the Fifth Dimension is a distributed literacy consortium of specially designed after-school enrichment programs that involve cooperation between local community organizations, such as school-based recreation centers, Boys' and Girls' Clubs, and YMCAs and YWCAs, all affiliated with colleges and universities in their communities. Currently Fifth Dimensions are located in the United States, Mexico, Brazil, Sweden, Poland, Russia, and Australia. After a decade of implementation and evaluation studies with a variety of communities and age groups, we believe the Fifth Dimension is a useful intervention for solving many of the cognitive, social, and personal problems confronting young adolescents.

What Would One See in a Fifth Dimension?

In your visit to the Fifth Dimension, you would see children engaged in a variety of activities, including playing computer and board games, drawing, reading stories, interacting with children at other sites through telecommunications, and using a variety of multimedia equipment and software, while working individually or in "ensembles" with other children. More accomplished others, such as university students enrolled in practica, adult volunteers, or high school students assist the younger participants in setting goals, making decisions, and developing strategies to achieve those goals. As a rule, a Fifth Dimension site contains a mix of Macs and PCs at a ratio of one computer for every two or three participants.

To the observer, the Fifth Dimension appears to be a group of kids actively engaged in computer games and other fun activities. In reality, much more is happening. The Fifth Dimension deliberately mixes play, education, peer interaction, and affiliation (Cole, 1996; Nicolopolou & Cole, 1993; Schustack, King, Gallego, & Vasquez, 1994). The make-believe world of the Fifth Dimension changes the way computer and board games are played. For most children, motivation for play and interaction with peers conflict with educational activity. By mixing these activities, we provide a way out of this natural bind for members of the Fifth Dimension.

The heart of the Fifth Dimension is a wooden or cardboard maze divided into 20 "rooms." Each room provides access to two or more kinds of activities. About 75% of the activities use educational software and computer games. Included are telecommunications activities for searching the Internet and tools for computer- and video-mediated conferences. The remaining activities are non-electronic. The software and accompanying task cards, indicating how to use software in the Fifth Dimension, represent its curricular core. Subject matter includes communication skills, math, social studies, health, science, technology, and the arts—all with an emphasis on problem solving. The maze may contain over 120 educational computer games, such as The Amazon Trail, Dino Park Tycoon, Opening Night, and Lego Logo, and board games, such as Battleship and Mastermind.

In the first step, Fifth Dimension participants decide on goals for engaging in activities. These goals are usually to have fun, meet friends, become better in a subject matter area, or become an expert in the Fifth Dimension. Next, children must decide where they will begin their journey in the maze. The task cards accompanying each game or activity help participants get started, specify expected achievements, and provide evidence necessary for obtaining credentials as an expert in the Fifth Dimension. The task cards also provide a variety of obligations that must be completed before moving to the next game, such as writing to others, writing in a personal journal, putting information in a hints book, making a video, or creating artwork representing the strategies used and knowledge gained in the activity. A record of each child's progress is kept in a Journey Log.

By having more than one activity in each room, as well as multiple paths through the maze, children are confronted with choices at every step in their Fifth Dimension activities. They are encouraged to set their own goals, develop their own strategies, and make their own decisions. Children travel through the maze by playing the games in each room to reach different levels of mastery, specified in the task cards. There are three levels of proficiency in each game. The beginning level is very easy—a way to get started. The good and excellent levels require children gradually to extend their problem-solving skills and acquire subject-matter knowledge. The choice of rooms to visit next is related to the level of mastery attained playing a game. As noted earlier, before players move to the next room, an obligation must be completed. Because children are required to complete this obligation, they are constantly confronted with the need to formulate and reflect on what they are doing and to communicate it to others in the Fifth Dimension community.

By the way, at any moment, a mythical prankster, curmudgeon, or wise one may appear as a helper. Names of these pranksters, which vary from site to site, include Wizard, Golem, Proteo, SunWiz, and El Maga. According to cyber legends told in the Fifth Dimension, these jokers appear when adults working with children cannot deal with the problems of operating and maintaining computers, software, and telecommunications networks that unite children in after-school programs around the world.

These mythical entities represent themselves as creators and custodians of the Fifth Dimension: the authors of the Fifth Dimension Constitution, providers of the computers and games, and the mediators of disputes between and among children and adults. Using different cyber pseudonyms, the pranksters communicate with the children on e-mail or engage them in live chats, often with a wild and playful sense of humor. Children write these cyber entities to tell them how they accomplished their tasks and what they learned, as well as to inquire about the pranksters' origins and to engage in playful banter. In return, the cyber entities provide encouragement and praise for the children. Like all cyber pranksters, they are extremely forgetful. As a result, they often neglect their responsibilities and things go wrong. In this role, they are an essential tool in reordering the power relations between adults and children. Adults need not confront children directly because it is the cyber pranksters who have the power to resolve disputes and make binding decisions. The pranksters provide an important element of the Fifth Dimension because they allow the adults to collude with the children and thereby construct a playful world with them. Most important, because technologies are often unreliable and often fail to work, adults can blame the cyber curmudgeons for breakdowns.

When Do the Children Participate?

Participation patterns vary greatly. Children typically visit a Fifth Dimension on a drop-in basis. Some children spend four to six hours per week of their after-school time at the Fifth Dimension, while others may only come once a week for a few hours. Opportunities and constraints vary a lot across locations, seasons, populations, and sites.

At some locations, adults expect the children to participate regularly in the Fifth Dimension and arrange for them to do so, while at other sites children are free to choose if and for how long to participate, with homework, basketball, reading, or other activities as some of their alternatives. Many children enter the Fifth Dimension directly after school or homework sessions and remain there until their parents or school transportation services take them home.

Why Is the Fifth Dimension an After-School Activity?

There is more than one answer to this question. We focus on after-school time for several reasons. First, our research has revealed that parents, schools, and community organizations have a strong desire to increase the amount of time children spend on academic tasks. Second, the changing nature of adult work has brought about significant changes in the organization of family life, making it difficult for adults to provide supervision for their children until 5:00 or 6:00 p.m. Third, after-school and community-based programs are self-supporting or rely on philanthropy. This form of support is usually limited, requiring adults to work for minimum wage or to volunteer their time to supervise large numbers of children. Level of funding and contexts make it difficult to organize and sustain educational programs. The Fifth Dimension provides a way to increase the educational programming of such institutions without substantially increasing operation costs.

Continuing education into the after-school hours is not easy. After school is, traditionally, a time to play and socialize with peers. It is the space between schoolwork and homework. We have accomplished this task by creating the Fifth Dimension as a "construction zone" where participants can engage in socially meaningful play and educational activity. We believe that in activity of this kind they boost their chances of success in school, and in life, by mastering a cultural tool kit that is transportable to communities beyond the walls of the Fifth Dimension.

Seymour Papert (1996) wrote, "Across the world there is a passionate love affair between children and computers" (p. 1). We take advantage of this love affair by arranging for children to learn while playing computer-based games and using telecommunications. Ultimately, we arrange for children to volunteer for a form of play in which they learn perseverance and how to organize their problem-solving skills in collaboration with others.

Here is an answer to a question you did not ask. By now, you are probably curious about the theoretical basis of our project. The Fifth Dimension continues the development of cultural-historical activity theory (CHAT) founded by Lev Vygotsky and his colleagues. From CHAT, we have derived a set of core principles for constituting a Fifth Dimension. We'll cover a few principles that might be of interest to your readers.

One interpretation we make of Vygotsky's work is that the mastery of cultural-historical tools, such as oral and written language, reading, and ways of thinking, appear first on the interpsychological plane (social), and later on the intrapsychological plane (personal) where "knowing" and "knowing how" are transformed. In Vygotsky's terms, the "zone of proximal development," which we interpret as a "zone of proximal education" (ZoPed), accounts for movement between the social plane and the personal plane. The ZoPed is the distance between a child's independent level of performance, say on a reading task, and his potential level of performance on more advanced reading tasks with the guided assistance of a more accomplished other.

As an illustration, a child might enter the Fifth Dimension with limited reading ability and be unable to focus on the meaning of written directions because she must direct attention to graphophonemic cues. However, her motivation to play computer games provides a rich learning resource. When the child engages in game play with a more knowledgeable adult or peer—who provides assistance with word recognition and game-playing strategies—a ZoPed is "coconstructed," and she masters more word-recognition strategies, expanding her word-recognition repertoire. Written directions begin to take on meaning for her at the point at which she understands that she must follow directions to perform well at the game. As she plays more difficult games, often accompanied by more complex directions, new ZoPeds are coconstructed.

Another of Vygotsky's ideas influencing our project is that "thought is completed in the word," or discourse, through communication (Vygotsky, 1987). Words are culturally shared objects. What we culturally share about them are their meanings. Communication with others in joint activity creates a ZoPed for one's thinking. More important, by engaging in the formulation and communication of thought, learning is not confined to one context.

In the Fifth Dimension, when children use telecommunications and multimedia as primary tools to formulate and communicate with others, the interaction leads to secondary tool use; for example, using writing to formulate one's thoughts makes explicit the relations between the key elements of what one knows. This helps one uncover elements thought to be clear that were not and formulate explanations that lead to a heightened level of consciousness about what one knows. In turn, knowledge is given a richer, more deepened structure and, therefore, may be more retrievable in other contexts.

There is considerable debate among reading educators and psychologists about what constitutes appropriate reading instruction. One side argues for explicit instruction in basic skills believed to be requisite for accomplished reading, such as decoding skills. Often the instruction called for is characterized as drill and practice, requiring lower order or bottom-up cognitive processes. The other side counters with holistic instruction, emphasizing meaning and requiring higher order or top-down cognitive processes. Obviously, the mastery of basic skills is essential to literate performance. Obviously, too, the mastery of basic skills must be meaningful to the learner.

Our view is that separating basic skills and meaning is undesirable. Learning activities should emphasize the interaction of both top-down and bottom-up processes (Griffin & Cole, 1987; Laboratory of Comparative Human Cognition, 1989).

Explicit instruction on basic skills is most often found on content and processes "inside" the heads of learners. This focus places a serious limitation on their transportability to other settings, as the history of research on transfer of learning has demonstrated. In contrast, the Fifth Dimension focus is on basic mediated *activity* in social practices "outside" the heads of learners (Padden & Ramsey, 1993). By embedding the mastery of basic skills in goal-oriented activities, children have an opportunity to master robust knowledge structures and skills that mediate the attainment of socially meaningful tasks. In turn, there is an opportunity to index knowledge and skill use to all the meaning-making resources in the context.

In the Fifth Dimension, learning and development are not seen as simply a process of knowledge and skill mastery, but as a way to become a literate person through participation in social practices. Participants in the Fifth Dimension master and appropriate a literacy tool kit, which includes not only skills and knowledge but also ways of knowing. For example, a child may enter the Fifth Dimension with the understanding that writing is nothing more than the laborious task of writing down a copy of what is inside one's head. However, he may have the potential, with the help of others, to grasp a deeper understanding of writing, particularly when a recurring social practice in the Fifth Dimension is to use writing as a tool for formulating, communicating, and reflecting. As more skillful others provide him with assistance in accomplishing writing tasks, he develops a new kind of knowing about writing—writing is used to mediate literate thinking.

What Research and Evaluation Have You Conducted on the Fifth Dimension?

Good question. We think you will find our results interesting. First, our research has demonstrated that students achieve at increasingly higher levels on tasks in which they participate (Nicolopoulou & Cole, 1993) and that they acquire proficiency in using technological tools in the process of attaining personal goals (Schustack et al., 1994). We have also learned that special education students who participate in the Fifth Dimension progress in the same manner as their regular education counterparts, with similar success (Blanton & Zimmerman, 1993).

Second, when Fifth Dimension citizens are compared with their counterparts in control groups, significant effects are found for participation in the Fifth Dimension on measures of near transfer, such as mastery of computer skills and knowledge (Schustack, Strauss, & Worden, 1997); solving math word problems (Mayer et al., 1997); and performing on measures of far transfer, such as statewide measures of reading and math achievement (Blanton, Moorman, Hayes, & Warner, 1997). Other research on following written directions and playing grammar games shows that participation in the Fifth Dimension can have a positive effect on certain aspects of language comprehension (Mayer, Schustack, & Blanton, 1999).

The Fifth Dimension offers its members another chance to work on subjects or concepts that often elude them in educational contexts. For the student who experiences anxiety with subjects in middle school or in other situations, the Fifth Dimension offers an opportunity for safe, supported engagement with problems and principles of logic, math, reading, writing, planning, and reflecting.

We also have demonstrated that the Fifth Dimension supports the acquisition of social competence and prosocial behavior in several deliberate ways. We build a multiple-literacy perspective into the play world. Practicing bilingualism, using computers, giving oral and written accounts of progress, being skilled in communicating, and collaborating with others are incorporated as essential tools for navigating paths to expertise. Even where there is friendly competition, expertise flows easily in different directions in the Fifth Dimension. No one knows everything, and citizens often find out that their own success is measured less by beating the other person at a game than by sharing their mastery of a new skill.

The play world offers numerous opportunities for children, undergraduates, adults, and the pranksters to engage in discussions of rules and norms of behavior (in the world and in the Fifth Dimension). Participants who have been coming to the Fifth Dimension for years are expert at things that baffle the new practicum students or adult volunteers each academic session: how to be a good citizen in the Fifth Dimension, how to move through the maze, how to work the computer, how to master a particular game. Undergraduates draw from their own general life skills and problem-solving experience to help participants coping with life's challenges in and out of the Fifth Dimension while learning the skills that are old hat to the computer-wise children.

Fifth Dimension citizens who experience themselves as nobodies or as outcasts in other social and educational settings become part of an imaginary world that deliberately de-emphasizes gender, ethnic class, and age-based normative cleavages (Gack, 1999). The journey to Fifth Dimension literacy offers enticement and help to escape the pressure to assign and receive labels or to engage in the sorts of activities that reflect and lead to forms of emotional or physical violence.

So there you have it. The middle school years have been referred to as the last best chance to make a difference in the lives of children. There is a critical need for alternative arrangements that meet their educational, social, and emotional needs. The Fifth Dimension is an innovation that meets these needs. Most important, it demonstrates that children will participate in after-school activity that is meaningful to them. In doing so, they master knowledge and skills for accomplishing educational goals, while having fun and interacting with peers in a supervised environment.

What Do I Do if I Want to Develop a Fifth Dimension Site?

We hoped you would ask this question. We have made it easy for you and your readers. All you have to do is log on to our Virtual Fifth Dimension Clearinghouse at http://129.171.53.1/blantonw/5dClhse/clearingh1.html.

Website of the Month

The Fifth Dimension Clearinghouse disseminates information on the Fifth Dimension and its principles to potential adopters, and it offers technical assistance for adoption and installation. The clearinghouse, at http://129.171.53.1/blantonw/5dClhse/clearingh1.html, is organized around five components: (1) diffusion of the Fifth Dimension, (2) Fifth Dimension Tool Kit, (3) Fifth Dimension Virtual Library, (4) technical assistance, and (5) development of Fifth Dimension publications and artifacts.

The Incomplete Guide and Starter Kit for the 5th Dimension CD-ROM is also available from the clearinghouse and provides information to universities, colleges, and communities interested in exploring the adoption of the Fifth Dimension. The CD-ROM presents an overview, video clips of sites in operation, and answers to questions such as What and who is the Fifth Dimension? What does the Fifth Dimension do? How do we do it? Who is using it? What are the results of using it? and How do we get started? One section presents different sites, highlighting both common and unique characteristics and daily routines. Another section shows children engaged in the kinds of interactions the Fifth Dimension promotes. These interactions also provide concrete examples of Fifth Dimension core principles.

REFERENCES

Blanton, W.E., Moorman, G.B., Hayes, B.A., & Warner, M.L. (1997). Effects of participation in the Fifth Dimension on far transfer. *Journal of Educational Computing Research, 16,* 371–396.

Blanton, W.E., & Zimmerman, S.J. (1993). *The effects of participation in a mixed activity system on the achievement of special needs students: A case study.* Paper presented at the annual meeting of the American Educational Research Association, New Orleans, LA.

Carnegie Council on Adolescent Development. (1989). *Turning points: Preparing American youth for the 21st century.* New York: Carnegie Corporation.

Cole, M. (1996). *Cultural psychology: A once and future discipline.* Cambridge, MA: The Belknap Press/Harvard University Press.

Donahue, P.L., Voelkl, K.E., Campbell, J.R., & Mazzeo, J. (1999). *NAEP 1998 reading report card for the nations and the states*. Washington, DC: Government Printing Office.

Gack, V.L. (1999). Mastery of fantasy or fantasies of mastery. In G.M. Smith (Ed.), *On a silver platter: CD-ROMs and the promises of a new technology* (pp. 211–238). New York: New York University Press.

Griffin, P., & Cole, M. (1987). New technologies, basic skills, and the underside of education: What's to be done? In J. Langer (Ed.), *Language literacy and culture: Issues of society and schooling* (pp. 199–231). Norwood, NJ: Ablex.

Laboratory of Comparative Human Cognition (LCHC). (1989). Kids and computers: A positive vision of the future. *Harvard Educational Review, 59*, 73–86.

Mayer, R.E., Quilici, J., Moreno, R., Duran, R., Woodbridge, S., Simon, R., Sanchez, D., & Lavezzo, A. (1997). Cognitive consequences of participation in a "Fifth Dimension" after-school computer club. *Journal of Educational Computing Research, 16*, 353–369.

Mayer, R.E., Schustack, M.W., & Blanton, W.E. (1999). What do children learn from using computers in an informal, collaborative setting? *Educational Technology, 39*(2), 27–31.

Nicolopoulou, A., & Cole, M. (1993). Generation and transmission of shared knowledge in the culture of collaborative learning: The Fifth Dimension, its play-world, and its institutional contexts. In E.A. Forman, N. Minick, & C.A. Stone (Eds.), *Contexts for learning: Sociocultural dynamics in children's development* (pp. 283–314). New York: Oxford University Press.

Padden, C., & Ramsey, C. (1993). Deaf culture and literacy. *American Annals of the Deaf, 138*, 86–99.

Papert, S. (1996). *The connected family: Bridging the digital generation gap*. Atlanta, GA: Longstreet Press.

Schustack, M.W., King, C., Gallego, M.A., & Vasquez, O.A. (1994). A computer-oriented after-school activity: Children's learning in the Fifth Dimension and La Clase Magica. In R.M. Lerner & A. Villaurruel (Eds.), *New directions for child development: Environments for socialization and learning* (pp. 35–50). San Francisco: Jossey-Bass.

Schustack, M.W., Strauss, R., & Worden, P.E. (1997). Learning about technology in a non-instructional environment. *Journal of Educational Computing Research, 16*, 337–351.

Vygotsky, L.S. (1987). *Thinking and speech*. New York: Plenum.

Guest Authors

Blanton teaches in the College of Education, Appalachian State University, Boone, North Carolina, USA. Greene also teaches at Appalachian State University, and Cole teaches at the University of California at San Diego in La Jolla, USA.

Education Online:
Learning Anywhere, Any Time

Editor's Message

Now that school is nearly out in most northern hemisphere countries, many students (and teachers) may be counting the days—for when the semester ends and the school doors close, the activity of schooling takes a vacation. We define schooling to be the activity that occurs within a certain space, the classroom, and a certain time, the school day. Despite our strong beliefs about learning beyond school walls and learning throughout life, it is difficult to step away from the equations of (a) learning with school and (b) learning with sitting at a hard classroom desk and staring at a chalkboard.

We have set the center of learning in the classroom, just as surely as the astronomers following Ptolemy placed the center of the solar system within the earth. Today, a heretical group proposes to abolish that placement—to deny the centrality of both the school building and the school calendar—and along the way the textbook and perhaps the teacher, too. These 20th-century Copernicans want to allow the earth to move. They see learning, even fully accredited, formal, certificate-driven learning, to be possible any time and anywhere.

Similar claims have been heard before, first with correspondence courses and external degree programs, later with educational radio and television, videocassettes, teleconferences, and similar media. But the integration and expansion of all these tools through the Internet and the dramatically increased accessibility of digital media should make even longtime skeptics look again at how education may change. Economic forces and new technologies may together bring about a Copernican revolution in the nature of formal education, and there is ample evidence of change already.

Many of these changes will be good, and many not so good. What is clear is that the disinterested position is an illusion. We will all be affected by these changes. We can ignore the decisions that are setting the path for 21st-century education, but they will still be made, more often for reasons of cost expediency or profit than for pedagogical principles. This month's column attempts to raise some of the issues that anyone involved in education today ought to consider.

Original version published May 1999 in the *Journal of Adolescent & Adult Literacy*
©1999 International Reading Association

Is the Center for Learning Shifting?

We put education into a frame, just as an art museum puts its paintings into frames. There is first of all a time frame. Lessons are defined as short time segments, with minilessons even briefer. The day is broken into periods, and school days are defined as specific portions of the week. We specify weeks to compose a semester and define courses or programs in terms of units that break down ultimately into numbers of minutes of study.

Then, there is a space frame. Learning occurs in the classroom, and then later in library carrels or study halls. Specific types of learning occur in certain spaces, such as laboratories or auditoriums. The school building is clearly defined and separate from other structures. Often, there is even a fence around its grounds.

We use other frames as well. Knowledge is typically framed within books, or even within the sole "textbook." The teacher and students are framed within certain roles, as are other participants such as administrators and classroom aides. What we do with what we learn is usually framed as well, perhaps as what's written in a "blue book" or as checkmarks on a multiple-choice quiz.

What would happen if we were to radically alter those frames? Such is the case with online learning today. The virtual school is already a reality; changes are occurring more rapidly than most of us can follow, much less shape. Let's consider just a few of the claims that are being made about these changes and see what they might mean for literacy development and education in general.

Students: Online learning will lead to significant changes in the population that has access to educational resources, especially at the secondary and higher levels. Distance learning has more than a 100-year history. External degrees from open universities are common and well accepted. These programs are particularly attractive to those living in rural areas far removed from centers of higher learning.

The advent of the Internet has now led to an exponential growth in the number of distance course offerings. Where once one could point to a few special cases such as the Open University in the United Kingdom, now virtually every institution of higher education is at least considering online course offerings. As the programs expand, we see the many ways that online education can expand learning opportunities. For many people, who must fit coursework within constraints of family and work, online courses make higher education attainable. Students with disabilities and those who work may all find increased opportunities to learn. One's country, even the language one speaks, may become only a minor barrier to educational access.

Teachers: The role of the teacher will change in dramatic ways. The lecture, already an endangered species in many contexts on pedagogical grounds, may have to be rethought entirely given the emerging technology for high-speed, low-cost delivery of video, or even virtual reality, on demand.

Schooling as an institution: Schools and universities will undergo fundamental reorganizations. The lines between schools, community colleges, technical colleges, universities, museums, nature centers, and workplaces are becoming fuzzy. As more courses are offered online, students will find it easier to continue full-time work while studying. There will be less need for the local college in each community or region. How many institutions of higher learning will survive? One-half of those in operation today? One-tenth? Will students even continue to study through public institutions, or will they turn to corporations or new organizations for coursework?

Commercialization: The technological revolution in the workplace is leading to an increased integration of schooling and work. Moreover, just to use the Internet is to enter into the commercial world. Online education is both a reflection of and a stimulus for a blurring of the lines between students as learners, workers, and consumers. For example, ZapMe! Corporation now offers schools (8,000 applications already) a package deal: a network server, a satellite dish, a laser printer, 15 networked personal computers with 17" monitors, software, a customized Web browser, e-mail and webpage accounts for students, and an educational website. The price? Schools agree to use the computer lab four hours a day and let students see the advertisements that pay for the equipment. Moreover, they agree to let ZapMe! collect aggregate data on student Web use and viewing preferences.

Curriculum: The nature of what is to be learned will also undoubtedly change. As schooling is tied more to work we will see the benefit of learning that can be used directly in careers. On the other hand, we risk diminishing the many other goals of education, such as promoting a common understanding, developing capable citizens, and enlarging the individual's capacity to appreciate and contribute to the larger culture.

As we think about all these changes, an interesting irony takes shape. The movement promoting learning anywhere and any time builds in part on our recognition that learning in life is much more than what occurs in the confines of a classroom or a designated time period for a class. Students graduating from a university often describe opportunities to learn from other students and informal learning experiences derived from the environment of the university as being even more important than their formal coursework.

This acknowledgment of life learning is part of what we think about when we respond positively to the rhetoric about learning beyond the walls of the classroom. And yet, the movement to online learning often means that formal education is then reduced to navigating courses divorced from any context of a social institution beyond that provided by an electronic community with limited functions. The concept of learning freed from the constraints of time and space is thus curiously reduced to learning confined within a new frame of asynchronous communication, without the serendipitous experiences that many of us most value. Despite the implicit claims to the contrary of traditional face-to-face education, its greatest contribution may be in what it affords, rather than what it delivers. The new frame may deliver just as well, but in so doing it excludes the anywhere, any time learning that characterizes much of the overall traditional experience.

Websites of the Month

The Globewide Network Academy at http://www.gnacademy.org has numerous annotated resource links for learners from preschool age through graduate school, as well as one of the most extensive course catalogs for distance learning. It lists more than 15,000 distance courses and 1,500 programs. This impressive array depends on submissions from course instructors and program directors. Thus, it includes online courses about South Africa from Spectrum Virtual University, Central Michigan University, and the University of Southern Colorado, but not the extensive set of course offerings from the University of South Africa itself.

Spectrum Virtual University at http://vu.org emerged from the free clinic movement in the 1960s, when that movement established counseling centers, "safe houses" for teen runaways, and drug education workshops. With the advent of affordable desktop computers, Spectrum began to offer free online courses. It is now one of the largest online learning communities; more than half a million people from 128 countries have attended its online classes.

The University of South Africa, also known as Unisa, at http://www.unisa.ac.za is the largest university in South Africa. In 1946, it pioneered tertiary distance education, and continues that now using the Internet. There are approximately 130,000 registered Unisa students all over the world.

The Open University at http://www.open.ac.uk is Great Britain's largest teaching institution, offering distance courses since 1971. Its videos and course modules are used worldwide. The OU image of virtual study offers an intriguing vision of what learning spaces could be, revealing both exciting possibilities and inherent limitations of digital technologies.

The Peterson's online guide has information about distance education programs at secondary and tertiary levels at http://www.petersons.com/distancelearning. About 100 colleges and universities in the United States are featured with in-depth descriptions of their online learning programs.

Yahoo has an excellent set of links to online learning off its education page at http://dir.yahoo.com/Education/Distance_Learning.

Online training is a rapidly growing area, but many sites are inaccessible, hidden behind corporate firewalls. Nevertheless, various resources are starting to appear in more public arenas. The Training & Development Community Centre at http://www.tcm.com/trdev has an excellent set of links and information about online training. Other sites offer a wide range of online computer classes and tutorials.

The Virtual High School at http://www.vhs.ucsc.edu describes an initiative in California to create an online, fully accredited high school. It has a virtual tour of the campus and a set of detailed annotations at http://www.vhs.ucsc.edu/vhs/hotlinks.htm on education sites supporting Internet-based learning.

The VHS is linked to the California Virtual University at http://www.cvc.edu, which ties together the online and distance education offerings of colleges and universities in California.

Glossary

Asynchronous communication: the exchange of messages in a medium that does not require the simultaneous presence of the sender and the receiver. By this definition, ordinary postal mail qualifies as asynchronous communication, but the term usually refers to asynchronous electronic communication, such as e-mail.

Distance learning: Distance education provides a unique opportunity for those who wish to study but cannot attend residential institutions because of personal circumstances or occupational obligations. The term was once synonymous with "correspondence course," and later with educational television, but has increasingly been used to refer to learning through an array of communication technologies, including video, teleconferences, e-mail, and the World Wide Web. As these tools have emerged as integral components of on-campus courses, distance (i.e., the physical location of the student with respect to the class) has become an increasingly peripheral factor. Thus, the concept of distance learning may fade away as its features are incorporated in learning in general.

Frequently Asked Question (FAQ): Many websites now include a list of questions that users commonly ask along with the answers that have been the most helpful. The compilation of questions and responses has thus become a new genre of collaborative writing.

Firewall: a network security system that allows a company, government, or other organization to keep its internal network files separate from the larger Internet community.

Sociotechnical system: a system comprising human activity, spaces, artifacts, tools, and communications media.

Synchronous communication: the exchange of messages in a medium that requires the simultaneous presence of the sender and the receiver (e.g., in an electronic chat system). The line between synchronous and asynchronous is a function of the sociotechnical system, not just the technologies per se. For example, one could use e-mail in a chat-like, synchronous fashion by requiring the "discussants" to be online at the same time.

Extending Literacy Through Participation in New Technologies

Guest Coauthors Umesh Thakkar, Maureen P. Hogan, Jo Williamson

Editor's Message

Literacy has always been an embodied, material act. Among other things, this means that it shapes and is shaped by its technologies. Today, we see changes in literacy practices as people gain access to new ways of communicating and making meaning. These changes raise many questions: How can we prepare students to participate in new literacies even as they are redefined by each new technological development? How can we build and sustain environments that promote the development of these new literacies?

One aspect of the new literacies is that it is easier now to produce, manipulate, and transmit images. In the past, many texts—memos, letters, reports—were created without pictures. The inclusion of images in children's literature or textbooks was often a major production. Today, images are routinely added to documents created using computers, including webpages and now e-mail messages. A related example is the ways that reading and writing can be more easily integrated with the use of online databases and interactive software.

This month, Umesh Thakkar, Maureen Hogan, Jo Williamson, and I look at a cross-curriculum innovation in which students engage in reading, writing, problem solving, interacting with simulations and databases, and performing various hands-on activities. A seemingly narrow focus on chicken eggs leads students to explore a broad array of questions in embryology, evolution, agriculture, economics, mathematics, and literature. The project provides students with the opportunity to participate in many of the new literacies. At the same time, teachers learn new skills as they use these same tools and participate with other teachers in a community of inquiry. Viewed retrospectively, the project also gives insights to how curriculum innovations can be implemented and sustained: What aspects of it can be scaled up? How can it continue beyond the initial excitement? What are the benefits and costs in creating a comprehensive learning environment?

We are especially indebted to our inservice and preservice teacher participants for their work as true collaborators and to all our colleagues who generously gave us their time and efforts on this project.

Original version published November 2001 in the *Journal of Adolescent & Adult Literacy*
©2001 International Reading Association

Inquiry Learning and Teaching With Chickscope

Because of the historical separation of disciplines in U.S. schools, K–12 science, mathematics, and technology reform programs might not be instantly associated with adolescent and adult literacy issues. However, the following description of one such project will illustrate how—in partnership—teachers, researchers, and practicing professionals are beginning to structure more authentic contexts to support students' literacy practices. In the Chickscope project, participants form a community of practice around common interests. Their interactions provide an opportunity to observe how the interplay of human activity and cultural tools, such as emerging technologies, influence the ever-changing definition of what it means to be literate. Through such activity, students and adults are immersed in the process of defining problems, answering questions, and communicating with others. During their collaborative inquiry, participants contextualize new tools and construct ways of talking, acting, and thinking that serve their purposes. As their work progresses and others move in and out of their community, their literacy practices evolve. Some practices are sustained and shared with others, while some fall out of use. In such situations, students not only practice literacy skills necessary for the future, but they also experience how language mediates meaningful and immediate tasks.

What Is Chickscope?

The Chickscope project allows students and teachers to study chicken embryo development using a variety of educational resources such as inquiry-based curriculum materials, interactive modules on egg mathematics, image processing, and a remote controlled magnetic resonance imaging (MRI) instrument. The project, an educational innovation of the World Wide Laboratory (WWL), was initiated by Clint Potter of the Beckman Institute for Advanced Science and Technology at the University of Illinois at Urbana-Champaign, USA. Potter collaborated with educators and researchers from several university departments. Using a standard Web browser, researchers in any location and at any time can access the latest scientific instruments without having to travel to a remote site or invest in the hardware. Accordingly, the Web becomes a laboratory—a WWL—for long-distance, interactive imaging, and scientific experimentation.

From laboratory to pilot implementation. The Chickscope project was initiated in the spring of 1996 to enable students and teachers in 10 classrooms ranging from kindergarten to high school (including an after-school science club and an out-of-state home school) to access and control the MRI system to study the maturation of a chicken embryo during its 21-day development. Classrooms were selected on the basis of the teachers' interest in the project, plans for integrating it with their curriculum, and access to the Internet from their classrooms. Prior to the start of the project, a training day was held at the university for teachers to familiarize themselves with project content and resources, as well as to receive materials such as classroom incubators. The project objectives were twofold: (1) to understand the impact of using remote scientific instrumentation in the classroom in light of then-current education reform initiatives recommending the use of the Internet for learning, teaching, and research (e.g., Hunter, 1995) and (2) to further develop a human and technological infrastructure for the MRI system for scientists. It was reasoned that if kindergartners could use the system easily, then so could busy scientists.

Using computers in their classrooms with access to the Internet, students and teachers were able to log in to the computers at the university, manipulate experimental conditions, and then view resulting MR images of a chicken embryo in real time. (See http://chickscope.beckman.uiuc.edu for a review of the project.) Researchers at the university answered students' questions about the images they acquired and about related issues (e.g., Why is the MR image black and white?). An evaluation report documented that Chickscope was successful in immersing about 210 students, 9 teachers, and 15 undergraduate students (including three preservice teachers) in a scientific community (Bruce et al., 1997). Students and teachers learned much about how to collect and analyze data, how to ask questions, and how to communicate their findings with others (Mason-Fossum & Thakkar, 1997). That is, Chickscope gave classrooms a human and technological infrastructure that is usually reserved for scientists. As a seventh-grade science teacher at one middle school in Urbana, Illinois, said,

> My students gained knowledge about embryonic development and MRI. They learned new skills in using the World Wide Web and e-mail. My students also felt as though they were a community of learners playing an integral role in a project. They felt like respected people who were given control of an expensive machine. This control of their learning in turn provides motivation and interest towards learning science.

The Chickscope project as initially conceived was not sustainable because of the large number of human and technological resources needed to support a small number of classrooms. Since the completion of the project, there have been continuing inquiries from around the world asking if the project would be repeated and requesting access to the resources and expertise.

From pilot to widespread implementation. To address growing interest in the project, we initiated Illinois Chickscope—a professional development program for K–12 teachers from east-central Illinois interested in integrating the Chickscope project with their curriculum. The Illinois Chickscope program began in the fall of 1997 with the introduction of the project to 57 preservice teachers (in two concurrent science methods courses—one taught by Chip Bruce) through a month-long unit on chicken embryo development. These teachers then took their new pedagogical knowledge into their student teaching. Over the next year, there were 11 all-day inservice sessions. Each session included interactive discussions and hands-on and computer-based activities related to chicken embryology, egg mathematics, and MR imaging. The Illinois Chickscope teachers shared the work they did during the summer with the new group of preservice teachers in the fall of 1998.

Thirty-two teachers from 15 schools collaborated with preservice teachers, graduate students, and faculty and staff from different departments to develop inquiry-based curriculum activities (Bruce, Thakkar, & Hogan, 1999). Thus grew a community of teachers—inservice and preservice—and scientists in a variety of disciplines. The project promoted an integrated understanding of science and mathematics and facilitated new ways of using the Internet for learning, teaching, and research.

The program continued in a similar way in the second year with another group of 23 teachers. This group included a high school teacher taking leave for a year to finish his graduate coursework as well as two preservice teachers who wanted to participate in all program activities. Eleven teachers in this group were continuing from the first year of the program, and they served as mentors to new teachers, especially those from their schools. For example, a learning disabilities teacher from an Urbana elementary school was the only teacher from her school in the program's first year. In the second year, she led a team of two teachers and a preservice teacher from her school on the Chickscope project. In a statement about participating again, she wrote,

Since I am familiar with the rich resources on the Chickscope page, I envision helping the classrooms to access appropriate materials. Teachers on the team identified technology as an area that they wish to have support. I have conducted several technology inservice opportunities for our staff and would collaborate with the participants as they begin using online resources in their classrooms related to this project. I see myself as a facilitator supporting these classroom teachers and student teacher and will act as a resource for their classrooms.

The levels taught by these four teachers ranged from kindergarten to fifth grade. In their joint statement about integrating Chickscope with their classroom curriculum, the teachers wrote as follows:

One of our school's goals is to integrate technology with the curriculum. Chickscope provides classrooms access to the MRI database and the embryology images to support the hands-on learning involved with hatching chicken eggs.

1. Classrooms would access the embryology page each day during the 21-day incubation and allow students to "see" inside the egg the changes that are occurring. This pairs hands-on experience with technology, allowing students to experience information that would not be available in any other way.

2. One idea is to have upper-grade students from the resource room act as mentors for students in the kindergarten and first-grade classrooms. During the computer lab time, the mentors could show students some Chickscope online features that support the chick hatching experience.

The students would be able to access information developed by scientists, mathematicians, or educators and have opportunities to ask questions of the project scientists. Students will (a) seek answers to their inquiry-based questions—visit the Roost for answers from University scientists; (b) explore online activities—complete symmetry activities on the Chickscope math pages; (c) explore the Inquiry Page for both fiction and nonfiction literature on chickens and eggs; and (d) compare egg sizes of various birds or other egg-laying animals.

The teachers also created webpages illustrating the Chickscope project activities. Through these pages, their students made predictions and collected data, wrote about egg development and chickens, and drew pictures based on their observations.

The classroom experiences imply that Chickscope not only provided a rich, innovative technological environment, but also extended literacy practices across the content areas. For example, in order to carry out the project, students needed to learn new vocabulary (e.g., *magnetic resonance imaging*, *germ spot*, *remote access*) and communicate what they found out with others, both orally and in written texts—sometimes electronically, sometimes not. They also read both fiction and nonfiction texts to complement and expand their learning. Through their drawings and image accessing, they also used visual literacy. All in all, this was a full multimedia literacy experience within a burgeoning scientific community.

Challenges of Inquiry-Based Learning and Teaching

Many experts and recent U.S. reports concur that inquiry-based projects successfully facilitate learning. One considered "peer Inquiry Groups" as a valuable professional resource for teachers (National Commission on Mathematics and Science Teaching, 2000), which can be envisioned as communities of learning. Another report on technology and inquiry has suggested that inquiry-based instruction "allows students [and teachers] to engage in practices of scientists and to construct their own scientific knowledge through investigation rather than memorization" (Linn, Slotta, & Baumgartner, 2000, p. 2). Yet another report has called for an emphasis on inquiry in teaching and learning in classrooms across K–12 (National Research Council, 2000). However, getting teachers interested and familiar with inquiry and inquiry-based learning and teaching, and providing support for them, can be challenging.

Illinois Chickscope attempts to offer a best practice professional development program model for inquiry-based learning and teaching with emerging technologies. During the inservice sessions, the teachers focused on a broad question: How do we build a community for inquiry learning? Each day during the summer inservice we began with an inquiry question to guide the discussion as well as design and development of teacher-driven curriculum materials. The questions included the following:

- How do we get students to engage in inquiry?
- How do we ensure that *all* students are involved in inquiry activities?
- How do teachers link to other teachers and student teachers to facilitate inquiry learning and teaching?
- What are roles for scientists in supporting inquiry in classrooms?
- How can teachers study their own inquiry practice and share what they learn with others?

These questions served to connect theory and practice. For instance, a working definition of inquiry may be as follows:

> Inquiry is one way of making sense out of what we experience.... Inquiry teaching is putting learners into situations in which they must engage in the intellectual operations that constitute inquiry. It requires learners to make their own meaning out of what they experience. (Beyer, 1971, p. 6)

Illinois Chickscope teachers seem to have different definitions yet some of the same general concepts. To one group of middle and high school teachers, inquiry learning refers to a "process to stimulate students' critical thinking skills in which the teacher serves as a facilitator. It helps to encourage a desire for learning, and problem solving." Teachers also noted that implementing inquiry-based learning was often a struggle because of institutional and scheduling constraints and overemphasis on behavioral management.

Despite these challenges, a sustained, scalable scientific discourse community emerged. During the two years of Illinois Chickscope, around 42 teachers from 17 schools, 150 preservice teachers, and 2,000 students became involved with the project. (Between 1996 and 1999, around 49 teachers from 24 schools have been involved with Chickscope.) In addition, several teachers involved their colleagues (such as librarians and technology coordinators), other classroom teachers, and their students' parents in their projects.

Inquiry Page Collaboratory

One outcome of the project has been the Inquiry Page, a collaboratory for curriculum development to support inquiry-based learning and teaching (Bruce, 2001). The website started in part because the teachers wanted to share their ongoing development of their inquiry units with one another and with the program staff. Each such inquiry unit starts with a guiding question and provides a space for activities of investigation, creation, discussion, and reflection. (To review teacher-created units, please search for Chickscope units on the Inquiry Page.) The Inquiry Page allows teachers (and students) to create their units using a Web-based inquiry unit generator. In addition, if a teacher wants to adapt an existing Chickscope unit, she or he can easily do this by using the Inquiry Page's spin-off feature.

The website has been instrumental in sustaining the community for inquiry learning among the program participants—preservice and inservice teachers across K–12 and teaching different subject areas, such as arts, mathematics, science, social studies, and technology; graduate and undergraduate students from different disciplines, such as curriculum and instruction, computer science, and mathematics education; and program staff with a diverse expertise, such as chicken embryology, egg mathematics, inquiry learning, and MR imaging. The Inquiry Page provides yet another way to promote literacy practices across content areas and extend the discourse community.

Challenges of Scalability and Sustainability

Studies of systemic change usually identify the following principles: (a) fundamental change takes time, (b) collegiality and cooperation are essential, (c) professional development has much in common with effective teaching, (d) there are many ways to learn and teach, and (e) the system needs to change if the individuals within are to have the room to make changes themselves (e.g., Loucks-Horsley, 1997).

Principles such as these were confirmed for us in the initial and continuing evaluation of Chickscope. The infrastructure for change was part and parcel of improving mathematics and science instruction. In one sense the infrastructure was necessary to bring about changes, and in another a new infrastructure was the major change itself. One piece of evidence for this impact is that teachers and schools that participated in Chickscope through the initial project or through the Illinois Chickscope program are continuing to use the project in different ways in their classrooms while supporting literacy practices. In addition, teachers from across the United States are contacting the program staff regularly about getting involved in the project and using its resources. One such person, a science teacher from a middle school in Texas City, Texas, wrote this e-mail:

> Hello Chickscope team,
>
> [I] would like a chance to work with Chickscope. We learned of your site from Bugscope, which my students thoroughly enjoyed working with. If it is possible for my students to work with Chickscope, could we hatch ducks in place of chickens?

This teacher later would invite people, via her homepage, to join her class during the hatching of chickens. For example, she sent Chip Bruce her URL and said, "We have the webcam ready, and you can see a demo on March 26 and 27. Find on my page where it says Live Presentations, and there you are. We plan to hatch baby chicks after Easter."

The project has expanded to other counties in Illinois, to schools across the United States, and even worldwide. A partial explanation for the sustained enthusiasm is that teachers at all levels see how Chickscope could promote an integrated understanding in different subjects beyond science, mathematics, and technology, to support literacy across the content areas.

Educational Reform and Chickscope

In writing about scaling educational reforms, Songer (2000) identified two approaches to scaling: maverick and systemic. The maverick approach suggests adaptation of a project innovation among teachers who are able to customize it to their needs and interests without extensive guidance. One can think of such teachers or administrators as early adopters or self-starters. The systemic approach suggests adaptation of a project innovation by using the local context to shape it (e.g., teachers in a single school district working with school administrators and university personnel to shape the innovation from within). Teachers in the systemic approach can also include self-starters (but that may not necessarily be the case), second-level adopters, and reluctant adopters.

Songer (2000) made a perceptive argument that the word *scaling* is a misnomer in the context of educational reform because it implies a replication of the same project innovation in many new locations. Instead, scaling within the context of systemic reform would occur only through customization and adoption of the project innovation. At the same time, it is important to note the interrelatedness between systemic reform and scalability. Songer's colleagues, Blumenfeld, Fishman, Krajcik, and Marx (2000) rightfully argued that systemic reform implies that the innovation is scalable but a scalable innovation may not be systemic. Our guiding assumption has been that an innovation (e.g., the Chickscope project) is realized, or comes into being, only through use (Bruce & Rubin, 1993). Thus, for the Illinois Chickscope teachers there are various forms of innovation-in-use through districtwide or schoolwide implementations (e.g., Hogan, 2000). This situation, in turn, has helped the project to address the issues relating to scalability and sustainability.

We concur with Songer's (2000) research with maverick populations that it takes a minimum of three years before a comprehensive adaptation of a project innovation occurs in a given classroom. However, we have found through our Chickscope and Illinois Chickscope experiences that such an adaptation of innovation can sometimes occur in less time. For instance, one high school teacher who participated throughout the Chickscope project continually integrates the project resources every academic year with her ninth graders in different ways, such as hatching chickens and using image processing with MR images to learn about the scientific method (e.g., forming a hypothesis that the eye of the chicken embryo grows larger each day and then using National Institute of Health Image to analyze the data and draw conclusions).

Final Thoughts

Our experiences working with Chickscope teachers led us to develop a deeper understanding about integrating technologies with classroom curriculum. For instance, only a few of the teachers were able to incorporate MR images with their classroom activities because this technology appeared narrow with respect to the curriculum and required extra technical resources and expertise. However, every teacher used the chicken incubator, which was highly adaptable to diverse curricular goals. This evidence suggests that flexible, trailing-edge technologies have a greater likelihood of being adopted.

Another important result of the project was that the teachers saw it as a boundary object, a means for them to come together to share ideas and problems. A boundary object is one that is flexible enough to be used in different ways by any teacher, yet stable and tangible enough to maintain a common identity. Star and Griesemer (1989) said such boundary objects allow both autonomy and trade across boundaries. A new technology means different things to a scientist, a technology specialist, a teacher educator, a teacher, a student, or a child, but it offers enough of a fixed reference point to enable new forms of interaction among all these parties.

Website of the Month

Bugscope (http://bugscope.beckman.uiuc.edu) is an educational outreach project that allows students and teachers across K–12 to study insects and other arthropods through remote access and control of an environmental scanning electron microscope from their classroom computers (Thakkar et al., 2000). Bugscope has been featured in a section of *The New York Times* and on National Public Radio's *All Things Considered*. There is no cost for classrooms to participate in the project.

Glossary

Innovation: "an idea, practice, or object that is perceived as new by an individual or another unit of adoption" (Rogers, 1995, p. 11).

Scaling up and scalability: scaling up occurs after an "implementation of a tested prototype program or design expands to many schools" (Datnow, Hubbard, & Mehan, 1998, p. 1). "Scalability means that an innovation can operate in more than a handful of select and resource-rich classrooms or schools" (Blumenfeld et al., 2000, p. 152).

REFERENCES

Beyer, B.K. (1971). *Inquiry in the social studies classroom*. Columbus, OH: Merrill.

Blumenfeld, P., Fishman, B.J., Krajcik, J., Marx, R.W., & Soloway, E. (2000). Creating usable innovations in systemic reform: Scaling up technology-embedded project-based science in urban schools. *Educational Psychologist, 35*, 149–164.

Bruce, B.C. (2001). The Inquiry Page: A collaboratory for curricular innovation. *Learning Technology, 3*(1). Retrieved from http://lttf.ieee.org/learn_tech/issues/january2001

Bruce, B.C., Carragher, B.O., Damon, B.M., Dawson, M.J., Eurell, J.A., Gregory, C.D., Lauterbur, P.C., Marjanovic, M.M., Mason-Fossum, B., Morris, H.D., Potter, C.S., & Thakkar, U. (1997). Chickscope: An interactive MRI classroom curriculum innovation for K–12. *Computers and Education Journal, 29*(2), 73–87.

Bruce, B.C., & Rubin, A. (1993). *Electronic quills: A situated evaluation of using computers for writing in classrooms*. Hillsdale, NJ: Erlbaum.

Bruce, B.C., Thakkar, U., & Hogan, M.P. (1999). Inquiry-based learning and teaching with new technologies. *Spectrum: Journal of the Illinois Science Teachers Association, 25*(2), 16–19.

Datnow, A., Hubbard, L., & Mehan, H. (1998). *Educational reform implementation: A co-constructed process* (Research Rep. No. 5). Center for Research on Education, Diversity, & Excellence, University of California, Santa Cruz. Retrieved from http://www.cal.org/crede/pubs/research/rr5.htm

Hogan, M.P. (2000). Chickscope realized: A situated evaluation of a sixth-grade classroom. *International Journal of Educational Technology, 2*(1). Retrieved from http://www.outreach.uiuc.edu/ijet/v2n1/hogan/index.html

Hunter, B. (1995). Learning and teaching on the Internet: Contributions to educational reform. In B. Kahin & J. Keller (Eds.), *Public access to the Internet* (pp. 85–114). Cambridge, MA: MIT Press.

Linn, M.C., Slotta, J.D., & Baumgartner, E. (2000). *Teaching high school science in the information age: A review of courses and technology for inquiry-based learning*. Santa Monica, CA: Milken Family Foundation. Retrieved from http://www.mff.org

Loucks-Horsley, S. (1997). Teacher change, staff development, and systemic change: Reflections from the eye of a paradigm shift. In S.N. Friel & G.W. Bright (Eds.), *Reflecting on our work: NSF teacher enhancement in K–6 mathematics* (pp. 133–149). Lanham, MD: University Press of America.

Mason-Fossum, B., & Thakkar, U. (1997). Primary school classroom and Chickscope: Studying the egg in the classroom and using the Internet. *Proceedings of the 3rd Conference on Human*

Factors and the Web. Denver, CO: US West Communications. Retrieved from http://www. inquiry.uiuc.edu/partners/chickscope/fossum.php3

National Commission on Mathematics and Science Teaching. (2000). *Before it's too late: A report to the nation*. Jessup, MD: U.S. Department of Education. Retrieved from http:// www.ed.gov/americacounts/glenn

National Research Council. (2000). *Inquiry and the National Science Education Standards*. Washington, DC: National Academy Press. Retrieved from http://books.nap.edu/html/ inquiry_addendum

Rogers, E.M. (1995). *Diffusions of innovations* (4th ed.). New York: Free Press.

Songer, N. (2000, October). Scaling beyond mavericks: What do our experiences tell us? Paper presented at the Workshop on Modeling and Visualization in Teacher Education, Arlington, VA. Retrieved from http://www.eot.org/edgrid/mvw.shtml

Star, S.L., & Griesemer, J.R. (1989). Institutional ecology: "Translations" and boundary objects: Amateurs and professionals in Berkeley's Museum of Vertebrate Zoology, 1907–39. *Social Studies of Science, 19*, 387–420.

Thakkar, U., Carragher, B., Carroll, L., Conway, C., Grosser, B., Kisseberth, N., Potter, C.S., Robinson, S., Sinn-Hanlon, J., Stone, D., & Weber, D. (2000). *Formative evaluation of Bugscope: A sustainable world wide laboratory for K–12*. Educational Resources Information Center. (ERIC Document Reproduction Service No. ED 441 018) Retrieved from http://www.itg.uiuc.edu/publications/techreports/00-008/00-008.pdf

Guest Coauthors

Thakkar is a research scientist at the National Center for Supercomputing Applications and a visiting assistant professor in the Graduate School of Library and Information Science at the University of Illinois at Urbana-Champaign. Hogan teaches at the University of Alaska in Fairbanks, and Williamson is a doctoral student in Curriculum & Instruction at the University of Illinois at Urbana-Champaign.

Case Studies of a Virtual School

Guest Coauthors D. Michelle Hinn, Kevin M. Leander

Editor's Message

Being a young person today means having to live in multiple worlds. As they move between home, school, and peer group, adolescents have to recalibrate their sense of what actions are appropriate, what is valued, and what is known. The conflicting forces represented in the mass media, on the street corner, and in one's immediate realm of rapid physical and social development create familiar difficulties for many young people.

George Gerbner, founder of the Cultural Environment Movement, along with other social critics, has argued that mass media exacerbate these problems. They see the global marketing strategy of television as creating an especially damaging and alienating environment. Others have pointed to video games or online chat rooms as new dangers for young people. At the same time, many educators have seen the learning potential of the Web, multimedia, and simulations.

The contrasting evaluations of new media remind us how little we actually know about what these different environments mean to adolescents, or to any of us, for that matter. What does it mean to develop and to explore social relationships with others in online environments? Can what one learns in a virtual environment apply to the real world? Can we draw a sharp line between real and virtual worlds?

This month, D. Michelle Hinn, Kevin M. Leander, and I explore a unique virtual world, which was created to help educators learn more about teaching adolescents using new technologies. As the project progressed, the simple question "Is this a good way to help students learn?" began to expand into a host of questions about what a simulation is, how to evaluate the use of new media, and how people learn.

The virtual world in question was initially only an object of study for a course for teachers called Evaluation of Information Technologies, which was designed by Michelle, Kevin, and me. But as students began to enter that virtual world and interact with it and within it, they changed it. Soon, it began to take on a life of its own, which we describe here and which we are still attempting to understand.

Original version published October 2001 in the *Journal of Adolescent & Adult Literacy*
©2001 International Reading Association

Learning the Art of Evaluation

What's it like to participate in a virtual world? What can one learn by interacting in a space in which participants are both themselves and constructed online personas? We explored these questions as we brought into being a virtual junior high school, and then were swept along in its ever more real life. Our experiences taught us many things about virtual reality, the use of the Web, and how to evaluate innovations.

Our course, Evaluation of Information Technologies, focused on evaluating technology use in instruction. Although the course was offered through an online master's program designed for educators, a mixture of 26 online master's degree students and 9 on-campus doctoral students were enrolled. The master's students were all practicing K–12 educators working full time while earning their master's degrees in instructional technology. The doctoral students were enrolled as full-time students in either the Writing Studies or the Technologies for Learning Program, now Technology Studies in Education program.

Our approach. The course had been taught once before as an on-campus doctoral seminar. However, because it was now going to be taught in the online master's degree sequence as a required research/evaluation course, one of our many challenges was how to adapt it for an online environment. But perhaps an even bigger challenge was how to make an evaluation methodologies course interesting and, in particular, interesting in an online context.

Key differences between student histories, communities, and interests were evident from the beginning of the course. The 26 master's students enrolled formed a cohort, for which this course was the third common experience in their degree program. Thus, the master's cohort was fairly accustomed to taking courses online. The doctoral students, on the other hand, were not taking this course as part of any particular sequence, and none had ever taken a course offered entirely online. Most of the doctoral students, however, had taken classes that used technology of some sort (such as an electronic mailing list or a Web board).

Why not have two separate sections for the course, such as one online and one on-site? Because of the way that the course emerged. Because the course had been offered once before, it triggered interest among the on-campus students, even though it was originally intended for the online master's cohort. We felt that it would be a particularly interesting challenge to include both groups in an online course.

As a response to the challenges of course enrollment, course contexts, and the processes and content we wished the students to experience, we created an online course community in the form of an evaluation center. We modeled the center after offline evaluation centers such as the Evaluation Center at Western Michigan University, led by James Sanders, and the Center for Instructional Reform and Curriculum Evaluation, led by Bob Stake at the University of Illinois at Urbana-Champaign. Our evaluation center would have its own online newsletter, evaluation teams, and projects that spanned on- and offline worlds. Each student in the course was considered to be a member of the evaluation center, and the course instructors would serve as the center facilitators. When we began the course we did not have a name for the evaluation center, preferring to leave it up to the students in the class. One student came up with CITIES (Central Illinois Technology and Instructional Evaluation Service), and the name stuck. CITIES comprised six teams of five or six students each. Because we wished to diversify the teams as much as possible, we assigned the students to teams. Each team had one or two doctoral students and four or five master's students. Team members represented diverse academic disciplines and professional positions in the schools.

As course instructors, the three of us served as another type of team. In discussions of technology in education we often hear a discourse of efficiency in instruction, in which teaching more students with fewer instructors and instructional time is held up as a value. However, in creating learning contexts and experiences that are experimental, efficiency should not be a goal at the outset. In our case, we put a lot of time into the course. We monitored and interacted very closely with two teams each while keeping one another informed of problems and successes occurring with our teams. We switched teams every few weeks so that we each had a chance to interact closely with all the students.

The center had a guiding theme—the words of Lee Cronbach (1982), who said that "evaluation is an art." As an art, because evaluation is also improvisational when one considers multiple contexts and the variety of stakeholder and client needs, we gave each team the surname of a famous jazz artist (e.g., Louis Armstrong, John Coltrane, Duke Ellington).

The virtual evaluation project. A large part of the course centered around a virtual evaluation project that the evaluation center had undertaken of a simulated U.S. school district given a technology grant by a simulated funding body. In this case study, we created a scenario in which our evaluation center received a request from the National Education Foundation (NEF) to conduct an evaluation of an Illinois school district's use of its funds. The school district receives funds from NEF to implement a Learning With Computer Technologies program. During each section, a different evaluation problem arose that each evaluation team worked to solve.

The purpose of the virtual case study was to allow each evaluation team to explore the intricacies of the evaluation of the use of information technologies in a virtual setting. Each student also worked on an individual real-world evaluation project, and the virtual and real evaluations helped give some richer context for textbook readings, which can otherwise be dry. Why not just have the individuals do such real-world evaluations and share them online? A number of different reasons influenced our design. First, the distance between students and instructors and accessibility of real-world evaluation sites was a primary consideration. With all the students online, and most at a fair distance from the home campus, finding a "live" project for the entire class to work on would have been extremely difficult. We also wanted to have a group project in the course as well as individual projects so that we could provide a type of in-class activity for the online course. We wanted something in common that they were all working on, something that we could all learn from. Ethical concerns were also at play: We wanted to ensure that we had prepared students for the ethical issues in a safe arena. Thus, we created a simulation of a virtual school, one that perhaps seemed more real in the end than it had in the beginning.

The scenario. The National Education Foundation is very similar to other government-supported agencies and departments in the United States, like the National Science Foundation and the Department of Education, and it existed solely in our imagination. Or did it? The students had a unique opportunity to interact with one of the representatives of the NEF. We kicked off the online course with one face-to-face meeting before going fully online. This was so that we could introduce the master's cohort to the on-campus doctoral students and explain the design of the course. During this live session, the NEF representative spoke to the members of the CITIES evaluation center, explaining what their charge was, and took questions. The NEF representative was played, in most people's opinions, very accurately in his governmental agency vagueness. The representative was played by a professor at the university who had no prior experience with any of the students in the class. An interesting side note is that, while we thought originally that we had created the NEF, we found out that life sometimes does follow fiction when we received an announcement from the "real" National Education Foundation.

The Wynne County Unified School District won a large grant from the National Education Foundation to start a Learning With Computer Technologies program in their county. Wildwood Junior High School was chosen as the main site for the evaluation, as it received the bulk of the funding. WJHS is a flagship school in the district, and its motto is "Without the students, we wouldn't be here." Sports play a big role at WJHS, and the principal is very supportive of the sports programs there. Because of his love of athletics, the principal takes a "team" attitude in his leadership of the school and tries to remain as accessible as possible to all the students and parents, stating on his homepage that "there's a PAL in principal." A visitor to the school principal's homepage will see an invitation to coffee as well as links to his favorite sports teams.

The staff at Wildwood worked extremely hard on their website, and it provided one of the main opportunities that the evaluation center members had for data collection. As the center members looked for more information when they began to focus their evaluations, the website often grew. The staff at Wildwood had not thought of including quite a bit of information on their website, and so for them the evaluation process was quite a learning experience and helped them communicate better with one another and the public through their Web resources.

Behind the scenes. Eighteen "live" volunteers at multiple campuses served as role-players (some playing multiple parts) for numerous faculty and staff of Wynne County and Wildwood Junior High School. The evaluation center members had access to the "e-mail addresses" of the Wynne County superintendent, the county technology director, and the county's evaluation specialist. At WJHS, the evaluators had access to the principal, the vice principal, 11 teachers, the school technology coordinator, two members of the PTA, and two students. In addition to being available via e-mail, several of the Wynne County and WJHS staff members were available to chat with the evaluation center members live through a synchronous text-based chat tool. This came about later as some teams wanted to "visit" Wildwood.

Wynne County and WJHS had "real" websites with which students could interact and from which they could try to glean as much information as possible. We didn't want to provide all information on the website because we wanted to encourage each team to interact with the role-players. Not only that, but we didn't even begin to know what "all information" was. We couldn't predict the directions teams would take in their evaluations. When one team would want to see the district's "report card" we would need to provide one. Thus the students helped create the reality of the simulation. We set the stage, and from then on the play became very improvisational. The role-players gave the simulation a new reality, and we no longer controlled it—just like in the real world.

In the beginning, the teams were uncertain about how to go about "talking" with the staff at Wildwood. So one person in one team contacted everyone at Wildwood with "Hi, I'm part of the evaluation team. I love your webpage" (paraphrasing). Another team responded with "I am a member of ____ evaluation team, and we are now ready to initiate electronic communication" (a survey was attached). In turn, the role-players either did not return e-mail at all (to the "Hi" team), and some only curtly responded to the survey (if at all). Both teams wondered why. So, in our commentaries for that week for the evaluation team members, we mentioned that the principal had called us and raised some concerns about the evaluation. Several teachers did not know the scope of the evaluation or even who these people were. Thus, WJHS school personnel were a bit unnerved by the survey without a proper introduction and the barrage of other e-mail. As instructors, we used this breakdown in communication as an occasion (a) to talk about how one initiates dialogue at an evaluation site and (b) to reconsider how real the people might be with whom the students were communicating.

Problems and Successes

Teams. It tended to be the best of times and the worst of times when it came to how team members interacted with one another and with the simulation. We had one team that needed a lot of encouragement and hand-holding in order for members to communicate with one another. On the other hand, members of another team worked amazingly well together, but there was a definite "Let's get things done as efficiently as possible" approach. Although its work was of very high quality, this team didn't spend a lot of time wrangling over process issues, nor did its members spend much time worrying about the authenticity of the simulation. As well as this team functioned to produce end results, perhaps it was the teams whose members didn't work as well together that were the most interesting to observe. Their members were often the most creative with respect to evaluation approaches. These teams questioned the simulation and fought against it. But they also often had the most creative solutions and asked the most probing questions, pushing the inquiry further than the best-of-times group.

Disorderly resources and perspectives. The simulation was constructed with a group of role-players who in many cases did not know one another and had different conceptions of WJHS, evaluation, and the course context and goals. The WJHS website was also developed by several different individuals with different perspectives on what the school might be, and these individuals drew from texts and images from the Web and other disparate sources. Moreover, the course was taught by three instructors who, while in constant communication with one another, had many different interactions going with different course members (in their own roles as both instructors and role-players). For course members, the experience of doing the evaluation could often be frustrating due to these disorderly resources and perspectives. WJHS, the Wynne County School District, the NEF, and even the course itself did not make for an entity with a clear perspective. Rather, the simulation created a type of deliberate confusion and set of contradictions that students were directed to puzzle over. For some students, this type of work was particularly challenging and even frustrating; they believed the experience needed to be more clear and manageable. We understand this issue as related to the histories of the students in other, more "tidy" educational experiences and also as a critical response to our own expectations for their creation of order from a disorderly set of texts and experiences.

At the same time, as an indication of success in the project, we believe that a measure of disorder and a number of conflicting perspectives among role-players and Web texts were resources for the simulation. In school or other organizational contexts, participants have limited knowledge of other participants, have widely different perspectives on so-called common goals, and have limited knowledge of others' perspectives and activity. These aspects were in fact built in by the designed disorder of the simulation. A simulation with a well-bounded design team, led by a hierarchical management that had complete knowledge of its own product, would have developed a very different simulation with its own set of strengths, but it would likely not have drawn as strongly on disorder and multiple perspectives.

Authenticity, boundaries, and pleasure. At times, the need for boundaries or sharper distinctions to be made between the virtual and the real emerged from student confusion. For example, when the Wildwood project was first introduced to the class in a face-to-face meeting, one student, showing a great deal of engagement in the activity but also in Wildwood as a location, expressed interest in applying for a job at WJHS. Chip Bruce, who wanted to represent the virtual space by borrowing upon a rhetoric of the "real," while at the same time keeping distinctions clear for course (and even career) purposes, used his own embodied space in the classroom as a response:

> (Chip, standing to one side of the room) Okay, I'm over here. This is Wildwood Junior High. It has a technology program that is funded from the National Education Foundation. This semester, evaluators are coming in to find out how this technology program is going so far.

> (Chip, moving to other side of the room—across the front) Now I'm over here. I'm in the class on the Evaluation of Information Technologies. As far as I know, Wildwood Junior High School and the National Education Foundation only exist on the Web— they're not real places.

Chip used his embodied positioning in the space of the room as a metaphoric means of making clearer distinctions between the various locations of the project. At the same time, he also slightly blurred these locations ("as far as I know"), as the entire project traded to some extent on the meanings in common between the virtual space of Wildwood, real schools, and real human relationships as well as virtual relations between members of the university class and the role-players of the school.

Because WJHS was shaped by many page designers' and role-players' experiences with schools in different parts of the United States, it was hard for some students in the class to buy some of the stories and images related to the school. A few times the instructors received comments such as "This isn't like a school," and we had to respond with "Wildwood isn't like all schools." In the end, however, we received comments such as "You know, we were looking at the websites of other schools in some other states and realized that Wildwood is like other schools in a lot of ways."

The lack of believability was also related to the manner in which the webpages and role-player interactions used humor to play at the boundaries of school life. For example, the school principal, Lee Daniels, was a caricature of a secondary principal whose primary interest was in athletics (having written a master's thesis titled "We're All on Your Team: Supporting Student Athletes in the Classroom.") Many examples of such humorous play existed in the experience, and pushing boundaries of parody in schooling was one of the pleasures of engaging in the simulation for role-players, instructors, and students alike. At the same time, students had to be willing to enter into this play for the simulation to be meaningful to them. Although some students enjoyed and even relished the experience, others seemed to critically distance themselves from it at times as not being "authentic" enough. These positions vis-à-vis the simulation are complex, and we have yet to work them out. One of the complexities, of course, involves understanding not just engaging in simulation, but engaging in simulated "play" as part of school "work," which constructs different relations of power and different consequences for making meaning among instructors, role-players, and students.

Reality of the virtual. A reality of sorts emerged out of the simulation that was not real in the sense that the evaluation teams could go and actually visit WJHS. But there emerged an alternative reality to the simulation, a community of real people doing real things (even if they were simply creating mock-ups) that other real people were evaluating. In some ways, the simulation in the end began to resemble the constant formative nature of most instructional technology projects. As such, the students had to approach the simulation in the same sort of way one might approach a new use of instructional technology. In any evaluation, there exists unknowns. One might go into an evaluation with a set impression of what quality will look like or what the developers say that quality will be and often miss the unexpected, or the unknown. It is important that the unexpected might be something more wonderful (or more terrible) than what was being deliberately sought after in the first place. With the simulation, we were trying to help the students look beyond what they feel is true from their past experiences and look for the unexpected.

Another general manner in which the simulation took on a real life of its own was that, as a set of texts and resources, WJHS and the evaluations of it were created in dialogue with one another. Wildwood was not fixed in advance of an evaluation of it, but responded to the questions asked of it and was created through them. For instance, Lee Daniels, the principal of Wildwood, had not properly prepared budget documents for the evaluators in advance. However, when asked about them, his postponement could be interpreted as his lack of preparation. Several days later the documents appeared and were posted to the website. This dialogic emergence (Holland, Holyoak, Nisbett, & Thagard, 1986) of resources, social contexts, persons, and social practices in the simulation is suggestive of how social life develops across on- and offline worlds.

Final Comments

Information technologies bring in a set of special issues for evaluation (Baker & O'Neil, 1994; Johnston, 1984; Rice, 1984). Among these are technical characteristics of the technologies, including collaborative tools, interface features, and hypertext structures. Additionally, as use scales up, the new media reshape geography through spatially dispersed contexts of use and variations in implementation. Thus, new modes of communication, whose effects modify with use, pose new challenges for understanding collaboration. At the same time, technology-based, collaborative learning projects, such as the one described in this column, typically experience continual revision throughout their implementation, implying that we are effectively engaged in perpetual formative evaluation (Bruce & Rubin, 1993).

Interpretations

Simulacrum and Simulation

Loosely defined, we might term any object or processes of a simulated world as a *simulacrum* (plural, *simulacra*). (*Simulacrum* derives from the Latin *simulare*, meaning to make like or to put on an appearance of.) Simulations make use of all manner of settings, characters, and action, which may strike us as copies of settings, characters, and action in the real world. However, as it turns out, the idea of a simulacrum as a copy of a real-world object is only one means of conceptualizing simulated and real relations. What are other possibilities, and where might they lead as we reconsider the dynamics of simulation? Below, we offer three contrasting perspectives.

1. Pragmatic: Copying reality. A pragmatic perspective is primarily concerned with the practical needs that drive our desire to create simulations. In the case of the Wildwood simulation, a pragmatic perspective would claim that doing an evaluation of an actual junior high school would be too costly or too difficult to coordinate for the course instructors and students. The technology enables one to surmount such practical difficulties and to create something that is very much like, or perhaps intensifies, encounters in real situations. A pragmatic perspective would generally assume that a simulacrum—such as the principal at WJHS—is a copy of something (in this case, a stereotypical principal, or perhaps caricature) in the real world.

2. *Pessimistic: Rupturing with reality*. French social theorist Jean Baudrillard (1983) has written much about simulacra and simulation, and he is perhaps best known for theorizing that in postmodern culture images and texts of all kinds have become separated from any relation to reality; signs no longer represent anything "out there" but merely refer to other signs. A postmodern world in which images no longer bear any relation to reality is termed "hyperreality." Disneyland, a self-perpetuating zone of images of images, copies of copies, is a prime example of hyperreality. The simulacra of Disneyland are cut off from anything real, and yet this rupture is not recognized in contemporary life-as-simulation.

3. *Productive: Appropriating reality*. Like Baudrillard, French theorists Gilles Deleuze (1983) and Felix Guattari (Deleuze & Guattari, 1977) considered the relation of copy to model as a starting point. However, they argued that the relation between simulacrum and model is external and deceptive. In the case of the simulacrum, the process of its production, its inner dynamism, is entirely different from that of its supposed model: Its resemblance to it is merely a surface effect, an illusion (Massumi, 1987). Resemblance in simulation—the ways in which Wildwood looks like the webpage of a junior high school—is only an entrée for considering how reality has been appropriated in the production of the simulacra. In this perspective, the copy/model binary breaks down: Reality cannot be understood apart from the processes of simulation operating behind it, and simulation both draws from and produces new realities.

Other Considerations

Although a pragmatic perspective describes something of our own work in creating Wildwood and the simulated evaluation, it tells us relatively little about the relation of simulated and real worlds as they are experienced by players, or about the unfolding of the simulation as an activity and sociotechnical space. Baudrillard's perspective on simulacra—signs made meaningful primarily in relation to other signs—is helpful in understanding the ways in which Wildwood is produced as a world of images and texts that becomes semi-independent from any "real world" we might nominate. Deleuze and Guattari (1977) prompt us to consider, at a deeper level, how Wildwood appropriates, rearranges, and effectively draws from actual junior high schools and teams of evaluators, but re-creates them in new ways and for new purposes. Copying reality, in this sense, is not the goal of the activity but merely an illusion masking the production of a new educational practice and space.

Website of the Month

Nowhere Road (http://www.nowhereroad.com) is the website of Lloyd Rieber, a professor of instructional technology at the University of Georgia, Athens, USA. The site contains numerous examples of games and simulations for education, including "Nowhere Road—The Game" (where the player assumes the role of a professor who must bike to work "without getting bit, run over, or emotionally scarred for life"), "Space Shuttle Commander" (a simulation designed to introduce Isaac Newton's laws of motion by giving students the role of a commander of a space shuttle), and "SimSchool" (a simulation that examines the philosophical perspectives of objectivism and constructivism and their influence on educational practice). "Nowhere Road" also hosts several papers and electronic texts on building simulations and games for educational settings.

Glossary

Avatar: something in electronic space, often an image but not always, that represents a user in a multiuser situation such as a multiplayer electronic game, simulation, or chat session.

Evaluation: the process of determining the merit, worth, or quality of the object of inquiry.

Role-playing games (RPGs): games in which each player assumes the role of a character (such as a principal or a student, as in the WJHS simulation) who can interact with other characters within the imaginary world of the game.

Virtual reality: in simplest terms, refers to a simulation of either a real or imagined environment or "world." Virtual reality has been used to describe many different activities including online collaboration through text or video, the imagined environments of a game, and three-dimensional representations of lifelike images displayed through technologies such as CAVEs (Cave Automated Virtual Environments).

REFERENCES

Baker, E.L., & O'Neil, H.F. (1994). *Technology assessment in education and training*. Hillsdale, NJ: Erlbaum.

Baudrillard, J. (1983). *Simulations* (P. Foss, P. Patton, & J. Johnston, Trans.). New York: Semiotexte.

Bruce, B.C., & Rubin, A.D. (1993). *Electronic quills: A situated evaluation of using computers for writing in classrooms*. Hillsdale, NJ: Erlbaum.

Cronbach, L. (1982). *Designing evaluations of educational and social programs*. San Francisco: Jossey-Bass.

Deleuze, G. (1983, Winter). Plato and the simulacrum. *October, 27,* 48–56.

Deleuze, G., & Guattari, F. (1977). *Anti-Oedipus* (R. Hurley, M. Seem, & H.R. Lane, Trans.). New York: Viking.

Holland, J.H., Holyoak, K.J., Nisbett, R.E., & Thagard, P.R. (1986). *Induction: Processes of inference, learning, and discovery*. Cambridge, MA: MIT Press.

Johnston, J. (Ed.). (1984). *Evaluating the new information technologies*. Washington, DC: Jossey-Bass.

Massumi, B. (1987). Realer than real: The simulacrum according to Deleuze and Guattari. Retrieved from http://www.anu.edu/HRC/first_and_last/works/realer.htm

Rice, R.E. (1984). Evaluating new media systems. In J. Johnston (Ed.), *Evaluating the new information technologies* (pp. 53–71). Washington, DC: Jossey-Bass.

Guest Coauthors

Hinn is a doctoral candidate in educational psychology at the University of Illinois, Urbana-Champaign. Leander teaches at Peabody College, Vanderbilt University in Nashville, Tennessee, USA.

Community

One theme that recurs throughout this book is that the technical is personal. Computers are not autonomous agents offering us unimagined pleasures or threatening us with misery. They may do either or both of those things, but only as they embody the choices we have made. That is not to say that our consciousness of the possibilities is ever complete, any more than that could be true in other areas. In addition to our choices, the new technologies also embody prejudice, greed, ignorance, division, and unreflective action.

Thus, when we look at technologies, even the most exotic models, we are looking at ourselves. For that reason, our technological situation is inescapable, but that does not mean it is unchangeable. Through processes of dialogue, engaged action, reflection, and critical consciousness, there is at least the hope that we can achieve a deeper or more fully articulated understanding of that technological situation, and hence, of ourselves, and our potential for change. Those processes are inevitably social ones, and it is thus fitting that the last section of the book focuses on the relation of new literacy technologies to community, from the local to the global.

In "Collaboratories: Working Together on the Web," Karen J. Lunsford and I examine new tools being used to facilitate collaboration across time and space. The next column, "How Worldwide Is the Web?" builds on an incident in which I was forced to ask whether my experience of the new literacy technologies bore any semblance to that of an elderly woman living in a remote village in Africa without telephone or electricity. Marc D. Wielansky continues the international theme in his column, "Internationalized Domain Names." Although aspects of his contribution are technical, they highlight an important concept—that we express our social relations through our technologies, in this case whose language counts. In the final column, "Communities for the New Century," Ann Peterson Bishop discusses the role of new literacy technologies in local communities. Systems such as Prairienet help community organizations support individuals within and connect with people and resources around the world.

Collaboratories: Working Together on the Web

Guest Coauthor Karen J. Lunsford

Editor's Message

It is entirely appropriate that this month's column represents a collaboration. Karen Lunsford and I are working together to study how people—scientists, writers, teachers, students—come together to share their expertise, to construct something more than they might have alone, and to learn from one another in the process. As we collaborate, we learn about the process, just as we learn by seeing how others do it.

In their collaborations, people increasingly make use of new information and communication technologies to augment their work. Technologies have always been used to support collaboration: At one time these may have been marks on a log or jottings on paper. More recently, we have seen telephones and e-mail as communication tools for collaboration, along with databases as information tools. Notes taped to the refrigerator door must be one of the most powerful of these collaborative technologies, if one can infer anything from the way such notes are relied on in so many homes and offices.

Today, even more powerful collaboration tools are being developed and explored. These are coming together into suites of tools that help create virtual workspaces. We take here a brief excursion into some of these spaces with the aim of understanding how they may be changing the way people communicate, make meaning, and work together.

Original version published September 2001 in the *Journal of Adolescent & Adult Literacy*
©2001 International Reading Association

Defining a Virtual Workspace—The Call to Collaborate

Within the past decade, attention has been increasingly paid to collaboration in business, research and development, and education. This interest has been driven to a great extent by economics: How might people work together more efficiently to accomplish what no single person could do? In light of a new information-based economy, how might organizations best capture the knowledge created tacitly by their members? How might nations better teach students to become more flexible employees who can move among projects and into new situations quickly? How might new technologies provide more effective ways to collaborate, especially ways to write collaboratively?

Long before these and similar issues surrounding collaboration caught the attention of the general public, they had become critical for scientists: Since World War II, basic research and development projects have proven more and more expensive to conduct. The image of the isolated Dr. Frankenstein in his laboratory, always something of a myth, has now become thoroughly displaced. Today's scientific enterprises often must rely on huge, multinational consortiums. For example, hundreds of high-energy physicists must work together to find massive funding for the super-colliders they need to conduct their experiments (Knorr-Cetina, 1999). Seeking to understand better how such collaborative enterprises work and to promote further collaborations, the U.S. National Science Foundation has recently funded new projects to study and to implement interdisciplinary teams (Hackett, 2000).

More broadly, educational institutions at all levels have begun to focus on collaborative issues. As funds for universities, colleges, and schools have shifted from the public to the private sector, new partnerships between educational institutions and industry have grown. Recently, the Boyer Commission on Educating Undergraduates (1998) called on research universities, particularly humanities departments, to include undergraduates more regularly in meaningful research projects. Speaking to K–12 teachers, Murnane and Levy (1996) have argued that students ought to be taught the "new basic skills" of communication, collaboration, and learning to prepare them for successful careers in this new economy.

In response to these increased calls for collaboration, new technological tools have been developed to promote better communication and the better sharing of data. Several tools have become routine for many Internet users: bulletin boards;

e-mail, with and without attachments; databases, usually with powerful search engines; electronic calendars and schedulers; and PowerPoint slides that can be displayed on the Web. Not only have these tools become common in the workplace, but they are also becoming more available to more students as school districts attempt to close the digital divide.

Yet, even though tools such as these may promote collaboration, they should not be viewed as simple, isolated answers to collaborative issues. Instead, a growing literature suggests that we should view tools and people as constituting complex activity systems that must be better understood if we are to understand collaboration. Distributed and situated cognition theorists such as Cole and Engeström (1993), Hutchins (1995), and Wenger (1998) have examined how collective knowledge is generated through interactions among and between people and the tools they employ. Similarly, Knorr-Cetina (1999), a sociologist of science, has described the *epistemic* (knowledge-building) cultures that form around collaborative, scientific projects. Latour (1996, 1999) has likewise studied how scientists, technologists, and city planners generate tacit assumptions that deeply affect the success of an experimental project. Ethnographers of writing such as Cintron (1997), Flower, Long, and Higgins (2000), Prior (1998), and Spigelman (2000) have focused on the complex engagements between "authors," "readers," and "texts" as people read and write—and they have challenged any single, stable definition of these terms, for the roles are constantly renegotiated. A single collaborative tool is always part of an activity system, as when writers exchange drafts of texts through e-mail for feedback.

Individual tools, however, may also be deliberately gathered together to form collective, virtual workspaces. When the tools are thus incorporated into a website, the site can be a central, quite visible locus for some of a community's activities. It provides a record of an activity system at the same time it supports that system. The site might also serve as a *boundary object* (Star & Griesemer, 1989; Wenger, 1998), or an artifact that can be shared among different communities and can act as an interface between those communities. The collective, virtual workspaces that most interest us here are called *collaboratories*, a coinage combining *collaboration* and *laboratory*.

What Counts as a Collaboratory?

There are many collective or potentially collective sites on the Web. For example, Web logs, or *blogs*, may range from individual diaries with regular readers to lists of annotated, bibliographic entries provided by various blog team members. Amateur, electronic magazines called Webzines may be collectively written; more important, they are often central to a fan club's activities. Yahoo! Groups, HotOffice, NBCi, and other commercially sponsored sites often provide a range of collaborative tools to support clubs or work groups. What distinguishes collaboratories from these collective sites?

The answer is complex. Defining the term *collaboratory* is rather like defining the term *game*, as Wittgenstein (1953–1958) described the problem. According to Wittgenstein, no single, objective dictionary definition can account for every specific example of something that English speakers might call a game. First of all, in this case a vast range of things might count: children's role-playing, sports, board games, bar stunts, puzzles, as well as things that have not yet been contemplated. But, beyond this there is the problem of the apparent exceptions to a single definition of *game*: What if most of the pieces are missing? What if people do not seem to be following rules? What about activities that might be called by some other name? Are these things still rightly called games? Wittgenstein responded that people do not keep precise dictionaries in their heads, but rather come to understand all words through their use. English speakers align with more or less agreement on the several attributes that might constitute a game, and negotiate, often tacitly, whether a particular activity with certain attributes is more or less game-like. Thus, an online site cannot be a collaboratory per se, but it may provide the means for enacting a collaboratory. The collective sites mentioned earlier may also support collaboratory activities.

The negotiations over *collaboratory* are perhaps more visible because the word's use is expanding. Several dictionary definitions, as well as the person credited with coining the word, point to the term's origins in science. William Wulf was working for the U.S. National Science Foundation when he originally described a *collaboratory* as a

> center without walls, in which the nation's researchers can perform their research without regard to geographical location—interacting with colleagues, accessing instrumentation, sharing data and computational resource[s], and accessing information in digital libraries. (cited in Kouzes, Myers, & Wulf, 1996)

A collaboratory was a set of resources—instruments, data, computers—that scientists could share to save expenses and to work on problems together. But the word is also beginning to appear in educational websites such as The

Collaboratory Project (Northwestern University, Chicago) and in research about those sites (Dorneich, 1999; Robins, 2000). Although vestiges of its scientific origins may remain, the term is no longer confined to scientific circles. Among teachers, the basic concept is familiar to many because it is a way to extend cooperative learning.

The term *collaboratory* is also particularly negotiable because its parent words—*collaboration* and *laboratory*—are themselves seen as flexible. For example, Ede and Lunsford (1983) named at least three general categories of activities that may be counted as collaborative writing:

> (1) intensive collaboration where two or more authors create one text by working closely together—often by talking through and writing the text together; (2) collaboration that does not depend on intensive and ongoing personal contacts but that may involve some work together but also considerable work completed separately; (3) group collaboration that occurs via a sequence of activities, as in the writing of a business's annual report or of a state or federal regulation. (http://www.stanford.edu/group/collaborate/wisdom.htm)

Similarly, Knorr-Cetina (1999) shifted the definition of *laboratory* away from a simple definition of a space: "We need to conceive of laboratories as *processes* through which reconfigurations [of objects of investigation] are negotiated, implemented, superseded, and replaced" (pp. 44–45, italics added). Just as *collaboration* and *laboratory* refer to activities that can be variously experienced and defined by participants, so does *collaboratory*.

Nevertheless, we would like to suggest some attributes that are found in a collaboratory, attributes that might be used to determine whether something is more or less collaboratory-like:

- *Shared inquiry*. Reflecting its origins in scientific communities, the term *collaboratory* suggests that participants share not just common goals (say, a social activity) but a common set of problems or issues— ones that interest them and that they are working together to study more deeply and perhaps to solve.

- *Intentionality*. Although people regularly work together under many circumstances, a collaboratory (as perhaps, collaboration) tends to be recognized by its participants as a joint venture; there is a shared consciousness of the site's status as a mutual project. This awareness can cause it to become a generative space in which each participant appears to gain as much or more than he or she gives. Thus, there is a "tipping point" (Gladwell, 2000), which leads to the critical mass awareness needed before a collective site is perceived by its members as a collaboratory.

- *Active participation and contribution*. A collaboratory exists to the extent that its members use and, more important, add to its resources. Members also continually negotiate with one another over their projects. Often, a collaboratory will contain member profiles to enable further communication and to identify common interests.

- *Access to shared resources*. A collaboratory provides the unique information (data, links, research findings) and tools needed by its participants.

- *Technologies*. Collaboratories involve technologies, whether they are scientific instruments shared by far-flung communities, the unique symbol systems used among participants, or the information technologies needed to communicate. A collaboratory is usually Web based.

- *Boundary-crossings*. Collaboratories bridge gaps and distances of (a) *geography*, by providing international access through the Internet; (b) *time*, by supplying both synchronous and asynchronous communication technologies; (c) *institutions*, by allowing groups access to tools and materials of common interest; and (d) *disciplines*, by enabling the participants to decide what resources are most relevant to a topic, without regard to traditional understandings of what constitutes a particular discipline.

Because collaboratories record and enable a community's activities, they are a potential boon to instructors, particularly science and writing instructors. On the one hand, a collaboratory often reflects the history of a community (e.g., the shared resources, completed projects, older documents). As a result, collaboratories demonstrate how people pursue and complete certain inquiries, as well as how they develop spin-off inquiries from the original plans. If the collaboratory contains many documents, it also models how different genres of writing—grant proposals, conference papers, lab reports, computer codes, presentations, bibliographies, informal drafts—work together to support and literally compose a research project. Such models may improve on those in textbook scenarios because the collaboratory provides more context—the activity systems—that informs how the documents achieve their rhetorical goals (or do not).

On the other hand, some collaboratories may welcome student participants, thus allowing them to engage directly in a meaningful collaboration. Classes are always free to set up their own collaboratories based on what they may find on the Web. Such course collaboratories may extend beyond the semester's end by enabling students to return to their work or by inviting new students and teachers to participate in them.

Website of the Month

The Space Physics and Aeronomy Research Collaboratory (SPARC) project (http://intel.si.umich.edu/sparc), according to the site, has brought together "an international community of space, computer, and behavioral scientists" to design the infrastructure needed on the Internet to support collaborative work on "space and upper atmospheric science." In addition to conducting scientific experiments, this collaboratory supports Windows to the Universe (http://www.windows.ucar.edu). This educational site, funded by the U.S. National Aeronautics and Space Administration, invites teachers, students, and the general public to explore the instruments, computer models, real-time data, and theories that scientists use. SPARC's section on Windows to the Universe offers outlines of classroom activities, opportunities to "Ask a Scientist" questions, rules for science-based games, images of the sun and earth, and a range of information about myths, fun facts, and ongoing SPARC experiments. Because it allows users to select an appropriate level of difficulty for content (beginning, intermediate, and advanced), it is a particularly enjoyable and accessible scientific site.

How You Can Participate

Collaborate! (http://stanford.edu/group/collaborate) is a new site designed by Corinne Arraez, Lisa Ede, and Andrea Lunsford to provide an alternative to the "adversarial academy." The editors hope to change institutional practices in the humanities that overlook collaborative research, writing, and teaching. To this end, the site provides models of collaboration, as well as resources to inform further research on collaboration. The editors invite your comments and contributions.

The Collaboratory Project (http://collaboratory.acns.nwu.edu/cwebdocs/index.html) is an example of a regional attempt to build a collaborative virtual environment to support education. Funded by Ameritech, this project is run by Northwestern University's Information Technology group. The project enables schools, museums, libraries, and other cultural institutions in the greater Chicago area to share information.

The Inquiry Page (http://inquiry.uiuc.edu) provides resources such as references, contacts with other teachers, lesson plans, and presentational material to support inquiry-based learning. The most important tool is the Inquiry Unit Generator, a Web-based template that helps users outline an inquiry-based course unit, including its lesson plans. The generator converts the information that teachers enter into a webpage that may be restricted to a few users or shared openly on the Web. Because the units contain keywords and standard fields, they are searchable; so teachers may view units on specific topics that interest them. The Inquiry Page is administered by a group of university professors, K–12 teachers, graduate students, and members of the National Center for Supercomputing Applications, but it is currently open to all.

Barbara and David Mikkelson's Urban Legends Reference Pages (http://www.snopes.com/index.html) track unlikely stories that appear in the media and on the Internet. The aim is to research the stories' origins to determine which are true (not many, although some contain germs of truth). The Reference Pages also debunk hoaxes, such as petitions against bills that have never been proposed. Associated with the California San Fernando Valley's Folklore Society, the Reference Pages are supported by "hundreds of readers." These readers alert the editors to new folklore resources, correct any errors they find in the reference pages, and report on the latest appearances of urban legends and hoaxes in such places as circulated e-mails, news reports, movies, or songs.

Glossary

Blog, Blogger: the term *blog* is short for *Web log*, which was initially a chronological, sometimes annotated listing of the URLs that a Web designer had visited. Blogs have evolved into a variety of Web-based logs, from online diaries to collections of jokes and annotated bibliographies kept by individuals or teams. Blogger is one software site that allows users to create, manage, and post their blogs to their own sites or to a Blogger server.

Cooperative learning: an instructional approach in which students work in groups to solve problems, thus developing the interpersonal skills of communication, leadership, decision making, and conflict resolution. Cooperative learning creates a community of inquiry in the classroom similar to what the philosopher C.S. Peirce described as he observed the work of scientists (see Johnson & Johnson, 1998). The Cooperative Learning Center is at the University of Minnesota.

E-zine, Webzine: an electronic, amateur magazine. E-zines derive from fanzines, literally cut-and-paste, home-produced magazines often devoted to discussing popular shows and fiction (especially science fiction) and to distributing spin-off texts. Now, e-zines encompass a wide range of topics, as well as a variety of delivery systems. Webzines are e-zines found on the Web, whereas other e-zines are still delivered as ASCII files through e-mail.

Yahoo! Groups: one of several commercial sites that offer various bulletin boards, e-mail, calendars, document storage, and chat rooms to support a community's online activities.

REFERENCES

Boyer Commission on Educating Undergraduates. (1998). *Reinventing undergraduate education: A blueprint for America's research universities*. Stony Brook, NY: State University of New York at Stony Brook for the Carnegie Foundation for the Advancement of Teaching.

Cintron, R. (1997). *Angels' town: Chero ways, gang life, and the rhetorics of the everyday*. Boston: Beacon Press.

Cole, M., & Engeström, Y. (1993). A cultural-historical approach to distributed cognition. In G. Salomon (Ed.), *Distributed cognitions: Psychological and educational considerations* (pp. 1–46). Cambridge, UK: Cambridge University Press.

Dorneich, M.C. (1999). *System design framework for a learning collaboratory*. Unpublished doctoral dissertation, University of Illinois at Urbana-Champaign.

Ede, L.S., & Lunsford, A.A. (1983). Why write...together? *Rhetoric Review 1*, 150–158.

Flower, L., Long, E., & Higgins, L. (2000). *Learning to rival: A literate practice for intercultural inquiry*. Mahwah, NJ: Erlbaum.

Gladwell, M. (2000). The tipping point: How little things can make a big difference. Boston: Little, Brown. Retrieved from http://www.usatoday.com/life/enter/books/fc/tippingpoint.htm

Hackett, E.J. (2000). Interdisciplinary research initiatives at the U.S. National Science Foundation. In P. Weingart & N. Stehr (Eds.), *Practising interdisciplinarity* (pp. 248–259). Toronto, ON: University of Toronto Press.

Hutchins, E. (1995). *Cognition in the wild*. Cambridge, MA: MIT Press.

Johnson, D.W., & Johnson, R.T. (1998). *Learning together and alone: Cooperative, competitive, and individualistic learning* (5th ed.). Needham Heights, MA: Allyn & Bacon.

Knorr-Cetina, K. (1999). *Epistemic cultures: How the sciences make knowledge*. Cambridge, MA: Harvard University Press.

Kouzes, R.T., Myers, J.D., & Wulf, W.A. (1996, August). Collaboratories: Doing science on the Internet. Published in *IEEE Computer*, *29*(8). Retrieved from http://www.emsl.pnl.gov:2080/docs/collab/presentations/papers/IEEECollaboratories.html

Latour, B. (1996). *ARAMIS, or the love of technology* (C. Porter, Trans.). Cambridge, MA: Harvard University Press.

Latour, B. (1999). *Pandora's hope: Essays on the reality of science studies*. Cambridge, MA: Harvard University Press.

Murnane, R.J., & Levy F. (1996). *Teaching the new basic skills: Principles for educating children to thrive in a changing economy*. New York: Free Press.

Prior, P.A. (1998). *Writing/disciplinarity: A sociohistoric account of literate activity in the academy*. Mahwah, NJ: Erlbaum.

Robins, J. (2000, November 3–5). The inquiry page: A K–12 collaboratory using socially intelligent agents. Paper presented at the American Association for Artificial Intelligence (AAAI) Fall Symposium, "Socially Intelligent Agents—The Human in the Loop," North Falmouth, MA. Retrieved from http://www.students.uiuc.edu/~jrobins/JRobins00.pdf.

Spigelman, C. (2000). *Across property lines: Textual ownership in writing groups*. Carbondale, IL: Southern Illinois University Press for the National Council of Teachers of English.

Star, S.L., & Griesemer, J. (1989). Institutional ecology, "translations" and boundary objects: Amateurs and professionals in Berkeley's museum of vertebrate zoology, 1907–1939. In *Social Studies of Science*, vol. 19 (pp. 387–420). London: Sage.

Wenger, E. (1998). *Communities of practice: Learning, meaning and identity*. Cambridge, UK: Cambridge University Press.

Wittgenstein, L. (1958). *Philosophical investigations* (3rd ed.). (G.E.M. Anscombe, Trans.). Englewood Cliffs, NJ: Prentice Hall. (Original work published 1953)

Guest Coauthor

Karen J. Lunsford is a doctoral candidate at the Center for Writing Studies, Department of English, University of Illinois at Urbana-Champaign.

Editor's Message

I once participated in a seminar about the implications of the new communication and information technologies for education around the world. The discussion began with some of the "gee whiz!" aspects of the World Wide Web. People shared descriptions of resources they had found on the Web as well as some of the statistics about how large it had become and how fast it was growing.

We talked about finding things such as the National Parks of Malaysia; the complete works of William Shakespeare; a directory listing international broadcasters present on the Internet; cameras in public settings such as zoos, which anyone can control from a desktop computer; museums, such as the Exploratorium in San Francisco, with interactive exhibits online; photographs taken by the space shuttle; art galleries; information about Carnevale in Venice; and interactive adventure stories you can write collaboratively. We also discussed finding courses in every subject imaginable, countless individuals, schools, companies, and offbeat sites of all sorts. Some participants shared their experiences with research—needing to find an address, an article, a quotation, or whatever, they learned that the Web was an invaluable tool.

Somewhere, in the midst of this conversation, I made the offhand comment that there was nothing that you could not find on the Web. Daisy Webster, a graduate student in this group, quickly said, "Well, you can't find my grandmother in Kenya!" This was a good challenge. Her grandmother didn't use computers and, for all I knew, was among the many people in the world who don't have telephones or electricity.

We decided to search to see what we could find. Using a Web search engine, we asked for a list of all the websites that included both "grandmother" and "Kenya." The Issue section this month explores the implications of what we found. Other sections examine other aspects of the *worldwide* in World Wide Web.

Original version published February 1999 in the *Journal of Adolescent & Adult Literacy*
©1999 International Reading Association

My Grandmother in Kenya

When Daisy and I searched the Web to locate her grandmother in Kenya, we found 4,815 sites. There were sites about travel in Kenya, about political events, about the plants and animals of East Africa. We found fiction, nonfiction, poetry, maps, and pictures. There was far more about Kenya than either of us expected to find.

Along the way, we were diverted to intriguing side paths. There was one site about the chain from early hominids to humans. It was a sort of thought experiment in which we were asked to imagine the first upright hominid mother holding hands with her daughter, then her daughter linking with her daughter, and so on, up to the present day. This chain would extend only 300 miles, from the ocean to the rift valley of Kenya. The site creates a beautiful metaphor about connections in nature and the marvel of evolution.

As we proceeded, we both learned new things about Kenya. And we found Kenyan grandmothers. There were stories about grandmothers and stories by grandmothers; there were pictures of grandmothers. There were even grandmothers from families known to Daisy. But we could not find her grandmother.

We also noticed something else. Of the 4,815 sites, only 7 had the domain .ke for Kenya. Many of the sites were commercial, such as European or North American travel agencies promoting tours to Kenya. Most of the sites were from the United States or the United Kingdom. Four of the 7 Kenyan sites were maintained by an Internet newspaper, the *Daily Nation*, and even that site seems now to be maintained in the general .com domain http://www.nationaudio.com/News/DailyNation/Today.

The *Daily Nation* contains many articles and pictures about Kenya, which enlarged my understanding of current events there. For example, looking at the September 14, 1998, issue, I saw an article titled "New plans to boost adult literacy" by Kariuki Waihenya, which began as follows:

> Plans are underway to strengthen adult education programmes and improve participation rates countrywide. During the International Literacy day observed last week, participants concurred that policies in adult education needed to be re-examined, curriculum revised and the Act reviewed in line with the changing global educational trends.... Minister Sharif Nassir said a report on the National Consultation on Post-Literacy Curriculum was complete and that it had proposed several changes to improve the adult education sub-sector.

This article in turn led me to others. I read about organizations providing food, medical care, and education; I read fiction; I viewed pictures; I began to learn at least a little about another people and place.

This kind of experience should be familiar to Web users. In fact, one of the glories as well as frustrations of using the Web is that it's very easy to find all kinds of things, but not necessarily what you wanted to find in the first place. However, this example tells us more than just that the Web is a large and disjointed repository of information. In fact, I would like to draw out at least four important lessons.

First, the Web contains immense amounts of material about almost any subject you can name. It is relatively easy to immerse yourself in learning about a topic you could barely name before. You can discover things about another country through rich materials available in only a specialized or very large print library. What is more, the Web materials have a currency and vitality because they are created by all types of people and sometimes change daily in response to events and to other websites. There is at least the promise that this richness can support global understanding and, at the very least, provide useful information about other countries, languages, and people.

Second, the knowledge encoded in the Web leads to serendipitous learning. There is no list of end-of-chapter questions with the accompanying certainty that the chapter contains the answers. Instead, there are endless answers, but to questions you never thought of asking. The Web encourages us to question our questions, to think about what we are trying to learn and why. Some might accept that as a reasonable formulation of the essence of learning, but it doesn't fit with some of the structures commonly employed in formal schooling.

Third, there is a need to critically examine the Web's bounty of knowledge. True, there is an amazing amount available on a topic such as grandmothers in Kenya, but there is also much missing. We found only 7 sites out of 4,815 that had the .ke domain. Even if many of the other sites were authored and maintained by Kenyans, this imbalance is one indication that the story of Kenya is told on the Web by people who are not themselves from Kenya. How would the representation of Kenya differ if Daisy's grandmother were telling the story? Moreover, many of the sites, regardless of the nationality of their authors, are commercial sites, designed to sell some product. The travel agency photographs, for example, do make me want to visit Kenya, but I need to remember that they tell only one aspect of what Kenya is today.

Fourth, these points and the investigation of the grandmothers in Kenya sites remind me that the Web today is still far from worldwide. Its users include perhaps 3% of the world's population, and most of those are concentrated in the wealthy countries and among the highly educated and wealthiest in those places. As the Web expands and as more voices enter this global conversation it will be fascinating to see how it changes. Will English continue to be the dominant language? Will we see more divergent perspectives on political and cultural debates? What will Daisy's grandmother have to say if she can tell her own story about Kenya?

Data

InfoNation is one of several "Resource Sources" at the United Nations CyberSchoolBus site (http://www.un.org/Pubs/CyberSchoolBus). It's an easy-to-use, two-step database that allows you to view and compare up-to-date statistical data for members of the United Nations. First, you select up to seven countries, using either a list or a world map. Then, you select statistics, and the site returns a table based on data from the UN publications *World Statistics Pocketbook and Statistical Yearbook*. What I like is that a very simple design based on a rich set of data results in a practical tool that can be used by literacy researchers, teachers, and students for a wide variety of tasks. One of the tables, for example, suggests many interesting ways to investigate questions such as, Is newspaper reading a valid indicator of literacy? Are developed countries investing more in education? and How does income relate to literacy?

Website of the Month

Literacy Web Australia: A valuable resource for schools and literacy educators by Neil Anderson (Queensland University of Technology, Centre for Cognitive Processes in Learning, School of Learning and Development, Brisbane, http://www.schools.ash.org.au/litweb).

This Internet site was created with the express purpose of providing teachers and researchers in the literacy field with practical case studies of teachers implementing the latest ideas and pedagogies in literacy education. Many of these teachers also use technology to enhance their work. The use of new technologies in classrooms is a secondary theme of this website. Many of these teachers are also concerned with equity issues and how these factors have an impact on outcomes for students—this provides another important secondary theme. Australia has a long history of schemes to assist students who are disadvantaged in schools, and initial funding for Literacy Web Australia came from one of these schemes. More details on Australian equity schemes can be found on the website.

The website has three distinct sections: (1) the cases, (2) a set of hyperlinks to relevant sites, and (3) a library of recently written articles by literacy researchers. This third section includes recent, often yet-to-be-published articles by leading Australian and international researchers in literacy and technology fields. Accordingly, users of Literacy Web Australia will be able to access papers that discuss or develop new theoretical and pedagogical trends in the literacy and technology education arenas, often before these ideas appear anywhere else.

The case study section will expand rapidly over the coming months but already includes sections on improving communication skills of children with disabilities through the use of technology, creating a multimedia history of a school, using peer mentoring to improve reading, and using the latest technology to improve the literacy outcomes of infant students. It also looks at the types of language used by teachers to effectively teach the new digital literacy skills.

Literacy links includes hyperlinks to library search engines and other Australian and international literacy Internet sites.

The Articles section will be expanding constantly to include the work of leading Australian and international researchers.

The site is stored on an Australian server at http://www.schools.ash.org.au/litweb.

Glossary

Domain name: a name that identifies an IP (Internet Protocol) address. For example, the domain name http://www.ed.gov represents a numerical address signifying a location in cyberspace. A domain name is the first part of the URL used to identify a webpage. Each host computer in the Domain Name System has a name, which allows computers using the World Wide Web to connect to the appropriate webpage.

Domain name server: a computer that accesses the Domain Name System in order to determine the correspondence between a domain name and an IP address.

Domain Name System (DNS): the online distributed database system that is used to map human-readable addresses into IP addresses.

continued

Glossary (cont.)

Internet Protocol (IP): a system of conventions that allows computers connected to the Internet to exchange data with one another regardless of the manufacturer, the operating system, or location.

Internet Protocol Address: a computer address in the form of four numbers, each one between 0 and 255, separated by dots. The Internet uses the numeric IP address to send data. For example, you may connect to a World Wide Web server with the domain name http://www.reading.org, but to the network you are connecting to the Web server with the IP address 207.97.47.101.

Note: There is a comprehensive online glossary of telecommunications terms maintained by The Institute for Telecommunication Sciences of the U.S. Department of Commerce at http://glossary.its.bldrdoc.gov/fs-1037.

Internationalized Domain Names

Guest Author Marc D. Wielansky

Editor's Message

I teach courses on topics such as literacy in the information age and learning technologies. One of the exciting aspects for me is that I learn so much from the students. One works with nonprofit groups to show them how they can deliver radio programs through the Internet and in turn has shared that expertise with his fellow students and me. Another manages electronic bulletin board systems and was able to lead a class discussion on how they work and the relative advantages of each. Others have extensive experiences with music on the Internet, the various digital divides, e-commerce, art on the Web, online fan clubs, free speech issues, and other topics currently reshaping literacy practices.

This month, one of those students, Marc Wielansky, reports on his own investigation of what may appear at first to be an arcane topic—the internationalization of domain names on the Internet. To many people who are only beginning to appreciate the potential of the Internet, domain names are just one of many strange concepts that fall in the realm of difficult and seemingly irrelevant technical discussions.

But domain names are the medium through which people access any resource on the Web. They are used to identify websites uniquely so that a user can easily explore webpages around the world. Without them, we would need to use a long sequence of numbers to specify a website. The domain naming system has become a significant factor in emerging literacy practices. For example, the use of alphabetic characters means that the International Reading Association can be found on the Web through its domain name, reading.org, instead of by specifying the sequence of numbers in its IP address, 24.104.0.35. This system makes the Web more accessible and easier to use, but only if you use Latin characters. Most people in the world use other writing scripts, so even the first step of Web access, getting to a webpage, requires them to use a writing script other than that of their own language.

Expanding the domain naming system to accommodate additional scripts would significantly improve access for those literate in Chinese, Arabic, and most other languages. Even most European languages use variants of the basic Latin alphabet, such as the German umlaut, the Spanish tilde, or the French cedilla. Yet, expanding in this way poses challenges to the inherent open structure of the Internet, to its ease of use for those accustomed to Latin-alphabet-only domain names, and to corporate interests. These are just a few of the issues Marc addresses this month.

Original version published December 2001 in the *Journal of Adolescent & Adult Literacy*
©2001 International Reading Association

Multilingual Access to the Internet

As with any major technological advance, the mass adoption of Internet technologies does not come without its own problems. Educational institutions have begun to take notice of social issues including concepts of the digital divide and information literacy. Arguments have been made that the Internet intensifies rather than decreases the differences between the haves and the have-nots of modern society. As a result, many philanthropic organizations have devoted themselves to addressing these newfound problems.

Although many of these problems are unavoidable, some are not. Many popular sources acknowledge the Internet as a global phenomenon, referring to the great number of users now and in the near future. As of year-end 2000 there were 374.9 million Internet users, and by 2002 this number is estimated to become 490 million (Pastore, 2001). However, most of the world still does not use the Internet. Although access to the Internet infrastructure may exist for many of these people, there is one major limitation to access: their language.

While webpages and other Internet media can be created in almost any existing language, their access is limited to English-based ASCII characters. This is due to the very technology that was designed to make the Internet more accessible—the domain naming system (DNS). Because phrases are generally easier to remember than series of numbers, the DNS was created to associate registered domain names with IP addresses. However, as helpful as this system was designed to be, it is limited because its original designers used the ASCII character set, restricting the DNS to only English characters. The original design was never intended for users of any other character set.

The international nature of the modern Internet calls for the development of a new DNS standard. There are multiple reasons for the development of a DNS that supports international domain names (IDNs). First of all, it allows the Internet to be the truly global phenomenon that so many people describe it to be. According to one prediction by *Computer Economics*, by 2005 there will be approximately 198 million nonnative English-speaking users on the Internet, compared with the 148 million native English-speaking users (Pastore, 2001). In other words, there will be 14% more non-English-speaking users than English-speaking users. As the number of international users continues to grow, the use of ASCII characters alone for identifying websites will be unreasonable. Restricting addresses to English characters creates an entry barrier for those who may be unfamiliar with the English character set, even for sites created entirely in other languages. In addition, it limits the site itself by forcing it to have registered a domain name based on English characters.

Providing increased access for those who speak languages with non-Roman characters allows users from multiple language backgrounds to tap into the power of the Internet, instantly increasing the level of technological literacy for millions of people worldwide. While it is important to note that it is impossible to recognize all character sets based on their sheer number, the majority of the world's character sets should be represented. The creation of IDNs will radically change the way these people use the Internet by allowing them access to the Web, e-mail addresses, FTP sites, and any other network applications based on network addresses in the same manner as many users of the ASCII character set.

In addition, the internationalization of domain names adds to the localization of sites. It gives people a choice in the language of their domain name so that they can address a certain audience. Creating a domain name in a specific language can reflect cultural elements onto a website. This helps individuals and businesses connect with their target markets and audiences. It also preserves cultural and linguistic integrity by allowing online identities, such as names and brands of products and organizations, to be represented in natural language and native script. Although the country code top-level domains also provide some localization, they are limited to national borders. International domain names, on the other hand, can appeal to people across the globe.

The Current Domain Naming System

In order to understand the challenges involved in rethinking the DNS, it is necessary to understand how the current system works. Only then can the several options for modifying or upgrading the system be analyzed according to their technical plausibility and effectiveness.

The DNS is one of the most crucial elements of the Internet. It provides an efficient method of matching IP addresses to domain names in a manner that is transparent to most users. It is based on a relatively simple concept: Each domain has a responsibility to provide its own DNS servers for each of its sites. Therefore, when a user wishes to access a site, his or her Web browser queries a directory based on the top-level domain name (such as .com or .net). This directory lists the DNS for an IP address that matches the URL the user requested on that particular domain. For example, when a user wants to access the site located at http://www.lis.uiuc.edu, the user's browser would go through several steps before loading the webpage. First, it recognizes uiuc.edu as the domain name. Next it queries that domain to find the address of the associated DNS server. After that it queries that DNS server (in this case DNS1.CSO.UIUC.EDU) for the correct IP address. Only then does the browser connect to its final destination, located at the IP address 128.174.4.10, in order to download the webpage. It is important to note that on many occasions ISPs will develop DNS tables of their own in order to speed up this process for commonly accessed sites, but will continue to use this process for uncommon or unvisited sites (Topping, 2000).

Once the need for domain names in international characters was recognized, several Internet organizations began working on the technical problems it poses. (I'll discuss this later under Solving the Technical Problems.)

Implementing a New System

Most of the aftereffects of implementing IDNs will result from the lack of a regulatory body for the Internet. However, the complexity of the modern Internet has made it virtually impossible to regulate. The nature of the Internet is based on the protocols involved being completely open source and on there being no central body responsible for maintaining its structure. Each of the hundreds of organizations worldwide is responsible for providing its part of the connectivity among the thousands of networks that make up the Internet. The openness of its design has allowed the Internet to take on an organic growth pattern as organizations have added technologies that have become standards, but the process has always been slow.

Although some official standards-making bodies exist, each lacks sufficient power to enforce the new standards as they are developed. As a result of the lack of a single responsible body for worldwide standards enforcement, it is extremely difficult, if not impossible, to impose a new worldwide standard or to change an existing one. In the past, most new Internet standards have followed a policy of backward compatibility so that adaptation was not necessary. Otherwise, a new standard would break the Internet for anyone who chose not to follow it.

Currently the Internet Corporation for Assigned Names and Numbers (ICANN) assumes most of the responsibility for "IP address space allocation, protocol parameter assignment, domain name system management, and root server system management functions" (Internet Corporation for Assigned Names and Numbers, 2001). Many other corporations have taken liberties as well. The role of i-DNS.net in creating IDN technology is a perfect example of corporate standards making. They have provided an active solution for IDN resolution since December 1999. Many governments also take liberties to make standards for the Internet. For example, the Chinese government has set up the China Internet Network Information Center and administrative divisions within the government to regulate standards in China. The Chinese government has even gone as far as attempting to regulate the use of the Chinese language on the Internet, believing it to be under its jurisdiction (Wang, 2001).

Domain Disputes

The most immediate problem that will result from a finalization of the IDN standard will be the resolution of the names registered by the many organizations that have already begun to register IDNs under the incomplete standards in existence today. Although there seems to be some organization to this process, in most cases it is merely a false impression. Because there are no standards yet, it is impossible for any organization to guarantee rights to any IDN. For example, the VeriSign Global Registry Services is currently "the exclusive provider of registry services for the .com, .net, and .org top-level domains (TLD)" for over 70 domain name registrars (VeriSign Global Registry Services, 2001a). So, one could reasonably assume that registering an IDN with VeriSign or one of its affiliates would be secure. However, this is not the case. As with any other organization involved in resolving the IDN issue, VeriSign is still in the testing phase of development. Therefore, it is impossible for them to guarantee a registry of any domain name because there is no accepted standard.

In recent years when domain registration disputes have arisen, the rights and responsibilities of registering a domain name have evolved differently in the courts of various countries. As mentioned earlier, a domain name is essentially just a phrase that serves as a reference to a specific address in the Internet. However, as the Internet has developed into a commercial entity, that name has come to signify much more. Domain names have reflected trademarks, brand names, corporate names, and marketing slogans.

Trademark rights have been a longstanding issue for domain names on the Internet, but many countries do not even recognize trademark or branding rights for domain names. Of the more than 240 countries heavily involved in the Internet, only 14 have adopted the Uniform Domain Dispute Resolution Policy (Lemanski-Valente & Majika, 2000). This policy and others like it allow trademark owners the right to have domains transferred if they can prove the following:

1. Their domain name is identical or confusingly similar to a trademark or service mark in which the complainant has rights.

2. They have no rights or legitimate interests in respect of the domain name.

3. Their domain name has been registered and is being used in bad faith. (Internet Corporation for Assigned Names and Numbers, 2000)

As the number and complexity of domain names increase, the likelihood of a domain dispute increases as well. This could occur as a coincidence, but would more likely occur as cybersquatting or cybercloning. Cybersquatting occurs when a domain is registered by a third party in bad faith. Cybercloning involves registering a domain name that is the same or similar to an existing brand name, effectively taking advantage of that brand image. The dot-com eBay encountered this problem when it attempted to expand internationally. Although it preferred the country-specific name ebay.fr, it was forced to accept ebayfrance.com because the former name was already registered. In an attempt to prevent these occurrences and avoid disputes, many organizations register many domain names for themselves based on their various brands and identities.

The introduction of multiple character sets to this situation would only increase the number of domain disputes and make resolution even more difficult. The new domain names present lucrative opportunities for those willing to commit cybersquatting or cybercloning. It also would be even more difficult to detect cases because of the character recognition barriers. Therefore, any organization that is global, or ever plans to be, would have to register its name(s) in every language available. This could put a great time and cost burden on those organizations that have already spent tremendous time and effort developing an online presence. For example, The Coca-Cola Company has built a strong brand image worldwide involving multiple languages. Therefore it would need to register its brand name(s) in all these languages. However, there is no guarantee that these rights would be granted.

Future Implications

The introduction of domain name usage in multiple character sets is a necessary step in the true globalization of the Internet. However, the development and implementation of this phase proves to be a rather difficult step in its evolution. Initial exploration of the idea might suggest that completing this task could be easy, although this is certainly not the case. Short-term and long-term solutions may be implemented, but the selection of any of these technologies will have many implications that go far beyond the implementation of a technical standard. Over the years, the Internet has developed from a technology into a social construct in which any major change raises serious political, legal, and social issues. In the history of the Internet, there has never been a case in which the fundamental technology was changed. In the past, technologies designed to enhance the Internet have been allowed to develop independently and yet have managed to work together in the end. The decentralized structure of the Internet has served as its strength. As the Internet develops in the future, its decentralization may also prove to be a major weakness. Important lessons can be learned from exploring the implementation of an internationalized DNS. This case is one of the first ever to address a fundamental change to the Internet and will not be the last. It is important to learn how to correctly implement similar fundamental changes, because the Internet will continue to require modifications as it evolves as a tool.

Solving the Technical Problems

The internationalized domain name working group of the Internet Engineering Task Force (IETF) has assumed the responsibility for evaluating the standards for IDNs that are developed by the multiple organizations involved (Internet Engineering Task Force, 2000). The first step to internationalizing domain names is to develop the new technology necessary for handling non-ASCII characters. There are three major views on possible solutions to the IDN problem:

1. Upgrade the DNS and every application that uses it in order to support international characters.

2. Modify the current domain naming conventions to handle international characters without affecting the current system.

3. Develop a new system that would be a hybrid of the two that would determine if the domain name that is sent to a DNS server is ASCII based or international. Then it would forward the address accordingly to a traditional or internationalized server.

Before selecting any of these options, however, it is important to recognize several requirements created by the IETF that must be met in order for a solution to be successful. First, solutions must be globally compatible. A person using language A must be able to access a computer in language B. Second, it must work for all applications, not just the Web. Finally, it must work through standards to preserve the globally unique naming system currently in place (Wenzel & Seng, 2001).

At first glance, one solution would be to upgrade the DNS to support Unicode rather than ASCII. Unicode is a widely accepted character set standard that incorporates most widely used modern languages, including Latin-based and Eastern Asian languages. Because it works essentially the same way that ASCII does, it could work with the DNS in a similar manner. However, there are two major problems with doing this. First, Unicode uses a much larger character set and therefore uses more bits to communicate each character. As a result, domain names will be limited to fewer characters than the 63 allowed with the current domain name size limits. Second, and more important, changing the character coding of domain names would require every system connected to the Internet to recognize this change. Because there is no regulatory body to enforce this, the capital requirements necessary to convert every system would prevent it from happening on a large scale. Consequently, this solution would break the current system preventing anyone who did not switch to Unicode from using the DNS. This solution may be possible in the long run, but it is ineffective for the immediate future.

A second solution would be to label the character sets used when submitting a query to the DNS. This method allows systems to continue using any character sets, so it involves little adaptation on the user's end. However, it would require all resolvers to be able to recognize all character sets. According to the working group, this is unacceptable because "the number of [character sets] would probably have to be limited and never expand" and "mapping of characters between charsets would have to be exact and not change over time." This could restrict certain users from accessing sites and would also add to the DNS's complexity. Although this idea was discouraged by the IETF, it's another possible long-run solution (Hoffman, 2000).

The solution, therefore, must remain within the boundaries of the ASCII character set. As a result, the only possible solution for IDN resolution would be to somehow map the international characters onto an ASCII character set. This is done through a process termed ASCII-compatible encoding or ACE. There were many proposed methods for the format of ACE, but row-based ACE (RACE) seems to be the most widely supported. RACE involves a "two-step algorithm that first compresses the name part, then converts the compressed string into an ACE." Although ACE is compatible with the existing ASCII-based DNS, there still are some drawbacks. First of all, the 63-character limit for a domain name is reduced to less than 20 characters in some languages. Because the domain names are encoded, there is also a potential for future problems with managing domain names. Despite these drawbacks, this method seems to be the best short-term solution (Hoffman, 2000).

Two companies are currently using the RACE method of encoding to provide IDN resolution. VeriSign Global Registry Services (2001b) has developed a testbed to test the resolution of IDNs on the .com, .net, and .org top-level domains. It registers international characters in its RACE encoded form with the prefix *bq*—added to signal that the domain name is international. For example, .com will be registered as bq—3b7vcv67.com. VeriSign requires that the IDN be converted to ASCII before it is queried on its DNS. On the other hand, i-DNS.net International (2001) has a fully functional solution in which domain names can be registered in their original languages complete with the TLD in their original language. i-DNS is even capable of recognizing character direction for languages that are written right to left, such as Hebrew and Arabic. i-DNS servers can do RACE conversion on the DNS side; however, the user must access an i-DNS server for this service. Therefore, the Hebrew address could be sent to an i-DNS, and the Web browser would resolve it in the same way that it would resolve http://www.info.gov.il. Both companies have been successful so far in the process and plan to continue testing their systems and solutions. According to their websites, both are working for the IETF and will support whichever standard is approved.

It is possible that neither company's plans will ever be put in place. Although both have provided solutions that correctly encode characters into ASCII, there is much more involved in IDN character conversion than these two companies represent. Case sensitivity is a significant issue when dealing with any form of text. The current domain naming system is case insensitive to ASCII characters. This has been a great advantage for those who use the Internet. However, this feature only works because case conversion for ASCII characters is simple; everything has a one-to-one match. However, not all languages are this simple. Each character set has special properties that must be considered in developing a DNS that supports international characters. For example, some Asian languages require spelling changes as the case changes, and many Middle Eastern languages have optional characters such as vowels. It is important for any international DNS to be able to resolve the domain name regardless of these issues. In addition, many character sets have common characters that may be represented differently after conversion to ASCII. Chinese, Japanese, and Korean all have similar characters, as do Latin, Cyrillic, and Greek. For these reasons, RACE might not be a permanent solution; one of the other two solutions mentioned may be more useful in the long run.

Website of the Month

Consult the Internet Engineering Task Force internationalized domain names working group's website (http://www.nsiregistry.net/idn) for continuing coverage of the development and implementation of international domain names.

REFERENCES

Hoffman, P. (2000, July 11). Comparison of internationalized domain name proposals. Retrieved May 1, 2001, from http://www.i-d-n.net/draft/draft-ietf-idn-compare-01.txt

i-DNS.net International. (2001). Samples. Retrieved May 1, 2001, from http://www.idns.net/tech/samples/index.html

Internet Corporation for Assigned Names and Numbers. (2000). ICANN uniform domain name dispute resolution policy. Retrieved May 1, 2001, from http://www.icann.org/udrp/udrp-policy-24oct99.htm

Internet Corporation for Assigned Names and Numbers. (2001). About ICANN. Retrieved May 1, 2001, from http://www.icann.org/general/abouticann.htm

Internet Engineering Task Force. (2000, June 20). Internationalized domain name (idn) charter. Retrieved May 1, 2001, from http://www.ietf.org/html.charters/idn-charter.html

Lemanski-Valente, K., & Majka, T. (2000, October). An overview of international Internet domain registrations. *E-Commerce*, 17(5), p. 1.

Pastore, M. (2001, July 2). The world's online populations. Retrieved May 1, 2001, from http://cyberatlas.Internet.com/big_picture/geographics/article/0,1323,5911_151151,00.html

Topping, S. (2000, December). The multilingual domain name race: On your mark..get set..WAIT! *BizWonk, Inc.* Retrieved May 1, 2001, from http://www-106.ibm.com/developerworks/unicode/library/u-domains.html

VeriSign Global Registry Services. (2001a). About VeriSign GRS. Retrieved May 1, 2001, from http://www.verisign-grs.com/aboutus

VeriSign Global Registry Services. (2001b). General information paper on multilingual domain name resolution. Retrieved May 1, 2001, from http://www.verisign-grs.com/multilingual/Gen_Info_Paper.pdf

Wang, J. (2001, January). The Internet and e-commerce in China: Regulations, judicial views, and government policies. *The Computer & Internet Lawyer*, 18(1), p. 12.

Wenzel, Z., & Seng, J. (2001, May 23). Requirements of internationalized domain names. Retrieved May 1, 2001, from http://www.i-d-n.net/draft/draft-ietf-idn-requirements-07.txt

Guest Author

Wielansky is a student at the Graduate School of Library and Information Science at the University of Illinois at Urbana-Champaign.

Communities for the New Century

Guest Author Ann Peterson Bishop

Editor's Message

New technologies present challenges to our relations with one another and to the communities in which we live, work, and learn. These technologies simultaneously offer new ways to stay connected with others through travel or communications and threaten those very connections by presenting new barriers to communication or by making it too easy to leave one's established community behind. As we look ahead in this new century, crucial questions arise. How will communities change? Will new technologies lead to greater access and connections, or to more fragmentation? Will they enable more social equity by connecting people to information and organizations?

Many people have written on these topics. For example, building on his experiences with an online community called the WELL at http://www.well.com, Howard Rheingold has examined the social and political implications of computer networking for ordinary people. In *The Virtual Community: Homesteading on the Electronic Frontier* (1994), he argued that computer-mediated communication restructures democratic discourse. Moreover, it has created a new form of human social life called "the virtual community"—a group of people who use computers to communicate with one another in lieu of face-to-face contact. Such a community redefines the constraints of time and place, and potentially the relations among those people and the institutions that frame their lives.

Until recently, most examples of virtual communities have come from privileged arenas. Participants tend to be computer enthusiasts and innovators, such as those in the WELL. New online communities have also arisen within university settings and in high-tech companies. Not surprisingly, most of those participants as well have been relatively prosperous and possess an advanced level of formal education. Although the virtual communities appear open and egalitarian, one could argue that rather than democratizing, they have become one more way to maintain privilege, to widen the digital divide.

But there are some notable exceptions to this pattern. Ann Peterson Bishop is one of the leaders in the U.S. effort to ensure that new communication technologies become a resource for all people, especially those who have had limited educational and employment opportunities. She studies the use and impact of computer-based information systems, including digital libraries and the World Wide Web. A striking characteristic of her work is a continuing concern for social equity in access to information. She recognizes that one cannot understand the meaning of a new technology through its technical features alone, but must consider seriously how users make sense of it and employ it in their daily practices. Moreover, users with different bases of knowledge, time, or access to other resources may experience the same technology very differently. In this month's column, Ann talks about work to make community networking a reality for all citizens.

Original version published February 2000 in the *Journal of Adolescent & Adult Literacy*
©2000 International Reading Association

Technology Literacy in Low-Income Communities

As digital services and resources continue to expand in quality and scope, more people are firing up their computers and turning to the Internet as a routine part of their work, learning, leisure, and healthcare activities. But studies published over the past few years have demonstrated that the online migration is characterized by a digital divide that segments computer use along socioeconomic lines (Kraut, Scherlis, Mukhopadhyay, Manning, & Kiesler, 1998; Novak & Hoffman, 1998; U.S. Department of Commerce, 1999). The danger is that disenfranchised members of society will become increasingly isolated from information, resources, and opportunities that are critical to their well-being and prosperity, yet available only to those with technology access and skills. As pointed out by James Katz in the Benton Foundation (1998) report on low-income communities in the information age, "The information poor will become more impoverished because government bodies, community organizations, and corporations are displacing resources from their ordinary channels of communication onto the Internet" (p. 5).

Community networking is a movement whose basic aim is to foster the advantageous and affordable use of computers by people and organizations within a particular local region (Schuler, 1996; see also the website for the Association for Community Networking at http://www.afcn.net). Community networking services are provided by and for local residents and typically include (a) the creation, consolidation, and management of local digital content (e.g., community calendars, personal and organizational websites, social service directories); (b) the provision of Internet access and e-mail accounts; (c) the establishment of public access computing sites; and (d) computer training and technical support. Although some community networking services may be offered in a piecemeal and ad hoc fashion in most towns in the United States today, a community network is a local organization exclusively devoted to providing such services, at little or no cost, in support of community development. Currently, hundreds of community networks are in operation around the world (see the Community Connector directory of community networks and community information systems at http://databases.si.umich.edu/cfdocs/community/DirSearch.cfm).

Community-based access and training programs have, in fact, been heralded by the Clinton administration as a promising step in reducing the digital divide (U.S. Department of Commerce, 1999):

> Community access centers (CACs)—such as schools, libraries, and other public access points—will play an important role. The 1998 data demonstrate that community access centers are particularly well used by those groups who lack access at home or at work. These same groups (such as those with lower incomes and education levels, certain minorities, and the unemployed) are also using the Internet at higher rates to search for jobs or take courses. Providing public access to the Internet will help these groups advance economically, as well as provide them the technical skills to compete professionally in today's digital economy. (Executive Summary)

Prairienet, begun in 1993 at the University of Illinois Graduate School of Library and Information Science, is the community network serving Champaign-Urbana and the surrounding region. With support from the Telecommunications and Information Infrastructure Assistance Program in the U.S. Department of Commerce and from the Kellogg Foundation, Prairienet and the Urban League of Champaign County have embarked on an integrated research and service program to expand technology access and literacy in low-income, predominantly African American neighborhoods. Our Community Networking Initiative is analyzing information exchange and computing practices, donating recycled computers to teens and adults who have completed basic technology training, providing technical assistance to small community organizations who wish to expand their use of computers and Prairienet, and revamping Prairienet's content and retrieval features to improve their usefulness and usability to low-income residents. Like the exciting program described by Allan Luke in Standpoints & Voices [in the February 2000 issue of the *Journal of Adolescent & Adult Literacy*, pp. 482–484], our aim is to build community locally by helping individuals and groups "get virtual."

Through household interviews, surveys, focus groups, training observations, evaluation questionnaires, and logs of user support interactions, we are studying the context and culture of community computing and knowledge exchange in low-income neighborhoods (Bishop, Tidline, Shoemaker, & Salela, in press). We feel our research has led to a number of insights—four are listed below—that may help in the design and implementation of community services devoted to computer access and training, regardless of whether they are offered by a community network or by other types of community-based organizations, such as schools, libraries, or social service agencies.

1. *Building participation of low-income residents in networked information services demands a community-wide approach.* Our CNI participants described a splintered ecology of access to technology and technical expertise. Equipment available for various uses is scattered across different locales, training is often superficial and not driven by individual needs and interests, and computers available at home may be only partially usable or temporarily available. Community information exchange and computing constitute a fabric of activity—no matter how fragile—that encompasses a wide range of local organizations. Outreach, access, training, and use must be woven into the fabric, not addressed piecemeal and not restricted to formal institutions. No single organization is likely to be completely effective in recruiting and supporting low-income residents, creating online information repositories that represent low-income needs and views, and providing public access and training centers that are convenient and hospitable to disenfranchised local residents. Networked information services should cross institutional boundaries, including all three "tiers" of community organizations (Venkatesh, 1997), from small, loosely organized, grass-roots groups (e.g., neighborhood watch) to large, wealthy, formal institutions (e.g., United Way).

2. *Community-based technology literacy efforts should recruit and support "local tailors" (Star & Ruhleder, 1996) to mediate the technology for their peers.* Moll's (1994) work to integrate indigenous household knowledge into the K–12 classroom was also suggestive for technology literacy programs. In the CNI project, we are striving to incorporate and capitalize on the enthusiasm, interest, insights, knowledge, and skills of low-income community members who want to contribute to promotional, training and support, or content development activities. People who have received training have volunteered as workshop facilitators at subsequent training sessions. This makes them more "homey," a word used by several community members. Many are eager to create their own webpages to spread information about upcoming events in their neighborhood parks and churches, share recipes, help parents select schools for their kids, or simply "encourage other single moms."

Around the United States, other projects are similarly fueled by the energy, talent, and knowledge of low-income teens and adults. For example, mentored teen groups have created webpages for local nonprofit organizations (see the Weblinks website at http://www.flint.lib.mi.us/weblinks) and community announcements (see the Access Newark website at http://www.lff.org/demo/access/huh.html). A number of community technology centers serving low-income neighborhoods are also run with substantial help from local residents (Chapman & Rhodes, 1997).

3. *Technology literacy flourishes through existing social connections and interactions.* Family and peer networks are key to community involvement and to the exchange of information and support (Agada, 1999; Chaskin, 1997; Uehara, 1990). It has also been recognized that informal collaboration and social exchange with peers help in learning how to use information technology (Agre, 1997; Twidale, Nichols, & Paice, 1997). In CNI, participants repeatedly stressed the importance of word-of-mouth communication with people in their close social circles for exchanging information about local resources and activities. As one local resident noted with a grin, "I talk with my neighbors out on the porch in the summer. That's what I call voice mail!" About half of our community trainees heard about the CNI project through family and friends; about a third heard of it through the Urban League; and only about 10% learned of the program through mass media, such as radio, television, or newspapers.

Preliminary results from our follow-up telephone survey indicated that project participants have been active in informally extending or getting help with CNI resources through their social networks. The majority of respondents said that someone besides themselves had used their CNI computer and that they had used their CNI computer to show someone else how to do something. About half of the survey respondents also said that someone other than a project staff member—primarily a family member or friend, with social proximity apparently more of a factor than physical proximity—had helped them in some way with their computer. Other indications we've seen of the importance of social bonds in technology training are requests from individuals to attend training sessions in family groups and an impromptu user support group set up by cohorts in one training session.

4. *Technology literacy flourishes with an open, "discovery" approach to training that permits people to develop their own meanings and uses for computers.* In order to understand how to make technology "disappear" (Bruce & Hogan, 1998) into the everyday life of low-income community members, we need to attend to the prevailing social context and practices in which computer use is embedded. In the CNI project, we have increasingly moved to develop a training curriculum and support services that are driven by low-income residents and fit with well-grounded community development programs. For example, in the most recent rounds of CNI training, teens have acquired computing skills through projects that involve creating their own digital music performances and planning a computer fair for their parents.

CNI program "graduates" host in-home, dish-to-pass social evenings attended by CNI trainers where people gather to explore new things on the computer or refresh their knowledge from training classes. CNI staff have also started incorporating training within community development programs offered by others (e.g., supplying relevant computer instruction—such as how to use spreadsheets for budgeting purposes and how to find information on the Web about nutritional requirements for lunches—for participants in a local program that prepares women to become home day-care providers).

Website of the Month

The Community Connector at http://www.si.umich.edu/Community is the most comprehensive online repository of information related to community networking. Managed by faculty and students at the University of Michigan School of Information (Ann Arbor), under the direction of Joan Durrance, it is an up-to-date and well-organized collection of a wide variety of resources. Included are directories, conference listings, papers and articles, news groups, and links to material that represents best practices in the field (e.g., exemplary online community information collections, evaluation instruments, training material). The Community Connector site also includes an online journal, *Connections*, devoted to community networking and created by people at the School of Information.

Other Views

Rethinking Communities and Networks

Recent literature exhibits some thoughtful analyses of how people adopt and adapt computers, raising questions about the meaning of *community* and *network* in today's society.

> The central tension between the concepts of community and network, perhaps, is that communities are supposed to define us, where networks are not. Communities are supposed to have boundaries and meanings; they are supposed to correlate with languages and identities, and to be the sites of collective cognition and solitary action. The antirationalist traditions of left and right both celebrate them for this reason, and view the boundlessness of networks as disruptive, or at best as a tool for recovering communitarian values. But none of these conceptual associations is quite true. Communities have always been more complicated than that, and it is precisely those intrinsic complexities that networks greatly amplify. The design of community networks can support positive values in this complicated world, but only so long as the designers understand what they are getting into. (P. Agre, 1999, reprinted with permission)

> For young people to become technologically fluent...they need to live in a "digital community," interacting not only with technological equipment but with people who know how to explore, experiment, and express themselves with the technology. (M. Resnick, N. Rusk, & S. Cooke, 1999, p. 277)

> Framing the issue as one of access is the ultimate success for people who have created a technology and are trying to sell it. If the poor and excluded need access, they mostly need reinvention for different aims. (B. Tardieu, 1999, p. 309)

> [T]echnology activists stress the importance of nurturing individuals and indigenous community organizations that already provide help and support in the community, rather than trying to impose technology from the outside. If an effort is aimed at providing new Internet access points in a certain community, they say, residents should have a say in where the stations are set up. Low-income people should decide for themselves how these tools can best serve their interests. (Benton Foundation, 1998, p. 21)

Data

As noted earlier, recent studies have documented the digital divide that segments computer use along socioeconomic dimensions. U.S. census data (U.S. Department of Commerce, 1999) demonstrates that such factors as race, income, and educational attainment affect computer access and use:

- Households with incomes of $75,000 and higher are more than *twenty times* more likely to have access to the Internet than those at the lowest income levels, and more than *nine times* as likely to have a computer at home.

- Black and Hispanic households are approximately *one-third* as likely to have home Internet access as households of Asian/Pacific Islander descent, and roughly *two-fifths* as likely as White households.

- The gaps between White and Hispanic households, and between White and Black households, are now more than six percentage points larger than they were in 1994.

- The digital divides based on education and income level have also increased in the last year alone. Between 1997 and 1998, the divide between those at the highest and lowest education levels increased 25 percent, and the divide between those at the highest and lowest income levels grew 29 percent. (Executive Summary)

A few years ago, the National Science Foundation in the United States supported a study of users of community technology centers nationwide (Chow, Ellis, Mark, & Wise, 1998). Survey results—with three-quarters of the respondents reporting annual household incomes less than US$30,000—demonstrated that centers set up to provide public access and training are helping local residents in a variety of ways:

- Eighty-seven percent of the 774 people who responded to the last survey question, "Has coming to this center made any difference in your life?" answered yes. Of these, 18% (139) reported the impact as a general improvement in their life, their confidence, their outlook on life, and their future prospects. Other major impacts described by survey respondents included work-related benefits such as improved job skills, improved computer skills, and educational benefits. Other common responses referred to improved perceptions of technology; social and community benefits; appreciation for access to hardware, software, and video; and general enjoyment and appreciation of the center.

- 65% of 707 survey respondents said they took computer classes at their technology center to improve their job skills.... Of the 586 respondents who held improving job skills as a goal, 39% said they were "a lot closer" and 8% said they had "reached" their goal.

- Of the 608 individuals who came to the center to pursue an educational goal, 6% said they had "reached" their goal and another 38% said they were "a lot closer" to it.

- A substantial 51% (of 799 respondents) said they felt "much more positive" about themselves as learners as a result of coming to the center.

- Most users said they were "a lot closer" [37%] to reaching or had "reached" [21%] their goals of increased self-confidence and overcoming computer fears or anxieties. (Reprinted with permission)

REFERENCES

Agada, J. (1999). Inner-city gatekeepers: An exploratory survey of their information use environment. *Journal of the American Society for Information Science, 50*, 74–85.

Agre, P. (1999, June 8). *Rethinking networks and communities in a wired society.* Paper presented at the midyear meeting of the American Society for Information Science, Pasadena, CA. Retrieved from http://dlis.gseis.ucla.edu/people/pagre/asis.html

Agre, P.E. (1997). Computing as social practice. In P.E. Agre & D. Schuler (Eds.), *Reinventing technology, rediscovering community* (pp. 1–17). Greenwich, CT: Ablex.

Benton Foundation. (1998). *Losing ground bit by bit: Low-income communities in the information age.* Washington, DC: Author. Retrieved from http://www.benton.org/Library/Low-Income

Bishop, A.P., Tidline, T.J., Shoemaker, S., & Salela, P. (in press). Public libraries and networked information services in low-income communities. *Library & Information Science Research.*

Bruce, B.C., & Hogan, M.P. (1998). The disappearance of technology: Toward an ecological model of literacy. In D. Reinking, M. McKenna, L. Labbo, & R. Kieffer (Eds.), *Handbook of literacy and technology: Transformations in a post-typographic world* (pp. 269–281). Hillsdale, NJ: Erlbaum. Retrieved from http://www.ed.uiuc.edu/facstaff/chip/Publications/Disappearance.html

Chapman, G., & Rhodes, L. (1997). Nurturing neighborhood nets. *Technology Review.* Retrieved from http://web.mit.edu/techreview/www/articles/oct97/chapman.html

Chaskin, R.J. (1997). Perspectives on neighborhood and community: A review of the literature. *Social Services Review, 71*, 522–547.

Chow, C., Ellis, J., Mark, J., & Wise, B. (1998, July). *Impact of CTCNet affiliates: Findings from a national survey of users of community technology centers.* Newton, MA: Community Technology Centers Network. Retrieved from http://www.ctcnet.org/impact98.htm

Kraut, R., Scherlis, W., Mukhopadhyay, T., Manning, J., & Kiesler, S. (1996). HomeNet: A field trial of residential Internet services. *Communications of the ACM, 39*(12), 55–63.

Moll, L.C. (1994). Mediating knowledge between homes and classrooms. In D. Keller-Cohen (Ed.), *Literacy: Interdisciplinary conversations* (pp. 385–410). Cresskill, NJ: Hampton.

Novak, T.P., & Hoffman, D.L. (1998). *Bridging the digital divide: The impact of race on computer access and Internet use.* Retrieved from http://www2000.ogsm.vanderbilt.edu/papers/race/science.html

Resnick, M., Rusk, N., & Cooke, S. (1999). The Computer Clubhouse: Technological fluency in the inner city. In D.A. Schön, B. Sanyal, & W.J. Mitchell (Eds.), *High technology and low-income communities: Prospects for the positive use of advanced information technology* (pp. 264–285). Cambridge, MA: MIT Press.

Schuler, D. (1996). *New community networks: Wired for change.* New York: ACM Press.

Star, S.L., & Ruhleder, K. (1996). Steps toward an ecology of infrastructure: Design and access for large information spaces. *Information Systems Research, 7*(1), 111–134.

Tardieu, B. (1999). Computer as community memory: How people in very poor neighborhoods made a computer their own. In D.A. Schön, B. Sanyal, & W.J. Mitchell (Eds.), *High technology and low-income communities: Prospects for the positive use of advanced information technology* (pp. 287–313). Cambridge, MA: MIT Press.

Twidale, M.B., Nichols, D.M., & Paice, C.D. (1997). Browsing is a collaborative process. *Information Processing & Management, 33*(6), 761–783. Retrieved from http://www.comp.lancs.ac.uk/computing/research/cseg/projects/ariadne/docs/bcp.html

Uehara, E. (1990). Dual exchange theory, social networks, and informal social support. *American Journal of Sociology, 9*, 521–527.

U.S. Department of Commerce. (1999). Falling through the net: Defining the digital divide. Washington, DC: National Telecommunications and Information Administration. Retrieved from http://www.ntia.doc.gov/ntiahome/fttn99

Venkatesh, S.A. (1997). The three-tier model: How helping occurs in urban, poor communities. *Social Service Review, 71*, 574–606.

Guest Author

Bishop teaches in the Graduate School of Library & Information Science at the University of Illinois at Urbana-Champaign.

IN CLOSING: WHAT IS LITERACY IN THE INFORMATION AGE?

Through the columns in this book, we have explored historical perspectives on the new literacies, evolving media practices, the impact on personal meaning making, ethical and policy issues, learning opportunities, and implications for community. To sum all this up in a neat package would be a prodigious task, but more than that it would wrap up something we need to be unwrapping instead. Our summation must be an opening, not a closing.

Openings and Closings

In 1986, a conference titled *The Linguistics of Writing*, was held at the The University of Strathclyde in Glasgow, Scotland, to bring together linguists and literary scholars, two groups who had little to say to each other, even though those outside their communities would have thought they were the same group. The linguists, who study ordinary language, were accustomed to looking for common patterns in language structure and use. For them, language was primarily spoken, not written. It comprised mostly the common grammar and vocabulary used by the ordinary person in unprepared circumstances, not the specialized language of the scholar, and especially not the language of the poet. In contrast, the literary scholars, who study poetic language, more often sought an understanding of the special nature of language represented in Chaucer, Shakespeare, or Austen. For them, language meant not talk, but prose, written language, with the occasional excursion into reading poetry aloud or the representation of dialogue in text.

The conference set out to explore what scholars in the two fields might have in common. There was a goal of understanding what each could contribute to the other, but also to create a synthesis that was neither the linguistics, nor the literary studies, of the past. In other words, the participants valued the work that had preceded the conference, but they saw the need to open new ways of thinking. Instead of beginning with an opening statement and finishing with a closing statement, as conferences usually do, the presenters decided to start instead with a closing, a wrapping up of a century of scholarship in which, to a large degree, the linguists and the literary scholars had diverged ever further from each other (Attridge, 1987). Then, instead of finishing with a closing, they offered an opening statement to a new field, "an exhortation to future work" (MacCabe, 1987, p. 286).

Rather than summarizing or concluding, I would like to see here an opening as well, one that invites a wider dialogue on the changes we are just beginning to experience. All too often, the discourse around new literacies is confined to those invested in promoting new technologies, or it is reduced to a set of competencies. The authors here neither extol nor excoriate the new media, but instead ask us to engage with those media to understand their meaning and to shape what they might become.

And how do we engage in that way? I think here of Miguel de Unamuno's classic work on skepticism, despair, and hope, *Tragic Sense of Life* (1954). The book is based on a diary the author wrote after the birth of his son Raimundo, who suffered from hydrocephalus plus meningitis and died at the age of six. de Unamuno was Rector-for-Life of the University of Salamanca, but was removed three times from that post for political reasons. His life experiences made him into a philosopher who was passionate about ideas, but also one who vigorously distrusted philosophy. He argues that the categories we create to organize our knowledge contest with our flesh-and-blood reality because "Our sense of the world of objective reality is necessarily subjective, human, anthropomorphic" (p. 115). Hence, these categories tend to divorce reason and feeling, often separating us from our lived experience. For us, it seems worthwhile to examine how the concepts we use enable or disable our understanding of "literacy in the information age." Let's begin with this phrase, also the title of this book.

Explaining the Title

At the end of a dissertation a Ph.D. student presents his or her work to a committee and subjects it to the questions of the committee members to ascertain whether the student has produced work that represents a significant contribution to knowledge. Typically, these questions probe details of the argument, aspects of the data, or links to major theories. One question, which opens up to all these and more, is a very simple question that often turns out to be the most challenging one of all for the student: What does your title mean?

The reason that this apparently innocuous question is so powerful is that by the end of dissertation research the student has begun to understand the complexities of his or her questions, such that what once had seemed simple is now rich and multifaceted. Students often recapitulate Perry's (1970) stages of intellectual development, moving from absolutism or dualism; through stages of multiplicity, in which many opinions can be equally valid; to relativism; and eventually to ethical commitment, in which fundamental principles define the contexts for evaluating truth. A student's growth means that the formerly simple act of explaining the title can become a challenge. Moreover, that explaining provides an opportunity to say in a concise way what the work was really about.

I considered many titles for this work, and cannot say for sure that I have arrived at the only, or best possible, one. But let me take on the role of the Ph.D. student here to see whether I can talk about the title, and thereby the book, in a way that opens rather than closes the dialogue.

Literacy

The first word, *literacy*, is enough to make me regret this path. Why not *literacies* if the topic includes *new-*, *information-*, *computer-*, *visual-*, *media-*, *Web-*, *technology-*, and various other hyphenated literacies? Why not *reading* or *writing*? Why *literacy* at all, instead of *technology* or *hyper* or *cyber*? The answer for me is that literacy, as represented here, encompasses a way of being in the world. If it is *reading*, then it is the kind of reading Hans-Georg Gadamer has in mind when he writes, "Not just occasionally but always, the meaning of a text goes beyond its author. That is why understanding is not merely a reproductive but always a productive attitude as well.... It is enough to say that we understand in a *different* way, *if we understand at all*" (1999, pp. 296–297). For Gadamer, reading is productive, by which he means that new meanings are inevitable. The reader understands in the light of his or her historical circumstances, which are unique for each reader, even for each reading. Reading is a continual search for meaning, growing out of the meanings we have experienced before.

If literacy is reading, it is also the reading of Paolo Freire, who showed that we read the world before reading the word, hence his claim that infants can read because they are already making sense of the world around them. Freire understood that reading was not simply decoding, but a political act, one based on an understanding of one's material circumstances and one that could become the practice of freedom. Richard Shaull (1970) states this well in the foreword to Freire's *Pedagogy of the Oppressed*:

> There is no such thing as a *neutral* educational process. Education functions as either an instrument which is used to facilitate the integration of the younger generation into the logic of the present order and bring about conformity to it, *or* it becomes the "practice of freedom," the means by which men and women learn to deal critically and creatively with reality to participate in the transformation of their world. (pp. 9–15)

Literacy is also the reading (and the writing) that we see in the new literacy studies (among many others: Barton & Hamilton, 1998; Gee, 1990; Green & Bloome, 1997; New London Group, 1996; Street, 1984). This work, employing ethnographic and discourse analysis techniques, helps us to see how literacy is social practice; how it is the means we use to construct and share meaning, to establish relationships, to gain power, to learn, and to participate in social worlds.

Literacy is not one thing, which one can attain and possess, any more than one can attain and possess culture. This is because we live within literacy: The literacy practices of a community are given historically. One can assimilate to them, but not abstract them from the lived experience. As Bakhtin (1984) shows, even the individual word is filled with the voice of others:

> No member of a verbal community can ever find words in the language that are neutral, exempt from the aspirations and evaluations of the other, uninhabited by the other's voice. On the contrary, he receives the word by the other's voice and it remains filled with that voice. He intervenes in his own context from another context, already penetrated by the other's intentions. His own intention finds a word already lived in. (p. 131)

Literacy as a whole is likewise filled with the voice of the other. That is why it can never be packaged as a set of skills or taught as a collection of competencies.

Moreover, literacy is an assortment of practices, or *multiliteracies*. The literacies are multiple in multiple ways: Different disciplines demand or define different ways to represent meaning; different social practices call on different communicative means, different cultures imply different primary literacies, and different media invoke different critical faculties. A recognition of these multiplicities and their import for understanding the growth of both individuals and societies is one reason that I have chosen to work in the area of multiliteracies.

And yet, there is still a value in thinking of the changes we see on the array of literacies as a whole. The transitions from oral communication to writing, from manuscript to print, from print to radio, movies, and television, all had far-reaching consequences across many communities. As we begin to employ computer-mediated communication, hypertext, the Web, virtual reality, interactive agents, and other new media, we may experience similar far-reaching changes to all our literacies. It is thus useful to investigate both the specific elements of particular literacies and what is happening with meaning-making and communication in general as a result of new technologies. Conversely, we need to understand how those technologies are shaped by our evolving literacy practices.

The word *literacy* then describes that space in which we make meaning in interaction with others. The processes for that meaning making are both subject and object: They enable us to communicate, to solve problems, and to achieve social ends—as we simultaneously reconstruct those processes for future use. That creative capacity in the processes of meaning making implies that new literacies are not simply tools to acquire, but tools to be created. Ann Berthoff (1990) writes about this capacity as providing the "ground of hope" for teachers:

> [The] species-specific capacity for thinking about thinking, for interpreting interpretations, for knowing our knowledge, is, I think, the chief resource for any teacher, and the ground of hope in the enterprise of teaching reading and writing. (p. 11)

The creative capacity is also the ground of hope for society as it both embraces and struggles with the new literacy processes it has foisted upon itself. We need to repeatedly ask both what is and what can be.

In

One should be forgiven for skipping over a word as short as *in*, but even a preposition raises important questions about our stance. For example, the title could have been *Literacy* for *the Information Age*. That would suggest a focus on developing the skills that one needs to cope with new technologies, perhaps what many mean when they say "information literacy." The American Library Association says that "[t]o be information literate, a person must be able to recognize when information is needed and have the ability to locate, evaluate, and use effectively the needed information" (1989, p. 1). I believe that this book contributes to an understanding of information literacy so defined, but its primary purpose is not to outline what one needs for the information age, but to explore what it means to exist within it already.

Another reasonable choice would have been *Literacy* Through *the Information Age*. One sense of that is historical—how literacy has changed during different periods of the information age. That aspect is certainly here, as in the first section of the book, and it could have been developed more. Another sense is pedagogical—how we learn literacy through, or by means of, new information tools. Again, a number of the chapters delve into how students develop their literacies through experiences with the new technologies.

Similarly, a case could be made for *Literacy* About *the Information Age* or *Literacy* of *the Information Age*. One might fruitfully ask about *Literacy* before and after *the Information Age*. But in the final analysis the simple word *in* seemed to capture best the sense of being immersed in a world we are simultaneously creating.

The

Even the simple article (or determiner) cannot escape. In fact, I have the greatest doubts about the appropriateness of the word *the* in the book title. *The* suggests a historical uniqueness that is hardly justified. There have been many "information ages," or, one might argue, there has been a single age, but it is the condition of being human that we live in a perpetual information age.

It is difficult to specify when the current information age began. Some place it as recently as the advent of Mosaic, the first graphical browser for the Web, only 10 years ago. Others mark it by the Internet, or the personal computer. Others go further back, to the Electronic Numerical Integrator and Computer (ENIAC) of World War II. Singh (1966) traces the information age to ideas about language and computing, which developed well before their physical manifestations. Many writers (e.g., Bell, 1973; Davis & McCormack, 1979; Machlup, 1962) focus more on the economic and societal changes associated with new kinds of work.

In a recent work, Daniel Headrick (2000) develops an interesting argument, essentially that the software of the information age preceded the hardware developments we see today. During the period 1700–1850, systems were created for organizing information (classification and scientific language), transforming it (the emergence of statistics), displaying it (maps and graphs), storing it (dictionaries and encyclopedias), and communicating (postal and semaphore systems). Today, with television, electronic databases, computers, the Internet, and computer-mediated communication, we can access that information more easily and rapidly, but we primarily use the systems of two or three centuries ago to organize it and make sense of it.

A historical perspective makes it difficult to maintain that the current information age is the only, or even the most significant, one. It may turn out to be the most momentous, but the evidence is not yet in to argue that it is more significant than the information technology developments of a century ago (e.g., telephone, telegraph, sound recording, motion pictures, radio, high-speed printing, and electricity to power it all), the systems described in Headrick's book, the printing press (see Eisenstein, 1979), the alphabet, or the invention of writing itself.

There is another problem with *the* applied to information age. As we saw in the column "How Worldwide Is the Web?" on page 300, Daisy's grandmother, whose village in Kenya, has no telephone or electricity, lives in a different information age from that of the students in my university classes, and not just the ones designing new software systems. All these university students have access to quantities of information and media that are almost unimaginable for large numbers of contemporaries around the world. But the extension of this argument is also true: No two of us live in the same information age. My 81-year-old grandmother, for example, rarely uses e-mail or browses the Web. Those technologies have had little direct meaning in her daily life. On the other hand, unlike me, she has a cell phone, cable television, and a car that knows far more than I do about where it is, what weather it is experiencing, and how it should adjust the seats to please different passengers.

The further we go along this path, the less plausible the notion is of a discrete information age, one that emerged sometime in the near past and affects us all in similar, dramatic ways. To the extent that we are in the midst of a major tectonic shift, it is even less likely that any of us can foresee its direction and extent. Nevertheless, there is clearly a lot happening right where we are, and *the* helps us focus our attention on the evolving world around us.

Information

Although different writers have focused on the hypertextual nature of the new media, its immediacy, its fluidity, its accessibility, or other features, one aspect they all identify is the growth of information. People point to the Web, the hidden or deep Web, the proliferation of video, peer-to-peer computing, or the multiple forms of computer-mediated communication as indicators of the vast and rapidly enlarging information space in which we live. But it may be time to question some of the easy rhetoric about the explosion of information.

One reason for caution in these pronouncements is our egocentricity. We see the aspects of information that are meaningful to us and tend to ignore those that are not. When my students created the Learning Technologies Time Line (see page 21), they noted that there were more entries for the twentieth century than for all the previous centuries, and that the 1990s were the most active decade. This might be taken as evidence for the accelerating pace of inventions or the growth of knowledge, and it's difficult to deny the pace seems faster. And yet, critical reflection on what had been noted in the time line began to show that we see changes as significant when they relate to things in our own lives. There are many references to radio and television in the time line and to their antecedent inventions, but there is nothing on building pyramids or castles. Nor are there extensive references to the details of writing system development (a more clearly identifiable literacy technology). We take for granted the intricacies of written language because they are given to us as a whole when we are children, whereas we see each new twist and turn on the Web as a discovery of note.

Moreover, only a pixelation of vision allows us to limit the term *information* to that which can be represented, manipulated, and transmitted by electronic means. Bill McKibben's famous experiment contrasting television with sitting by himself in the woods on a mountain is one example to make us pause in the celebration of the information age. McKibben asked his friends to tape roughly 2,000 hours of programming on 93 cable television channels. Then he watched all of it. He also spent a full 24 hours on a small mountain near his home in order to see what information was on the mountain that was missing from television. Where the television offered cartoons, soap operas, shopping channels, televangelists, and bite-sized news, the mountain spoke to McKibben about animals, plants, and human presence as part of nature. In his memoir about this comparison of two "information spaces," McKibben concludes,

> We believe that we live in the "age of information," that there has been an information "explosion," an information "revolution." While in a certain narrow sense this is the case, in many important ways just the opposite is true. We also live at a moment of deep ignorance, when vital knowledge that humans have always possessed about who we are and where we live seems beyond our reach. An Unenlightenment. An age of missing information. (p. 9)

McKibben leads us to question the value of the new information age. However, suppose that we do see a burgeoning of information along some dimensions and that we do value that information. Suppose further that we are concerned about how to respond critically and how to make the best use of that information, including how to assess it relative to a broader perspective on human values. We might then want to focus on the ways that we produce and access information in the digital era.

We still have a problem of terminology. Although *information age* and *information technology* are widely used terms, we need to be aware of the baggage they carry and don't carry. For example, the term *information and communication technologies* (ICT) is used in some circles, notably in Europe more than in the United States. ICT highlights the inherent plurality of the technologies and also the communicative function. Although information seems somewhat meaningless without some notion of communication, including the "C" reminds us that these technologies need not be simply one-way modes of delivering information, but truly two-way avenues for dialogue.

Age

The earlier comments should be enough to alert us to the dangers in the concept of an Age of Information, particularly if that is conceived as one that breaks sharply with the past, signifies momentous changes, and has universal import. But the word *age* suggests other questions as well: When did it start? Now that we are in it, when will it end? And what would ending mean, or does it go on forever? What sustains it—the technologies, or the way we use them?

Age is also a curious concept in terms of long-term meanings. If one were to return to an early point in the Age of the Dinosaurs, one might see not only the famous creatures, but also many gymnosperms, or plants without flowers, such as seed ferns, cycads, ginkgos, and conifers. It was not until the middle of the Cretaceous period that flowering plants appeared. Later in that period, the first mammals began to appear, while the age still belonged to the dinosaurs. Thus, although most people think of that time as the Age of the Dinosaurs, it was the age in which the flowering plants of today and the mammals had their beginning. We may be in the Internet age or the personal computer era, and able to see only the creatures that will disappear, not the fantastic ones evolving in our midst.

Constructing Literacy

It is often said that significant changes in social practices are overestimated in the short term and underestimated in the long term. The reasons for this are the same. We think a new idea or process will make a difference, but that cannot occur until other things change as well. For example, the automobile meant little until there were paved roads and service stations. However, as concurrent technologies developed, they, together with the automobile, began to define major shifts in the culture of modern countries. The situation with the new literacies is similar. Today, we see changes in the practices of teaching and learning in work and in leisure. But we cannot know where these will all lead; they derive from much more than the technology in isolation.

One might then ask, If literacy and technology are defined so broadly, isn't there a danger that our investigation results in a mystical statement that the world is an unanalyzable whole, which cannot be broken down into parts? Are we left with Wittgenstein's call to silence: "What we cannot speak about we must pass over in silence" (1974, p. 74)? How do we develop a stance toward literacy, which is not so general as to encompass all human activity, yet recognizes its many facets, interconnections, and open nature?

Richard Lewontin (2000) discusses a similar problem that arises in the analysis of biological systems. He questions the reductionist claim that genes determine the organism, which then adapt to the environment—the neat linear path from chemistry to situated life. He argues that genes, organisms, and environments coconstruct themselves. Rather than selection, he sees construction as the fundamental process:

> the actual process of evolution seems best captured by the process of <u>construction</u>. Just as there can be no organism without an environment, so there can be no environment without an organism. (p. 48)

John Dewey (1916) discusses an analogous process when he talks about a situation being apprehended as a whole. Rather than thinking of a situation as something one is placed in, which then affects the individual, and then can later be analyzed in terms of how well the individual adapted to it, Dewey argues that "the functional development of a situation alone constitutes a 'whole' for the purpose of mind" (p. 207). Translating this to our discussion, we might say that the literacy in the information age, that which we experience, is not a collection of materials, nor tools, nor competencies, nor technical processes, nor even new affordances, but rather, a whole determined by our purpose at a given moment. There is then a coevolution of individual, society, literacy, and technology, given coherence by the processes of construction. As Dewey writes,

> For the person approaching a subject, the simple thing is his purpose—the use he [or she] desires to make of material, tool, or technical process, no matter how complicated the process of execution may be. The unity of the purpose, with the concentration upon details which it entails, confers simplicity upon the elements which have to be reckoned with in the course of action. (p. 207)

Literacy is that which we actively construct. As we *see* new possibilities in the emerging media of the information age, we begin to *change* our literacy. In turn, as literacy practices of a community evolve they shape the very media in which they are immersed. This coevolutionary process means that we can never freeze the activity of literacy and say that these are exactly the skills that need to be learned. Such a conclusion bodes ill for educational reform efforts based on monolithic definitions of literacy, predefined accountability criteria, or the linear accumulation of skills and knowledge.

On the other hand, the unity of purpose, as Dewey suggests, does confer a simplicity upon the elements of a situation. And there can be unity to literacy to the extent that there is a shared unity of purpose within a community. Our goal for education must be more than technocratic competency, conformity to established ideas, or a social sorting mechanism. If we seek instead to help people learn how to participate actively in understanding themselves and those around them; to learn how to express their ideas and aspirations; to communicate with others, including those who have different backgrounds and ideals; to acquire a critical, socially engaged intelligence; and to approach the world with a sense of wonder and to enjoy learning in depth about it, then we need to recognize and support the constructive process whereby individuals come to make their world. If our purpose is the former, we will find that literacy in the information age supports us all too well. If the latter, we will find its potential is limited only by our imaginations.

REFERENCES

American Library Association. (1989). *Presidential Committee on Information Literacy. Final report*. Chicago: American Library Association. Retrieved December 2, 2001, from http://www.ala.org/acrl/nili/ilit1st.html

Attridge, D. (1987). Closing statement: Linguistics and poetics in retrospect. In N. Fabb, D. Attridge, A. Durant, & C. MacCabe (Eds.), *The linguistics of writing: Arguments between language and literature* (pp. 15–32). New York: Metheun.

Bakhtin, M. (1984). *Problems of Dostoevsky's poetics* (C. Emerson, Trans.). Minneapolis, MN: University of Minnesota Press.

Barton, D., & Hamilton, M. (1998). *Local literacies*. London: Routledge.

Bell, D. (1973). *The coming of post-industrial society: A venture in social forecasting*. New York: Basic.

Berthoff, A.E. (1990). *The sense of learning*. Portsmouth, NH: Boynton/Cook.

Davis, W.S., & McCormack, A. (1979). *The information age*. Reading, MA: Addison-Wesley.

de Unamuno, M. (1954). *Tragic sense of life* (J.E.C. Flitch, Trans.). New York: Dover. (Original work published 1921)

Dewey, J. (1916). *Democracy and education*. New York: Macmillan.

Eisenstein, E. (1979). *The printing press as an agent of change: Communications & cultural transformation in early-modern Europe*. Cambridge: Cambridge University Press.

Fabb, N., Attridge, D., Durant, A., & MacCabe, C. (Eds.). (1987). *The linguistics of writing: Arguments between language and literature*. New York: Metheun.

Gadamer, H.-G. (1999). *Truth and method* (2nd ed.) (J. Wiensheimer & D.G. Marshall, Trans.). New York: Continuum. (Original work published 1960)

Gee, J.P. (1990). *Social linguistics and literacies: Ideology in discourses*. London: Falmer

Green, J.L., & Bloome, D. (1997). A situated perspective on ethnography and ethnographers of and in education. In S.B. Heath, J. Flood, & D. Lapp (Eds.), *Handbook of research on teaching literacy through the communicative and visual arts* (pp. 181–202). New York: Macmillan.

Headrick, D.R. (2000). *When information came of age: Technologies of knowledge in the age of reason and revolution 1700–1850*. New York: Oxford University Press.

Lankshear, C., & Knobel, M. (2003). *New literacies: Changing knowledge in the classroom*. Buckingham, UK: Open University Press.

Lewontin, R.C. (2000). *The triple helix: Gene, organism, and environment*. Cambridge, MA: Harvard University Press.

MacCabe, C. (1987). Opening statement: Theory and practice. In N. Fabb, D. Attridge, A. Durant, & C. MacCabe (Eds.), *The linguistics of writing: Arguments between language and literature* (pp. 286–306). New York: Metheun.

Machlup, F. (1962). *The production and distribution of knowledge in the United States*. Princeton, NJ: Princeton University Press.

McKibben, B. (1993). *The age of missing information*. New York: Penguin.

New London Group. (1996). A pedagogy of multiliteracies: Designing social futures. *Harvard Educational Review, 66*(1), 60–92.

Perry, W. (1970). *Forms of intellectual and ethical development in the college years*. New York: Holt, Rinehart and Winston.

Shaull, R. (1970). Foreword. In P. Freire, *Pedagogy of the oppressed* (pp. 9–15). New York: Seabury.

Singh, J. (1966). *Great ideas in information theory, language and cybernetics*. New York: Dover.

Street, B. (1984). *Literacy in theory and practice*. Cambridge, UK: Cambridge University Press.

Wittgenstein, L. (1974). *Tractatus logico-philosophicus* (D.F. Pears & B.F. McGuinness, Trans.). London: Routledge & Kegan Paul. (Original work published 1921)

GLOSSARY

It is vain to think that one could include here a complete glossary for *Literacy in the Information Age*. Even a half-serious attempt would fill the entire book, and moreover, the corpus of technology terminology is expanding rapidly. One indication of this can be seen by examining the new and revised entries in the *Oxford English Dictionary* (available through online subscription at http://www.oed.com). For example, the summer 2002 quarter alone saw new words or new meanings for words such as *biochip, biocircuit, biocomputer, bioinformatics, bitstream, globality, global positioning system, grey out, modulize, spintronics, technoscience,* and the new meanings of *tool* in *software tool, programming tool, toolbar, toolbox,* and *toolkit*. Those are only a few of the additions to one dictionary.

Nevertheless, the staff editors and I felt that a combined glossary would be useful not only for reading this book, but as a starting point for entering the literature in this area. Some of the entries here have definitions that are specialized to the column in which the term appeared; others apply fairly well across all the columns and beyond. Together, they provide a broad sweep of both specific technical terms and concepts that help in thinking about the issues raised.

We identified the author of the entry unless it came from one of my single-authored columns. For those cases in which more than one author defined a term, I selected a version or synthesized a new entry.

Acceptable Use Policy (AUP): the policy of a company, school district, or owners of computer networks that explicitly states what is and is not acceptable, including, for instance, how and when computers might be used for personal use, what sort of sites can and cannot be viewed, what sorts of e-mail are allowed, and what specifically may be posted on a website. (Kehus)

Aesthetic: People adopt any of various stances toward a new technology, or toward any change. These stances include skeptical, utilitarian, oppositional, and transformational. Others adopt an essentially aesthetic stance toward change. They believe change should be described and commented on but not fully engaged. This stance is similar to what Rosenblatt called the "aesthetic response" to reading.

Affiliate, reseller, or Value Added Reseller (VAR): a website that links to another site for profit. For example, TeenLit.com links to Amazon.com with a special code that tracks visitors so that TeenLit makes a commission on any purchases they make there. (Kehus; pp. 148–158)

Alternative text for images (ALT text): a term used in webpage design, referring to the use of text to convey information to a user of the webpage, primarily when the image is not being displayed. This can be useful for a blind reader who can still understand the webpage content with a speech synthesizer. But it is also helpful to a user who has a text-only browser, such as Lynx, or for one who has set the browser not to load images (as might be done with a slow Internet connection). Nearly everyone who has looked into the issue of webpage accessibility strongly recommends the use of ALT text. For example, the following HTML code

```
<a href=next.html> <img src="downarrow.gif" alt="more"></a>
```

might be used on a webpage to indicate a link to additional information in the file "next.html." Assume here that the image represented in the file "downarrow.gif" shows a down-pointing arrow to a sighted reader who is using an appropriate browser, while the word *more* provides comparable information to other users.

Unfortunately, most editing programs for webpages do not treat ALT text as the norm, but rather as the exception. So, authors of webpages need to remember to include the text alternative. In addition, they need to think about the function of the image. In the example above, both a down-pointing arrow and the word *more* or *next* would indicate to most users that additional information could be found by clicking on the hyperlink. Sometimes, the designer simply says something like "link" or "image17" that turns out worse than no ALT text at all. (pp. 172–181, 182–190)

The American Standard Code for Information Interchange (ASCII): a code for computers, which was developed in the days of teletype machines. It allows programmers to represent familiar symbols in terms of numbers, on virtually all computers. Using eight bits, ASCII can represent 128 characters, including upper- and lowercase letters, numbers, punctuation, and other symbols. ASCII significantly expands access to computers. It makes possible the use of familiar characters, such as the letter *a* instead of a string of binary symbols, such as "1100001."

But ASCII also defines classes of users in terms of ease of access. Because it is limited to representing characters in use in the American alphabet, it cannot fully represent the characters in the major European languages (e.g., Spanish tilde, French cedilla, German umlaut) much less ideographic languages such as Chinese. U.S. users can represent the dollar sign (36), but there is no representation for the British pound. Nevertheless, ASCII is the primary code used on the Internet and in many software packages. Thus, it enables, but differentially enables, access to the tools of the new information age. (pp. 129–131, 175, 317–319)

Arpanet: a network of computers designed to allow researchers to share expensive computer resources. It was created in 1969 at Bolt Beranek and Newman in Cambridge, Massachusetts, USA, and was the forerunner of the Internet, the infrastructure for the World Wide Web.

Asynchronous communication: the exchange of messages in a medium that does not require the simultaneous presence of the sender and the receiver. By this definition, ordinary postal mail qualifies as asynchronous communication, but the term usually refers to asynchronous electronic communication, such as e-mail. (pp. 2–4)

Authority: a website that is linked from many other pages (see *Hub*).

Avatar: something in electronic space, often an image but not always, that represents a user in a multiuser situation such as a multiplayer electronic game, simulation, or chat session. (Hinn, Leander, & Bruce)

Bazaar model: a style of interaction, originally applied to software development, in which large numbers of people contribute, often without monetary compensation, to build some larger whole. Proponents accept and applaud diversity. They argue that people committed to a particular area will produce results whose value far offsets any problems due to lack of uniformity of overall structure. See *Cathedral model*. (pp. 102, 195)

Berkeley Software Distribution (BSD): an offshoot of the ill-fated Unix development collaboration between the computer-science department of the University of California at Berkeley and AT&T. BSD Unix is the core of free operating systems like FreeBSD, NetBSD, and OpenBSD, as well as commercial operating systems such as Sun's Solaris and Apple's Mac OS X. (Brunelle)

Blog, Blogger: the term *blog* is short for *Web log*, which was initially a chronological, sometimes annotated listing of the URLs that a Web designer had visited. Blogs have evolved into a variety of Web-based logs, from online diaries to collections of jokes and annotated bibliographies kept by individuals or teams. Blogger is one software site that allows users to create, manage, and post their blogs to their own sites or to a Blogger server. (Lunsford & Bruce)

Boolean expression: an expression that evaluates to true or false; for example, used in a Web search, the expression *travel and France* is true for every webpage that contains both *travel* and *France*. Expressions that contain logical operators such as *and*, *or*, and *not* are explicitly Boolean, but all Web searches implicitly involve Boolean expressions. Boolean logic was developed by the English mathematician George Boole.

Call number: a unique code displayed on the spine of library materials that represents the item in the library catalog and allows the user to locate the resource on the shelf. (Kapitzke; Glossary adapted from Reitz, 2000)

Cascade effect: a series of effects of an initial perturbation of a social system. This happens, for example, when a new technology is introduced and practices shift to accommodate it. Then, there are effects of that initial change, which lead to even less predictable changes. This is one reason that it is often said that people overestimate the short-term impact of innovations, but underestimate the long-term effects.

In a school, we might observe small initial changes with the introduction of Web browsing. Students would spend some time doing a new activity. But, over time, teachers might see how students could use the Web for research, and later for publishing. As these new uses develop, the entire ecology of reading and writing could shift to a new center of activity. (pp. 193–194)

Case sensitive: the property of paying attention to uppercase and lowercase letters; each search engine has its own policy about this (e.g., is *White House* the same as *white house*?).

Cathedral model: a style of interaction, originally applied to software development, in which a dedicated few work within a guiding structure. Proponents argue that the need for consistency and quality control outweighs the advantages of enlisting vast contingents of volunteers. See *Bazaar model*. (pp. 102, 195)

Collaboratory: a "center without walls, in which the nation's researchers can perform their research without regard to geographical location—interacting with colleagues, accessing instrumentation, sharing data and computational resources[s], and accessing information in digital libraries" (Kouzes, Myers, & Wulf, 1996). (pp. 294–303)

Cookie: a small file placed on the user's computer by a website that allows it to track and remember visitors. Cookies must be enabled and can be disabled on your browser. They are relatively harmless in that they can't damage or even access your system and do not contain high-stakes information (such as credit card numbers), but they are a way of tracking and thus infringing on your privacy. (Kehus)

Cooperative learning: an instructional approach in which students work in groups to solve problems, thus developing the interpersonal skills of communication, leadership, decision making, and conflict resolution. Cooperative learning creates a community of inquiry in the classroom similar to what the philosopher C.S. Peirce described as he observed the work of scientists (see Johnson & Johnson, 1998). The Cooperative Learning Center is at the University of Minnesota. (Lunsford & Bruce)

Copyright: the exclusive legal right granted by a government to an author, editor, composer, playwright, publisher, or distributor to publish, produce, sell, or distribute a literary, musical, dramatic, or artistic work. Copyright law also governs the right to prepare derivative works, to reproduce a work or portions of it, and to display or perform a work in public. (Kapitzke; Glossary adapted from Reitz, 2000)

Cyberart: a term used to denote art that uses, builds on, talks about, or in some other interesting way relates to the computer, Internet, or Web. See Rodney Chang's list of 72 propositions in his definition of *cyberart* (http://www.lastplace.com/page48.htm). (pp. 51–58)

Cyberspace: as coined by science fiction writer William Gibson, a computer network in which users mentally traverse large data matrices; now commonly used to describe the Internet or the Web.

Cyborg: usually refers to a being that is half machine, half living entity. Donna Haraway wrote that "a cyborg is a cybernetic organism, a hybrid of machine and organism, a creature of social reality as well as a creature of fiction" (1991, p. 149). (Hawisher)

Cybrary: an electronic gateway or portal for clients physically located anywhere to access information located everywhere. (Kapitzke; Glossary adapted from Reitz, 2000; pp. 60–67)

Deterritorialized: stripped from a relation to local place. (Leander)

Dewey Decimal Classification System (DDC): a system of classifying books and other works first published in 1876 by librarian Melvil Dewey, who divided human knowledge into 10 basic categories with subdivisions indicated by decimal notation. (Kapitzke; Glossary adapted from Reitz, 2000)

Digital divide: the disparities in access to new information and communication technologies across race, class, gender, nationality, and other social dimensions. (pp. 15, 172–181, 321–330)

Digital library: a concept with varying definitions; the Association of Research Libraries (http://www.arl.org) has a definition (http://www.libnet.sh.cn/diglib/definition.htm) that suggests synonymy with "electronic library" or "virtual library"; a key element is that the library uses new technologies to link diverse resources in a manner transparent to the user.

Discourse: recurrent statements that constitute material and social relations of power. (Kapitzke; Glossary adapted from Reitz, 2000)

Distance learning: Distance education provides a unique opportunity for those who wish to study but cannot attend residential institutions because of personal circumstances or occupational obligations. The term was once synonymous with "correspondence course," and later with educational television, but has increasingly been used to refer to learning through an array of communication technologies, including video, teleconferences, e-mail, and the World Wide Web. As these tools have emerged as integral components of on-campus courses, distance (i.e., the physical location of the student with respect to the class) has become an increasingly peripheral factor. Thus, the concept of distance learning may fade away as its features are incorporated in learning in general. (pp. 261–266)

Domain name: a name that identifies an IP (Internet Protocol) address. For example, the domain name http://www.ed.gov represents a numerical address signifying a location in cyberspace. A domain name is the first part of the URL used to identify a webpage. Each host computer in the Domain Name System has a name, which allows computers using the World Wide Web to connect to the appropriate webpage. (pp. 310–320)

Domain name server: a computer that accesses the Domain Name System in order to determine the correspondence between a domain name and an IP address.

Domain Name System (DNS): the online distributed database system that is used to map human-readable addresses into IP addresses.

Dynabook: the Dynabook was Alan Kay's vision of a "personal dynamic medium," a powerful personal computer that could be used by children and adults to explore and create words, music, sounds, and images and animations. (Sharples)

Dynamic (Web) page: a webpage that changes in response to user input, the time of day, or other variable information, a consequence being that it cannot be indexed easily by a Web search engine.

E-art: electronic art, such as ASCII pictorial representations. (Hawisher; pp. 51–58, 129–138)

E-book and e-book reader: an e-book is a book presented in electronic form to be read primarily on a screen. It may provide interactivity through dynamic links, quizzes, or simulations. An e-book reader is a device, which may be in the form of a simulated book with two foldout screens, for viewing e-books. (Sharples; pp. 46–49)

Egalitarianism: the term refers to equality for human beings across different social settings. When applied to electronic environments, the term is used to argue that a lack of social context cues in online discourse results automatically in nonhierarchical structures across gender, race, sexual orientation, and a host of our other differences. In other words, because paralinguistic cues (e.g., appearance, facial expressions, and tone of voice) are absent online, what is said supposedly becomes more important than who says it. (Hawisher; pp. 129–138)

Einstein's Theory of Relativity: In 1905 Albert Einstein published his famous Special Theory of Relativity and overthrew common-sense assumptions about space and time. Relative to the observer, both are altered near the speed of light: Distances appear to stretch; clocks tick more slowly. Einstein's General Theory of Relativity is a separate theory about a very different topic—the effects of gravity. (Jungwirth)

E-journal: a journal in electronic form. In some cases, an e-journal may appear as a World Wide Web page, with a URL; in others it is delivered by electronic mail, usually through a listserv. (pp. 39, 42–43)

E-mail: a service that allows users to send and receive messages via computer and network; many services now support styled text, graphics, audio, or video.

Embedded systems: computer processors that work in appliances, cars, telephones, lights, and other devices; they are often invisible to the user and mean that nearly everyone is becoming a user of computer technologies, even without realizing it.

Evaluation: the process of determining the merit, worth, or quality of the object of inquiry. (Hinn, Leander, & Bruce; pp. 182–198, 279–291)

E-zine, Webzine: an electronic, amateur magazine. E-zines derive from fanzines, literally cut-and-paste, home-produced magazines often devoted to discussing popular shows and fiction (especially science fiction) and to distributing spin-off texts. Now, e-zines encompass a wide range of topics, as well as a variety of delivery systems. Webzines are e-zines found on the Web, whereas other e-zines are still delivered as ASCII files through e-mail. (Lunsford & Bruce)

File Transfer Protocol (FTP): the most widely used way of moving files from one computer to another over a network. There is a set of commands in FTP for making and changing directories, and for transferring, copying, moving, and deleting files. Formerly, all FTP connections were text based, but graphical applications are now available that make FTP commands as easy as dragging and dropping. Numerous FTP clients exist for a number of platforms. Common FTP clients include Fetch (Macintosh) and ws_ftp (Windows). (Zhao, Tan, & Mishra)

Filter: a program that takes a list of documents and removes those that meet certain prespecified criteria; family filters are used to remove objectionable Web material, other filters are used to focus a search to retrieve the most relevant items, and any filter will occasionally let through unwanted items and screen out desirable ones.

Firewall: a network security system that allows a company, government, or other organization to keep its internal network files separate from the larger Internet community.

First-wave technologies: communication/information technologies, such as radio, television, audio recording, video recording, cinema, and telephone, which operate primarily with analog representations of information. These technologies have been primarily used for one-way delivery of information, but there are many exceptions. *See Second-wave technologies.*

Flaming: any derogatory message sent online, either posted to a message board or e-mailed. A particularly harsh flame might include a deluge of such messages. (Kehus)

Formative evaluation: evaluation applied to a program under development in order to find ways to improve it; widely employed for technology-based programs because of the rapid technological changes. (pp. 182–190)

Forum: an online discussion group, sometimes called a newsgroup or a conference. Web-based forums are often archived so that participants can follow and post to past and current threads. (Leander)

Frames: a technique for webpage design that allows information to be displayed and manipulated in different portions of the screen; while useful, it makes webpages inaccessible to those whose browsers cannot process the frames and also makes it impossible to bookmark specific subsections of the site.

Free software: software is considered free if users can run the program for any purpose, study how the program works (by looking at the source code), adapt it to their needs (by modifying that source code), and freely redistribute modified or unmodified copies to anyone, all without having to ask or pay for permission. (Brunelle; pp. 108–113)

Future studies: a form of inquiry in which futurists forecast a variety of alternative possible futures (see Dator, 1998). The goal is to help people invent and then move toward a preferred future. One approach to this is called scenario planning.

GNU (GNU's Not Unix): a "Unix-workalike" development effort by the Free Software Foundation headed by Richard Stallman. (Brunelle)

Header: information included with an e-mail message such as who sent it, the date of sending, and the subject of the message. A full header can show the path that the message traveled, where an automatic reply will be sent, the message priority, and other features.

Heisenberg's relations of uncertainty: Heisenberg formulated the relations of uncertainty concerning the simultaneous precise measurement of the position and velocity of microscopic particles and, consequently, the unpredictability of their behavior. (Jungwirth)

Host: a computer connected to the Internet with a registered name, such as http://www.reading.org. The term is used to refer to any single machine on the Internet, but a single machine can act as multiple systems, each with its own domain name and IP address, so the definition now typically includes virtual hosts as well.

Hub: a website with many links to other sites (see *Authority*).

Hybrid library: a library in which a significant proportion of the resources are available in digital format, as opposed to print or microform. (Kapitzke; Glossary adapted from Reitz, 2000; pp. 60–67, 71–75)

Hybrid literacy: a way of producing and interpreting texts that combines aspects of two or more sets of literate practices. For example, discussion on a moderated list may call for a unique blend of certain academic conventions for writing along with other conventions about friendly social interchange. The particular blend is in turn dependent on technological features such as how the listserv program displays messages and headers. (pp. 40–41; 223–233)

Hypermedia: a combination of hypertext and multimedia that creates interactive experiences with media. (Beach & Myers; pp. 234–248)

Hypertext: a text in which "hot links" allow the reader to move to another text; these texts can be sounds, images, and video, as well as familiar printed texts. Hypertext blurs the line between author and reader, as each collaborates in the construction of the text to be read. It is the format for World Wide Web resources.

Hypertext Markup Language (HTML): a language for writing webpages. The first webpages had to be written directly in this language, with an expression such as the following to indicate a hyperlink: "<A HREF="http://io.advanced.org/thinkquest/">ThinkQuest</A>." In this case, were the above link active, the reader of the webpage would see only ThinkQuest. When he or she clicked on that word, the Web browser would automatically connect to the Web server containing the ThinkQuest site.

Idealization: the set of practices originally envisioned for a technology, rather than the realized practices. This is analogous to an intended, as opposed to an enacted, curriculum.

Image viewer: a program that allows the computer to display and control a visual image. There are many varieties. The major ones have plug-in versions that can be incorporated into a Web browser. Some simply display an image; others allow seamless panning and zooming on an image.

Information science: a branch of knowledge that investigates the sources, development, dissemination, use, and management of information in all its forms. (Kapitzke; Glossary adapted from Reitz, 2000)

Innovation: "an idea, practice, or object that is perceived as new by an individual or another unit of adoption" (Rogers, 1995, p. 11). (Thakkar, Bruce, Hogan, & Williamson; pp. 274–276)

Inquiry Page: a Web resource containing a database of units for inquiry-based instruction across grade levels and subjects. (Bishop & Bruce; pp. 209–221)

Instant Messenger: a type of software that enables instant messaging, a type of communications service that lets one user create a private chat room with another individual. Typically, the instant messaging system alerts the user whenever somebody on his or her private list is online. The user can then initiate a chat session with that person. AOL Instant Messenger (AIM) was the first instant messaging system to become popular on the Internet. (Zhao, Tan, & Mishra; pp. 2, 171)

Intentional stance: how people respond to interactive media as if it were a psychological being or actor. There is increasing evidence that this intentional stance appears to be an unconscious response, independent of age and expertise. (Mishra, Nicholson, & Wojcikiewicz)

Interactive agents: semi-autonomous, proactive, and adaptive computer programs. Agents do not necessarily have human-like qualities (such as language-processing abilities and so on). However the development of human-like agents (with beliefs, intentions, knowledge, and even emotions) is a growing area of research. (Mishra, Nicholson, & Wojcikiewicz; p. 125)

Internet: the global communications network that supports the World Wide Web and, increasingly, voice and video communications. (p. 17)

Internet Protocol (IP): a system of conventions that allows computers connected to the Internet to exchange data with one another regardless of the manufacturer, the operating system, or location.

Internet Protocol address: a computer address in the form of four numbers, each one between 0 and 255, separated by dots. The Internet uses the numeric IP address to send data. For example, you may connect to a World Wide Web server with the domain name http://www.reading.org, but to the network you are connecting to the Web server with the IP address 207.97.47.101.

Internet Relay Chat (IRC): a system of clients and servers allowing people all over the world to communicate via typed messages. IRC allows multiple users to converse in real time on different "channels." Channels vary in traffic and content. IRC clients are available for nearly all platforms. (Zhao, Tan, & Mishra)

Invisible Web: the portion of the Web not accessible through Web search engines. It mainly consists of a broad variety of databases. Its content tends to be more qualitative and larger in comparison to the visible Web. Sometimes it is also called the deep Web. (Jungwirth)

Java applets: Java is a full-fledged programming language, similar to C++ or Pascal. An applet is a Java program that runs directly within a Web browser, rather than as an independent program. Many Java applets are available free across the Internet.

JavaScript: JavaScript is an authoring language for Netscape browsers, which extends HTML with more interactive features. Authors add JavaScript code directly to their pages. Microsoft browsers can understand Jscript, a similar but not identical language.

Latent function: a function of a new technology that becomes apparent only through practice. For example, complex computer technology may lead to greater collaboration as people are forced to help one another in order to use it at all. That collaboration might be considered desirable or might not, but it was not a conscious motivation of the system designers. (pp. 192–193)

Learning technology: a tool or medium that helps learners construct new knowledge. It usually refers to a new information or communication technology such as visualization software, virtual reality, electronic bulletin board, simulation, tutorial, or interactive game. Depending on the use, practically any technology can be considered a learning technology.

The term *learning technology* is ambiguous in at least four ways. It can mean (1) the tool that helps one learn and thus enables *learning through* technology, (2) *learning how to use* technology, (3) *learning about* technology, or (4) a technology that itself learns. In (4) for example, genetic algorithms in effect learn how to perform more effectively in some environments based on feedback about their success and failure; thus, they are *technologies that learn*. (pp. 162–171, 202–204, 209–221, 249–292)

Legacy system: a computer system that was developed long ago, but still has value today. Typically, the organization has invested considerable resources in its development or in collecting data in a particular form for use with the system.

    As conditions change, these systems risk losing some of their capabilities, or, in the case of the Y2K problem, begin to produce errors they never did in the past. A large amount of software and hardware development is devoted to maintaining and updating legacy applications, or to designing new products that can work with existing applications or import data from them. (p. 193)

Lexia: the different pages linked together in hypertext, triggered by clicking on words or buttons. (Beach & Myers)

Library of Congress Classification: a system of classifying books and other works devised by the Library of Congress in Washington, D.C., USA, which divides human knowledge into broad categories indicated by letters of the Roman alphabet, with further subdivisions indicated by decimal notation. Most research and academic libraries use Library of Congress Classification, whereas public and school libraries use the DDC. (Kapitzke; Glossary adapted from Reitz, 2000)

Linux operating system (http://www.linux.org): a version of the Unix operating system, which works with a variety of computers, including PCs, Macintoshes, and Amigas. As an operating system, it enables the user to invoke word processors, Web browsers, and other programs, as needed. In that sense, Linux is similar to Windows or MacOS. However, it is unusual in the way it has been created and in its cost. Linux development has been led by Linus Torvalds, but its continuing development occurs through an unusual collaborative arrangement in which programmers around the globe contribute pieces of the system. The software is free and represents the bazaar approach to software development.

Listserv: an Internet service that allows a group of people to communicate via e-mail by sending mail to a single electronic address and having it redistributed to individual e-mail accounts. Messages are forwarded to each person on a designated list and are often archived for future reference. Listserv communications vary greatly, including informal conversations, moderated list discussions, and formal publications, such as e-journals. The term today has been generalized to refer to the electronic discussion group itself, such as WAC-L, a list or listserv on writing across the curriculum. (Hawisher & Bruce)

Logo: a programming language, essentially a version of the language Lisp, which was designed as a tool for learning. It is notable for its emphasis on modular design, extensibility, interactivity, and flexibility, all features that enhance its potential for learning. Wallace Feurzeig at Bolt Beranek and Newman led a team that created the first version of Logo in 1967. Seymour Papert, who had worked with Feurzeig and also with Jean Piaget in Geneva, led further developments of Logo at the Massachusetts Institute of Technology, Cambridge.

Logo has been used across the curriculum, notably in mathematics, language, music, robotics, telecommunications, and science. The most popular Logo environments have involved the turtle, either as a robot that moves around on the floor or as an icon that moves about a computer screen and can be used to draw pictures.

Additional developments have included LogoWriter (adding word processing), LEGO Logo (connecting Logo to machines built out of LEGO bricks, motors, and sensors), MicroWorlds (adding drawing tools, a shape editor, and a melody maker), the Programmable Brick (with a computer inside it), and StarLogo (a massively parallel version of Logo in which thousands of turtles can carry on independent processes and interact with one another).

Manifest function: the purpose built into the design of a new technology or inherent in the reasons for its adoption. These are the expected or desired functions of the innovation, which may or may not be realized. (pp. 192–193)

Megabytes, gigabytes, terabytes, exabytes: A megabyte consists of 1,024 kilobytes, 1,024 megabytes are one gigabyte, and 1,024 gigabytes are one terabyte. One exabyte in turn is 1,024 times 1,024 terabytes. One terabyte is about the equivalent to the textual content of a million books. The number 1,024 is a result of the fact that computers use binaries (1,024 is 2 to the power of 10). (Jungwirth)

Metasearch engine: a computer program, such as Dogpile, that collects the results from several search engines at once. This is especially valuable because no search engine indexes more than one sixth of the Web.

Metcalfe's Law: the value of a network for users is proportional to the square of the number of users.

Mirror site: a website that maintains a copy of another site so that the access load is distributed more evenly across the Internet, or users in a distant part of the world can have faster connections.

Moderated list: an electronic e-mail list with a moderator who may initiate and guide discussions, review messages for appropriateness, or issue periodic summaries.

MOO: an acronym for MUD, Object Oriented. A MUD is a Multiple-User Dimension (also Domain, Dungeon, or Dialogue), a computer database that permits multiple users to log in by Telnet and interact in real time. In MOOs, users can also create, manipulate, and move among virtual objects (including rooms). (Leander)

Moore's Law: the processing power on a microchip will double every 18 months.

MP3 (or MPEG3): a scheme for compressing audio signals without sacrificing sound quality. This allows a sound file to be small and easily transferred over the Internet. A musician could use MP3 to distribute a performance directly to a listener without need of a record company.

Multimedia: music, sound, images, artwork, graphics, or video, for example, in-corporated into hypermedia. (Beach & Myers; pp. 234–248)

Multisemiotic: several modes, including the visual, aural, and written, are all part of the society's meaning-making apparatus. With the rise of electronic com-munication technologies, increasingly our senses are assaulted with sound, images, and even smells that conspire to gain our attention. (Hawisher)

Network effects: the phenomenon that the effects of a particular technology may depend on how it is interconnected with other devices, and how those effects depend on the structure, size, and operating characteristics of the network.

Neutrality: Some say no specific stance toward change is needed, implicitly ad-vocating a neutral stance. They fear the allure of today's fashion, stressing instead what they see as enduring values. Thus, they give little consideration to how events might alter their practices. In traumatic changes, it is often difficult to distinguish neutrality from denial.

Oeuvre: The French cultural psychologist Ignace Meyerson used the plural *oeuvres* to refer to artifacts, activities, and events of a culture that bear its identity. In *The Culture of Education*, Bruner (1996) applied the term in an educational context to refer to authentic products and events of schools. (Zhao, Tan, & Mishra)

Online catalog: a library catalog consisting of bibliographic records in digital format maintained on a dedicated computer that provides uninterrupted access via workstations that are in direct, continuous communication with the central computer during each transaction. (Kapitzke; Glossary adapted from Reitz, 2000)

Online Public Access Catalog (OPAC): a computer catalog of the materials in a library. (Kapitzke; Glossary adapted from Reitz, 2000)

Online services: the branch of library services concerned with selecting and providing access to electronic resources such as online databases and CD-ROMs, including mediated searching, which is usually handled by an online services librarian. (Kapitzke; Glossary adapted from Reitz, 2000)

Online writing center: a Web space containing resources to support student writing and information about on-campus services. (pp. 223–233)

Open source: a concept about how knowledge is constructed and shared, with implications for whether it is seen as intellectual property or collaborative inquiry. See the Open Directory category: http://dmoz.org/Computers/Open_Source (pp. 101–106, 195)

Open-world learning: highlights the need for students to learn how to engage in productive inquiry within dynamic contexts, which accommodate massive amounts of richly interrelated data. Open-world learning sets up learning experiences that go beyond working on fully specified problems, static and restricted databases, and predetermined answers. But these approaches do not guarantee clear learning outcomes, and require greater access to information resources and more educator support. New computational tools such as Biology Workbench highlight the need for open-world learning: They make powerful tools available to learners—tools that make possible exploration of new and complex domains.

Opposition: Others go beyond the neutral position to stand in active opposition to change. In many cases, their concern is that humanistic values will be subsumed by technocratic or economic forces. Kaufmann (1977) used the term *dogmatic* in a similar way in his discussion of the art of reading.

Opt-out: Most reputable companies using e-mail lists usually give directions somewhere in their e-mail and/or on their site to allow you to remove yourself from such lists. This is known as the opt-out or option to get out. (Kehus)

Physiognomy: the art of studying outward appearance (such as facial features and expression) in order to discover temperament, character, and personality. (Mishra, Nicholson, & Wojcikiewicz)

Picts: a term used here to refer to the ASCII representations women created on the listserv women@waytoofast. (Hawisher)

Planet eBook: a comprehensive and independent website exclusively focused on electronic books (eBooks) and eBook-related technologies (http://www.planetebook.com). (Sharples)

Platform for Internet Content Selection (PICS): developed as a common symbol system of rating content, specifically to allow control over what sorts of Web content a browser is allowed to view, mostly by parents controlling their children's Web viewing. (Kehus)

Quick take: a photograph or image that may misrepresent the person or event being captured digitally or on film. Sound bytes and quick takes are often stripped of the context necessary for adequately understanding what's at hand. (Hawisher)

Ranking function: a means used by a search engine to order documents found in a search in terms of potential relevance, quality, or other criteria.

Realization: the set of practices associated with actual use of a technology. These may differ markedly from the idealization represented in documentation, a curriculum unit, or a teachers' guide.

Reterritorialized: a dynamic and complex relation to developing spaces. (Leander)

Revenge effect: an effect of using a new technology, which we never anticipated or wanted. This occurs when we use a new tool to accomplish one purpose without realizing how it would affect other aspects of our lives. For example, the introduction of gypsy moths to the United States was intended to make silk production a reality, yet led to massive destruction of hardwood trees in the Northeast. This is more than a simple side effect that would have been anticipated and conceived as part of the bargain in adopting the innovation. (p. 193)

Reverse revenge effect: a revenge effect that appears with an older technology. This can be positive, as when we realize a benefit that was invisible until the new technology took it away. The benefits of a high-fiber diet are one example: As technology to refine foods became more commonplace, we created health problems that earlier food technologies had not created without our recognizing it. (p. 193)

Role-playing games (RPGs): games in which each player assumes the role of a character (such as a principal or a student, as in the WJHS simulation) who can interact with other characters within the imaginary world of the game. (Bruce, Hinn, & Leander)

Scaling up and scalability: scaling up occurs after an "implementation of a tested prototype program or design expands to many schools" (Datnow, Hubbard, & Mehan, 1998, p. 1). "Scalability means that an innovation can operate in more than a handful of select and resource-rich classrooms or schools" (Blumenfeld et al., 2000, p. 152). (Bruce, Hogan, & Thakkar; pp. 274–275)

Scenario planning: "an approach to planning that starts from the assumption that, much as we try, we simply cannot predict or control the future. We can only imagine different ways in which the future might turn, stake out a course that makes sense today, and try to be flexible and alert when the unexpected inevitably occurs," according to the website http://www.marin.cc.ca.us/scenario. The site, Scenario Planning at College of Marin, provides a good introduction to scenario planning and shows its application to planning in the context of uncertain levels of state funding for California's community colleges.

Scientific visualization: the use of data-driven computer graphics to aid in the understanding of scientific information.

Search directory: a database that organizes documents according to categories and, usually, subcategories; it provides an alternative to general searching for finding particular items.

Search engine: a program that searches a database to locate all the documents that meet certain specifications given in search keys or a search query. It is commonly used to refer to programs for searching the Web. Most search engines return a list of webpages ordered by how well they match the specifications and by other heuristics, such as the number of sites that link to that page. (pp. 79–84)

Search index: a large database of document locations based on the words contained in each document; the index facilitates efficient, meaningful searches and is created by a program within the search engine.

Search key: a string of text used to guide a search engine (see *Search engine*) to find webpages. The keys can include phrases as well as individual words or parts of words. Users can specify keys that must be present in the webpage as well as those that must not be present and with some search engines, use Boolean operators (and, or).

Second-wave technologies: communication/information technologies, such as computers, the Internet, the World Wide Web, and digital video, which operate primarily with digital representations of information. These technologies present great opportunities for two-way communication. See *First-wave technologies*.

Semiotics: a theory of signs aimed at studying how images and other kinds of social discourse are produced, interpreted, and come to "mean." (Hawisher)

Situated evaluation: an approach to evaluation of technology use that assumes the technology is not set a priori, but comes into being through use. Situated evaluation is a "new framework for understanding innovation and change. This framework has several key ingredients: It emphasizes contrastive analysis and seeks to explore differences in use. It assumes that the object of study is neither the innovation alone nor its effects, but rather, the realization of the innovation—the innovation-in-use. Finally, it produces hypotheses supported by detailed analyses of actual practices. These hypotheses make possible informed plans for use and change of innovations" (Bruce & Rubin, 1993, p. 215).

Situated studies: a research method that explicitly incorporates an analysis of the context in which literacy is practiced or learning occurs. It is particularly appropriate for investigations of the use of new technologies, because users typically find diverse ways to realize their potentials. In fact, to the extent that new technologies for learning truly empower students and teachers, we would expect that they would be used in unexpected ways. (pp. 185–187)

Skeptical: The pessimistic side of utilitarianism is practical skepticism. Proponents point to past unfulfilled promises and to the inertia of large systems as justification for their doubts.

Social informatics: the study of how information technologies are used in social contexts, how that use leads to social changes, and, conversely, how social practices influence that use.

Social spreadsheets: a term that arose when people saw that spreadsheets could be a learning tool as well as a tool for accounting and business planning. Used by an individual, a spreadsheet could fit in a category such as "data analysis," but it could also serve as a collaborative medium. Students in a class might each collect data for one piece of a larger problem and then combine their data in a class spreadsheet.

An interesting example of this arose among small rural schools in Queensland, Australia. There is heavy rainfall there along the coast and an informal competition to see what town deserves the title of "wettest place" took place. Teachers had students measure rain in gauges and then add their weekly totals to a spreadsheet containing statewide data. Students everywhere could then make comparisons, analyze trends, and develop arguments for why their town was the wettest, the driest, most variable, or whatever. Projects such as this engage learners and afford opportunities for many kinds of learning. The spreadsheet tools and the network for sharing data made possible activities that would have been difficult to accomplish otherwise.

Sociotechnical analysis: an approach to the study of human activity that explicitly accounts for both social practices and the influence of material objects, such as artifacts, tools, and communications media.

Sociotechnical system: a system comprising human activity, spaces, artifacts, tools, and communications media.

Specialty search engine: a search engine that searches a limited database of documents, such as the telephone white pages; such an engine can be made more efficient for limited purposes and is more likely to return only the sorts of data that a user would want.

Spiders (search robots): a computer program sent out by a search engine to index documents on the Web to facilitate efficient search later on.

Static (Web) page: a webpage that does not change and can thus be indexed by a Web search engine.

Streaming: Using streaming protocols, computer programs such as RealPlayer compress audio and video files and transfer them to a Web browser a little at a time. The first few seconds of the file begin playing while the next sections are brought in. Most such programs are available as plugins for Web browsers.

Summative evaluation: evaluation applied to judge the overall effect of a developed program; most suitable for the uniform impacts perspective on a learning program. (pp. 182–190)

Synchronous communication: the exchange of messages in a medium that requires the simultaneous presence of the sender and the receiver (e.g., in an electronic chat system). The line between synchronous and asynchronous is a function of the sociotechnical system, not just the technologies per se. For example, one could use e-mail in a chat-like, synchronous fashion by requiring the "discussants" to be online at the same time. (pp. 2–4)

Technocentrism: a way of thinking about the use of technology that attributes all important changes to the technology itself.

Telnet: a program that allows a personal computer to link to another computer, via the Internet or other network. Telnet has a history of being used for connecting smaller machines to larger mainframe computers, but is currently used to remotely access and control computer servers of all size via the Internet. (Leander)

Terabyte: a trillion bytes of information, enough to represent a trillion characters; about 100 fairly large personal computer hard drives would be needed to hold this much information.

Topffer's Law: as defined by Gombrich (1972) and based on work by Rodolphe Topffer: Any human face, however poorly drawn, possesses necessarily, by the mere fact of existing, some perfectly definite expression and character. In the present context, we extend Topffer's Law to include the perception of personality and character in interactive artifacts (such as animatronic toys or computer software), however poorly they may be designed. (Mishra, Nicholson, & Wojcikiewicz; pp. 118–124)

Transaction: a phenomenon in which mind and reality, or a "knowing" and the "known," are conceived as a unified entity; from Dewey and Bentley's (1949) *Knowing and the Known*. Their theory of transaction provided one more way to respond to change, whether that be in the form of new ideas in a text, a new technology, another person, or events in the world. In this theory, a transaction is the encounter of a person's unique, situated history with something new. Every transaction is different, and holds the seeds of new meaning (see McDermott, 1981, p. x). A transactional stance means a welcoming attitude toward change, opening oneself to the significance inherent in such encounters.

Transformational: In contrast to the oppositional position toward change is the transformational one, especially when that stance conceives the transformation as positive. In extreme versions, we get what Kaufmann called the "exegetical response," a faith in the transformative powers of the new. The transformationalist argues that our task is to understand and guide the transformation.

Unicode: The Unicode Standard specifies the representation of text in software. It works in principle as ASCII does, but by using 16 bits a programmer can represent 128 times as many characters. Unicode can represent European alphabetic scripts, Middle Eastern right-to-left scripts, and scripts of Asia, as well as punctuation marks and mathematical and technical symbols. It provides codes for diacritics, such as the Spanish tilde (ñ). There are currently codes for 49,194 characters. With Unicode it is possible to provide a unique number for every character, regardless of computing platform or program. The code is currently supported in many operating systems, all modern browsers, and many other products.

The Unicode Consortium is a nonprofit organization founded to develop and promote this standard. Membership includes organizations and individuals in the computer and information processing industry throughout the world. (pp. 310–320)

Uniform Resource Locator (URL): an electronic address, typically one designating a computer file on the World Wide Web, such as http://www.reading.org. The URL system allows millions of computers, each containing thousands of files, to refer consistently to specific resources.

Unix: a multiuser, multitasking 32-bit operating system written in the computer programming language C and developed in the late 1960s at AT&T's Bell Labs; later development split between BSD variants and AT&T's own System V. (Brunelle)

Utilitarian: Some argue for a utilitarian stance (for Kaufmann, agnostic), saying that new tools or ideas need to be incorporated intelligently into practice. The utilitarian stance toward change is much like Rosenblatt's (1978) efferent stance in reading—a view of the text as a repository of information.

Virtual library: a "library without walls" in which the collection and resources are accessible only electronically and are not kept in paper, microform, or any tangible form. (Kapitzke; Glossary adapted from Reitz, 2000; pp. 60–67)

Virtual reality: in simplest terms, refers to a simulation of either a real or imagined environment or "world." Virtual reality has been used to describe many different activities including online collaboration through text or video, the imagined environments of a game, and three-dimensional representations of life-like images displayed through technologies such as CAVEs (Cave Automated Virtual Environments). Current systems include 360-degree, 3-D visualization, surround sound, and even physical touch effects (haptic sensations). (Hinn, Leander, & Bruce)

Virtual Reality Markup Language (VRML): VRML allows users to navigate around a webpage with the perception of three dimensions, as in games such as Doom or Quake. Educational uses for VRML include 3-D modeling of phenomena in science and history.

Visual discourse: pictorial representation of language in action. (Hawisher)

VRML art: art integrating audio and video for 3D digital imaging. Many different forms exist, making use of various "viewers" to display the art. The person experiencing the artwork can do so in a manner akin to exploring a real space, hence the "VR," or virtual reality, designator. Today, VRML art is included in many websites as a supplement to other content, not only as a separate art presentation. It is also being integrated with physical exhibitions of art in galleries and museums.

[Web] browser: a computer program that allows the user to explore the World Wide Web by interpreting documents written in HTML or other hypertext languages.

Webcam: a digital camera for transmitting real-time digital images (usually at speeds much slower than video) over the Internet. (Leander)

[Web] client: a computer that allows the user to connect to a server program in order to retrieve (download) or post (upload) Web documents.

Webopedia: a good online glossary of computer terms.

WebPac: a public access online catalog with a graphical user interface (GUI) accessible via the World Wide Web, as opposed to a text-based catalog interface accessible via Telnet. (Kapitzke; Glossary adapted from Reitz, 2000)

Webpage accessibility: the degree to which the content of a webpage is available to people in different groups, such as those who speak a language other than the author or who have a low-speed network connection. (pp. 188–189)

[Web] server: a program running on a host computer that maintains Web documents accessible via a Web browser.

World Wide Web (WWW): an Internet service based on hypertext links to organize and connect to Internet resources; as the Web begins to incorporate e-mail, telephone, recorded music and movies, radio, and television, it appears poised to become the all-encompassing communications media framework. (pp. 79–86, 90–94, 304–309)

WYSIWYG (pronounce wizzywig): What You See Is What You Get is the slang-term title for software, in this case webpage creation software, that is very user friendly and straightforward. (Kehus)

Yahoo! Groups: one of several commercial sites that offer various bulletin boards, e-mail, calendars, document storage, and chat rooms to support a community's online activities. (Lunsford & Bruce)

Y2K problem: a class of problems related to how computers represent and manipulate dates, which became apparent in the move from 1999 to 2000. The most common cause of this is that many programs written to minimize data storage used only the last two digits of the year, thus "05" means "1905." On January 1, 2000, some users of computers encountered difficulties because the programs were not be able to distinguish 1900 from 2000. There are a variety of similar problems, such as programs that use "99" to indicate missing data, but also use two digits to represent a year. (p. 191)